A. E. HOUSMAN

COLLECTED POEMS
AND
SELECTED PROSE

Edited with an Introduction
and Notes by
CHRISTOPHER RICKS

PENGUIN BOOKS

PENGUIN BOOKS

Published by the Penguin Group
Penguin Books Ltd, 27 Wrights Lane, London W8 5TZ, England
Viking Penguin, a division of Penguin Books USA Inc.
375 Hudson Street, New York, New York 10014, USA
Penguin Books Australia Ltd, Ringwood, Victoria, Australia
Penguin Books Canada Ltd, 10 Alcorn Avenue, Toronto, Ontario, Canada M4V 3B2
Penguin Books (NZ) Ltd, 182–190 Wairau Road, Auckland 10, New Zealand

Penguin Books Ltd, Registered Offices: Harmondsworth, Middlesex, England

First published by Allen Lane The Penguin Press 1988
Published in Penguin Books 1989
3 5 7 9 10 8 6 4 2

For permission to reproduce copyright works,
grateful acknowledgement is made to the following:
For *Additional Poems* XIX and XX; 'It is a fearful thing to be',
'Purple William' and 'Aunts and Nieces' (Light Verse and Parodies);
'Cambridge Inaugural Lecture', 'Matthew Arnold', 'Swinbourne'
(Selected Prose); and extracts from *The Letters of A. E. Housman*
(edited by Henry Maas, 1971) to The Socierty of Authors as the
literary representative of the Estate of A. E. Housman
and Jonathan Cape Ltd, publishers of A. E. Housman's *Collected Poems*.
For 'Dream Song 205' from *His Toy, His Dream, His Rest* by John Berryman,
which appears on p. 8 to Faber and Faber Ltd. The text of the Classical Papers section
is from *The Classical Papers of A. E. Housman: Vols 1–3*, eds. J. Diggle and F. R. D. Goodyear
(CUP, 1972), reprinted by permission, copyright © Cambridge University Press, 1972.

Printed in England by Clays Ltd, St Ives plc

PENGUIN TWENTIETH-CENTURY CLASSICS

HOUSMAN: COLLECTED POEMS AND
SELECTED PROSE

A. E. Housman was born in 1859, the eldest son of a Worcester-
shire solicitor. He was educated at Bromsgrove School and won a
scholarship to St John's College, Oxford. He gained first-class
honours in Classical Moderations, his first public examination at
Oxford, but then failed in Greats, the Final School, and so left
Oxford without a degree. From 1882 he worked for ten years as a
clerk in Her Majesty's Patent Office, proving himself by the
publications of his leisure hours a superb scholar in Latin and
Greek. In 1892 he was appointed Professor of Latin at University
College, London. He was to publish editions of Manilius (1903–
30), Juvenal (1905) and Lucan (1926), as well as magisterial papers
on a range of classical authors, with the focus particularly on
questions of principle, fact and tact within textual scholarship. He
became Professor of Latin at Cambridge in 1911 and died there in
1936.

His scholarship won admiration and fear; his poetry, love and
fame. He published his first book of poems, *A Shropshire Lad*, in
1896 and followed it only with *Last Poems* in 1922. Fortunately his
brother, Laurence Housman, permitted the posthumous publica-
tion of *More Poems* and of some 'Additional Poems'. Three years
before Housman died he gave delight and offence with his vivid,
lucid lecture on 'The Name and Nature of Poetry'. He declined
honours, including the Order of Merit.

Christopher Ricks was born in 1933. He was formerly a Fellow of
Worcester College, Oxford, and later a professor first at Bristol
and then at Cambridge where he was a Fellow of Christ's College.
Since 1986 he has been at Boston University. He is a Fellow of the
British Academy.

He edited a collection of critical essays on Housman in 1968.

He is the author of *Milton's Grand Style* (1963), *Tennyson* (1972),
Keats and Embarrassment (1974), and *The Force of Poetry* (1984). He
edited *The Poems of Tennyson* (1969, revised 1987) and *The New
Oxford Book of Victorian Verse* (1987) and was co-editor of *The State
of the Language* (1980). He is the general editor of the annotated
Penguin Poets.

CONTENTS

INTRODUCTION

A.E. Housman had integrity, and he was deeply divided. Housman the poet thrives upon division. Sometimes he sets classical form against romantic impulse; sometimes he plays a bleak statement against an exquisite measure; sometimes he newly lays bare an age-old conflict between head and heart, or between Saxon and Celt, or between masculine and feminine, or between shame and pride. A.E. Housman the classical scholar appears so intransigently different a figure as to have made people in his lifetime deny that this could be one and the same Housman.

The man himself valued the *cordon sanitaire*. He was grateful to his colleagues at Trinity College, Cambridge, for the kindness which they did him in never mentioning his poems. Some of his self-reproach at having agreed in old age to give the Leslie Stephen Lecture in Cambridge, on *The Name and Nature of Poetry*, came from a sense that he was blurring the severe distinction, scholar *or* poet, within which he felt so austerely comfortable. Yet the scholar, like the poet, has seized the imagination, mythically edged and etched.

A successor of Housman's in the Kennedy Professorship of Latin at Cambridge, C.O. Brink, has given Housman plaudits that are both full-handed and even-handed:

Each activity alone – the making of pure verse and of pure scholarship – would have brought justified fame to anyone unusually gifted; their concurrence is astounding. The two gifts came out of one root; I should be tempted to call it a quite extraordinary sensitivity and alertness that allowed him to touch, as it were, the very quick of language, both in forming poetry and in doing the criticism of poetry already formed. That is how the observer may see it. Himself he kept the two gifts as separate as possible.

A volume like the present one, which brings together the collected poems and a selection of the prose, has some obligation to try to join together what Housman, or God, has put asunder.

John Berryman spoke of Housman as one of his heroes. Or rather as two of his heroes, since for Berryman there was a total split between Housman the 'absolutely marvellous minor poet' and Housman the 'great scholar'. 'You are dealing with an absolute schizophrenic.' These terms, though, are coarse compared with what Berryman makes of all this in a poem, 'Dream Song 205', comic, admiring, rueful, and staging Housman (not upstaging him) in a verse-style as far as possible – and perhaps slightly further than is altogether decent – from Housman's own:

> Come & dance, Housman's hopeless heroine
> bereft of all: I take you in me arms
> burnt-cork:
> your creator is studying his celestial sphere,
> he never loved you, he never loved a woman
> or a man, save one: he was a fork
>
> saved by his double genius & certain emendations
> All his long life, hopeless lads grew cold
> He drew their death-masks
> To listen to him, you'd think that growing old
> at twenty-two was horrible, and the ordinary tasks
> of people didn't exist.
>
> He did his almost perfect best with what he had
> Shades are sorrowing, as not called up
> by in his genius him
> Others are for his life-long omission glad
> & published their works as soon as he came to a stop
> & could not review them.

Within Housman's prose, this double genius is shown to be truly forked when he bends his imaginative attention upon exactly what a poet wrote and meant. From the happy banter played upon the verses of his brother Laurence in an affectionate letter, through to the high professional scorn visited upon mindless defences of indefensible readings in classical texts, the most marked characteristic of Housman's prose is its preternatural stringency – except only that Housman would have thought that things had come to a pretty pass when such stringency appears to be preternatural rather than natural. How uncommon are such feats of common sense as Housman everywhere effects. Common sense, and exacting exactitude. 'I did not praise Bechert's accuracy, because accuracy is a duty

and not a virtue; but if I could have foreseen the shameful careless-
ness of Breiter and van Wageningen I should have said with
emphasis, as I do now, that he was very accurate indeed.'

What repeatedly holds together the prose, and holds it in living
relation to the poetry, is the conviction that poets are not the slovens
and buffoons whom commentators are happy to fabricate rather
than abandon a foolish reading or a foolish interpretation. 'But to
say that a thing *is not yet begun but is still going on* is such nonsense as
not one of us can conceive himself uttering in the loosest negligence
of conversation; only when centuries of transcription by barbarians
have imputed it to an incomparable poet, then we accept it as a
matter of course.'

There is nonsense and nonsense. Housman was disgusted by the
imputation to great poets of such null nonsense, and many of his
fiercest and funniest exuberances light up, with level incandescence,
the absurdity of these 'professional' incomprehensions. Such vib-
rant dismay at the wrong sort of nonsense is at one with Housman's
delight in the right sort, from his pleasure in nonsense verse (others'
and his own), through to the tone of sincere surprise with which he
used the word 'nonsense' for the transcendence by the greatest
poetry of exactly that common sense which must be admiringly
possessed if it is ever to be astonishingly transcended. It is in this
sense that Christina Rossetti's poems, or Shakespeare's, or Blake's,
are for Housman 'nonsense'.

The prose, then, is alive with principles, impulses and sensi-
tivities that are apt to the poems' achievements. And vice versa.
Housman demanded for the published text of his poems what
classical texts deserved, the most minute and responsible exacti-
tude. This is to the point, not least in its sardonic comedy: in the
words of the prefatory note to *Last Poems*, 'it is best that what I have
written should be printed while I am here to see it through the press
and control its spelling and punctuation'. At this point he later had
to write in the margin of his own copy, 'Vain hope!'

But the 'double genius' is more, since this last is a matter only of
printing and not of writing. The weight and nuance of the poems
are often created and enforced in ways that are sustained by the same
powers and direction of mind that animate Housman's classical
arguments. Many of Housman's best poems are in essence a text
and an unexpected construction put upon it, unexpected because at

once glossing the text and laying it bare as something other than its easy traditional acceptation. The very first poem of *A Shropshire Lad* takes and turns a fundamental or constitutional text of England, 'God Save the Queen'; turns it in an act of supreme editorial imagination. An old text newly apprehended: this is the plot, for instance, of *More Poems* XXXI, 'Because I liked you better / Than suits a man to say'. What did he mean when he made his promise?

> 'Goodbye,' said you, 'forget me.'
> 'I will, no fear,' said I.

The insistence at the end, that the speaker 'was one that kept his word', is so grounded as to be unanswerably true, but only because the words 'I will, no fear' are seen – again by something like an editorial elucidation – to mean something very different from the mere placation which they had seemed to offer. Again, the lovely poem upon Robert Louis Stevenson's death, 'R.L.S.', in its relation to Stevenson's 'Requiem' is an act of editorial reprise, an unenvious uncompetitive re-requiem, with the first prefix re- being that of reiteration, and the second prefix re- (in requiem itself) being 'in response to a stimulus, with intensive force'. Housman as a poet is engaged in the principled re-writing (writing again and in response to this stimulus) which editors all too seldom achieve.

But these filaments between the poetry and the prose, though strong, are slender compared with the steely knot that most bitingly binds the two: blasphemy.

The blasphemy of the poems is their central energy. In light verse it can take an impudently light form, as when Lieutenant-Colonel Mary Jane, of the Salvation Army, 'was cut in little pieces by the train': 'We will gather up the fragments that remain.' The blasphemous comedy is nourished, as if miraculously, by the feeding of the five thousand.

From the Salvation Army to salvation: *A Shropshire Lad* I broods smoulderingly on whether God saves anything or anybody, including the Queen. *Last Poems* IX joins in cursing 'Whatever brute and blackguard made the world', quivering with the preposterous comedy of (in Samuel Beckett's words) an atheist chipping the deity. *Last Poems* XII scorns equally, levelly, 'The laws of God, the laws of man,' and *Additional Poems* XVIII has as its climax a line limited neither to its absurd literal sense nor to Housman's immediate application to sexual perversity: 'He can curse the God that made him for the colour of his hair.' Much of Housman can be read as an unfolding of the double sense of perversion: the sexual turning-aside from one form of the straight, or strait, and narrow, and the religious turning-aside, 'specifically change to error in religious belief', the old opposite of conversion.

The poems are steeped in the Bible, and a bitter drench it is. Housman has, in both senses, gall. The calculated inoffensiveness of his verse-forms, of his diction, of his rhythms even, is his stalking-horse, and under the presentation of that he shoots his wit, the fiery darts of the wicked. But then if he has eisell and gall, so have the many anthologists who include his poems in books of religious verse. Yet it is true that there is no great religious poetry that does not – as crucial to its enterprise – raise the question of whether it is open to the charge of blasphemy; and true too that (as T.S. Eliot said) blasphemy is itself possible only to a believer – or at least to someone who half-fears he may be a believer, and kicks against the pricks. For Eliot, the decay of blasphemy is a symptom of the decay of belief. On Baudelaire: 'Genuine blasphemy, genuine in spirit and not purely verbal, is the product of partial belief, and is as impossible to the complete atheist as to the perfect Christian.' (This last, it may be added, explains why the *possibility* of being accused of blasphemy is essential to Christian poetry, since without such a possibility the poetry would announce itself as that of a perfect Christian, something no good Christian could claim.) Eliot's words in 1927 have their applicability to the poet (not 'versifier') who published *Last Poems* five years before; Eliot saw 'the twelfth century anomaly – and yet the essential congruity – of the finest religious verse and the most brilliant blasphemous verse. To the present generation of versifiers, so deficient in devotion and so feeble in blasphemy, the twelfth century might offer an edifying subject of study.'

Housman is more creatively conscious of the principled absurdity of his position (to use Beckett's words again, or rather his character's: 'The bastard! He doesn't exist!') than are the anthologists who baptise him with their blithe hose. What truly saves the best poems is their gravity in contemplating the depths of their – and, at least on occasion, our – longing for oblivion. 'Easter Hymn'

(*More Poems* I) prays to Christ, in its way, and ends: 'Bow hither out of heaven and see and save.' *Save*, how? In the only real way, by granting oblivion, the gift of eternal death, such as Christ himself must now or would now yearn for. Housman is a poet with a very long memory, and 'Easter Hymn' gets some of its power from the knowledge that Easter antedates Christianity, and that it was a brilliant but perilous coup of the Christian missionaries which took over the name of the goddess whose feast was celebrated at the vernal equinox.

'For My Funeral' (*More Poems* XLVII) is supremely grateful for the fact that Christianity is true not at all. Housman will have savoured in anticipation the thought of its ringing through Trinity College Chapel as the 'Hymn' at his funeral service.

These profoundly irreligious and blasphemous energies animated the man, and they can be seen in many an authenticated anecdote and in the styptic comedy of his letters. Of *A Shropshire Lad*: 'Kate writes to say that she likes the verse better than the sentiments. The sentiments, she then goes on to say, appear to be taken from the book of Ecclesiastes. To prefer my versification to the sentiments of the Holy Ghost is decidedly flattering, but strikes me as a trifle impious.' Years later, *Nunc dimittis* runs in his head as he awaits the fifth and last volume of his edition of Manilius: 'It ought to be out in a year's time, and then I shall have done what I came on earth to do, and can devote the rest of my days to religious meditation.' Not much religious devotion in 'devote' there – except that, in devoting himself to classical scholarship, Housman was as devoted and devout as any believer could be.

For here too the strongest presence of the poet within the editing is as blasphemer. The wit, hostility and even obsessiveness of the religious allusions are unremitting. The poet who deplored the Christian God is at one with the scholar who is profoundly blasphemous. Christ says of himself, 'a greater than Solomon is here'; Housman wrests it to a matter of self-deluding scholarly pre-eminence: 'a greater than Lachmann is here'. The believers say, 'Lighten our darkness, we beseech thee, O Lord'; Housman says of those who press him with questions which they hope he will be unable to answer,

When these scholars ask me these questions, they are not beseeching me to lighten their darkness; nothing is further from their desire. They hope and believe that they are asking me awkward questions, questions which I in my precipitancy have forgotten to ask myself; and accordingly, like Pilate of old, they do not stay for an answer.

In Housman's world, it is not Christ who was 'despised and rejected', but certain manuscript readings. One particular manuscript is more three than one, and 'its devotees, believing themselves good unitarians, have been engaged in worshipping a trinity'. Of the great scholar Bentley, Housman says that as he grew older he 'acquired the worst habits of deity'.

Gibbon, as Housman acknowledged, was one of the masters from whom he learnt how to write. Like Gibbon, Housman was engaged in what has been half-sneered at as 'sapping a solemn creed with solemn sneer'. Yet sustaining the arrogance there is an angry humility:

Communion with the ancients is purchasable at no cheaper rate than the kingdom of heaven; we must be born again. But to be born again is a process exceedingly repugnant to all right-minded Englishmen. I believe they think it improper, and they have a strong and well-grounded suspicion that it is arduous.

Yet Housman's anger often precipitates the comedy not only of extravagance but of a burgeoning extravaganza. The finest blasphemy in his classical writings is his unfolding, in a many-petalled comedy, of how H.W. Garrod's inconsistency and chicanery had betrayed Garrod into positing something that he had not bargained for; Housman, all silk, says: 'By putting together his scattered utterances, dotting his *i*'s and crossing his *t*'s, I think I have constructed what is surely the most eventful history in the annals of literature: the life, death, and resurrection of Alfenus Varus.'

What elevates such comedy above a merely professional combat or contempt is Housman's passion not only for sense and for responsibility but for truth. When he avers that 'the faintest of all human passions is the love of truth', we are heart-warmed and we heed him because it is unmistakable that nothing could be further from the truth in his amazing case. Yet the greatness of the blasphemy in Housman's prose, unremitting and diverse, is not only a matter of his personal imaginative convictions but also of his being charged by a whole tradition that relates editing to blasphemy. Housman brings over the energies which had shone in the fictitious or imaginary edition; brings them over into the world of real – albeit endlessly factitious, inaccurate and self-deceiving – scholarship.

If we scan the writers who have most powerfully been drawn to the fictitious edition as a literary form, we find that one of the few things which they have in common is an equivocal fascination with religion. They may not be simply irreligious; they may indeed possess that exacerbated spirituality which Lionel Trilling has seen as especially characteristic of modernism; but at any rate they are not staunchly devout. Jonathan Swift with both *A Tale of a Tub* and *Gulliver's Travels* invoked the idea of the fictitious editor, and both – to say the least – are religiously disconcerting. Alexander Pope created a monstrous parody of the learned edition in *The Dunciad* and concluded it with his own creative parody of the apocalyptic uncreation. Pope was willing to outrage the conventional religionists by speaking of textual cruces in the same breath as the Crucifixion; not satisfied with his first try ('And crucify poor Shakespeare once a week'), he tried again: 'The frippery of crucified Molière'. It is no surprise that Pope's *Dunciad Variorum* includes in its prefatory material a fierce accusation by John Dennis about Pope's being a professing Roman Catholic: 'Though he is a professor of the worst religion, yet he laughs at it.' And the poet who 'edited' *The Dunciad* was the poet who could meet the accusations of godlike arrogance with godlike arrogance:

> Yes, I am proud; I must be proud to see
> Men not afraid of God, afraid of me.

Or there is Laurence Sterne, whose *Tristram Shandy* is at once one of the important precursors of Carlyle's *Sartor Resartus* and a work which persistently – and, most would say, blasphemously – juxtaposes God's creative powers, the writer's creative powers, and everybody's procreative powers.

'Shame on us degenerate Editors!' – how crucial that cry of Carlyle's was. Carlyle's apprenticeship as reviewer and encyclopaedist was to be transformed into his persistent role as editor-translator. In an essay on Jean Paul Richter, he was happy to quote his own earlier words as those of 'one of Richter's English critics'. The culmination was *Sartor Resartus* – not only 'the tailor retailored' and 'the patcher patched', but also 'the clothes volume edited'. The

Editor wrestles with the problems of Teufelsdröckh's manuscript, scattered through the paper bags marked with the signs of the zodiac. The fictitious Editor's 'critical endeavours are less important than Teufelsdröckh's creative ones', as G.B. Tennyson has said, but Carlyle's creative endeavours encircle it all: 'Carlyle can create any materials he wants, but the Editor has no such power.'

Or if we leap from Carlyle into the modern, there is Jorge Luis Borges. In his Preface to *Fictions*, Borges discusses fiction-within-fiction: 'A better course of procedure is to pretend that these books already exist, and then to offer a résumé, a commentary. Thus proceeded Carlyle in *Sartor Resartus*.' Borges is perhaps the greatest of those modern writers who are fictitious editors or commentators, whether of the complete history of an unknown planet, the works of Herbert Quain, the bibliography of Pierre Menard (author of the *Quixote*) or *The Approach to Al-Mu'tasim*. And just as Borges is the most insatiable commentator on fictitious books, so is he the most sceptical of religious devotees. Quain's imagined book is called *The God of the Labyrinth*. Biblical scholarship illuminates 'Three Versions of Judas'. The spurious (not just fictitious) history of Tlön was the creation of a nineteenth-century irreligious maniac: 'Buckley did not believe in God, but nevertheless wished to demonstrate to the non-existent God that mortal men were capable of conceiving a world.'

Then there is Nabokov and *Pale Fire*. Whatever else it may be, *Pale Fire* is obviously a glittering example of the fictitious edition – and of the fictitious edition as especially concerned with the absence or presence of God. 'While snubbing gods, including the big G': Shade's line receives Kinbote's *imprimatur*: 'Here indeed is the Gist of the matter.' The characters of *Pale Fire* are mostly people who think they are God or who have what is charmingly called a religion of their own.

> My God died young. Theolatry I found
> Degrading, and its premises, unsound.

But what then of the Author of our being?

> Man's life as commentary to abstruse
> Unfinished poem, Note for further use.

Which note Kinbote has to annotate: 'If I correctly understand the sense of this succinct observation, our poet suggests here that human life is but a series of footnotes to a vast obscure unfinished masterpiece.' Nabokov's fictitious edition has evident affinities with *Sartor Resartus*, and with the refrain of Carlyle's poem 'Peter Nimmo': 'Life's a variorum.'

Yet why should 'snubbing gods, including the big G' be so much a concern of the fictitious edition? Because God may indeed be our Author, but there is one person who can (with guilty pride) trump even authors: an editor. In the beginning was the Word, and the Word was with God, and the Word was God – and I edited it, cackles the lunatic editor. The godlike pride of the real-life editor can be evident enough. Take those real-life editors whom Lewis Mumford berated for their assumption 'that Emerson's own intentions need not be respected, and that he has no right to have the final word'. Their assumption is godlike in the way it overrides; they, like God, have the right to the final word. Man proposes, his editor disposes.

Such is the impious tendency which Benjamin Franklin opposed when he made sure that God would be acknowledged to be at once the author of our being, and the publisher, and the editor.

> The Body of
> B. Franklin Printer,
> (Like the cover of an Old Book
> Its contents torn out
> And stript of its Lettering and Gilding)
> Lies here, Food for Worms.
> But the work shall not be lost;
> For it will, (as he believ'd) appear
> once more
> In a new and more elegant Edition
> Revised and Corrected
> By the Author.

Coleridge said of the imagination that it was 'a repetition in the finite mind of the eternal act of creation in the infinite I A M'. But if it is happily natural for us to worship creators, it is no less unhappily natural for us to fear and snub them, and the editor can embody the revenge of the uncreative. The antagonism between Carlyle's

Editor and Teufelsdröckh is quite as real as their co-operation – and the same is true of Nabokov's Shade and Kinbote. Kinbote's Preface ends with the classic Olympian *hauteur* of the editor, who may suspect that he is only a living dog, but who knows that his author (like his God, perhaps) is only a dead lion:

> Let me state that without my notes Shade's text simply has no human reality at all since the human reality of such a poem as his (being too skittish and reticent for an autobiographical work), with the omission of many pithy lines carelessly rejected by him, has to depend entirely on the reality of its author and his surroundings, attachments and so forth, a reality that only my notes can provide. To this statement my dear poet would probably not have subscribed, but, for better or worse, it is the commentator who has the last word.

Instead of the infinite patience of God, we have come to 'a commentator's infinite patience and disgust'. God may be the author; he may even be the papermaker ('every page in the book of one's personal fate bears His watermark'), but he isn't for the impious Kinbote what he was for the pious Benjamin Franklin, His own editor and bibliographer. So that when Borges says of the invention of the planet Tlön, 'we have unanimously rejected the idea of a single creator', the point about fictions is a point about gods.

Tennyson was seen by Carlyle as 'carrying a bit of Chaos about him, which he is manufacturing into Cosmos' – the poetic power is analogous to, or partakes of, the divine one, and Nabokov's Shade wishes to 'plunge back into his chaos and drag out of it with all its wet stars, his cosmos'. Housman for his part sees the positive anti-creative power of Pope's Dullness in the new scholarly dunces: 'This ends what I have to say on Dr Postgate's spirited attempt to re-establish chaos amongst Propertius' manuscripts.'

Well before Anthony Burgess's excellent fable of literary blasphemy, *ABBA ABBA*, Housman knew that people could invest their zealotry elsewhere than in religion, and that blasphemy might therefore fall within and upon the auspices of institutionalised literature or learning. R.W. Chambers has an anecdote which brings home that there was more than one piety upon which Housman was willing to visit his blasphemy.

I had just been appointed Librarian [at University College] and, with some friends, made a pretty thorough search of the then very neglected College Library, in the course of which we discovered, among other treasures, a quite unknown Coverdale Bible. I reported this to the Library Committee, possibly with an excess of self-satisfaction which Housman thought ought to be discountenanced. 'Would it not be as well,' said Housman, 'to sell these and buy some really useful books with the proceeds?' 'Judas Iscariot once said something of that sort,' retorted W.P. Ker, and Housman left it at that.

But left it at what exactly? At having provoked the pious Ker into a blasphemy more shocking than Housman's own? For Housman both practised and incited 'genuine blasphemy'.

> Ho, everyone that thirsteth
>   And hath the price to give,
> Come to the stolen waters,
>   Drink and your soul shall live.

'And as for him that wanteth understanding, she saith to him, stolen waters are sweet, and bread eaten in secret is pleasant. But he knoweth not that the dead are there; and that her guests are in the depths of hell.' Housman, in poetry and prose, writes as a paying guest in the depths of hell.

COLLECTED
POEMS

——

A SHROPSHIRE LAD

I

1887

From Clee to heaven the beacon burns,
    The shires have seen it plain,
From north and south the sign returns
    And beacons burn again.

Look left, look right, the hills are bright,
    The dales are light between,
Because 'tis fifty years to-night
    That God has saved the Queen.

Now, when the flame they watch not towers
    About the soil they trod,
Lads, we'll remember friends of ours
    Who shared the work with God.

To skies that knit their heartstrings right,
    To fields that bred them brave,
The saviours come not home to-night:
    Themselves they could not save.

It dawns in Asia, tombstones show
    And Shropshire names are read;
And the Nile spills his overflow
    Beside the Severn's dead.

We pledge in peace by farm and town
    The Queen they served in war,
And fire the beacons up and down
    The land they perished for.

'God save the Queen' we living sing,
    From height to height 'tis heard;
And with the rest your voices ring,
    Lads of the Fifty-third.

Oh, God will save her, fear you not:
    Be you the men you've been,
Get you the sons your fathers got,
    And God will save the Queen.

II

Loveliest of trees, the cherry now
Is hung with bloom along the bough,
And stands about the woodland ride
Wearing white for Eastertide.

Now, of my threescore years and ten,
Twenty will not come again,
And take from seventy springs a score,
It only leaves me fifty more.

And since to look at things in bloom
Fifty springs are little room,
About the woodlands I will go
To see the cherry hung with snow.

III

THE RECRUIT

Leave your home behind, lad,
  And reach your friends your hand,
And go, and luck go with you
  While Ludlow tower shall stand.

Oh, come you home of Sunday
  When Ludlow streets are still
And Ludlow bells are calling
  To farm and lane and mill,

Or come you home of Monday
  When Ludlow market hums
And Ludlow chimes are playing
  'The conquering hero comes',

Come you home a hero,
  Or come not home at all,
The lads you leave will mind you
  Till Ludlow tower shall fall.

And you will list the bugle
  That blows in lands of morn,
And make the foes of England
  Be sorry you were born.

And you till trump of doomsday
  On lands of morn may lie,
And make the hearts of comrades
  Be heavy where you die.

Leave your home behind you,
  Your friends by field and town:
Oh, town and field will mind you
  Till Ludlow tower is down.

IV

REVEILLE

Wake: the silver dusk returning
  Up the beach of darkness brims,
And the ship of sunrise burning
  Strands upon the eastern rims.

Wake: the vaulted shadow shatters,
  Trampled to the floor it spanned,
And the tent of night in tatters
  Straws the sky-pavilioned land.

Up, lad, up, 'tis late for lying:
  Hear the drums of morning play;
Hark, the empty highways crying
  'Who'll beyond the hills away?'

Towns and countries woo together,
  Forelands beacon, belfries call;
Never lad that trod on leather
  Lived to feast his heart with all.

Up, lad: thews that lie and cumber
  Sunlit pallets never thrive;
Morns abed and daylight slumber
  Were not meant for man alive.

Clay lies still, but blood's a rover;
  Breath's a ware that will not keep.
Up, lad: when the journey's over
  There'll be time enough to sleep.

V

Oh see how thick the goldcup flowers
    Are lying in field and lane,
With dandelions to tell the hours
    That never are told again.
Oh may I squire you round the meads
    And pick you posies gay?
– 'Twill do no harm to take my arm.
    'You may, young man, you may.'

Ah, spring was sent for lass and lad,
    'Tis now the blood runs gold,
And man and maid had best be glad
    Before the world is old.
What flowers to-day may flower to-morrow,
    But never as good as new.
– Suppose I wound my arm right round –
    ''Tis true, young man, 'tis true.'

Some lads there are, 'tis shame to say,
    That only court to thieve,
And once they bear the bloom away
    'Tis little enough they leave.
Then keep your heart for men like me
    And safe from trustless chaps.
My love is true and all for you.
    'Perhaps, young man, perhaps.'

Oh, look in my eyes then, can you doubt?
    – Why, 'tis a mile from town.
How green the grass is all about!
    We might as well sit down.
– Ah, life, what is it but a flower?
    Why must true lovers sigh?
Be kind, have pity, my own, my pretty, –
    'Good-bye, young man, good-bye.'

VI

When the lad for longing sighs,
   Mute and dull of cheer and pale,
If at death's own door he lies,
   Maiden, you can heal his ail.

Lovers' ills are all to buy:
   The wan look, the hollow tone,
The hung head, the sunken eye,
   You can have them for your own.

Buy them, buy them: eve and morn
   Lovers' ills are all to sell.
Then you can lie down forlorn;
   But the lover will be well.

VII

When smoke stood up from Ludlow,
  And mist blew off from Teme,
And blithe afield to ploughing
  Against the morning beam
  I strode beside my team,

The blackbird in the coppice
  Looked out to see me stride,
And hearkened as I whistled
  The trampling team beside,
  And fluted and replied:

'Lie down, lie down, young yeoman;
  What use to rise and rise?
Rise man a thousand mornings
  Yet down at last he lies,
  And then the man is wise.'

I heard the tune he sang me,
  And spied his yellow bill;
I picked a stone and aimed it
  And threw it with a will:
  Then the bird was still.

Then my soul within me
  Took up the blackbird's strain,
And still beside the horses
  Along the dewy lane
  It sang the song again:

'Lie down, lie down, young yeoman;
  The sun moves always west;
The road one treads to labour
  Will lead one home to rest,
  And that will be the best.'

VIII

'Farewell to barn and stack and tree,
    Farewell to Severn shore.
Terence, look your last at me,
    For I come home no more.

'The sun burns on the half-mown hill,
    By now the blood is dried;
And Maurice amongst the hay lies still
    And my knife is in his side.

'My mother thinks us long away;
    'Tis time the field were mown.
She had two sons at rising day,
    To-night she'll be alone.

'And here's a bloody hand to shake,
    And oh, man, here's good-bye;
We'll sweat no more on scythe and rake,
    My bloody hands and I.

'I wish you strength to bring you pride,
    And a love to keep you clean,
And I wish you luck, come Lammastide,
    At racing on the green.

'Long for me the rick will wait,
    And long will wait the fold,
And long will stand the empty plate,
    And dinner will be cold.'

IX

On moonlit heath and lonesome bank
　　The sheep beside me graze;
And yon the gallows used to clank
　　Fast by the four cross ways.

A careless shepherd once would keep
　　The flocks by moonlight there, [1]
And high amongst the glimmering sheep
　　The dead man stood on air.

They hang us now in Shrewsbury jail:
　　The whistles blow forlorn,
And trains all night groan on the rail
　　To men that die at morn.

There sleeps in Shrewsbury jail to-night,
　　Or wakes, as may betide,
A better lad, if things went right,
　　Than most that sleep outside.

And naked to the hangman's noose
　　The morning clocks will ring
A neck God made for other use
　　Than strangling in a string.

And sharp the link of life will snap,
　　And dead on air will stand
Heels that held up as straight a chap
　　As treads upon the land.

So here I'll watch the night and wait
　　To see the morning shine,
When he will hear the stroke of eight
　　And not the stroke of nine;

And wish my friend as sound a sleep
　　As lads' I did not know,
That shepherded the moonlit sheep
　　A hundred years ago.

[1] Hanging in chains was called keeping sheep by moonlight.

X

MARCH

The Sun at noon to higher air,
Unharnessing the silver Pair
That late before his chariot swam,
Rides on the gold wool of the Ram.

So braver notes the storm-cock sings
To start the rusted wheel of things,
And brutes in field and brutes in pen
Leap that the world goes round again.

The boys are up the woods with day
To fetch the daffodils away,
And home at noonday from the hills
They bring no dearth of daffodils.

Afield for palms the girls repair,
And sure enough the palms are there,
And each will find by hedge or pond
Her waving silver-tufted wand.

In farm and field through all the shire
The eye beholds the heart's desire;
Ah, let not only mine be vain,
For lovers should be loved again.

XI

On your midnight pallet lying,
    Listen, and undo the door:
Lads that waste the light in sighing
    In the dark should sigh no more;
Night should ease a lover's sorrow;
Therefore, since I go to-morrow,
    Pity me before.

In the land to which I travel,
    The far dwelling, let me say –
Once, if here the couch is gravel,
    In a kinder bed I lay,
And the breast the darnel smothers
Rested once upon another's
    When it was not clay.

XII

When I watch the living meet,
　　And the moving pageant file
Warm and breathing through the street
　　Where I lodge a little while,

If the heats of hate and lust
　　In the house of flesh are strong,
Let me mind the house of dust
　　Where my sojourn shall be long.

In the nation that is not
　　Nothing stands that stood before;
There revenges are forgot,
　　And the hater hates no more;

Lovers lying two and two
　　Ask not whom they sleep beside,
And the bridegroom all night through
　　Never turns him to the bride.

XIII

When I was one-and-twenty
  I heard a wise man say,
'Give crowns and pounds and guineas
  But not your heart away;
Give pearls away and rubies
  But keep your fancy free.'
But I was one-and-twenty,
  No use to talk to me.

When I was one-and-twenty
  I heard him say again,
'The heart out of the bosom
  Was never given in vain;
'Tis paid with sighs a plenty
  And sold for endless rue.'
And I am two-and-twenty,
  And oh, 'tis true, 'tis true.

XIV

There pass the careless people
  That call their souls their own:
Here by the road I loiter,
  How idle and alone.

Ah, past the plunge of plummet,
  In seas I cannot sound,
My heart and soul and senses,
  World without end, are drowned.

His folly has not fellow
  Beneath the blue of day
That gives to man or woman
  His heart and soul away.

There flowers no balm to sain him
  From east of earth to west
That's lost for everlasting
  The heart out of his breast.

Here by the labouring highway
  With empty hands I stroll:
Sea-deep, till doomsday morning,
  Lie lost my heart and soul.

XV

Look not in my eyes, for fear
  They mirror true the sight I see,
And there you find your face too clear
  And love it and be lost like me.
One the long nights through must lie
  Spent in star-defeated sighs,
But why should you as well as I
  Perish? gaze not in my eyes.

A Grecian lad, as I hear tell,
  One that many loved in vain,
Looked into a forest well
  And never looked away again.
There, when the turf in springtime flowers,
  With downward eye and gazes sad,
Stands amid the glancing showers
  A jonquil, not a Grecian lad.

XVI

It nods and curtseys and recovers
　When the wind blows above,
The nettle on the graves of lovers
　That hanged themselves for love.

The nettle nods, the wind blows over,
　The man, he does not move,
The lover of the grave, the lover
　That hanged himself for love.

XVII

Twice a week the winter thorough
    Here stood I to keep the goal:
Football then was fighting sorrow
    For the young man's soul.

Now in Maytime to the wicket
    Out I march with bat and pad:
See the son of grief at cricket
    Trying to be glad.

Try I will; no harm in trying:
    Wonder 'tis how little mirth
Keeps the bones of man from lying
    On the bed of earth.

XVIII

Oh, when I was in love with you,
　　Then I was clean and brave,
And miles around the wonder grew
　　How well did I behave.

And now the fancy passes by,
　　And nothing will remain,
And miles around they'll say that I
　　Am quite myself again.

XIX

TO AN ATHLETE DYING YOUNG

The time you won your town the race
We chaired you through the market-place;
Man and boy stood cheering by,
And home we brought you shoulder-high.

To-day, the road all runners come,
Shoulder-high we bring you home,
And set you at your threshold down,
Townsman of a stiller town.

Smart lad, to slip betimes away
From fields where glory does not stay
And early though the laurel grows
It withers quicker than the rose.

Eyes the shady night has shut
Cannot see the record cut,
And silence sounds no worse than cheers
After earth has stopped the ears:

Now you will not swell the rout
Of lads that wore their honours out,
Runners whom renown outran
And the name died before the man.

So set, before its echoes fade,
The fleet foot on the sill of shade,
And hold to the low lintel up
The still-defended challenge-cup.

And round that early-laurelled head
Will flock to gaze the strengthless dead,
And find unwithered on its curls
The garland briefer than a girl's.

XX

Oh fair enough are sky and plain,
  But I know fairer far:
Those are as beautiful again
  That in the water are;

The pools and rivers wash so clean
  The trees and clouds and air,
The like on earth was never seen,
  And oh that I were there.

These are the thoughts I often think
  As I stand gazing down
In act upon the cressy brink
  To strip and dive and drown;

But in the golden-sanded brooks
  And azure meres I spy
A silly lad that longs and looks
  And wishes he were I.

XXI

BREDON[1] HILL

In summertime on Bredon
  The bells they sound so clear;
Round both the shires they ring them
  In steeples far and near,
  A happy noise to hear.

Here of a Sunday morning
  My love and I would lie,
And see the coloured counties,
  And hear the larks so high
  About us in the sky.

The bells would ring to call her
  In valleys miles away:
'Come all to church, good people;
  Good people, come and pray.'
  But here my love would stay.

And I would turn and answer
  Among the springing thyme,
'Oh, peal upon our wedding,
  And we will hear the chime,
  And come to church in time.'

But when the snows at Christmas
  On Bredon top were strown,
My love rose up so early
  And stole out unbeknown
  And went to church alone.

They tolled the one bell only,
  Groom there was none to see,
The mourners followed after,
  And so to church went she,
  And would not wait for me.

[1] Pronounced Breedon.

The bells they sound on Bredon,
    And still the steeples hum.
'Come all to church, good people,' –
    Oh, noisy bells, be dumb;
    I hear you, I will come.

XXII

The street sounds to the soldiers' tread,
    And out we troop to see:
A single redcoat turns his head,
    He turns and looks at me.

My man, from sky to sky's so far,
    We never crossed before;
Such leagues apart the world's ends are,
    We're like to meet no more;

What thoughts at heart have you and I
    We cannot stop to tell;
But dead or living, drunk or dry,
    Soldier, I wish you well.

XXIII

The lads in their hundreds to Ludlow come in for the fair,
   There's men from the barn and the forge and the mill and the
      fold,
The lads for the girls and the lads for the liquor are there,
   And there with the rest are the lads that will never be old.

There's chaps from the town and the field and the till and the
      cart,
   And many to count are the stalwart, and many the brave,
And many the handsome of face and the handsome of heart,
   And few that will carry their looks or their truth to the grave.

I wish one could know them, I wish there were tokens to tell
   The fortunate fellows that now you can never discern;
And then one could talk with them friendly and wish them
      farewell
   And watch them depart on the way that they will not return.

But now you may stare as you like and there's nothing to scan;
   And brushing your elbow unguessed-at and not to be told
They carry back bright to the coiner the mintage of man,
   The lads that will die in their glory and never be old.

XXIV

Say, lad, have you things to do?
  Quick then, while your day's at prime.
Quick, and if 'tis work for two,
  Here am I, man: now's your time.

Send me now, and I shall go;
  Call me, I shall hear you call;
Use me ere they lay me low
  Where a man's no use at all;

Ere the wholesome flesh decay,
  And the willing nerve be numb,
And the lips lack breath to say,
  'No, my lad, I cannot come.'

XXV

This time of year a twelvemonth past,
   When Fred and I would meet,
We needs must jangle, till at last
   We fought and I was beat.

So then the summer fields about,
   Till rainy days began,
Rose Harland on her Sundays out
   Walked with the better man.

The better man she walks with still,
   Though now 'tis not with Fred:
A lad that lives and has his will
   Is worth a dozen dead.

Fred keeps the house all kinds of weather,
   And clay's the house he keeps;
When Rose and I walk out together
   Stock-still lies Fred and sleeps.

XXVI

Along the field as we came by
A year ago, my love and I,
The aspen over stile and stone
Was talking to itself alone.
'Oh who are these that kiss and pass?
A country lover and his lass;
Two lovers looking to be wed;
And time shall put them both to bed,
But she shall lie with earth above,
And he beside another love.'

And sure enough beneath the tree
There walks another love with me,
And overhead the aspen heaves
Its rainy-sounding silver leaves;
And I spell nothing in their stir,
But now perhaps they speak to her,
And plain for her to understand
They talk about a time at hand
When I shall sleep with clover clad,
And she beside another lad.

XXVII

'Is my team ploughing,
  That I was used to drive
And hear the harness jingle
  When I was man alive?'

Ay, the horses trample,
  The harness jingles now;
No change though you lie under
  The land you used to plough.

'Is football playing
  Along the river shore,
With lads to chase the leather,
  Now I stand up no more?'

Ay, the ball is flying,
  The lads play heart and soul;
The goal stands up, the keeper
  Stands up to keep the goal.

'Is my girl happy,
  That I thought hard to leave,
And has she tired of weeping
  As she lies down at eve?'

Ay, she lies down lightly,
  She lies not down to weep:
Your girl is well contented.
  Be still, my lad, and sleep.

'Is my friend hearty,
  Now I am thin and pine,
And has he found to sleep in
  A better bed than mine?'

Yes, lad, I lie easy,
  I lie as lads would choose;
I cheer a dead man's sweetheart,
  Never ask me whose.

XXVIII

THE WELSH MARCHES

High the vanes of Shrewsbury gleam
Islanded in Severn stream;
The bridges from the steepled crest
Cross the water east and west.

The flag of morn in conqueror's state
Enters at the English gate:
The vanquished eve, as night prevails,
Bleeds upon the road to Wales.

Ages since the vanquished bled
Round my mother's marriage-bed;
There the ravens feasted far
About the open house of war:

When Severn down to Buildwas ran
Coloured with the death of man,
Couched upon her brother's grave
The Saxon got me on the slave.

The sound of fight is silent long
That began the ancient wrong;
Long the voice of tears is still
That wept of old the endless ill.

In my heart it has not died,
The war that sleeps on Severn side;
They cease not fighting, east and west,
On the marches of my breast.

Here the truceless armies yet
Trample, rolled in blood and sweat;
They kill and kill and never die;
And I think that each is I.

None will part us, none undo
The knot that makes one flesh of two,
Sick with hatred, sick with pain,
Strangling – When shall we be slain?

When shall I be dead and rid
Of the wrong my father did?
How long, how long, till spade and hearse
Put to sleep my mother's curse?

XXIX

THE LENT LILY

'Tis spring; come out to ramble
  The hilly brakes around,
For under thorn and bramble
  About the hollow ground
  The primroses are found.

And there's the windflower chilly
  With all the winds at play,
And there's the Lenten lily
  That has not long to stay
  And dies on Easter day.

And since till girls go maying
  You find the primrose still,
And find the windflower playing
  With every wind at will,
  But not the daffodil,

Bring baskets now, and sally
  Upon the spring's array,
And bear from hill and valley
  The daffodil away
  That dies on Easter day.

XXX

Others, I am not the first,
Have willed more mischief than they durst:
If in the breathless night I too
Shiver now, 'tis nothing new.

More than I, if truth were told,
Have stood and sweated hot and cold,
And through their reins in ice and fire
Fear contended with desire.

Agued once like me were they,
But I like them shall win my way
Lastly to the bed of mould
Where there's neither heat nor cold.

But from my grave across my brow
Plays no wind of healing now,
And fire and ice within me fight
Beneath the suffocating night.

XXXI

On Wenlock Edge the wood's in trouble;
  His forest fleece the Wrekin heaves;
The gale, it plies the saplings double,
  And thick on Severn snow the leaves.

'Twould blow like this through holt and hanger
  When Uricon the city stood:
'Tis the old wind in the old anger,
  But then it threshed another wood.

Then, 'twas before my time, the Roman
  At yonder heaving hill would stare:
The blood that warms an English yeoman,
  The thoughts that hurt him, they were there.

There, like the wind through woods in riot,
  Through him the gale of life blew high;
The tree of man was never quiet:
  Then 'twas the Roman, now 'tis I.

The gale, it plies the saplings double,
  It blows so hard, 'twill soon be gone:
To-day the Roman and his trouble
  Are ashes under Uricon.

XXXII

From far, from eve and morning
   And yon twelve-winded sky,
The stuff of life to knit me
   Blew hither: here am I.

Now – for a breath I tarry
   Nor yet disperse apart –
Take my hand quick and tell me,
   What have you in your heart.

Speak now, and I will answer;
   How shall I help you, say;
Ere to the wind's twelve quarters
   I take my endless way.

XXXIII

If truth in hearts that perish
  Could move the powers on high,
I think the love I bear you
  Should make you not to die.

Sure, sure, if stedfast meaning,
  If single thought could save,
The world might end to-morrow,
  You should not see the grave.

This long and sure-set liking,
  This boundless will to please,
– Oh, you should live for ever
  If there were help in these.

But now, since all is idle,
  To this lost heart be kind,
Ere to a town you journey
  Where friends are ill to find.

XXXIV

THE NEW MISTRESS

'Oh, sick I am to see you, will you never let me be?
You may be good for something but you are not good for me.
Oh, go where you are wanted, for you are not wanted here.
And that was all the farewell when I parted from my dear.

'I will go where I am wanted, to a lady born and bred
Who will dress me free for nothing in a uniform of red;
She will not be sick to see me if I only keep it clean:
I will go where I am wanted for a soldier of the Queen.

'I will go where I am wanted, for the sergeant does not mind;
He may be sick to see me but he treats me very kind:
He gives me beer and breakfast and a ribbon for my cap,
And I never knew a sweetheart spend her money on a chap.

'I will go where I am wanted, where there's room for one or
    two,
And the men are none too many for the work there is to do;
Where the standing line wears thinner and the dropping dead lie
    thick;
And the enemies of England they shall see me and be sick.'

XXXV

On the idle hill of summer,
   Sleepy with the flow of streams,
Far I hear the steady drummer
   Drumming like a noise in dreams.

Far and near and low and louder
   On the roads of earth go by,
Dear to friends and food for powder,
   Soldiers marching, all to die.

East and west on fields forgotten
   Bleach the bones of comrades slain,
Lovely lads and dead and rotten;
   None that go return again.

Far the calling bugles hollo,
   High the screaming fife replies,
Gay the files of scarlet follow:
   Woman bore me, I will rise.

XXXVI

White in the moon the long road lies,
  The moon stands blank above;
White in the moon the long road lies
  That leads me from my love.

Still hangs the hedge without a gust,
  Still, still the shadows stay:
My feet upon the moonlit dust
  Pursue the ceaseless way.

The world is round, so travellers tell,
  And straight though reach the track,
Trudge on, trudge on, 'twill all be well,
  The way will guide one back.

But ere the circle homeward hies
  Far, far must it remove:
White in the moon the long road lies
  That leads me from my love.

XXXVII

As through the wild green hills of Wyre
The train ran, changing sky and shire,
And far behind, a fading crest,
Low in the forsaken west
Sank the high-reared head of Clee,
My hand lay empty on my knee.
Aching on my knee it lay:
That morning half a shire away
So many an honest fellow's fist
Had well-nigh wrung it from the wrist.
Hand, said I, since now we part
From fields and men we know by heart,
For strangers' faces, strangers' lands, —
Hand, you have held true fellows' hands.
Be clean then; rot before you do
A thing they'd not believe of you.
You and I must keep from shame
In London streets the Shropshire name;
On banks of Thames they must not say
Severn breeds worse men than they;
And friends abroad must bear in mind
Friends at home they leave behind.
Oh, I shall be stiff and cold
When I forget you, hearts of gold;
The land where I shall mind you not
Is the land where all's forgot.
And if my foot returns no more
To Teme nor Corve nor Severn shore,
Luck, my lads, be with you still
By falling stream and standing hill,
By chiming tower and whispering tree,
Men that made a man of me.
About your work in town and farm
Still you'll keep my head from harm,
Still you'll help me, hands that gave
A grasp to friend me to the grave.

XXXVIII

The winds out of the west land blow,
  My friends have breathed them there;
Warm with the blood of lads I know
  Comes east the sighing air.

It fanned their temples, filled their lungs,
  Scattered their forelocks free;
My friends made words of it with tongues
  That talk no more to me.

Their voices, dying as they fly,
  Loose on the wind are sown;
The names of men blow soundless by,
  My fellows' and my own.

Oh lads, at home I heard you plain,
  But here your speech is still,
And down the sighing wind in vain
  You hollo from the hill.

The wind and I, we both were there,
  But neither long abode;
Now through the friendless world we fare
  And sigh upon the road.

XXXIX

'Tis time, I think, by Wenlock town
   The golden broom should blow;
The hawthorn sprinkled up and down
   Should charge the land with snow.

Spring will not wait the loiterer's time
   Who keeps so long away;
So others wear the broom and climb
   The hedgerows heaped with may.

Oh tarnish late on Wenlock Edge,
   Gold that I never see;
Lie long, high snowdrifts in the hedge
   That will not shower on me.

XL

Into my heart an air that kills
  From yon far country blows:
What are those blue remembered hills,
  What spires, what farms are those?

This is the land of lost content,
  I see it shining plain,
The happy highways where I went
  And cannot come again.

XLI

In my own shire, if I was sad,
Homely comforters I had:
The earth, because my heart was sore,
Sorrowed for the son she bore;
And standing hills, long to remain,
Shared their short-lived comrade's pain.
And bound for the same bourn as I,
On every road I wandered by,
Trod beside me, close and dear,
The beautiful and death-struck year:
Whether in the woodland brown
I heard the beechnut rustle down,
And saw the purple crocus pale
Flower about the autumn dale;
Or littering far the fields of May
Lady-smocks a-bleaching lay,
And like a skylit water stood
The bluebells in the azured wood.

Yonder, lightening other loads,
The seasons range the country roads,
But here in London streets I ken
No such helpmates, only men;
And these are not in plight to bear,
If they would, another's care.
They have enough as 'tis: I see
In many an eye that measures me
The mortal sickness of a mind
Too unhappy to be kind.
Undone with misery, all they can
Is to hate their fellow man;
And till they drop they needs must still
Look at you and wish you ill.

XLII

THE MERRY GUIDE

Once in the wind of morning
  I ranged the thymy wold;
The world-wide air was azure
  And all the brooks ran gold.

There through the dews beside me
  Behold a youth that trod,
With feathered cap on forehead,
  And poised a golden rod.

With mien to match the morning
  And gay delightful guise
And friendly brows and laughter
  He looked me in the eyes.

Oh whence, I asked, and whither?
  He smiled and would not say,
And looked at me and beckoned
  And laughed and led the way.

And with kind looks and laughter
  And nought to say beside
We two went on together,
  I and my happy guide.

Across the glittering pastures
  And empty upland still
And solitude of shepherds
  High in the folded hill,

By hanging woods and hamlets
  That gaze through orchards down
On many a windmill turning
  And far-discovered town,

With gay regards of promise
  And sure unslackened stride
And smiles and nothing spoken
  Led on my merry guide.

By blowing realms of woodland
    With sunstruck vanes afield
And cloud-led shadows sailing
    About the windy weald,

By valley-guarded granges
    And silver waters wide,
Content at heart I followed
    With my delightful guide.

And like the cloudy shadows
    Across the country blown
We two fare on for ever,
    But not we two alone.

With the great gale we journey
    That breathes from gardens thinned,
Borne in the drift of blossoms
    Whose petals throng the wind;

Buoyed on the heaven-heard whisper
    Of dancing leaflets whirled
From all the woods that autumn
    Bereaves in all the world.

And midst the fluttering legion
    Of all that ever died
I follow, and before us
    Goes the delightful guide,

With lips that brim with laughter
    But never once respond,
And feet that fly on feathers,
    And serpent-circled wand.

XLIII

THE IMMORTAL PART

When I meet the morning beam
Or lay me down at night to dream,
I hear my bones within me say,
'Another night, another day.

'When shall this slough of sense be cast,
This dust of thoughts be laid at last,
The man of flesh and soul be slain
And the man of bone remain?

'This tongue that talks, these lungs that shout,
These thews that hustle us about,
This brain that fills the skull with schemes,
And its humming hive of dreams, –

'These to-day are proud in power
And lord it in their little hour:
The immortal bones obey control
Of dying flesh and dying soul.

''Tis long till eve and morn are gone:
Slow the endless night comes on,
And late to fulness grows the birth
That shall last as long as earth.

'Wanderers eastward, wanderers west,
Know you why you cannot rest?
'Tis that every mother's son
Travails with a skeleton.

'Lie down in the bed of dust;
Bear the fruit that bear you must;
Bring the eternal seed to light,
And morn is all the same as night.

'Rest you so from trouble sore,
Fear the heat o' the sun no more,
Nor the snowing winter wild,
Now you labour not with child.

'Empty vessel, garment cast,
We that wore you long shall last.
– Another night, another day.'
So my bones within me say.

Therefore they shall do my will
To-day while I am master still,
And flesh and soul, now both are strong,
Shall hale the sullen slaves along,

Before this fire of sense decay,
This smoke of thought blow clean away,
And leave with ancient night alone
The stedfast and enduring bone.

XLIV

Shot? so quick, so clean an ending?
  Oh that was right, lad, that was brave:
Yours was not an ill for mending,
  'Twas best to take it to the grave.

Oh you had forethought, you could reason,
  And saw your road and where it led,
And early wise and brave in season
  Put the pistol to your head.

Oh soon, and better so than later
  After long disgrace and scorn,
You shot dead the household traitor,
  The soul that should not have been born.

Right you guessed the rising morrow
  And scorned to tread the mire you must:
Dust's your wages, son of sorrow,
  But men may come to worse than dust.

Souls undone, undoing others, –
  Long time since the tale began.
You would not live to wrong your brothers:
  Oh lad, you died as fits a man.

Now to your grave shall friend and stranger
  With ruth and some with envy come:
Undishonoured, clear of danger,
  Clean of guilt, pass hence and home.

Turn safe to rest, no dreams, no waking;
  And here, man, here's the wreath I've made:
'Tis not a gift that's worth the taking,
  But wear it and it will not fade.

XLV

If it chance your eye offend you,
    Pluck it out, lad, and be sound:
'Twill hurt, but here are salves to friend you,
    And many a balsam grows on ground.

And if your hand or foot offend you,
    Cut it off, lad, and be whole;
But play the man, stand up and end you,
    When your sickness is your soul.

XLVI

Bring, in this timeless grave to throw,
No cypress, sombre on the snow;
Snap not from the bitter yew
His leaves that live December through;
Break no rosemary, bright with rime
And sparkling to the cruel clime;
Nor plod the winter land to look
For willows in the icy brook
To cast them leafless round him: bring
No spray that ever buds in spring.

But if the Christmas field has kept
Awns the last gleaner overstept,
Or shrivelled flax, whose flower is blue
A single season, never two;
Or if one haulm whose year is o'er
Shivers on the upland frore,
– Oh, bring from hill and stream and plain
Whatever will not flower again,
To give him comfort: he and those
Shall bide eternal bedfellows
Where low upon the couch he lies
Whence he never shall arise.

XLVII

THE CARPENTER'S SON

'Here the hangman stops his cart:
Now the best of friends must part.
Fare you well, for ill fare I:
Live, lads, and I will die.

'Oh, at home had I but stayed
'Prenticed to my father's trade,
Had I stuck to plane and adze,
I had not been lost, my lads.

'Then I might have built perhaps
Gallows-trees for other chaps,
Never dangled on my own,
Had I but left ill alone.

'Now, you see, they hang me high,
And the people passing by
Stop to shake their fists and curse;
So 'tis come from ill to worse.

'Here hang I, and right and left
Two poor fellows hang for theft:
All the same's the luck we prove,
Though the midmost hangs for love.

'Comrades all, that stand and gaze,
Walk henceforth in other ways;
See my neck and save your own:
Comrades all, leave ill alone.

'Make some day a decent end,
Shrewder fellows than your friend.
Fare you well, for ill fare I:
Live, lads, and I will die.'

XLVIII

Be still, my soul, be still; the arms you bear are brittle,
   Earth and high heaven are fixt of old and founded strong.
Think rather, – call to thought, if now you grieve a little,
   The days when we had rest, O soul, for they were long.

Men loved unkindness then, but lightless in the quarry
   I slept and saw not; tears fell down, I did not mourn;
Sweat ran and blood sprang out and I was never sorry:
   Then it was well with me, in days ere I was born.

Now, and I muse for why and never find the reason,
   I pace the earth, and drink the air, and feel the sun.
Be still, be still, my soul; it is but for a season:
   Let us endure an hour and see injustice done.

Ay, look: high heaven and earth ail from the prime foundation;
   All thoughts to rive the heart are here, and all are vain:
Horror and scorn and hate and fear and indignation –
   Oh why did I awake? when shall I sleep again?

XLIX

Think no more, lad; laugh, be jolly:
  Why should men make haste to die?
Empty heads and tongues a-talking
Make the rough road easy walking,
And the feather pate of folly
  Bears the falling sky.

Oh, 'tis jesting, dancing, drinking
  Spins the heavy world around.
If young hearts were not so clever,
Oh, they would be young for ever:
Think no more; 'tis only thinking
  Lays lads underground.

L

Clunton and Clunbury,
Clungunford and Clun,
Are the quietest places
Under the sun.

In valleys of springs of rivers,
  By Ony and Teme and Clun,
The country for easy livers,
  The quietest under the sun,

We still had sorrows to lighten,
  One could not be always glad,
And lads knew trouble at Knighton
  When I was a Knighton lad.

By bridges that Thames runs under,
  In London, the town built ill,
'Tis sure small matter for wonder
  If sorrow is with one still.

And if as a lad grows older
  The troubles he bears are more,
He carries his griefs on a shoulder
  That handselled them long before.

Where shall one halt to deliver
  This luggage I'd lief set down?
Not Thames, not Teme is the river,
  Nor London nor Knighton the town:

'Tis a long way further than Knighton,
  A quieter place than Clun,
Where doomsday may thunder and lighten
  And little 'twill matter to one.

LI

Loitering with a vacant eye
Along the Grecian gallery,
And brooding on my heavy ill,
I met a statue standing still.
Still in marble stone stood he,
And stedfastly he looked at me.
'Well met,' I thought the look would say,
'We both were fashioned far away;
We neither knew, when we were young,
These Londoners we live among.'

Still he stood and eyed me hard,
An earnest and a grave regard:
'What, lad, drooping with your lot?
I too would be where I am not.
I too survey that endless line
Of men whose thoughts are not as mine.
Years, ere you stood up from rest,
On my neck the collar prest;
Years, when you lay down your ill,
I shall stand and bear it still.
Courage, lad, 'tis not for long:
Stand, quit you like stone, be strong.'
So I thought his look would say;
And light on me my trouble lay,
And I stept out in flesh and bone
Manful like the man of stone.

LII

Far in a western brookland
  That bred me long ago
The poplars stand and tremble
  By pools I used to know.

There, in the windless night-time,
  The wanderer, marvelling why,
Halts on the bridge to hearken
  How soft the poplars sigh.

He hears: no more remembered
  In fields where I was known,
Here I lie down in London
  And turn to rest alone.

There, by the starlit fences,
  The wanderer halts and hears
My soul that lingers sighing
  About the glimmering weirs.

LIII

THE TRUE LOVER

The lad came to the door at night,
 When lovers crown their vows,
And whistled soft and out of sight
 In shadow of the boughs.

'I shall not vex you with my face
 Henceforth, my love, for aye;
So take me in your arms a space
 Before the east is grey.

'When I from hence away am past
 I shall not find a bride,
And you shall be the first and last
 I ever lay beside.'

She heard and went and knew not why;
 Her heart to his she laid;
Light was the air beneath the sky
 But dark under the shade.

'Oh do you breathe, lad, that your breast
 Seems not to rise and fall,
And here upon my bosom prest
 There beats no heart at all?'

'Oh loud, my girl, it once would knock,
 You should have felt it then;
But since for you I stopped the clock
 It never goes again.'

'Oh lad, what is it, lad, that drips
 Wet from your neck on mine?
What is it falling on my lips,
 My lad, that tastes of brine?'

'Oh like enough 'tis blood, my dear,
 For when the knife has slit
The throat across from ear to ear
 'Twill bleed because of it.'

Under the stars the air was light
　　But dark below the boughs,
The still air of the speechless night,
　　When lovers crown their vows.

LIV

With rue my heart is laden
　　For golden friends I had,
For many a rose-lipt maiden
　　And many a lightfoot lad.

By brooks too broad for leaping
　　The lightfoot boys are laid;
The rose-lipt girls are sleeping
　　In fields where roses fade.

LV

Westward on the high-hilled plains
   Where for me the world began,
Still, I think, in newer veins
   Frets the changeless blood of man.

Now that other lads than I
   Strip to bathe on Severn shore,
They, no help, for all they try,
   Tread the mill I trod before.

There, when hueless is the west
   And the darkness hushes wide,
Where the lad lies down to rest
   Stands the troubled dream beside.

There, on thoughts that once were mine,
   Day looks down the eastern steep,
And the youth at morning shine
   Makes the vow he will not keep.

LVI

THE DAY OF BATTLE

'Far I hear the bugle blow
To call me where I would not go,
And the guns begin the song,
"Soldier, fly or stay for long."

'Comrade, if to turn and fly
Made a soldier never die,
Fly I would, for who would not?
'Tis sure no pleasure to be shot.

'But since the man that runs away
Lives to die another day,
And cowards' funerals, when they come,
Are not wept so well at home,

'Therefore, though the best is bad,
Stand and do the best, my lad;
Stand and fight and see your slain,
And take the bullet in your brain.'

LVII

You smile upon your friend to-day,
    To-day his ills are over;
You hearken to the lover's say,
    And happy is the lover.

'Tis late to hearken, late to smile,
    But better late than never:
I shall have lived a little while
    Before I die for ever.

LVIII

When I came last to Ludlow
    Amidst the moonlight pale,
Two friends kept step beside me,
    Two honest lads and hale.

Now Dick lies long in the churchyard,
    And Ned lies long in jail,
And I come home to Ludlow
    Amidst the moonlight pale.

LIX

THE ISLE OF PORTLAND

The star-filled seas are smooth to-night
  From France to England strown;
Black towers above the Portland light
  The felon-quarried stone.

On yonder island, not to rise,
  Never to stir forth free,
Far from his folk a dead lad lies
  That once was friends with me.

Lie you easy, dream you light,
  And sleep you fast for aye;
And luckier may you find the night
  Than ever you found the day.

LX

Now hollow fires burn out to black,
    And lights are guttering low:
Square your shoulders, lift your pack,
    And leave your friends and go.

Oh never fear, man, nought's to dread,
    Look not left nor right:
In all the endless road you tread
    There's nothing but the night.

LXI

HUGHLEY STEEPLE

The vane on Hughley steeple
  Veers bright, a far-known sign,
And there lie Hughley people,
  And there lie friends of mine.
Tall in their midst the tower
  Divides the shade and sun,
And the clock strikes the hour
  And tells the time to none.

To south the headstones cluster,
  The sunny mounds lie thick;
The dead are more in muster
  At Hughley than the quick.
North, for a soon-told number,
  Chill graves the sexton delves,
And steeple-shadowed slumber
  The slayers of themselves.

To north, to south, lie parted,
  With Hughley tower above,
The kind, the single-hearted,
  The lads I used to love.
And, south or north, 'tis only
  A choice of friends one knows,
And I shall ne'er be lonely
  Asleep with these or those.

LXII

'Terence, this is stupid stuff:
You eat your victuals fast enough;
There can't be much amiss, 'tis clear,
To see the rate you drink your beer.
But oh, good Lord, the verse you make,
It gives a chap the belly-ache.
The cow, the old cow, she is dead;
It sleeps well, the horned head:
We poor lads, 'tis our turn now
To hear such tunes as killed the cow.
Pretty friendship 'tis to rhyme
Your friends to death before their time
Moping melancholy mad:
Come, pipe a tune to dance to, lad.'

Why, if 'tis dancing you would be,
There's brisker pipes than poetry.
Say, for what were hop-yards meant,
Or why was Burton built on Trent?
Oh many a peer of England brews
Livelier liquor than the Muse,
And malt does more than Milton can
To justify God's ways to man.
Ale, man, ale's the stuff to drink
For fellows whom it hurts to think:
Look into the pewter pot
To see the world as the world's not.
And faith, 'tis pleasant till 'tis past:
The mischief is that 'twill not last.
Oh I have been to Ludlow fair
And left my necktie God knows where,
And carried half-way home, or near,
Pints and quarts of Ludlow beer:
Then the world seemed none so bad,
And I myself a sterling lad;
And down in lovely muck I've lain,
Happy till I woke again.
Then I saw the morning sky:

Heigho, the tale was all a lie;
The world, it was the old world yet,
I was I, my things were wet,
And nothing now remained to do
But begin the game anew.

  Therefore, since the world has still
Much good, but much less good than ill,
And while the sun and moon endure
Luck's a chance, but trouble's sure,
I'd face it as a wise man would,
And train for ill and not for good.
'Tis true, the stuff I bring for sale
Is not so brisk a brew as ale:
Out of a stem that scored the hand
I wrung it in a weary land.
But take it: if the smack is sour,
The better for the embittered hour;
It should do good to heart and head
When your soul is in my soul's stead;
And I will friend you, if I may,
In the dark and cloudy day.

  There was a king reigned in the East:
There, when kings will sit to feast,
They get their fill before they think
With poisoned meat and poisoned drink.
He gathered all that springs to birth
From the many-venomed earth;
First a little, thence to more,
He sampled all her killing store;
And easy, smiling, seasoned sound,
Sate the king when healths went round.
They put arsenic in his meat
And stared aghast to watch him eat;
They poured strychnine in his cup
And shook to see him drink it up:
They shook, they stared as white's their shirt:
Them it was their poison hurt.
– I tell the tale that I heard told.
Mithridates, he died old.

LXIII

I hoed and trenched and weeded,
  And took the flowers to fair:
I brought them home unheeded;
  The hue was not the wear.

So up and down I sow them
  For lads like me to find,
When I shall lie below them,
  A dead man out of mind.

Some seed the birds devour,
  And some the season mars,
But here and there will flower
  The solitary stars,

And fields will yearly bear them
  As light-leaved spring comes on,
And luckless lads will wear them
  When I am dead and gone.

LAST POEMS

I publish these poems, few though they are, because it is not likely that I shall ever be impelled to write much more. I can no longer expect to be revisited by the continuous excitement under which in the early months of 1895 I wrote the greater part of my other book, nor indeed could I well sustain it if it came; and it is best that what I have written should be printed while I am here to see it through the press and control its spelling and punctuation. About a quarter of this matter belongs to the April of the present year, but most of it to dates between 1895 and 1910.

September 1922

We'll to the woods no more,
The laurels all are cut,
The bowers are bare of bay
That once the Muses wore;
The year draws in the day
And soon will evening shut:
The laurels all are cut,
We'll to the woods no more.
Oh we'll no more, no more
To the leafy woods away,
To the high wild woods of laurel
And the bowers of bay no more.

I

THE WEST

Beyond the moor and mountain crest
– Comrade, look not on the west –
The sun is down and drinks away
From air and land the lees of day.

The long cloud and the single pine
Sentinel the ending line,
And out beyond it, clear and wan,
Reach the gulfs of evening on.

The son of woman turns his brow
West from forty counties now,
And, as the edge of heaven he eyes,
Thinks eternal thoughts, and sighs.

Oh wide's the world, to rest or roam,
With change abroad and cheer at home,
Fights and furloughs, talk and tale,
Company and beef and ale.

But if I front the evening sky
Silent on the west look I,
And my comrade, stride for stride,
Paces silent at my side.

Comrade, look not on the west:
'Twill have the heart out of your breast;
'Twill take your thoughts and sink them far,
Leagues beyond the sunset bar.

Oh lad, I fear that yon's the sea
Where they fished for you and me,
And there, from whence we both were ta'en,
You and I shall drown again.

Send not on your soul before
To dive from that beguiling shore,
And let not yet the swimmer leave
His clothes upon the sands of eve.

Too fast to yonder strand forlorn
We journey, to the sunken bourn,
To flush the fading tinges eyed
By other lads at eventide.

Wide is the world, to rest or roam,
And early 'tis for turning home:
Plant your heel on earth and stand,
And let's forget our native land.

When you and I are spilt on air
Long we shall be strangers there;
Friends of flesh and bone are best:
Comrade, look not on the west.

II

As I gird on for fighting
  My sword upon my thigh,
I think on old ill fortunes
  Of better men than I.

Think I, the round world over,
  What golden lads are low
With hurts not mine to mourn for
  And shames I shall not know.

What evil luck soever
  For me remains in store,
'Tis sure much finer fellows
  Have fared much worse before.

So here are things to think on
  That ought to make me brave,
As I strap on for fighting
  My sword that will not save.

III

Her strong enchantments failing,
　　Her towers of fear in wreck,
Her limbecks dried of poisons
　　And the knife at her neck,

The Queen of air and darkness
　　Begins to shrill and cry,
'O young man, O my slayer,
　　To-morrow you shall die.'

O Queen of air and darkness,
　　I think 'tis truth you say,
And I shall die to-morrow;
　　But you will die to-day.

IV

ILLIC JACET

Oh hard is the bed they have made him,
    And common the blanket and cheap;
But there he will lie as they laid him:
    Where else could you trust him to sleep?

To sleep when the bugle is crying
    And cravens have heard and are brave,
When mothers and sweethearts are sighing
    And lads are in love with the grave.

Oh dark is the chamber and lonely,
    And lights and companions depart;
But lief will he lose them and only
    Behold the desire of his heart.

And low is the roof, but it covers
    A sleeper content to repose;
And far from his friends and his lovers
    He lies with the sweetheart he chose.

V

GRENADIER

The Queen she sent to look for me,
  The sergeant he did say,
'Young man, a soldier will you be
  For thirteen pence a day?'

For thirteen pence a day did I
  Take off the things I wore,
And I have marched to where I lie,
  And I shall march no more.

My mouth is dry, my shirt is wet,
  My blood runs all away,
So now I shall not die in debt
  For thirteen pence a day.

To-morrow after new young men
  The sergeant he must see,
For things will all be over then
  Between the Queen and me.

And I shall have to bate my price,
  For in the grave, they say,
Is neither knowledge nor device
  Nor thirteen pence a day.

VI

LANCER

I 'listed at home for a lancer,
  Oh who would not sleep with the brave?
I 'listed at home for a lancer
  To ride on a horse to my grave.

And over the seas we were bidden
  A country to take and to keep;
And far with the brave I have ridden,
  And now with the brave I shall sleep.

For round me the men will be lying
  That learned me the way to behave,
And showed me my business of dying:
  Oh who would not sleep with the brave?

They ask and there is not an answer;
Says I, I will 'list for a lancer,
  Oh who would not sleep with the brave?

And I with the brave shall be sleeping
  At ease on my mattress of loam,
When back from their taking and keeping
  The squadron is riding at home.

The wind with the plumes will be playing,
  The girls will stand watching them wave,
And eyeing my comrades and saying
  Oh who would not sleep with the brave?

They ask and there is not an answer;
Says you, I will 'list for a lancer,
  Oh who would not sleep with the brave?

VII

In valleys green and still
  Where lovers wander maying
They hear from over hill
  A music playing.

Behind the drum and fife,
  Past hawthornwood and hollow,
Through earth and out of life
  The soldiers follow.

The soldier's is the trade:
  In any wind or weather
He steals the heart of maid
  And man together.

The lover and his lass
  Beneath the hawthorn lying
Have heard the soldiers pass,
  And both are sighing.

And down the distance they
  With dying note and swelling
Walk the resounding way
  To the still dwelling.

VIII

Soldier from the wars returning,
   Spoiler of the taken town,
Here is ease that asks not earning;
   Turn you in and sit you down.

Peace is come and wars are over,
   Welcome you and welcome all,
While the charger crops the clover
   And his bridle hangs in stall.

Now no more of winters biting,
   Filth in trench from fall to spring,
Summers full of sweat and fighting
   For the Kesar or the King.

Rest you, charger, rust you, bridle;
   Kings and kesars, keep your pay;
Soldier, sit you down and idle
   At the inn of night for aye.

IX

The chestnut casts his flambeaux, and the flowers
   Stream from the hawthorn on the wind away,
The doors clap to, the pane is blind with showers.
   Pass me the can, lad; there's an end of May.

There's one spoilt spring to scant our mortal lot,
   One season ruined of our little store.
May will be fine next year as like as not:
   Oh ay, but then we shall be twenty-four.

We for a certainty are not the first
   Have sat in taverns while the tempest hurled
Their hopeful plans to emptiness, and cursed
   Whatever brute and blackguard made the world.

It is in truth iniquity on high
   To cheat our sentenced souls of aught they crave,
And mar the merriment as you and I
   Fare on our long fool's-errand to the grave.

Iniquity it is; but pass the can.
   My lad, no pair of kings our mothers bore;
Our only portion is the estate of man:
   We want the moon, but we shall get no more.

If here to-day the cloud of thunder lours
   To-morrow it will hie on far behests;
The flesh will grieve on other bones than ours
   Soon, and the soul will mourn in other breasts.

The troubles of our proud and angry dust
   Are from eternity, and shall not fail.
Bear them we can, and if we can we must.
   Shoulder the sky, my lad, and drink your ale.

X

Could man be drunk for ever
 With liquor, love, or fights,
Lief should I rouse at morning
 And lief lie down of nights.

But men at whiles are sober
 And think by fits and starts,
And if they think, they fasten
 Their hands upon their hearts.

XI

Yonder see the morning blink:
  The sun is up, and up must I,
To wash and dress and eat and drink
And look at things and talk and think
  And work, and God knows why.

Oh often have I washed and dressed
  And what's to show for all my pain?
Let me lie abed and rest:
Ten thousand times I've done my best
  And all's to do again.

XII

The laws of God, the laws of man,
He may keep that will and can;
Not I: let God and man decree
Laws for themselves and not for me;
And if my ways are not as theirs
Let them mind their own affairs.
Their deeds I judge and much condemn,
Yet when did I make laws for them?
Please yourselves, say I, and they
Need only look the other way.
But no, they will not; they must still
Wrest their neighbour to their will,
And make me dance as they desire
With jail and gallows and hell-fire.
And how am I to face the odds
Of man's bedevilment and God's?
I, a stranger and afraid
In a world I never made.
They will be master, right or wrong;
Though both are foolish, both are strong.
And since, my soul, we cannot fly
To Saturn nor to Mercury,
Keep we must, if keep we can,
These foreign laws of God and man.

XIII

THE DESERTER

'What sound awakened me, I wonder,
    For now 'tis dumb.'
'Wheels on the road most like, or thunder:
    Lie down; 'twas not the drum.'

Toil at sea and two in haven
    And trouble far:
Fly, crow, away, and follow, raven,
    And all that croaks for war.

'Hark, I heard the bugle crying,
    And where am I?
My friends are up and dressed and dying,
    And I will dress and die.'

'Oh love is rare and trouble plenty
    And carrion cheap,
And daylight dear at four-and-twenty:
    Lie down again and sleep.'

'Reach me my belt and leave your prattle:
    Your hour is gone;
But my day is the day of battle,
    And that comes dawning on.

'They mow the field of man in season:
    Farewell, my fair,
And, call it truth or call it treason,
    Farewell the vows that were.'

'Ay, false heart, forsake me lightly:
    'Tis like the brave.
They find no bed to joy in rightly
    Before they find the grave.

'Their love is for their own undoing,
    And east and west
They scour about the world a-wooing
    The bullet to their breast.

'Sail away the ocean over,
  Oh sail away,
And lie there with your leaden lover
  For ever and a day.'

XIV

THE CULPRIT

The night my father got me
　His mind was not on me;
He did not plague his fancy
　To muse if I should be
　The son you see.

The day my mother bore me
　She was a fool and glad,
For all the pain I cost her,
　That she had borne the lad
　That borne she had.

My mother and my father
　Out of the light they lie;
The warrant would not find them,
　And here 'tis only I
　Shall hang so high.

Oh let not man remember
　The soul that God forgot,
But fetch the county kerchief
　And noose me in the knot,
　And I will rot.

For so the game is ended
　That should not have begun.
My father and my mother
　They had a likely son,
　And I have none.

XV

EIGHT O'CLOCK

He stood, and heard the steeple
  Sprinkle the quarters on the morning town.
One, two, three, four, to market-place and people
  It tossed them down.

Strapped, noosed, nighing his hour,
  He stood and counted them and cursed his luck;
And then the clock collected in the tower
  Its strength, and struck.

XVI

SPRING MORNING

Star and coronal and bell
  April underfoot renews,
And the hope of man as well
  Flowers among the morning dews.

Now the old come out to look,
  Winter past and winter's pains,
How the sky in pool and brook
  Glitters on the grassy plains.

Easily the gentle air
  Wafts the turning season on;
Things to comfort them are there,
  Though 'tis true the best are gone.

Now the scorned unlucky lad
  Rousing from his pillow gnawn
Mans his heart and deep and glad
  Drinks the valiant air of dawn.

Half the night he longed to die,
  Now are sown on hill and plain
Pleasures worth his while to try
  Ere he longs to die again.

Blue the sky from east to west
  Arches, and the world is wide,
Though the girl he loves the best
  Rouses from another's side.

XVII

ASTRONOMY

The Wain upon the northern steep
　　Descends and lifts away.
Oh I will sit me down and weep
　　For bones in Africa.

For pay and medals, name and rank,
　　Things that he has not found,
He hove the Cross to heaven and sank
　　The pole-star underground.

And now he does not even see
　　Signs of the nadir roll
At night over the ground where he
　　Is buried with the pole.

XVIII

The rain, it streams on stone and hillock,
    The boot clings to the clay.
Since all is done that's due and right
Let's home; and now, my lad, good-night,
    For I must turn away.

Good-night, my lad, for nought's eternal;
    No league of ours, for sure.
To-morrow I shall miss you less,
And ache of heart and heaviness
    Are things that time should cure.

Over the hill the highway marches
    And what's beyond is wide:
Oh soon enough will pine to nought
Remembrance and the faithful thought
    That sits the grave beside.

The skies, they are not always raining
    Nor grey the twelvemonth through;
And I shall meet good days and mirth,
And range the lovely lands of earth
    With friends no worse than you.

But oh, my man, the house is fallen
    That none can build again;
My man, how full of joy and woe
Your mother bore you years ago
    To-night to lie in the rain.

XIX

In midnights of November,
   When Dead Man's Fair is nigh,
And danger in the valley,
   And anger in the sky,

Around the huddling homesteads
   The leafless timber roars,
And the dead call the dying
   And finger at the doors.

Oh, yonder faltering fingers
   Are hands I used to hold;
Their false companion drowses
   And leaves them in the cold.

Oh, to the bed of ocean,
   To Africk and to Ind,
I will arise and follow
   Along the rainy wind.

The night goes out and under
   With all its train forlorn;
Hues in the east assemble
   And cocks crow up the morn.

The living are the living
   And dead the dead will stay,
And I will sort with comrades
   That face the beam of day.

XX

The night is freezing fast,
　　To-morrow comes December;
　　　And winterfalls of old
Are with me from the past;
　　And chiefly I remember
　　　How Dick would hate the cold.

Fall, winter, fall; for he,
　　Prompt hand and headpiece clever,
　　　Has woven a winter robe,
And made of earth and sea
　　His overcoat for ever,
　　　And wears the turning globe.

XXI

The fairies break their dances
　And leave the printed lawn,
And up from India glances
　The silver sail of dawn.

The candles burn their sockets,
　The blinds let through the day,
The young man feels his pockets
　And wonders what's to pay.

XXII

The sloe was lost in flower,
  The April elm was dim;
That was the lover's hour,
  The hour for lies and him.

If thorns are all the bower,
  If north winds freeze the fir,
Why, 'tis another's hour,
  The hour for truth and her.

XXIII

In the morning, in the morning,
   In the happy field of hay,
Oh they looked at one another
   By the light of day.

In the blue and silver morning
   On the haycock as they lay,
Oh they looked at one another
   And they looked away.

XXIV

EPITHALAMIUM

He is here, Urania's son,
Hymen come from Helicon;
God that glads the lover's heart,
He is here to join and part.
So the groomsman quits your side
And the bridegroom seeks the bride:
Friend and comrade yield you o'er
To her that hardly loves you more.

Now the sun his skyward beam
Has tilted from the Ocean stream.
Light the Indies, laggard sun:
Happy bridegroom, day is done,
And the star from Œta's steep
Calls to bed but not to sleep.

Happy bridegroom, Hesper brings
All desired and timely things.
All whom morning sends to roam,
Hesper loves to lead them home.
Home return who him behold,
Child to mother, sheep to fold,
Bird to nest from wandering wide:
Happy bridegroom, seek your bride.

Pour it out, the golden cup
Given and guarded, brimming up,
Safe through jostling markets borne
And the thicket of the thorn;
Folly spurned and danger past,
Pour it to the god at last.

Now, to smother noise and light,
Is stolen abroad the wildering night,
And the blotting shades confuse
Path and meadow full of dews;
And the high heavens, that all control,

Turn in silence round the pole.
Catch the starry beams they shed
Prospering the marriage bed,
And breed the land that reared your prime
Sons to stay the rot of time.
All is quiet, no alarms;
Nothing fear of nightly harms.
Safe you sleep on guarded ground,
And in silent circle round
The thoughts of friends keep watch and ward,
Harnessed angels, hand on sword.

XXV

THE ORACLES

'Tis mute, the word they went to hear on high Dodona
    mountain
  When winds were in the oakenshaws and all the cauldrons
    tolled,
And mute's the midland navel-stone beside the singing
    fountain,
  And echoes list to silence now where gods told lies of old.

I took my question to the shrine that has not ceased from
    speaking,
  The heart within, that tells the truth and tells it twice as plain;
And from the cave of oracles I heard the priestess shrieking
  That she and I should surely die and never live again.

Oh priestess, what you cry is clear, and sound good sense I
    think it;
  But let the screaming echoes rest, and froth your mouth no
    more.
'Tis true there's better boose than brine, but he that drowns
    must drink it;
  And oh, my lass, the news is news that men have heard
    before.

The King with half the East at heel is marched from lands of morning;
  Their fighters drink the rivers up, their shafts benight the air,
And he that stands will die for nought, and home there's no returning.
  The Spartans on the sea-wet rock sat down and combed their
    hair.

XXVI

The half-moon westers low, my love,
    And the wind brings up the rain;
And wide apart lie we, my love,
    And seas between the twain.

I know not if it rains, my love,
    In the land where you do lie;
And oh, so sound you sleep, my love,
    You know no more than I.

XXVII

The sigh that heaves the grasses
    Whence thou wilt never rise
Is of the air that passes
    And knows not if it sighs.

The diamond tears adorning
    Thy low mound on the lea,
Those are the tears of morning,
    That weeps, but not for thee.

XXVIII

Now dreary dawns the eastern light,
　　And fall of eve is drear,
And cold the poor man lies at night,
　　And so goes out the year.

Little is the luck I've had,
　　And oh, 'tis comfort small
To think that many another lad
　　Has had no luck at all.

XXIX

Wake not for the world-heard thunder
   Nor the chime that earthquakes toll.
Star may plot in heaven with planet,
Lightning rive the rock of granite,
Tempest tread the oakwood under:
   Fear not you for flesh nor soul.
Marching, fighting, victory past,
Stretch your limbs in peace at last.

Stir not for the soldiers drilling
   Nor the fever nothing cures:
Throb of drum and timbal's rattle
Call but man alive to battle,
And the fife with death-notes filling
   Screams for blood but not for yours.
Times enough you bled your best;
Sleep on now, and take your rest.

Sleep, my lad; the French are landed,
   London's burning, Windsor's down;
Clasp your cloak of earth about you,
We must man the ditch without you,
March unled and fight short-handed,
   Charge to fall and swim to drown.
Duty, friendship, bravery o'er,
Sleep away, lad; wake no more.

XXX

SINNER'S RUE

I walked alone and thinking,
  And faint the nightwind blew
And stirred on mounds at crossways
  The flower of sinner's rue.

Where the roads part they bury
  Him that his own hand slays,
And so the weed of sorrow
  Springs at the four cross ways.

By night I plucked it hueless,
  When morning broke 'twas blue:
Blue at my breast I fastened
  The flower of sinner's rue.

It seemed a herb of healing,
  A balsam and a sign,
Flower of a heart whose trouble
  Must have been worse than mine.

Dead clay that did me kindness,
  I can do none to you,
But only wear for breastknot
  The flower of sinner's rue.

XXXI

HELL GATE

Onward led the road again
Through the sad uncoloured plain
Under twilight brooding dim,
And along the utmost rim
Wall and rampart risen to sight
Cast a shadow not of night,
And beyond them seemed to glow
Bonfires lighted long ago.
And my dark conductor broke
Silence at my side and spoke,
Saying, 'You conjecture well:
Yonder is the gate of hell.'

Ill as yet the eye could see
The eternal masonry,
But beneath it on the dark
To and fro there stirred a spark.
And again the sombre guide
Knew my question, and replied:
'At hell gate the damned in turn
Pace for sentinel and burn.'

Dully at the leaden sky
Staring, and with idle eye
Measuring the listless plain,
I began to think again.
Many things I thought of then,
Battle, and the loves of men,
Cities entered, oceans crossed,
Knowledge gained and virtue lost,
Cureless folly done and said,
And the lovely way that led
To the slimepit and the mire
And the everlasting fire.
And against a smoulder dun
And a dawn without a sun

Did the nearing bastion loom,
And across the gate of gloom
Still one saw the sentry go,
Trim and burning, to and fro,
One for women to admire
In his finery of fire.
Something, as I watched him pace,
Minded me of time and place,
Soldiers of another corps
And a sentry known before.

Ever darker hell on high
Reared its strength upon the sky,
And our footfall on the track
Fetched the daunting echo back.
But the soldier pacing still
The insuperable sill,
Nursing his tormented pride,
Turned his head to neither side,
Sunk into himself apart
And the hell-fire of his heart.
But against our entering in
From the drawbridge Death and Sin
Rose to render key and sword
To their father and their lord.
And the portress foul to see
Lifted up her eyes on me
Smiling, and I made reply:
'Met again, my lass,' said I.
Then the sentry turned his head,
Looked, and knew me, and was Ned.

Once he looked, and halted straight,
Set his back against the gate,
Caught his musket to his chin,
While the hive of hell within
Sent abroad a seething hum
As of towns whose king is come
Leading conquest home from far
And the captives of his war,

And the car of triumph waits,
And they open wide the gates.
But across the entry barred
Straddled the revolted guard,
Weaponed and accoutred well
From the arsenals of hell;
And beside him, sick and white,
Sin to left and Death to right
Turned a countenance of fear
On the flaming mutineer.
Over us the darkness bowed,
And the anger in the cloud
Clenched the lightning for the stroke;
But the traitor musket spoke.

And the hollowness of hell
Sounded as its master fell,
And the mourning echo rolled
Ruin through his kingdom old.
Tyranny and terror flown
Left a pair of friends alone,
And beneath the nether sky
All that stirred was he and I.

Silent, nothing found to say,
We began the backward way;
And the ebbing lustre died
From the soldier at my side,
As in all his spruce attire
Failed the everlasting fire.
Midmost of the homeward track
Once we listened and looked back;
But the city, dusk and mute,
Slept, and there was no pursuit.

XXXII

When I would muse in boyhood
  The wild green woods among,
And nurse resolves and fancies
  Because the world was young,
It was not foes to conquer,
  Nor sweethearts to be kind,
But it was friends to die for
  That I would seek and find.

I sought them far and found them,
  The sure, the straight, the brave,
The hearts I lost my own to,
  The souls I could not save.
They braced their belts about them,
  They crossed in ships the sea,
They sought and found six feet of ground,
  And there they died for me.

XXXIII

When the eye of day is shut,
   And the stars deny their beams,
And about the forest hut
   Blows the roaring wood of dreams,

From deep clay, from desert rock,
   From the sunk sands of the main,
Come not at my door to knock,
   Hearts that loved me not again.

Sleep, be still, turn to your rest
   In the lands where you are laid;
In far lodgings east and west
   Lie down on the beds you made.

In gross marl, in blowing dust,
   In the drowned ooze of the sea,
Where you would not, lie you must,
   Lie you must, and not with me.

XXXIV

THE FIRST OF MAY

The orchards half the way
  From home to Ludlow fair
Flowered on the first of May
  In Mays when I was there;
And seen from stile or turning
  The plume of smoke would show
Where fires were burning
  That went out long ago.

The plum broke forth in green,
  The pear stood high and snowed,
My friends and I between
  Would take the Ludlow road;
Dressed to the nines and drinking
  And light in heart and limb,
And each chap thinking
  The fair was held for him.

Between the trees in flower
  New friends at fairtime tread
The way where Ludlow tower
  Stands planted on the dead.
Our thoughts, a long while after,
  They think, our words they say;
Theirs now's the laughter,
  The fair, the first of May.

Ay, yonder lads are yet
  The fools that we were then;
For oh, the sons we get
  Are still the sons of men.
The sumless tale of sorrow
  Is all unrolled in vain:
May comes to-morrow
  And Ludlow fair again.

XXXV

When first my way to fair I took
    Few pence in purse had I,
And long I used to stand and look
    At things I could not buy.

Now times are altered: if I care
    To buy a thing, I can;
The pence are here and here's the fair,
    But where's the lost young man?

– To think that two and two are four
    And neither five nor three
The heart of man has long been sore
    And long 'tis like to be.

XXXVI

REVOLUTION

West and away the wheels of darkness roll,
　　Day's beamy banner up the east is borne,
Spectres and fears, the nightmare and her foal,
　　Drown in the golden deluge of the morn.

But over sea and continent from sight
　　Safe to the Indies has the earth conveyed
The vast and moon-eclipsing cone of night,
　　Her towering foolscap of eternal shade.

See, in mid heaven the sun is mounted; hark,
　　The belfries tingle to the noonday chime.
'Tis silent, and the subterranean dark
　　Has crossed the nadir, and begins to climb.

XXXVII

EPITAPH ON AN ARMY OF MERCENARIES

These, in the day when heaven was falling,
   The hour when earth's foundations fled,
Followed their mercenary calling
   And took their wages and are dead.

Their shoulders held the sky suspended;
   They stood, and earth's foundations stay;
What God abandoned, these defended,
   And saved the sum of things for pay.

XXXVIII

Oh stay at home, my lad, and plough
  The land and not the sea,
And leave the soldiers at their drill,
And all about the idle hill
  Shepherd your sheep with me.

Oh stay with company and mirth
  And daylight and the air;
Too full already is the grave
Of fellows that were good and brave
  And died because they were.

XXXIX

When summer's end is nighing
   And skies at evening cloud,
I muse on change and fortune
   And all the feats I vowed
   When I was young and proud.

The weathercock at sunset
   Would lose the slanted ray,
And I would climb the beacon
   That looked to Wales away
   And saw the last of day.

From hill and cloud and heaven
   The hues of evening died;
Night welled through lane and hollow
   And hushed the countryside,
   But I had youth and pride.

And I with earth and nightfall
   In converse high would stand,
Late, till the west was ashen
   And darkness hard at hand,
   And the eye lost the land.

The year might age, and cloudy
   The lessening day might close,
But air of other summers
   Breathed from beyond the snows,
   And I had hope of those.

They came and were and are not
   And come no more anew;
And all the years and seasons
   That ever can ensue
   Must now be worse and few.

So here's an end of roaming
   On eves when autumn nighs:
The ear too fondly listens
   For summer's parting sighs,
   And then the heart replies.

XL

Tell me not here, it needs not saying,
   What tune the enchantress plays
In aftermaths of soft September
   Or under blanching mays,
For she and I were long acquainted
   And I knew all her ways.

On russet floors, by waters idle,
   The pine lets fall its cone;
The cuckoo shouts all day at nothing
   In leafy dells alone;
And traveller's joy beguiles in autumn
   Hearts that have lost their own.

On acres of the seeded grasses
   The changing burnish heaves;
Or marshalled under moons of harvest
   Stand still all night the sheaves;
Or beeches strip in storms for winter
   And stain the wind with leaves.

Possess, as I possessed a season,
   The countries I resign,
Where over elmy plains the highway
   Would mount the hills and shine,
And full of shade the pillared forest
   Would murmur and be mine.

For nature, heartless, witless nature,
   Will neither care nor know
What stranger's feet may find the meadow
   And trespass there and go,
Nor ask amid the dews of morning
   If they are mine or no.

XLI

FANCY'S KNELL

When lads were home from labour
   At Abdon under Clee,
A man would call his neighbour
   And both would send for me.
And where the light in lances
   Across the mead was laid,
There to the dances
   I fetched my flute and played.

Ours were idle pleasures,
   Yet oh, content we were,
The young to wind the measures,
   The old to heed the air;
And I to lift with playing
   From tree and tower and steep
The light delaying,
   And flute the sun to sleep.

The youth toward his fancy
   Would turn his brow of tan,
And Tom would pair with Nancy
   And Dick step off with Fan;
The girl would lift her glances
   To his, and both be mute:
Well went the dances
   At evening to the flute.

Wenlock Edge was umbered,
   And bright was Abdon Burf,
And warm between them slumbered
   The smooth green miles of turf;
Until from grass and clover
   The upshot beam would fade,
And England over
   Advanced the lofty shade.

The lofty shade advances,
  I fetch my flute and play:
Come, lads, and learn the dances
  And praise the tune to-day.
To-morrow, more's the pity,
  Away we both must hie,
To air the ditty,
  And to earth I.

MORE POEMS

They say my verse is sad: no wonder;
  Its narrow measure spans
Tears of eternity, and sorrow,
  Not mine, but man's.

This is for all ill-treated fellows
  Unborn and unbegot,
For them to read when they're in trouble
  And I am not.

I

EASTER HYMN

If in that Syrian garden, ages slain,
You sleep, and know not you are dead in vain,
Nor even in dreams behold how dark and bright
Ascends in smoke and fire by day and night
The hate you died to quench and could but fan,
Sleep well and see no morning, son of man.

But if, the grave rent and the stone rolled by,
At the right hand of majesty on high
You sit, and sitting so remember yet
Your tears, your agony and bloody sweat,
Your cross and passion and the life you gave,
Bow hither out of heaven and see and save.

II

When Israel out of Egypt came
    Safe in the sea they trod;
By day in cloud, by night in flame,
    Went on before them God.

He brought them with a stretched out hand
    Dry-footed through the foam,
Past sword and famine, rock and sand,
    Lust and rebellion, home.

I never over Horeb heard
    The blast of advent blow;
No fire-faced prophet brought me word
    Which way behoved me go.

Ascended is the cloudy flame,
    The mount of thunder dumb;
The tokens that to Israel came,
    To me they have not come.

I see the country far away
    Where I shall never stand;
The heart goes where no footstep may
    Into the promised land.

The realm I look upon and die
    Another man will own;
He shall attain the heaven that I
    Perish and have not known.

But I will go where they are hid
    That never were begot,
To my inheritance amid
    The nation that is not.

III

For these of old the trader
   Unpearled the Indian seas,
The nations of the nadir
   Were diamondless for these;

A people prone and haggard
   Beheld their lightnings hurled:
All round, like Sinai, staggered
   The sceptre-shaken world.

But now their coins are tarnished,
   Their towers decayed away,
Their kingdom swept and garnished
   For haler kings than they;

Their arms the rust hath eaten,
   Their statutes none regard:
Arabia shall not sweeten
   Their dust, with all her nard.

They cease from long vexation,
   Their nights, their days are done,
The pale, the perished nation
   That never see the sun;

From the old deep-dusted annals
   The years erase their tale,
And round them race the channels
   That take no second sail.

IV

THE SAGE TO THE YOUNG MAN

O youth whose heart is right,
  Whose loins are girt to gain
The hell-defended height
  Where Virtue beckons plain;

Who seest the stark array
  And hast not stayed to count
But singly wilt assay
  The many-cannoned mount:

Well is thy war begun;
  Endure, be strong and strive;
But think not, O my son,
  To save thy soul alive.

Wilt thou be true and just
  And clean and kind and brave?
Well; but for all thou dost,
  Be sure it shall not save.

Thou, when the night falls deep,
  Thou, though the mount be won,
High heart, thou shalt but sleep
  The sleep denied to none.

Others, or ever thou,
  To scale those heights were sworn;
And some achieved, but now
  They never see the morn.

How shouldst thou keep the prize?
  Thou wast not born for aye.
Content thee if thine eyes
  Behold it in thy day.

O youth that wilt attain,
  On, for thine hour is short.
It may be thou shalt gain
  The hell-defended fort.

V

DIFFUGERE NIVES

Horace, *Odes* I V 7

The snows are fled away, leaves on the shaws
   And grasses in the mead renew their birth,
The river to the river-bed withdraws,
   And altered is the fashion of the earth.

The Nymphs and Graces three put off their fear
   And unapparelled in the woodland play.
The swift hour and the brief prime of the year
   Say to the soul, *Thou wast not born for aye.*

Thaw follows frost; hard on the heel of spring
   Treads summer sure to die, for hard on hers
Comes autumn, with his apples scattering;
   Then back to wintertide, when nothing stirs.

But oh, whate'er the sky-led seasons mar,
   Moon upon moon rebuilds it with her beams:
Come *we* where Tullus and where Ancus are,
   And good Aeneas, we are dust and dreams.

Torquatus, if the gods in heaven shall add
   The morrow to the day, what tongue has told?
Feast then thy heart, for what thy heart has had
   The fingers of no heir will ever hold.

When thou descendest once the shades among,
   The stern assize and equal judgment o'er,
Not thy long lineage nor thy golden tongue,
   No, nor thy righteousness, shall friend thee more.

Night holds Hippolytus the pure of stain,
   Diana steads him nothing, he must stay;
And Theseus leaves Pirithoüs in the chain
   The love of comrades cannot take away.

VI

I to my perils
   Of cheat and charmer
   Came clad in armour
    By stars benign.
Hope lies to mortals
   And most believe her,
   But man's deceiver
    Was never mine.

The thoughts of others
   Were light and fleeting,
   Of lovers' meeting
    Or luck or fame.
Mine were of trouble,
   And mine were steady,
   So I was ready
    When trouble came.

VII

Stars, I have seen them fall,
   But when they drop and die
No star is lost at all
   From all the star-sown sky.
The toil of all that be
   Helps not the primal fault;
It rains into the sea,
   And still the sea is salt.

VIII

Give me a land of boughs in leaf,
  A land of trees that stand;
Where trees are fallen, there is grief;
  I love no leafless land.

Alas, the country whence I fare,
  It is where I would stay;
And where I would not, it is there
  That I shall be for aye.

And one remembers and forgets,
  But 'tis not found again,
Not though they hale in crimsoned nets
  The sunset from the main.

IX

When green buds hang in the elm like dust
   And sprinkle the lime like rain,
Forth I wander, forth I must,
   And drink of life again.
Forth I must by hedgerow bowers
   To look at the leaves uncurled,
And stand in the fields where cuckoo-flowers
   Are lying about the world.

X

The weeping Pleiads wester,
   And the moon is under seas;
From bourn to bourn of midnight
   Far sighs the rainy breeze:

It sighs from a lost country
   To a land I have not known;
The weeping Pleiads wester,
   And I lie down alone.

XI

The rainy Pleiads wester,
  Orion plunges prone,
The stroke of midnight ceases,
  And I lie down alone.

The rainy Pleiads wester
  And seek beyond the sea
The head that I shall dream of,
  And 'twill not dream of me.

XII

I promise nothing: friends will part;
   All things may end, for all began;
And truth and singleness of heart
   Are mortal even as is man.

But this unlucky love should last
   When answered passions thin to air;
Eternal fate so deep has cast
   Its sure foundation of despair.

XIII

I lay me down and slumber
   And every morn revive.
Whose is the night-long breathing
   That keeps a man alive?

When I was off to dreamland
   And left my limbs forgot,
Who stayed at home to mind them,
   And breathed when I did not?

. . .

— I waste my time in talking,
   No heed at all takes he,
My kind and foolish comrade
   That breathes all night for me.

XIV

The farms of home lie lost in even,
    I see far off the steeple stand;
West and away from here to heaven
    Still is the land.

There if I go no girl will greet me,
    No comrade hollo from the hill,
No dog run down the yard to meet me:
    The land is still.

The land is still by farm and steeple,
    And still for me the land may stay:
There I was friends with perished people,
    And there lie they.

XV

Tarry, delight, so seldom met,
    So sure to perish, tarry still;
Forbear to cease or languish yet,
    Though soon you must and will.

By Sestos town, in Hero's tower,
    On Hero's heart Leander lies;
The signal torch has burned its hour
    And sputters as it dies.

Beneath him, in the nighted firth,
    Between two continents complain
The seas he swam from earth to earth
    And he must swim again.

XVI

How clear, how lovely bright,
How beautiful to sight
    Those beams of morning play;
How heaven laughs out with glee
Where, like a bird set free,
Up from the eastern sea
    Soars the delightful day.

To-day I shall be strong,
No more shall yield to wrong,
    Shall squander life no more;
Days lost, I know not how,
I shall retrieve them now;
Now I shall keep the vow
    I never kept before.

Ensanguining the skies
How heavily it dies
    Into the west away;
Past touch and sight and sound,
Not further to be found,
How hopeless under ground
    Falls the remorseful day.

XVII

Bells in tower at evening toll,
And the day forsakes the soul;
Soon will evening's self be gone
And the whispering night come on.

Blame not thou the blinded light
Nor the whisper of the night:
Though the whispering night were still
Yet the heart would counsel ill.

XVIII

Delight it is in youth and May
    To see the morn arise,
And more delight to look all day
    A lover in the eyes.
Oh maiden, let your distaff be,
And pace the flowery meads with me,
    And I will tell you lies.

'Tis blithe to see the sunshine fail,
    And hear the land grow still
And listen till the nightingale
    Is heard beneath the hill.
Oh follow me where she is flown
Into the leafy woods alone,
    And I will work you ill.

XIX

The mill-stream, now that noises cease,
Is all that does not hold its peace;
Under the bridge it murmurs by,
And here are night and hell and I.

Who made the world I cannot tell;
'Tis made, and here am I in hell.
My hand, though now my knuckles bleed,
I never soiled with such a deed.

And so, no doubt, in time gone by,
Some have suffered more than I,
Who only spend the night alone
And strike my fist upon the stone.

XX

Like mine, the veins of these that slumber
   Leapt once with dancing fires divine;
The blood of all this noteless number
   Ran red like mine.

How still, with every pulse in station,
   Frost in the founts that used to leap,
The put to death, the perished nation,
   How sound they sleep!

These too, these veins which life convulses,
   Wait but a while, shall cease to bound;
I with the ice in all my pulses
   Shall sleep as sound.

XXI

The world goes none the lamer,
  For ought that I can see,
Because this cursed trouble
  Has struck my days and me.

The stars of heaven are steady,
  The founded hills remain,
Though I to earth and darkness
  Return in blood and pain.

Farewell to all belongings
  I won or bought or stole;
Farewell, my lusty carcase,
  Farewell, my aery soul.

Oh worse remains for others,
  And worse to fear had I
Than here at four-and-twenty
  To lay me down and die.

XXII

Ho, everyone that thirsteth
   And hath the price to give,
Come to the stolen waters,
   Drink and your soul shall live.

Come to the stolen waters,
   And leap the guarded pale,
And pull the flower in season
   Before desire shall fail.

It shall not last for ever,
   No more than earth and skies;
But he that drinks in season
   Shall live before he dies.

June suns, you cannot store them
   To warm the winter's cold,
The lad that hopes for heaven
   Shall fill his mouth with mould.

XXIII

Crossing alone the nighted ferry
  With the one coin for fee,
Whom, on the wharf of Lethe waiting,
  Count you to find? Not me.

The brisk fond lackey to fetch and carry,
  The true, sick-hearted slave,
Expect him not in the just city
  And free land of the grave.

XXIV

Stone, steel, dominions pass,
  Faith too, no wonder;
So leave alone the grass
  That I am under.

All knots that lovers tie
  Are tied to sever;
Here shall your sweetheart lie,
  Untrue for ever.

XXV

Yon flakes that fret the eastern sky
   Lead back my day of birth;
The far, wide-wandered hour when I
   Came crying upon earth.

Then came I crying, and to-day,
   With heavier cause to plain,
Depart I into death away,
   Not to be born again.

XXVI

Good creatures, do you love your lives
    And have you ears for sense?
Here is a knife like other knives,
    That cost me eighteen pence.

I need but stick it in my heart
    And down will come the sky,
And earth's foundations will depart
    And all you folk will die.

XXVII

To stand up straight and tread the turning mill,
To lie flat and know nothing and be still,
Are the two trades of man; and which is worse
I know not, but I know that both are ill.

XXVIII

He, standing hushed, a pace or two apart,
  Among the bluebells of the listless plain,
Thinks, and remembers how he cleansed his heart
  And washed his hands in innocence in vain.

XXIX

From the wash the laundress sends
My collars home with ravelled ends:
I must fit, now these are frayed,
My neck with new ones London-made.

Homespun collars, homespun hearts,
Wear to rags in foreign parts.
Mine at least's as good as done,
And I must get a London one.

XXX

Shake hands, we shall never be friends, all's over;
    I only vex you the more I try.
All's wrong that ever I've done or said,
And nought to help it in this dull head:
    Shake hands, here's luck, good-bye.

But if you come to a road where danger
    Or guilt or anguish or shame's to share,
Be good to the lad that loves you true
And the soul that was born to die for you,
    And whistle and I'll be there.

XXXI

Because I liked you better
    Than suits a man to say,
It irked you, and I promised
    To throw the thought away.

To put the world between us
    We parted, stiff and dry;
'Good-bye,' said you, 'forget me.'
    'I will, no fear,' said I.

If here, where clover whitens
    The dead man's knoll, you pass,
And no tall flower to meet you
    Starts in the trefoiled grass,

Halt by the headstone naming
    The heart no longer stirred,
And say the lad that loved you
    Was one that kept his word.

XXXII

With seed the sowers scatter
    The furrows as they go;
Poor lads, 'tis little matter
    How many sorts they sow,
    For only one will grow.

The charlock on the fallow
    Will take the traveller's eyes,
And gild the ploughland sallow
    With flowers before it dies,
    But twice 'twill not arise.

The stinging nettle only
    Will still be found to stand:
The numberless, the lonely,
    The thronger of the land,
    The leaf that hurts the hand.

It thrives, come sun, come showers,
    Blow east, blow west, it springs;
It peoples towns, and towers
    About the courts of Kings,
    And touch it and it stings.

XXXIII

On forelands high in heaven,
  'Tis many a year gone by,
Amidst the fall of even
  Would stand my friends and I.
Before our foolish faces
  Lay lands we did not see;
Our eyes were in the places
  Where we should never be.

'Oh, the pearl seas are yonder,
  The amber-sanded shore;
Shires where the girls are fonder,
  Towns where the pots hold more.
And here fret we and moulder
  By grange and rick and shed
And every moon are older,
  And soon we shall be dead.'

Heigho, 'twas true and pity;
  But there we lads must stay.
Troy was a steepled city,
  But Troy was far away.
And round we turned lamenting
  To homes we longed to leave,
And silent hills indenting
  The orange band of eve.

I see the air benighted
  And all the dusking dales,
And lamps in England lighted,
  And evening wrecked on Wales;
And starry darkness paces
  The road from sea to sea,
And blots the foolish faces
  Of my poor friends and me.

XXXIV

Young is the blood that yonder
  Strides out the dusty mile,
And breasts the hillside highway
  And whistles loud the while,
  And vaults the stile.

Yet flesh, now too, has thorn-pricks,
  And shoulders carry care,
Even as in other seasons,
  When I and not my heir
  Was young and there.

On miry meads in winter
  The football sprang and fell;
May stuck the land with wickets:
  For all the eye could tell,
  The world went well.

Yet well, God knows, it went not,
  God knows, it went awry;
For me, one flowery Maytime,
  It went so ill that I
  Designed to die.

And if so long I carry
  The lot that season marred,
'Tis that the sons of Adam
  Are not so evil-starred
  As they are hard.

Young is the blood that yonder
  Succeeds to rick and fold,
Fresh are the form and favour
  And new the minted mould:
  The thoughts are old.

XXXV

Half-way, for one commandment broken,
    The woman made her endless halt,
And she to-day, a glistering token,
    Stands in the wilderness of salt.
Behind, the vats of judgment brewing
    Thundered, and thick the brimstone snowed;
He to the hill of his undoing
    Pursued his road.

XXXVI

Here dead lie we because we did not choose
   To live and shame the land from which we sprung.
Life, to be sure, is nothing much to lose;
   But young men think it is, and we were young.

XXXVII

I did not lose my heart in summer's even,
  When roses to the moonrise burst apart:
When plumes were under heel and lead was flying,
  In blood and smoke and flame I lost my heart.

I lost it to a soldier and a foeman,
  A chap that did not kill me, but he tried;
That took the sabre straight and took it striking
  And laughed and kissed his hand to me and died.

XXXVIII

By shores and woods and steeples
   Rejoicing hearts receive
Poured on a hundred peoples
   The far-shed alms of eve.

Her hands are filled with slumber
   For world-wide labourers worn;
Yet those are more in number
   That know her not from morn.

Now who sees night for ever,
   He sees no happier sight:
Night and no moon and never
   A star upon the night.

XXXIX

My dreams are of a field afar
　And blood and smoke and shot.
There in their graves my comrades are,
　In my grave I am not.

I too was taught the trade of man
　And spelt the lesson plain;
But they, when I forgot and ran,
　Remembered and remain.

XL

Farewell to a name and a number
    Recalled again
To darkness and silence and slumber
    In blood and pain.

So ceases and turns to the thing
    He was born to be
A soldier cheap to the King
    And dear to me;

So smothers in blood the burning
    And flaming flight
Of valour and truth returning
    To dust and night.

XLI

He looked at me with eyes I thought
  I was not like to find,
The voice he begged for pence with brought
  Another man to mind.

Oh no, lad, never touch your cap;
  It is not my half-crown:
You have it from a better chap
  That long ago lay down.

Turn east and over Thames to Kent
  And come to the sea's brim,
And find his everlasting tent
  And touch your cap to him.

XLII

A.J.J.

When he's returned I'll tell him – oh,
    Dear fellow, I forgot:
Time was you would have cared to know,
    But now it matters not.

I mourn you, and you heed not how;
    Unsaid the word must stay;
Last month was time enough, but now
    The news must keep for aye.

Oh, many a month before I learn
    Will find me starting still
And listening, as the days return,
    For him that never will.

Strange, strange to think his blood is cold
    And mine flows easy on:
And that straight look, that heart of gold,
    That grace, that manhood gone.

The word unsaid will stay unsaid
    Though there was much to say;
Last month was time enough: he's dead,
    The news must keep for aye.

XLIII

I wake from dreams and turning
   My vision on the height
I scan the beacons burning
   About the fields of night.

Each in its stedfast station
   Inflaming heaven they flare;
They sign with conflagration
   The empty moors of air.

The signal-fires of warning
   They blaze, but none regard;
And on through night to morning
   The world runs ruinward.

XLIV

Far known to sea and shore,
   Foursquare and founded well,
A thousand years it bore,
   And then the belfry fell.
      The steersman of Triest
      Looked where his mark should be,
      But empty was the west
      And Venice under sea.

From dusty wreck dispersed
   Its stature mounts amain;
On surer foot than first
   The belfry stands again.
      At to-fall of the day
      Again its curfew tolls
      And burdens far away
      The green and sanguine shoals.

It looks to north and south,
   It looks to east and west;
It guides to Lido mouth
   The steersman of Triest.
      Andrea, fare you well;
      Venice, farewell to thee.
      The tower that stood and fell
      Is not rebuilt in me.

XLV

Smooth between sea and land
Is laid the yellow sand,
And here through summer days
The seed of Adam plays.

Here the child comes to found
His unremaining mound,
And the grown lad to score
Two names upon the shore.

Here, on the level sand,
Between the sea and land,
What shall I build or write
Against the fall of night?

Tell me of runes to grave
That hold the bursting wave,
Or bastions to design
For longer date than mine.

Shall it be Troy or Rome
I fence against the foam,
Or my own name, to stay
When I depart for aye?

Nothing: too near at hand,
Planing the figured sand,
Effacing clean and fast
Cities not built to last
And charms devised in vain,
Pours the confounding main.

XLVI

THE LAND OF BISCAY

Hearken, landsmen, hearken, seamen,
　to the tale of grief and me,
Looking from the land of Biscay
　on the waters of the sea.

Looking from the land of Biscay
　over Ocean to the sky
On the far-beholding foreland
　paced at even grief and I.
There, as warm the west was burning
　and the east uncoloured cold,
Down the waterway of sunset
　drove to shore a ship of gold.
Gold of mast and gold of cordage,
　gold of sail to sight was she,
And she glassed her ensign golden
　in the waters of the sea.

Oh, said I, my friend and lover,
　take we now that ship and sail
Outward in the ebb of hues and
　steer upon the sunset trail;
Leave the night to fall behind us
　and the clouding counties leave:
Help for you and me is yonder,
　in a haven west of eve.

Under hill she neared the harbour,
　till the gazer could behold
On the golden deck the steersman
　standing at the helm of gold,
Man and ship and sky and water
　burning in a single flame;
And the mariner of Ocean,
　he was calling as he came:
From the highway of the sunset
　he was shouting on the sea,

'Landsman of the land of Biscay,
   have you help for grief and me?'

When I heard I did not answer,
   I stood mute and shook my head:
Son of earth and son of Ocean,
   much we thought and nothing said.
Grief and I abode the nightfall,
   to the sunset grief and he
Turned them from the land of Biscay
   on the waters of the sea.

XLVII

FOR MY FUNERAL

O thou that from thy mansion,
  Through time and place to roam,
Dost send abroad thy children,
  And then dost call them home,

That men and tribes and nations
  And all thy hand hath made
May shelter them from sunshine
  In thine eternal shade:

We now to peace and darkness
  And earth and thee restore
Thy creature that thou madest
  And wilt cast forth no more.

XLVIII

PARTA QUIES

Good–night; ensured release,
Imperishable peace,
    Have these for yours,
While sea abides, and land,
And earth's foundations stand,
    And heaven endures.

When earth's foundations flee,
Nor sky nor land nor sea
    At all is found,
Content you, let them burn:
It is not your concern;
    Sleep on, sleep sound.

ADDITIONAL POEMS

I

ATYS

'Lydians, lords of Hermus river,
  Sifters of the golden loam,
See you yet the lances quiver
  And the hunt returning home?'

'King, the star that shuts the even
  Calls the sheep from Tmolus down;
Home return the doves from heaven,
  And the prince to Sardis town.'

From the hunting heavy laden
  Up the Mysian road they ride;
And the star that mates the maiden
  Leads his son to Croesus' side.

'Lydians, under stream and fountain
  Finders of the golden vein,
Riding from Olympus mountain,
  Lydians, see you Atys plain?'

'King, I see the Phrygian stranger
  And the guards in hunter's trim,
Saviours of thy son from danger;
  Them I see. I see not him.'

'Lydians, as the troop advances,
  – It is eve and I am old –
Tell me why they trail their lances,
  Washers of the sands of gold.

'I am old and day is ending
  And the wildering night comes on;
Up the Mysian entry wending,
  Lydians, Lydians, what is yon?'

Hounds behind their master whining,
  Huntsmen pacing dumb beside,
On his breast the boar-spear shining,
  Home they bear his father's pride.

II

Oh were he and I together,
   Shipmates on the fleeted main,
Sailing through the summer weather
   To the spoil of France or Spain.

Oh were he and I together,
   Locking hands and taking leave,
Low upon the trampled heather
   In the battle lost at eve.

Now are he and I asunder
   And asunder to remain;
Kingdoms are for others' plunder,
   And content for other slain.

III

When Adam walked in Eden young,
  Happy, 'tis writ, was he,
While high the fruit of knowledge hung
  Unbitten on the tree.

Happy was he the livelong day;
  I doubt 'tis written wrong:
The heart of man, for all they say,
  Was never happy long.

And now my feet are tired of rest,
  And here they will not stay,
And the soul fevers in my breast
  And aches to be away.

IV

It is no gift I tender,
　A loan is all I can;
But do not scorn the lender;
　Man gets no more from man.

Oh, mortal man may borrow
　What mortal man can lend;
And 'twill not end to-morrow,
　Though sure enough 'twill end.

If death and time are stronger,
　A love may yet be strong;
The world will last for longer,
　But this will last for long.

V

Here are the skies, the planets seven,
And all the starry train:
Content you with the mimic heaven,
And on the earth remain.

VI

Ask me no more, for fear I should reply;
   Others have held their tongues, and so can I:
Hundreds have died, and told no tale before:
   Ask me no more, for fear I should reply –

How one was true and one was clean of stain
   And one was braver than the heavens are high,
And one was fond of me: and all are slain.
   Ask me no more, for fear I should reply.

VII

He would not stay for me; and who can wonder?
   He would not stay for me to stand and gaze.
I shook his hand and tore my heart in sunder
   And went with half my life about my ways.

VIII

Now to her lap the incestuous earth
  The son she bore has ta'en.
And other sons she brings to birth
  But not my friend again.

IX

When the bells justle in the tower
   The hollow night amid,
Then on my tongue the taste is sour
   Of all I ever did.

X

Oh on my breast in days hereafter
　Light the earth should lie,
Such weight to bear is now the air,
　So heavy hangs the sky.

XI

GOD'S ACRE

Morning up the eastern stair
Marches, azuring the air,
And the foot of twilight still
Is stolen toward the western sill.
Blithe the maids go milking, blithe
Men in hayfields stone the scythe;
All the land's alive around
Except the churchyard's idle ground.
There's empty acres west and east,
But aye 'tis God's that bears the least:
This hopeless garden that they sow
With the seeds that never grow.

XIA

They shall have breath that never were,
But he that was shall have it ne'er;
The unconceived and unbegot
Shall look on heaven, but he shall not.
The heart with many wildfires lit,
Ice is not so cold as it.
The thirst that rivers could not lay
A little dust has quenched for aye;
And in a fathom's compass lie
Thoughts much wider than the sky.

ADDITIONAL POEMS

XII

AN EPITAPH

Stay, if you list, O passer by the way;
Yet night approaches; better not to stay.
  I never sigh, nor flush, nor knit the brow,
  Nor grieve to think how ill God made me, now.
Here, with one balm for many fevers found,
Whole of an ancient evil, I sleep sound.

XIII

Oh turn not in from marching
   To taverns on the way.
The drought and thirst and parching
   A little dust will lay,
   And take desire away.

Oh waste no words a-wooing
   The soft sleep to your bed;
She is not worth pursuing,
   You will so soon be dead;
   And death will serve instead.

XIV

'Oh is it the jar of nations,
    The noise of a world run mad,
The fleeing of earth's foundations?'
    Yes, yes; lie quiet, my lad.

'Oh is it my country calling,
    And whom will my country find
To shore up the sky from falling?'
    My business; never you mind.

'Oh is it the newsboys crying
    Lost battle, retreat, despair,
And honour and England dying?'
    Well, fighting-cock, what if it were?

The devil this side of the darnels
    Is having a dance with man,
And quarrelsome chaps in charnels
    Must bear it as best they can.

XV

'Tis five years since, 'An end,' said I;
'I'll march no further, time to die.
All's lost; no worse has heaven to give.'
Worse it has given, and yet I live.

I shall not die to-day, no fear:
I shall live yet for many a year,
And see worse ills and worse again,
And die of age and not of pain.

When God would rear from earth aloof
The blue height of the hollow roof,
He sought him pillars sure and strong,
And ere he found them sought them long.

The stark steel splintered from the thrust,
The basalt mountain sprang to dust,
The blazing pier of diamond flawed
In shards of rainbows all abroad.

What found he, that the heavens stand fast?
What pillar proven firm at last
Bears up so light that world-seen span?
The heart of man, the heart of man.

XVI

Some can gaze and not be sick,
But I could never learn the trick.
There's this to say for blood and breath,
They give a man a taste for death.

XVII

The stars have not dealt me the worst they could do:
My pleasures are plenty, my troubles are two.
But oh, my two troubles they reave me of rest,
The brains in my head and the heart in my breast.

Oh grant me the ease that is granted so free,
The birthright of multitudes, give it to me,
That relish their victuals and rest on their bed
With flint in the bosom and guts in the head.

XVIII

Oh who is that young sinner with the handcuffs on his wrists?
And what has he been after that they groan and shake their fists?
And wherefore is he wearing such a conscience-stricken air?
Oh they're taking him to prison for the colour of his hair.

'Tis a shame to human nature, such a head of hair as his;
In the good old time 'twas hanging for the colour that it is;
Though hanging isn't bad enough and flaying would be fair
For the nameless and abominable colour of his hair.

Oh a deal of pains he's taken and a pretty price he's paid
To hide his poll or dye it of a mentionable shade;
But they've pulled the beggar's hat off for the world to see and
    stare,
And they're haling him to justice for the colour of his hair.

Now 'tis oakum for his fingers and the treadmill for his feet
And the quarry-gang on Portland in the cold and in the heat,
And between his spells of labour in the time he has to spare
He can curse the God that made him for the colour of his hair.

XIX

THE DEFEATED

In battles of no renown
My fellows and I fell down,
And over the dead men roar
The battles they lost before.

The thunderstruck flagstaffs fall,
The earthquake breaches the wall,
The far-felled steeples resound,
And we lie under the ground.

Oh, soldiers, saluted afar
By them that had seen your star,
In conquest and freedom and pride
Remember your friends that died.

Amid rejoicing and song
Remember, my lads, how long,
How deep the innocent trod
The grapes of the anger of God.

XX

I shall not die for you,
   Another fellow may;
Good lads are left and true
   Though one departs away.
   But he departs to-day
And leaves his work to do,
   For I was luckless aye
And shall not die for you.

XXI

NEW YEAR'S EVE

The end of the year fell chilly
   Between a moon and a moon;
Thorough the twilight shrilly
   The bells rang, ringing no tune.

The windows stained with story,
   The walls with miracle scored,
Were hidden for gloom and glory
   Filling the house of the Lord.

Arch and aisle and rafter
   And roof-tree dizzily high
Were full of weeping and laughter
   And song and saying good-bye.

There stood in the holy places
   A multitude none could name,
Ranks of dreadful faces
   Flaming, transfigured in flame.

Crown and tiar and mitre
   Were starry with gold and gem;
Christmas never was whiter
   Than fear on the face of them.

In aisles that emperors vaulted
   For a faith the world confessed,
Abasing the Host exalted,
   They worshipped towards the west.

They brought with laughter oblation;
   They prayed, not bowing the head;
They made without tear lamentation,
   And rendered me answer and said:

'O thou that seest our sorrow,
   It fares with us even thus:
To-day we are gods, to-morrow
   Hell have mercy on us.

'Lo, morning over our border
  From out of the west comes cold;
Down ruins the ancient order
  And empire builded of old.

'Our house at even is queenly
  With psalm and censers alight:
Look thou never so keenly
  Thou shalt not find us to-night.

'We are come to the end appointed
  With sands not many to run;
Divinities disanointed
  And kings whose kingdom is done.

'The peoples knelt down at our portal,
  All kindreds under the sky;
We were gods and implored and immortal
  Once; and to-day we die.'

They turned them again to their praying,
  They worshipped and took no rest,
Singing old tunes and saying
  'We have seen his star in the west,'

Old tunes of the sacred psalters,
  Set to wild farewells;
And I left them there at their altars
  Ringing their own dead knells.

XXII

R.L.S.

Home is the sailor, home from sea.
    Her far-borne canvas furled
The ship pours shining on the quay
    The plunder of the world.

Home is the hunter from the hill:
    Fast in the boundless snare
All flesh lies taken at his will
    And every fowl of air.

'Tis evening on the moorland free,
    The starlit wave is still:
Home is the sailor from the sea,
    The hunter from the hill.

XXIII

THE OLIVE

The olive in its orchard
  Should now be rooted sure,
To cast abroad its branches
  And flourish and endure.

Aloft amid the trenches
  Its dressers dug and died
The olive in its orchard
  Should prosper and abide.

Close should the fruit be clustered
  And light the leaf should wave,
So deep the root is planted
  In the corrupting grave.

TRANSLATIONS

Aeschylus, *Septem Contra Thebas* (lines 848–60)

Now do our eyes behold
  The tidings which were told:
Twin fallen kings, twin perished hopes to mourn,
  The slayer, the slain,
The entangled doom forlorn
  And ruinous end of twain.
Say, is not sorrow, is not sorrow's sum
On home and hearthstone come?
  O waft with sighs the sail from shore,
O smite the bosom, cadencing the oar
That rows beyond the rueful stream for aye
    To the far strand,
  The ship of souls, the dark,
  The unreturning bark
Whereon light never falls nor foot of Day,
Ev'n to the bourne of all, to the unbeholden land.

Sophocles, *Oedipus Coloneus* (lines 1211–48)

What man is he that yearneth
   For length unmeasured of days?
Folly mine eye discerneth
   Encompassing all his ways.
For years over-running the measure
   Shall change thee in evil wise:
Grief draweth nigh thee; and pleasure,
   Behold, it is hid from thine eyes.
   This to their wage have they
   Which overlive their day.
And He that looseth from labour
   Doth one with other befriend,
   Whom bride nor bridesmen attend,
Song, nor sound of the tabor,
   Death, that maketh an end.

Thy portion esteem I highest,
   Who wast not ever begot;
Thine next, being born who diest
   And straightway again art not.
With follies light as the feather
   Doth Youth to man befall;
Then evils gather together,
   There wants not one of them all –
   Wrath, envy, discord, strife,
   The sword that seeketh life.
And sealing the sum of trouble
   Doth tottering Age draw nigh,
   Whom friends and kinsfolk fly,
Age, upon whom redouble
   All sorrows under the sky.

This man, as me, even so,
Have the evil days overtaken;
And like as a cape sea-shaken
With tempest at earth's last verges
And shock of all winds that blow,
His head the seas of woe,
The thunders of awful surges
Ruining overflow;
Blown from the fall of even,
    Blown from the dayspring forth,
Blown from the noon in heaven,
    Blown from night and the North.

Euripides, *Alcestis* (lines 962–1005)

In heaven-high musings and many,
  Far seeking and deep debate,
Of strong things find I not any
  That is as the strength of Fate.
Help nor healing is told
In soothsayings uttered of old,
In the Thracian runes, the verses
  Engraven of Orpheus' pen;
No balm of virtue to save
Apollo aforetime gave,
Who stayeth with tender mercies
  The plagues of the children of men.

She hath not her habitation
  In temples that hands have wrought;
Him that bringeth oblation,
  Behold, she heedeth him naught.
Be thou not wroth with us more,
O mistress, than heretofore;
For what God willeth soever,
  That thou bringest to be;
Thou breakest in sunder the brand
Far forged in the Iron Land;
Thine heart is cruel, and never
  Came pity anigh unto thee.

Thee too, O King, hath she taken
  And bound in her tenfold chain;
  Yet faint not, neither complain:
The dead thou wilt not awaken
  For all thy weeping again.

They perish, whom gods begot;
The night releaseth them not.
Beloved was she that died
And dear shall ever abide,
For this was the queen among women, Admetus, that lay by thy
  side.

Not as the multitude lowly
   Asleep in their sepulchres,
   Not as their grave be hers,
But like as the gods held holy,
   The worship of wayfarers.
Yea, all that travel the way
Far off shall see it and say,
Lo, erst for her lord she died,
To-day she sitteth enskied;
Hail, lady, be gracious to usward; that alway her honour abide.

LIGHT VERSE AND PARODIES:
A SELECTION

The shades of night were falling fast,
    And the rain was falling faster,
When through an Alpine village passed
    An Alpine village pastor:
A youth who bore mid snow and ice
    A bird that wouldn't chirrup,
And a banner with the strange device –
    'Mrs Winslow's soothing syrup.'

'Beware the pass,' the old man said,
    'My bold, my desperate fellah;
Dark lowers the tempest overhead,
    And you'll want your umberella;
And the roaring torrent is deep and wide –
    You may hear how loud it washes.'
But still that clarion voice replied:
    'I've got my old goloshes.'

'Oh, stay,' the maiden said, 'and rest
    (For the wind blows from the nor'ward)
Thy weary head upon my breast –
    And please don't think I'm forward.'
A tear stood in his bright blue eye,
    And he gladly would have tarried;
But still he answered with a sigh:
    'Unhappily I'm married.'

FRAGMENT OF A GREEK TRAGEDY

Alcmaeon.   Chorus.

Cho. O suitably attired in leather boots
       Head of a traveller, wherefore seeking whom
       Whence by what way how purposed art thou come
       To this well-nightingaled vicinity?
       My object in inquiring is to know.
       But if you happen to be deaf and dumb
       And do not understand a word I say,
       Nod with your hand to signify as much.
Alc.   I journeyed hither a Boeotian road.
Cho. Sailing on horseback or with feet for oars?
Alc.   Plying by turns my partnership of legs.
Cho. Beneath a shining or a rainy Zeus?
Alc.   Mud's sister, not himself, adorns my shoes.
Cho. To learn your name would not displease me much.
Alc.   Not all that men desire do they obtain.
Cho. Might I then hear at what your presence shoots?
Alc.   A shepherd's questioned mouth informed me that –
Cho. What? for I know not yet what you will say.
Alc.   Nor will you ever, if you interrupt.
Cho. Proceed, and I will hold my speechless tongue.
Alc.   – This house was Eriphyla's, no one's else.
Cho. Nor did he shame his throat with hateful lies.
Alc.   May I then enter, passing through the door?
Cho. Go, chase into the house a lucky foot.
       And, O my son, be, on the one hand, good,
       And do not, on the other hand, be bad;
       For that is very much the safest plan.
Alc.   I go into the house with heels and speed.

Chorus.

          In speculation   *Strophe*
       I would not willingly acquire a name
            For ill-digested thought,

236

But after pondering much
To this conclusion I at last have come:
   Life is uncertain.
   This truth I have written deep
   In my reflective midriff
   On tablets not of wax,
Nor with a pen did I inscribe it there
For many reasons: *Life*, I say, *is not*
   A stranger to uncertainty.
Not from the flight of omen-yelling fowls
   This fact did I discover,
Nor did the Delphic tripod bark it out,
   Nor yet Dodona.
Its native ingenuity sufficed
   My self-taught diaphragm.

   Why should I mention   *Antistrophe*
The Inachean daughter, loved of Zeus?
   Her whom of old the gods,
   More provident than kind,
Provided with four hoofs, two horns, one tail,
   A gift not asked for,
   And sent her forth to learn
   The unfamiliar science
   Of how to chew the cud.
She therefore, all about the Argive fields,
Went cropping pale green grass and nettle-tops,
   Nor did they disagree with her.
Yet, howsoe'er nutritious, such repasts
   I do not hanker after.
Never may Cypris for her seat select
   My dappled liver!
Why should I mention Io? Why indeed?
   I have no notion why.

   But now does my boding heart   *Epode*
   Unhired, unaccompanied, sing
   A strain not meet for the dance.
   Yea, even the palace appears
   To my yoke of circular eyes

(The right, nor omit I the left)
Like a slaughterhouse, so to speak,
Garnished with woolly deaths
And many shipwrecks of cows.
I therefore in a Cissian strain lament,
And to the rapid,
Loud, linen-tattering thumps upon my chest
Resounds in concert
The battering of my unlucky head.

Eriphyla (within). O, I am smitten with a hatchet's jaw;
And that in deed and not in word alone.
Cho. I thought I heard a sound within the house
Unlike the voice of one that jumps for joy.
Eri. He splits my skull, not in a friendly way,
Once more: he purposes to kill me dead.
Cho. I would not be reputed rash, but yet
I doubt if all be gay within the house.
Eri. O! O! another stroke! That makes the third.
He stabs me to the heart against my wish.
Cho. If that be so, thy state of health is poor;
But thine arithmetic is quite correct.

238

iii

I shall be interested to see the Devotional Poems. Perhaps I myself may write a Hymn-book for use in the Salvation Army:

> There is Hallelujah Hannah
>   Walking backwards down the lane,
> And I hear the loud Hosanna
>   Of regenerated Jane;
> And Lieutenant Isabella
>   In the centre of them comes,
> Dealing blows with her umbrella
>   On the trumpets and the drums.

Or again:

> 'Hallelujah!' was the only observation
> That escaped Lieutenant-Colonel Mary Jane,
> When she tumbled off the platform in the station,
> And was cut in little pieces by the train.
>   Mary Jane, the train is through yer:
>   Hallelujah, Hallelujah!
> We will gather up the fragments that remain.

It seems to come quite easy.

THE AFRICAN LION

To meet a bad lad on the African waste
   Is a thing that a lion enjoys;
But he rightly and strongly objects to the taste
   Of good and uneatable boys.

When he bites off a piece of a boy of that sort
   He spits it right out of his mouth,
And retires with a loud and dissatisfied snort
   To the east, or the west, or the south.

So lads of good habits, on coming across
   A lion, need feel no alarm,
For they know they are sure to escape with the loss
   Of a leg, or a head, or an arm.

THE PARALLELOGRAM
OR, INFANT OPTIMISM

The parallelogram, and what
The nature of its earthly lot,
Are themes on which a light we seek
From Euclid, the intrepid Greek.

That dauntless sage describes it as
A quadrilateral which has
(How he found out, he does not tell)
Its opposite sides parallel.

And seemingly the fact is such.
Oh, when I recollect how much
Strange information, true or no,
To that geometer we owe –

Surprising things, which I, alone,
Unaided, never should have known, –
My cheeks have often been bedewed
With tears of thoughtful gratitude.

Aɪ ˙ cause of thankfulness I find
Abounding in my infant mind,
Whenever I consider what
The parallelogram is not.

It is not (as it might have been)
A monster of appalling mien:
The hand of Providence confines
Its form by parallel straight lines.

It does not scratch, it does not bite,
It does not make a noise at night;
It would attempt these acts in vain:
And why? because it is a plane.

Nor let me peevishly repine
And wish its peaceful life were mine:
It suffers, blameless though it is,
From many disadvantages.

Wherever placed, it matters not
In how unsuitable a spot,
The parallelogram must stay:
It is too weak to crawl away.

If with a syringe you should go
And water it, it would not grow;
And nothing else can it become,
Not even a trapezium.

Then morn and evening let me raise
My little hands in duteous praise,
Because a Christian child I am,
And not a parallelogram.

THE AMPHISBÆNA
OR, THE LIMITS OF HUMAN KNOWLEDGE

Amphisbæna: a serpent supposed to have two heads, and by consequence to move with either end foremost.   – Johnson

If you should happen to descry
An Amphisbæna drawing nigh,
You may remain upon the spot,
But probably had better not.
The prudent its approach avoid
And do not stop to be annoyed,
For all who see it are perplexed
And wonder what will happen next.
Both ends, unfortunately, are
So singularly similar.
It has indeed a head in front
(As has the Indian elephant),
But then, to our alarm, we find
It has another head behind;
And hence zoologists affirm
That it is not a pachyderm.
Until it starts, you never know
In which direction it will go,
Nor can you even then maintain
That it will not come back again.
The sportsman, in amaze profound
Collapsing on his faithful hound,
Exclaims, as soon as he can speak,
'The Amphisbæna is unique.'
Unique no doubt it is; but oh,
That is not what distracts me so.
No: when before my musing eye
The Amphisbæna rambles by,
The question which bereaves of bliss
My finite intellect is this:

Who, who, oh, who will make it clear
Which is the front and which the rear?
Whether, at any given date,
The reptile is advancing straight,
Or whether it is hind-before,
Remains obscure for evermore.
Philosophy, with head of snow,
Confesses that it does not know;
Logicians have debated long,
Which is the right end, which the wrong;
But all their efforts are in vain.
They will not ever ascertain.

FRAGMENT OF AN ENGLISH OPERA

(Designed as a model for young librettists)

Dramatis personae:
Father (bass)
Mother (contralto)
Daughter (soprano)

Scene: a room. *Time*: Evening

Father:	Retire, my daughter;
	Prayers have been said;
	Take your warm water
	And go to bed.
Daughter:	But I had rather
	Sit up instead.
Father:	I am your father,
	So go to bed.
Daughter:	Are you my father?
Father:	I think so, rather:
	You go to bed.
Mother:	My daughter, vanish;
	You hear me speak:
	This is not Spanish,
	Nor is it Greek.
Daughter:	Oh, what a bother!
	Would I were dead!
Mother:	I am your mother,
	So go to bed.
Daughter:	Are you my mother?
Mother:	You have no other:
	You go to bed.
Father:	Take your bed-candle
	And take it quick.
	This is the handle.

Daughter:	Is *this* the handle?
Father:	No, that's the wick.
	This is the handle,
	At this end here.
	Take your bed-candle
	And disappear.
Daughter:	Oh dear, oh dear!
Father & Mother:	Take your warm water,
	As we have said;
	You are our daughter,
	So go to bed.
Daughter:	Am I your daughter?
Father & Mother:	If not, you oughter:
	You go to bed.

Daughter:

I am their daughter;
If not, I oughter:
   Prayers have been said.
This is my mother;
I have no other:
   Would I were dead!
That is my father;
He thinks so, rather:
   Oh dear, oh dear!
I take my candle;
This is the handle:
   I disappear.

Father & Mother: The coast is clear.

THE CROCODILE
OR, PUBLIC DECENCY

Though some at my aversion smile,
I cannot love the crocodile.
Its conduct does not seem to me
Consistent with sincerity.

Where Nile, with beneficial flood,
Improves the desert sand to mud,
The infant child, its banks upon,
Will run about with nothing on.
The London County Council not
Being adjacent to the spot,
This is the consequence. Meanwhile,
What is that object in the Nile
Which swallows water, chokes and spits?
It is the crocodile in fits.

'Oh infant! oh my country's shame!
Suppose a European came!
Picture his feelings, on his pure
Personally conducted tour!
The British Peer's averted look,
The mantling blush of Messrs. Cook!
Come, awful infant, come and be
Dressed, if in nothing else, in me.'

Then disappears into the Nile
The infant, clad in crocodile,
And meekly yields his youthful breath
To darkness, decency, and death.
His mother, in the local dells,
Deplores him with Egyptian yells:
Her hieroglyphic howls are vain,
Nor will the lost return again.
The crocodile itself no less
Displays, but does not feel, distress,

And with its tears augments the Nile;
The false, amphibious crocodile.

'Is it that winds Etesian blow,
Or melts on Ethiop hills the snow?'
So, midst the inundated scene,
Inquire the floating fellaheen.
From Cairo's ramparts gazing far
The mild Khedive and stern Sirdar
Say, as they scan the watery plain,
'There goes that crocodile again.'
The copious tribute of its lids
Submerges half the pyramids,
And over all the Sphinx it flows,
Except her non-existent nose.

It is a fearful thing to be
    The Pope.
That cross will not be laid on me,
    I hope.
A righteous God would not permit
    It.
The Pope himself must often say,
After the labours of the day,
'It is a fearful thing to be
    Me.'

PURPLE WILLIAM
OR, THE LIAR'S DOOM

The hideous hue which William is
Was not originally his:
So long as William told the truth
He was a usual-coloured youth.

He now is purple. One fine day
His tender father chanced to say
'What colour is a whelp, and why?'
'Purple' was William's false reply.

'Pooh' said his Pa, 'You silly elf,
'It's no more purple than yourself.
'Dismiss the notion from your head.'
'I, too, am purple' William said.

And he *was* purple. With a yell
His mother off the sofa fell
Exclaiming 'William's purple! Oh!'
William replied 'I told you so.'

His parents, who could not support
The pungency of this retort,
Died with a simultaneous groan.
The purple orphan was alone.

AUNTS AND NIECES
OR, TIME AND SPACE

Some nieces won't, some nieces can't
Imbibe instruction from an aunt.
Eliza scorned her good Aunt Clare.
Where is Eliza now? Ah, where?
  'Avoid, at the approach of dark,
Eliza, the umbrageous park.
During the daytime, lairs and dens
Conceal its direr denizens.
But when that brilliant orb, the Sun,
His useful journey nearly done,
Approaches the horizon's verge,
They will, my dearest niece, emerge;
And forth the cockatrice will frisk,
And out will bounce the basilisk,
And the astoundingly absurd
Yet dangerous cockyoly-bird
Will knock you, with its baneful beak,
Into the middle of next week.'
  'Pooh,' said Eliza, 'that it can't.
Still, if you think so, thank you, Aunt.
Now, after this exhausting talk,
I think that I will take a walk.'
  She therefore fetched her parasol,
Her gloves and reticule and all,
And need I specify the spot
Which drew her footsteps? I need not.

★   ★   ★

'Eliza,' said her aunt, 'is late.
Jane, place the crumpets by the grate.
What was that distant crow I heard?
Was it the cockyoly-bird?
I think so. There it goes again.
You may remove the crumpets, Jane.'

Meanwhile Eliza took the air.
(Shall I? – I will not – mention where),
And as the afternoon progressed
She sat upon the grass to rest,
Drew from her reticule a bun,
And bit it in the setting sun.
Soon, with her mouth full, she
   perceives
Movements and rustlings in the leaves
Which spoil the situation's charm
And tend to substitute alarm.
She dropped the bun and said 'Dear me!
I fear I shall be late for tea.'
Then, from behind, a vicious peck
Descended on Eliza's neck.
Eliza into the azure distance
Followed the line of least resistance.

★   ★   ★

In the middle of next week
There will be heard a piercing shriek,
And looking pale and weak and thin
Eliza will come flying in.

APPENDIX: THE LATIN VERSE DEDICATION TO M.J. JACKSON, WITH A TRANSLATION BY EDMUND WILSON

———

Dedication of Housman's *M. Manilii Astronomicon Liber Primus* (1903). Housman sent it to Grant Richards, 12 February 1903 (*Letters*, p. 64). On Moses Jackson, see the note to *Last Poems* XXIV. The translation by Edmund Wilson that follows is from the *Bookman*, October 1927.

SODALI MEO

M.I. IACKSON

HARVM LITTERARVM CONTEMPTORI

Signa pruinosae uariantia luce cauernas
  noctis et extincto lumina nata die
solo rure uagi lateque tacentibus aruis
  surgere nos una uidimus oceano.
uidimus: illa prius, cum luce carebat uterque,
  uiderat in latium prona poeta mare,
seque memor terra mortalem matre creatum
  intulit aeternis carmina sideribus,
clara nimis post se genitis exempla daturus
  ne quis forte deis fidere uellet homo.
nam supero sacrata polo complexaque mundum
  sunt tamen indignam carmina passa luem,
et licet ad nostras enarint naufraga terras
  scriptoris nomen uix tenuere sui.
non ego mortalem uexantia sidera sortem
  aeternosue tuli sollicitare deos,
sed cito casurae tactus uirtutis amore
  humana uolui quaerere nomen ope,
uirque uirum legi fortemque breuemque sodalem

253

qui titulus libro uellet inesse meo.
o uicture meis dicam periturene chartis,
  nomine sed certe uiuere digne tuo,
haec tibi ad auroram surgentia signa secuto
  hesperia trado munera missa plaga.
en cape: nos populo uenit inlatura perempto
  ossa solo quae det dissoluenda dies
fataque sortitas non inmortalia mentes
  et non aeterni uincla sodalicii.

Those starry signs that freak with light
The frosty caverns of the night,
Sea-born and bright when daylight dies –
Together we have watched them rise,
Late wandering, where fields lay wide,
The lone and silent countryside.
So once, while still our place was blank,
The poet watched them where they sank,
Setting below the Latian sea;
And, mindful of mortality,
Earth-sprung nor spared from earth for long,
He looked aloft and launched his song
Against the everlasting stars –
Alas! to leave, with many scars,
A warning, all too plain, of odds
Which mock the man who trusts the gods.
For, though to Heaven dedicate,
With all the universe for freight,
His verses found misfortune fast
And, washed upon our strand at last,
Shipwrecked and battered, blurred and lame,
They scarce can tell their maker's name.

I have not plied, importunate,
The stars that harass human fate
Nor, begging guidance from above,
Besieged the gods, but, touched with love
Of mortal glory swift to fade,
Have sought a name through human aid

And, man, have chosen among men,
To stead no heaven-assailing pen,
A comrade, mortal-lived but stout,
Whose name shall bring my volume out.
– 'O comrade,' let me say, 'whose name
May perish with my pages' fame,
Yet worthy through thine own to live:
From human hand to hand, I give –
To thee who followest away
Those rising signs, to seek the day –
This present from a western shore:
Take it: to-morrow runs before,
With those whom life no longer owns
To lay our flesh and loose our bones –
To dull with all-benumbing thrust
Our wits that wake not from the dust,
Nor spare, with learning's lettered leaf,
The bonds of fellowship as brief.'

SELECTED PROSE

Introductory Lecture (1892)

Every exercise of our faculties, says Aristotle, has some good for its aim; and if he speaks true it becomes a matter of importance that when we exert any special faculty we should clearly apprehend the special good at which we are aiming. What now is the good which we set before us as our end when we exercise our faculties in acquiring knowledge, in learning? The answers differ, and they differ for this reason, – that people seldom approach the question impartially, but usually bring with them a prepossession in favour of this or that department of knowledge. Everyone has his favourite study, and he is therefore disposed to lay down, as the aim of learning in general, the aim which his favourite study seems specially fitted to achieve, and the recognition of which as the aim of learning in general would increase the popularity of that study and the importance of those who profess it. This method, conclusion first, reasons afterwards, has always been in high favour with the human race: you write down at the outset the answer to the sum; then you proceed to fabricate, not for use but for exhibition to the public, the ciphering by which you can pretend to have arrived at it. The method has one obvious advantage, – that you are thus quite sure of reaching the conclusion you want to reach: if you began with your reasons there is no telling where they might lead you, and like enough you would never get to the desired conclusion at all. But it has one drawback, – that unanimity is thus unattainable: every man gives the answer which seems right in his own eyes. And accordingly we find that the aim of acquiring knowledge is differently defined by different people. In how many different ways, I do not know; but it will be sufficient for to-day to consider the answers given by two great parties: the advocates of those sciences which have now succeeded in arrogating to themselves the name of Science, and of those studies which call themselves by the title, perhaps equally arrogant, of Humane Letters.

The partisans of Science define the aim of learning to be utility. I do not mean to say that any eminent man of science commits himself to this opinion: some of them have publicly and scornfully repudiated it, and all of them, I imagine, reject it in their hearts. But there is no denying that this is the view which makes Science popular; this is the impression under which the British merchant or manufacturer dies and leaves his money to endow scientific education. And since this impression, though false, is nevertheless beneficent in its results, those who are interested in scientific pursuits may very well consider that it is no business of theirs to dispel a delusion which promises so well for the world in general and for themselves in particular. The popular view, I say, is that the aim of acquiring knowledge is to equip one's self for the business of life; that accordingly the knowledge most to be sought after is the knowledge which equips one best; and that this knowledge is Science. And the popular view has the very distinguished countenance of Mr Herbert Spencer. Mr Spencer, in his well-known treatise on Education, pronounces that education to be of most value which prepares us for self-preservation by preparing us for securing the necessaries of life; and that is education in the sciences. 'For,' says he, 'leaving out only some very small classes, what are all men employed in? They are employed in the production, preparation and distribution of commodities. And on what does efficiency in the production, preparation and distribution of commodities depend? It depends on the use of methods fitted to the respective natures of these commodities; it depends on an adequate acquaintance with their physical, chemical and vital properties, as the case may be; that is, it depends on Science.' And then he proceeds with his usual exactness of detail to shew in what way each several science serves to render one efficient in producing, preparing or distributing commodities.

Now to begin with, it is evident that if we are to pursue Science simply in order to obtain an adequate acquaintance with the physical, chemical and vital properties of the commodities which we produce, prepare or distribute, we shall not need to pursue Science far. Mr Spencer duly rehearses the list of the sciences, and is at much pains to demonstrate the bearing of each science on the arts of life. Take one for a specimen. I suppose that in no science have Englishmen more distinguished themselves than in astronomy: one need but mention the name of Isaac Newton. And it is a science which has not only fascinated the profoundest intellects but has always laid a strong hold on the popular imagination, so that, for example, our newspapers found it paid them to fill a good deal of space with articles about the present apposition of the planet Mars. And now listen to the reasons why we are to study astronomy. 'Of the concrete sciences we come first to Astronomy. Out of this has grown that art of navigation which has made possible the enormous foreign commerce that supports a large part of our population, while supplying us with many necessaries and most of our luxuries.' That is all there is to say about astronomy: that navigation has grown out of it. Well then, we want no Isaac Newtons; let them carry their Principias to another market. Astronomy is a squeezed orange as far as we are concerned. Astronomers may transfer their residence to the remotest world they can discover, and welcome, for all the need we have of them here: the enormous foreign commerce which Mr Spencer speaks of will still enable this island to be over-populated, and our currants and cocoanuts will continue to arrive with their former regularity. Hundreds and hundreds of years ago astronomy had reached the point which satisfies our modest requirements: it had given birth to navigation. They were conversing in Athens four centuries before Christ, and a young Spencerian named Glaucon already found more than this to say in praise of the utility of astronomy. 'Shall we make astronomy one of our studies,' asked Socrates, 'or do you dissent?' 'No, I agree,' said Glaucon, 'for to have an intimate acquaintance with seasons, and months, and years, is an advantage not only to the farmer and the navigator, but also, in an equal degree, to the general,' – an aspect of astronomical science which appears to have escaped Mr Spencer's notice.

Astronomy, you may say, is not a fair example to take, because of all sciences it is perhaps the one which least concerns the arts of life. May be; but this difference between astronomy and other sciences is a difference of degree alone. Just as even astronomy, though it touches practical life but little, does nevertheless touch it, so those sciences, such as chemistry and physics, which are the most intimately and widely concerned with practical life, nevertheless throughout a great portion of their range have no contact with it at all. If it is in order to secure the necessaries of life that we are to study chemistry and physics, we shall study them further no doubt than we shall for that reason study astronomy, but not so far by a long way as chemists and physicists do in fact study them now. Electric lighting and aniline dyes and other such magnificent alleviations of human destiny do not spring into being at every forward step in our knowledge of the physical forces and chemical composition of the universe: they are merely occasional incidents, flowers by the way. Much in both sciences which the chemist and the physicist study with intense interest and delight will be set aside as curious and unprofitable learning by our producer, preparer or distributor of commodities. In short, the fact is, that what man will seek to acquaint himself with in order to prepare him for securing the necessaries of life is not Science, but the indispensable minimum of Science.

And just as our knowledge of Science need not be deep, so too it need not be wide. Mr Spencer shews that every science is of some use to some man or another. But not every science is of use to every man. Geometry, he points out, is useful to the carpenter, and chemistry to the calico-printer. True; but geometry is not useful to the calico-printer, nor chemistry to the carpenter. If it is to secure the necessaries of life that men pursue Science, the sciences that each man needs to pursue are few. In addition to the initial studies of reading, writing and arithmetic, he needs to acquaint himself with those sciences, or rather, as I said before, with the indispensable minimum of those sciences, which concern the trade or the art he earns his bread by: the dyer with chemistry, the carpenter with geometry, the navigator with astronomy. But there he can stop. Mr Spencer appears to apprehend this; and since such a result is far from his desires, he attempts, in the case of one or two sciences, to shew that no one can neglect them with impunity. The following, for instance, is the method by which he endeavours to terrorise us into studying geology. We may, any of us, some day, take shares in a joint-stock company; and that company may engage in mining operations; and those operations may be directed to the discovery of coal; and for want of geological information the joint-stock company may go mining for coal under the old red sandstone, where there is no coal; and then the mining operations will be fruitless, and the joint-stock company will come to grief, and where shall we be then? This is, indeed, to eat the bread of carefulness. After all, men have been known to complete their pilgrimage through this vale of tears without taking shares in a joint-stock company. But the true reply to Mr Spencer's intimidations I imagine to be this: that the attempt to fortify man's estate against all contingencies by such precautions as these is in the first place interminable and in the second place hopeless. As Sarpedon says to Glaucus in the *Iliad*, a hundred thousand fates stand close to us always, which none can flee and none avoid. The complexity of the universe is infinite, and the days of a man's life are threescore years and ten. One lifetime, nine lifetimes are not long enough for the task of blocking every cranny through which calamity may enter. And say that we could thus triumphantly succeed in the attempt at self-preservation; say that we could thus impregnably secure the necessaries of existence; even then the true business of life is not so much as begun. Existence is not itself a good thing, that we should spend a lifetime securing its necessaries: a life spent, however victoriously, in securing the necessaries of life is no more than an elaborate furnishing and decoration of apartments for the reception of a guest who is never to come. Our business here is not to live, but to live happily. We may seem to be occupied, as Mr Spencer says, in the production, preparation and distribution of commodities; but our true occupation is to manufacture from the raw material of life the fabric of happiness; and if we are ever to set about our work we must make up our minds to risk something. Absolute security for existence is unattainable, and no wise man will pursue it; for if we must go to these lengths in the attempt at self-preservation we shall die before ever we have begun to live. Reasonable security is attainable; but it is attainable without any wide study of Science.

And if we grant for the moment that to secure the necessaries of life is the true aim of Science, and if we also grant, as we well may, that Science is really of some use in compassing that aim, still it is apparent that other things compass it much more effectually than Science. It is not found in experience that men of science are those who make the largest fortunes out of the production, preparation and distribution of commodities. The men who have risen, if you can call it rising, from barge-boys to millionaires, have not risen by their knowledge of science. They have sometimes risen by other people's knowledge of science, but their own contribution to their success, so far as it consists in knowledge at all, consists rather in their knowledge of business and their knowledge of men. Therefore, to sum up, when we find that for purposes of practical utility we need no wide knowledge of the sciences and no deep knowledge of any science, and that even for these purposes Science is not the most serviceable sort of knowledge, surely we are justified in concluding that the true aim of Science is something other than utility.

While the partisans of Science define the end of education as the useful, the partisans of the Humanities define it, more sublimely, as the good and the beautiful. We study, they say, not that we may earn a livelihood, but that we may transform and beautify our inner nature by culture. Therefore the true and the really valuable knowledge is that which is properly and distinctively human; the knowledge, as Matthew Arnold used to call it, of the best which has been said and thought in the world, – the literature which contains the history of the spirit of man.

Here indeed is an aim which no one will pretend to despise. The names of the good and the beautiful are treated with respect even by those who give themselves little trouble about the things; and if the study of the Humanities will really transform and beautify our inner nature, it will be acknowledged that so soon as we have acquired, with all possible despatch, that minimum of scientific knowledge which is necessary to put our material welfare in a state of reasonable security, we ought to apply ourselves earnestly and long to the study of the Humanities. And as a man should always magnify his own office, nothing could be more natural or agreeable to me than to embrace this opinion and to deliver here a panegyric of the Humanities and especially of that study on which the Humanities are founded, the study of the dead languages of Greece and Rome. I am deterred from doing so, in the first place, because it is possible that a partisan harangue of that sort might not be relished by the united Faculties of Arts, Laws and Science; and secondly because to tell the truth I do not much believe in these supposed effects of classical studies. I do not believe that the proportion of the human race whose inner nature the study of the classics will specially transform and beautify is large; and I am quite sure that the proportion of the human race on whom the classics will confer that benefit can attain the desired end without that minute and accurate study of the classical tongues which affords Latin professors their only excuse for existing.

How shall we judge whether a man's nature has been transformed and beautified? and where will the transformation and beautification begin? I never yet heard it maintained by the wildest enthusiast for Classics that the standard of morality or even of amiability is higher among classical scholars than among men of Science. The special benefit which these studies are supposed, and

in some cases justly supposed, to confer, is to quicken our appreci-
ation of what is excellent and to refine our discrimination between
what is excellent and what is not. And since literature is the
instrument by which this education is imparted, it is in the domain
of literature that this quickened appreciation and sharpened dis-
crimination ought first to display themselves. And so in fact they
do. If anyone wants convincing of the inestimable value of a
classical education to those who are naturally qualified to profit by
it, let him compare our two greatest poets, Shakespeare and Milton,
and see what the classics did for one and what the lack of the classics
did for the other. Milton was steeped through and through with
classical literature; and he is the one English poet from whom an
Englishman ignorant of Greek and Latin can learn what the great
classics were like. Mark: the classics cannot be said to have suc-
ceeded altogether in transforming and beautifying Milton's inner
nature. They did not sweeten his naturally disagreeable temper;
they did not enable him to conduct controversy with urbanity or
even with decency. But in the province of literature, where their
influence is soonest and most powerfully exerted, they conferred on
him all the benefits which their encomiasts ascribe to them. The
dignity, the sanity, the unfaltering elevation of style, the just
subordination of detail, the due adaptation of means to ends, the
high respect of the craftsman for his craft and for himself, which
ennoble Virgil and the great Greeks, are all to be found in Milton,
and nowhere else in English literature are they all to be found:
certainly not in Shakespeare. In richness of natural endow-
ment Shakespeare was the superior even of Milton; but he had
small Latin and less Greek, and the result – I do not know that
Samuel Johnson states the result too harshly when he has the noble
courage to say that Shakespeare has nowhere written more than
six consecutive lines of good poetry. It is told in a Christian
legend that when St Paul was in Italy he was led to Virgil's grave at
Parthenope, and that he wept over it and said 'O Chief of
poets, what would not I have made of thee, had I but found thee
living!'

> Ad Maronis mausoleum
> Ductus, fudit super eum
> Piae rorem lacrimae:

'Quem te' inquit 'reddidissem,
Si te vivum invenissem,
Poetarum maxime!'

I can imagine Virgil himself, in the year 1616, when he welcomed Shakespeare to the Elysian fields, I can imagine Virgil weeping and saying,

'Quem te reddidissem,
Si te vivum invenissem,
Poetarum maxime!'

Virgil and the Greeks would have made Shakespeare not merely a great genius, which he was already, but, like Milton, a great artist, which he is not. He would have gained from the classics that virtue in which he and all his contemporaries are so wofully deficient, sobriety. He would have learnt to discriminate between what is permanently attractive and what is merely fashionable or popular. And perhaps it is not too much to hope that with the example of the classics before him he would have developed a literary conscience and taken a pride in doing his best, instead of scamping his work because he knew his audience would never find out how ill he was writing. But it was not to be; and there is only too much justice in the exclamation of that eminent Shakespearian critic King George III, 'Was there ever such stuff as great part of Shakespeare?' Shakespeare, who at his best is the best of all poets, at his worst is almost the worst. I take a specimen not from any youthful perform-ance but from one of his maturest works, a play which contains perhaps the most beautiful poetry that even Shakespeare ever wrote, *The Winter's Tale*. He desires to say that a lady shed tears; and thus he says it: 'Her eyes became two spouts.' That was the sort of atrocity the Elizabethan audience liked, and Shakespeare gave it them to their hearts' content: sometimes, no doubt, with the full knowledge that it was detestable; sometimes, I greatly fear, in good faith, because he had no worthy model to guide him.

The classics, I say, must have done for Shakespeare what they did for Milton; but what proportion of mankind are even accessible to this influence? What proportion offer even a foothold for the entrance of literary culture into their minds? The classics can indeed quicken our appreciation of what is excellent; but can they implant it? They can refine our discrimination between good and bad; but can they create it? Take the greatest scholar that England or perhaps that Europe ever bred; a man so great that in his own province he serves for a touchstone of merit and has always been admired by all admirable scholars and despised by all despicable scholars: Richard Bentley. Bentley was born in the year 1662, and he brought with him into the world, like most men born near that date, a prosaic mind; nor did all his immense study of the classics avail to confer on him a true appreciation of poetry. While he dealt with the classical poets he was comparatively safe, for in dealing with these a prosaic mind is not so grave a disqualification as a dithyrambic mind; and Bentley had lived with the ancients till he understood them as no one will ever understand them who brings to their study a taste formed on the poetry of Elizabeth's time or ours. But that jealous deity which loves, Herodotus tells us, to strike down towering things, put it into his heart to invade a literature with which he was ill acquainted, and to edit *Paradise Lost*. He persuaded himself that Milton in his blindness had become the victim of an unscrupulous person, who had introduced into the poem a great deal that Milton never wrote, and had altered for the worse a great deal that he did write. Accordingly, whenever Milton's poetry failed to come up to Bentley's prosaic notions of what poetry ought to be, he detected the hand, or, as he preferred to call it, the fist, of this first editor. Milton relates how 'four speedy Cherubim' were sent out with trumpets to summon an assembly. 'Four *speedy* Cherubim' says Bentley: 'Not much need of swiftness to be a good trumpeter. For *speedy* I suspect the poet gave "Four *sturdy* Cherubim." Stout, robust, able to blow a strong blast.' Milton relates how Uriel at sunset came to Paradise to warn the guards of the approach of Satan: 'Thither came Uriel, gliding through the even.' Bentley insists on altering *even* to *heaven*, because, as he acutely observes, evening is a division of time, not of space, and consequently you cannot come gliding through it: you might as well say, he exclaims, 'came gliding through six o'clock.' Milton relates how Ithuriel found Satan disguised as a toad whispering at the ear of Eve: 'Him, thus intent, Ithuriel with his spear Touched lightly.' But Bentley cannot be happy without Ithuriel's motive for doing so, and accordingly inserts a verse of his own composition: 'Him, thus intent, Ithuriel with his spear, *Knowing no real toad durst there intrude*, Touched lightly.' Here was a man of true and even colossal genius, yet you see in matters poetical the profoundest knowledge of the classics profited him nothing, because he had been born without the organs by which poetical excellence is perceived. And so are most men born without them; and the quickening and refining influences special to literature run off them like water off a duck's back. It is the magnet and the churn in the song: 'If I can wheedle a knife or a needle, Why not a silver churn?' quoth the magnet; but he found his mistake; and where literature is the magnet most men are silver churns. It is nothing to be ashamed of, though on the other hand it is not much to be conceited about, as some people seem to think it. Different men have different aptitudes, and this aptitude happens to be uncommon; and the majority, not only of other men, but the majority also of professed students of the classics, whatever else they may get from those studies, do not get from them a just appreciation of literary excellence. True, we are not all so easily found out as Bentley, because we have not Bentley's intrepid candour. There is a sort of savage nobility about his firm reliance on his own bad taste: we on the other hand usually fit our judgments not to the truth of things nor even to our own impressions of things, true or false, but to the standard of convention. There are exceptions, but in general, if a man wants really penetrating judgments, really illuminating criticism on a classical author, he is ill advised if he goes to a classical scholar to get them. Again: You might perhaps expect that those whose chief occupation is the study of the greatest masters of style would insensibly acquire a good style of their own. It is not so: there are again exceptions, but as a rule the literary faculty of classical scholars is poor, and sometimes worse. A distinguished teacher of the classics, who now holds one of the most august positions in these realms, had occasion to give his reason for disapproving something or other, and he gave it in these words: 'It aggravates a tendency to let the thing slide.' We do not all of us write so ill as this, but we mostly write a style which is seldom graceful and not always grammatical: probably no class of students write English much worse. And as among the blind the one-eyed man is king, so the possessors of a very humble skill and grace in writing find themselves highly extolled if it is on classical themes that they write, because these merits are so unexpected, the standard is so low.

And while on the one hand no amount of classical learning can create a true appreciation of literature in those who lack the organs of appreciation, so on the other hand no great amount of classical learning is needed to quicken and refine the taste and judgment of those who do possess such organs. Who are the great critics of the classical literatures, the critics with real insight into the classical spirit, the critics who teach with authority and not as the scribes? They are such men as Lessing or Goethe or Matthew Arnold, scholars no doubt, but not scholars of minute or profound learning. Matthew Arnold went to his grave under the impression that the proper way to spell *lacrima* was to spell it with a γ, and that the words ἀνδρὸς παιδοφόνοιο ποτὶ στόμα χεῖϱ᾽ ὀϱέγεσθαι meant 'to carry to my lips the hand of him that slew my son.' We pedants know better: we spell *lacrima* with an *i*, and we know that the verse of Homer really means 'to reach forth my hand to the chin of him that slew my son.' But when it comes to literary criticism, heap up in one scale all the literary criticism that the whole nation of professed scholars ever wrote, and drop into the other the thin green volume of Matthew Arnold's Lectures on Translating Homer, which has long been out of print because the British public does not care to read it, and the first scale, as Milton says, will straight fly up and kick the beam.

It appears then that upon the majority of mankind the classics can hardly be said to exert the transforming influence which is claimed for them. The special effect of a classical education on the majority of those who receive it, is not to transform and beautify their inner nature, but rather to confer a certain amount of polish on their surface, by teaching them things that one is expected to know and enabling them to understand the meaning of English words and use them properly. If a man has learnt Greek and Latin and has to describe the blowing up of a powder mill, he will not describe it as a cataclysm; if he is irritated he will say so, and will not say that he is aggravated; if the conversation turns on the Muse who is supposed to preside over dancing, he will call her Terpsíchŏre, and not Térpsitshoar. We shall probably therefore think it advisable to acquire a tincture of Classics, for ornament, just as we shall think it advisable to acquire a modicum of Science, for use. There, in both cases, we shall most of us stop; because to pursue the classics further in the expectation of transforming and beautifying our inner natures is, for most of us, to ask from those studies what they

269

cannot give; and because, if practical utility be our aim in studying Science, a very modest amount of Science will serve our turn.

So we find that the two fancied aims of learning laid down by these two parties will not stand the test of examination. And no wonder; for these are the fabrications of men anxious to impose their own favourite pursuits on others, or of men who are ill at ease in their conscience until they have invented some external justification for those pursuits. The acquisition of knowledge needs no such justification: its true sanction is a much simpler affair, and inherent in itself. People are too prone to torment themselves with devising far-fetched reasons: they cannot be content with the simple truth asserted by Aristotle: 'all men possess by nature a craving for knowledge,' πάντες ἄνθρωποι τοῦ εἰδέναι ὀρέγονται φύσει. This is no rare endowment scattered sparingly from heaven that falls on a few heads and passes others by: curiosity, the desire to know things as they are, is a craving no less native to the being of man, no less universal in diffusion through mankind, than the craving for food and drink. And do you suppose that such a desire means nothing? The very definition of the good, says Aristotle again, is that which all desire. Whatever is pleasant is good, unless it can be shewn that in the long run it is harmful, or, in other words, not pleasant but unpleasant. Mr Spencer himself on another subject speaks thus: 'So profound an ignorance is there of the laws of life, that men do not even know that their sensations are their natural guides, and (when not rendered morbid by long continued disobedience) their trustworthy guides.' The desire of knowledge does not need, nor could it possibly possess, any higher or more authentic sanction than the happiness which attends its gratification.

Perhaps it will be objected that we see, every day of our lives, plenty of people who exhibit no pleasure in learning and experience no desire to know; people, as Plato agreeably puts it, who wallow in ignorance with the complacency of a brutal hog. We do; and here is the reason. If the cravings of hunger and thirst are denied satisfaction, if a man is kept from food and drink, the man starves to death, and there is an end of him. This is a result which arrests the attention of even the least observant mind; so it is generally recognised that hunger and thirst cannot be neglected with impunity, that a man ought to eat and drink. But if the craving for knowledge is denied satisfaction, the result which follows is not so striking to the eye.

270

The man, worse luck, does not starve to death. He still preserves the aspect and motions of a living human being; so people think that the hunger and thirst for knowledge can be neglected with impunity. And yet, though the man does not die altogether, part of him dies, part of him starves to death: as Plato says, he never attains completeness and health, but walks lame to the end of his life and returns imperfect and good for nothing to the world below.

But the desire of knowledge, stifle it though you may, is none the less originally born with every man; and nature does not implant desires in us for nothing, nor endow us with faculties in vain. 'Sure,' says Hamlet,

> Sure, He that made us with such large discourse,
> Looking before and after, gave us not
> That capability and godlike reason
> To fust in us unused.

The faculty of learning is ours that we may find in its exercise that delight which arises from the unimpeded activity of any energy in the groove nature meant it to run in. Let a man acquire knowledge not for this or that external and incidental good which may chance to result from it, but for itself; not because it is useful or ornamental, but because it is knowledge, and therefore good for man to acquire. 'Brothers,' says Ulysses in Dante, when with his old and tardy companions he had left Seville on the right hand and Ceuta on the other, and was come to that narrow pass where Hercules assigned his landmarks to hinder man from venturing farther: 'Brothers, who through a hundred thousand dangers have reached the West, deny not, to this brief vigil of your senses that remains, experience of the unpeopled world behind the sunset. Consider of what seed ye are sprung: ye were not formed to live like brutes, but to follow virtue and knowledge.' For knowledge resembles virtue in this, and differs in this from other possessions, that it is not merely a means of procuring good, but is good in itself simply: it is not a coin which we pay down to purchase happiness, but it has happiness indissolubly bound up with it. Fortitude and continence and honesty are not commended to us on the ground that they conduce, as on the whole they do conduce, to material success, nor yet on the ground that they will be rewarded hereafter: those whose office it is to exhort mankind to virtue are ashamed to degrade the cause they plead by proffering such lures as these. And let us too disdain to take lower ground in commending knowledge: let us insist that the pursuit of knowledge, like the pursuit of righteousness, is part of man's duty to himself; and remember the Scripture where it is written: 'He that refuseth instruction despiseth his own soul.'

I will not say, as Prof. Tyndall has somewhere said, that all happiness belongs to him who can say from his heart 'I covet truth.' Entire happiness is not attainable either by this or by any other method. Nay it may be urged on the contrary that the pursuit of truth in some directions is even injurious to happiness, because it compels us to take leave of delusions which were pleasant while they lasted. It may be urged that the light shed on the origin and destiny of man by the pursuit of truth in some directions is not altogether a cheerful light. It may be urged that man stands to-day in the position of one who has been reared from his cradle as the child of a noble race and the heir to great possessions, and who finds at this coming of age that he has been deceived alike as to his origin and his expectations; that he neither springs of the high lineage he fancied, nor will inherit the vast estate he looked for, but must put off his towering pride, and contract his boundless hopes, and begin the world anew from a lower level: and this, it may be urged, comes of pursuing knowledge. But even conceding this, I suppose the answer to be that knowledge, and especially disagreeable knowledge, cannot by any art be totally excluded even from those who do not seek it. Wisdom, said Aeschylus long ago, comes to men whether they will or no. The house of delusions is cheap to build, but draughty to live in, and ready at any instant to fall; and it is surely truer prudence to move our furniture betimes into the open air than to stay indoors until our tenement tumbles about our ears. It is and it must in the long run be better for a man to see things as they are than to be ignorant of them; just as there is less fear of stumbling or of striking against corners in the daylight than in the dark.

Nor again will I pretend that, as Bacon asserts, 'the pleasure and delight of knowledge and learning far surpasseth all other in nature.' This is too much the language of a salesman crying his own wares. The pleasures of the intellect are notoriously less vivid than either the pleasures of sense or the pleasures of the affections; and

272

therefore, especially in the season of youth, the pursuit of knowledge is likely enough to be neglected and lightly esteemed in comparison with other pursuits offering much stronger immediate attractions. But the pleasure of learning and knowing, though not the keenest, is yet the least perishable of pleasures; the least subject to external things, and the play of chance, and the wear of time. And as a prudent man puts money by to serve as a provision for the material wants of his old age, so too he needs to lay up against the end of his days provision for the intellect. As the years go by, comparative values are found to alter: Time, says Sophocles, takes many things which once were pleasures and brings them nearer to pain. In the day when the strong men shall bow themselves, and desire shall fail, it will be a matter of yet more concern than now, whether one can say 'my mind to me a kingdom is;' and whether the windows of the soul look out upon a broad and delightful landscape, or face nothing but a brick wall.

Well then, once we have recognised that knowledge in itself is good for man, we shall need to invent no pretexts for studying this subject or that; we shall import no extraneous considerations of use or ornament to justify us in learning one thing rather than another. If a certain department of knowledge specially attracts a man, let him study that, and study it because it attracts him; and let him not fabricate excuses for that which requires no excuse, but rest assured that the reason why it most attracts him is that it is best for him. The majority of mankind, as is only natural, will be most attracted by those sciences which most nearly concern human life; those sciences which, in Bacon's phrase, are drenched in flesh and blood, or, in the more elegant language of the *Daily Telegraph*, palpitate with actuality. The men who are attracted to the drier and the less palpitating sciences, say logic or pure mathematics or textual criticism, are likely to be fewer in number; but they are not to suppose that the comparative unpopularity of such learning renders it any the less worthy of pursuit. Nay they may if they like console themselves with Bacon's observation that 'this same *lumen siccum* doth parch and offend most men's watery and soft natures,' and infer, if it pleases them, that their natures are less soft and watery than other men's. But be that as it may, we can all dwell together in unity without crying up our own pursuits or depreciating the pursuits of others on factitious grounds. We are not like the Ottoman sultans of old time, who thought they could never enjoy a moment's security till they had murdered all their brothers. There is no rivalry between the studies of Arts and Laws and Science but the rivalry of fellow soldiers in striving which can most victoriously achieve the common end of all, to set back the frontier of darkness.

It is the glory of God, says Solomon, to conceal a thing: but the honour of kings is to search out a matter. Kings have long abdicated that province; and we students are come into their inheritance: it is our honour to search out the things which God has concealed. In Germany at Easter time they hide coloured eggs about the house and the garden that the children may amuse themselves in hunting after them and finding them. It is to some such game of hide-and-seek that we are invited by that power which planted in us the desire to find out what is concealed, and stored the universe with hidden things that we might delight ourselves in discovering them. And the pleasure of discovery differs from other pleasures in this, that it is shadowed by no fear of satiety on the one hand or of frustration on the other. Other desires perish in their gratification, but the desire of knowledge never: the eye is not satisfied with seeing nor the ear filled with hearing. Other desires become the occasion of pain through dearth of the material to gratify them, but not the desire of knowledge: the sum of things to be known is inexhaustible, and however long we read we shall never come to the end of our story-book. So long as the mind of man is what it is, it will continue to exult in advancing on the unknown throughout the infinite field of the universe; and the tree of knowledge will remain for ever, as it was in the beginning, a tree to be desired to make one wise.

Matthew Arnold

On the last day of October 1891 a bust of Matthew Arnold was unveiled in Westminster Abbey by his friend and contemporary Lord Coleridge. Lord Coleridge on that occasion delivered an address in which, by way of conveying to his audience a clear conception of what Matthew Arnold was, he explained to them with great particularity what Matthew Arnold was not. 'Thackeray' said he 'may have written more pungent social satire, Tennyson may be a greater poet, John Morley may be a greater critical biographer, Cardinal Newman may have a more splendid style, Lightfoot or Ellicott or Jowett may be greater ecclesiastical scholars and have done more for the interpretation of St Paul.' Here the list ends: I cannot imagine why; for it appears to me that if I were once started I could go on like that for ever. Mr Chevallier may be a more accomplished vocalist, Mr Gladstone may be an older Parliamentary hand, Mr Stoddart may have made higher scores against the Australians, the Lord Chief Justice may have sentenced a greater number of criminals to penal servitude – where is one to stop? all those personages have as much business here as that great biographer Mr John Morley. And as for the superb constellation of divines, – Lightfoot and Ellicott and Jowett, – what I want to know is, where is Archdeacon Farrar? But if, after all, Lord Coleridge's account of what Arnold was not, leaves it still a trifle vague what Arnold was, let me take you to the *Daily Chronicle* of April 17, 1888. I copied down its remarks that same day; and ever since, I carry them about with me wherever I go as a sort of intellectual salvolatile. Whenever I am in any ways afflicted or distressed in mind, body or estate, I take out this extract and read it; and then, like the poet Longfellow when he gazed on the planet Mars, I am strong again. The following are the salient characteristics of Matthew Arnold's poetry – 'His muse mounted upward with bright thoughts, as the skylark shakes dewdrops from its wing as it carols at "Heaven's Gate," or like a mountain brooklet carrying many a wildflower on its wavelets, his melody flowed cheerily on. Sometimes too his music rises like that of the mysterious ocean casting up pearls as it rolls.'

Now at last I hope you have a clear conception of the real Matthew Arnold: now you will be able to recognise his poetry when you come across it; and no doubt you will easily distinguish between his three poetical manners, – that in which he shakes the dewdrops from his wing, that in which he carries wildflowers on his wavelets, and that in which he casts up pearls as he rolls. I declare, I can liken such writing to nothing but the orgies in which the evil genii may be supposed to have indulged when they heard of the death of Solomon. The great critic of our land and time is dead, and the uncritical spirit of the English nation proceeds to execute this dance of freedom over his grave. He spent a lifetime trying to teach his countrymen how to use their minds, and the breath is hardly out of his body before the sow that was washed returns with majestic determination to her wallowing in the mire.

I can find no better words in which to speak of the loss of Arnold than those which were used by Gerard Hamilton at the death of Johnson. 'He has made a chasm which not only nothing can fill up, but which nothing has a tendency to fill up. Johnson is dead. Let us go to the next best: there is nobody; no man can be said to put you in mind of Johnson.' I will not compare Arnold with the mob of gentlemen who produce criticism ('quales ego vel Chorinus'), such woful stuff as I or Lord Coleridge write: I will compare him with the best. He leaves men behind him to whom we cannot refuse the name of critic; but then we need to find some other name for him and to call him more than a critic, as John the Baptist was called more than a prophet. I go to Mr Leslie Stephen, and I am always instructed, though I may not be charmed. I go to Mr Walter Pater, and I am always charmed, though I may not be instructed. But Arnold was not merely instructive or charming nor both together: he was what it seems to me no one else is: he was illuminating.

Swinburne

The publication, in 1866, of the late Mr Swinburne's *Poems and Ballads* may fairly be called the most conspicuous event in the literary history of the reign of Queen Victoria. We now see that it was not so important an event as it once appeared: its results were not permanent, nor even of long duration; but it was the most moving novelty that the world of letters had seen for many a day or is likely to see for many another. At a time when Victorian verse was at its very tamest, when the two most widely read of recent poems were *Enoch Arden* and *Hiawatha*, this trumpet of insurrection excited in young and ardent minds an emotion comparable to what Wordsworth and Coleridge had felt as they witnessed the beginning of the French Revolution. Mr Thomas Hardy has told me that in those days, when he was a young man of six-and-twenty living in London, there was a whole army of young men like himself, not mutually acquainted, who nevertheless, as they met in the streets, could recognise one another as spiritual brethren by a certain outward sign. This sign was an oblong projection at the breast-pocket of the coat. To the gross world of London, enslaved by commerce, respectability, and middle-age, it might have been anything; but the sons of fire who had similar oblongs protruding from their own breast-pockets knew what it was: it was Moxon's first edition of *Poems and Ballads*, worn where it should be worn, just over the heart.

When Mr Swinburne died, April 1909, at the age of 72, he might as well have been dead for a quarter of a century. For a quarter of a century and more he had written nothing that mattered. There were not many to buy his books, and fewer still to read them; the poetasters, except the very poorest, had ceased to try to imitate him; the literary world was much interested in many other things, good, bad and indifferent, but little interested in the poetry of Mr Swinburne. He still commanded the lip-service of the journalists, who would describe him from time to time as our only great living poet; but this they said, not because they knew anything about such matters or even believed it to be true, but because they hoped, by so saying, to inflict mental anguish on Mr William Watson or Mr Stephen Phillips.

Swinburne in fact was one of those not very numerous poets

whom their contemporaries have treated with justice. The different attention which he received at different periods very fairly corresponded to differences, at those periods, in the quality of his writing. He was neither steadily overrated, like Byron, nor steadily underrated, like Shelley, nor, like Wordsworth, derided while he wrote well and celebrated when he wrote well no longer: he received the day's wage for the day's work. His first book fell dead, as it deserved; his first good book, *Atalanta in Calydon*, earned him celebrity; his best book, *Poems and Ballads*, was his most famous and influential book; and the decline of his powers, slow in *Songs before Sunrise* and *Bothwell* and *Erectheus*, accelerated in his later writings, was followed, not immediately, but after an interval sufficient to give him the chance of recovery, by a corresponding decline, first slow and then rapid, in public interest and esteem.

There can be no doubt that the enthusiasm provoked by the *Poems and Ballads*, like the loud and transient outcry which frightened its first publisher into withdrawing it from circulation, was due in great measure to adventitious circumstances and to a feature of the book which is now seen to be merely accidental. The poems were largely and even chiefly concerned with a thing which one set of people call love, and another set of people call immorality, each set declaring that the other name is quite wrong, so that people who belong to neither set do not exactly know what to call it; but perhaps one may avoid extremes by calling it Aphrodite. Now in the general life of mankind Aphrodite is quite able to take care of herself; but in literature, at any rate in the literature of that Anglo-Saxon race to which we have the high privilege and heavy responsibility of belonging, she wages an unequal contest with another great divinity, who is called purity by her friends and hypocrisy by her enemies, and whom, again to avoid extremes, one may perhaps call Mrs Grundy. In the year 1866 the vicissitudes of their secular conflict had brought Mrs Grundy to the top: she appeared to be sitting on Aphrodite as firmly as the Babylonian woman on her seven mountains in the Book of Revelations; and Swinburne's *Poems and Ballads* were a powerful and timely demonstration in favour of the under dog – if indeed I may apply such a term to either of the fair antagonists. Here was a subject which most poets had ceased to talk about at all, and here was a poet talking about it at the very top of a very sonorous voice: the stone which the builders rejected was become the head of the corner. And although the enthusiasm which this intervention evoked in one camp, like the scandal which it occasioned in the other, was excessive – for Aphrodite has the knack of causing both her friends and her enemies to lose their heads and to make more fuss about her than she is worth – still the stroke was both effective and salutary, and entitles Swinburne to a secure though modest place among the liberators of mankind. The reasonable licence which English literature enjoys to-day, and which it so seldom abuses, is the result of a gradual emancipation which began with Swinburne's *Poems and Ballads*.

Those to whom this work appealed by its subject and contents, as distinct from its form, were of two classes: there were the simple adherents of Aphrodite, and there were many of those grave men, correct in behaviour and earnest in thought, who regard the relations of the sexes as the most serious and important element in human life. It was the irony of the situation that Swinburne himself belonged to neither class. He was not a libertine, and he was not an earnest thinker about life: he was merely a writer in search of a subject, and a tinder-box that any spark would set on fire. When he had written his book upon this subject, he had done with it, and it hardly appears again in the twenty volumes of his later verse: he was ready for a new subject. In *Songs before Sunrise*, his next volume, his attitude towards Aphrodite was austere, and the finest poem in the book is the Prelude in which he takes his leave of her. *Poems and Ballads* were the effervescence with which a quick and shallow nature responded to a certain influence issuing partly from the Greek and Latin classics, partly from medieval legend, partly from the French literature of the nineteenth century. That effervescence subsided, and around a new subject, Liberty, a new influence, chiefly Mazzini's, provoked a fresh effervescence, not nearly so sparkling. The fact is that, whatever may be the comparative merits of the two deities, Liberty is by no means so interesting as Aphrodite, and by no means so good a subject for poetry. There is a lack of detail about Liberty, and she has indeed no positive quality at all. Liberty consists in the absence of obstructions; it is merely a preliminary to activities whose character it does not determine; and to write poems about Liberty is very much as if one should write an Ode to Elbow-room or a panegyric on space of three dimensions.

And in truth poets never do write poems about Liberty, they only pretend to do so: they substitute images.

> Thy face is as a sword smiting in sunder
>> Shadows and chains and dreams and iron things;
> The sea is dumb before thy face, the thunder
>> Silent, the skies are narrower than thy wings.

Then, when they feel that the reader is starving for something more tangible, they generally begin to talk of Athens, which, as it happens, was a slave-state; and in the last resort they fall back on denunciation of tyranny, an abominable institution, no doubt, but at any rate less featureless than Liberty, and a godsend to people who have to pretend to write about her.

But even tyranny is an exhaustible subject, and seven thousand verses exhaust it; and Swinburne, since he could not be still, was forced to be eloquent about other things. He appointed himself to the laureateship of the sea; he cultivated a devotion to babies and young children; finally, under stress of famine and in desperation at the dearth of themes, he fled to what Johnson calls the last refuge of a scoundrel: he conceived a tardy enthusiasm for his native land, and wrote patriotic poems in imitation of Campbell. And, in addition to all this, he composed a great number of verses about the verses of other poets.

Not one of these subjects was well chosen. The sea is a natural object; and Swinburne had no eye for nature and no talent for describing it. Children and babies are not appropriately celebrated in verse so ornate and so verbose as Swinburne's. As for his patriotic poetry, it may be unfair to call it insincere, but certainly it has no air of sincerity: it is the sort of patriotic poetry one would expect from a man who had written volumes in honour of other nations before he wrote a line in honour of his own.

In truth there was only one theme which Swinburne thoroughly loved and understood; and that was literature. Here was the true centre of his interests, and the source of his genuine and spontaneous emotions. But literature, unfortunately, is neither a fruitful nor even an appropriate subject for poetry. Swinburne himself was uneasily aware of this; and consequently, when he heard it said that his work was grounded not upon life but upon books, it made him angry, and he began to splutter as follows: 'The half-brained creature to whom books are other than living things may see with the eyes of a bat and draw with the fingers of a mole his dullard's distinction between books and life: those who live the fuller life of a higher animal than he, know that books are to poets as much part of that life as pictures are to painters or as music is to musicians, dead matter though they may be to the spiritually still-born children of dirt and dullness who find it possible and natural to live while dead in heart and brain.' Well, of course it is a sad thing to be a spiritually still-born child of dirt and dullness, and it is peculiarly depressing to be dead in heart and brain when one has only half a brain to be dead in; but it is no use bemoaning one's condition, and we must pass on to consider the parallel which Swinburne draws.

Books, he says, are to poets as much part of life as pictures are to painters. Just so: they are to poets that part of life which is not fitted to become the subject of their art. Painters do not paint pictures of pictures, and similarly poets had better not write poems on poems. And Swinburne did worse than take books for his subject: he dragged this subject into the midst of all other subjects, and covered earth and sky and man with the dust of the library. He cannot watch a sunset at sea without beginning to think of Beaumont and Fletcher. He walks along a country road at Midsummer, and it sets him talking about Chaucer, because Chaucer may possibly have done the same thing. He writes an ode for the four hundred and fiftieth anniversary of the foundation of his own school, Eton, in which he contrives to drag in Shakespeare (who was educated at Harrow) but mentions only one Etonian. And who do you think that one Etonian is? Shelley, whom Eton did not quite succeed in tormenting out of his mind: Shelley, who except for his father's influence and intervention, would twice have been expelled: Shelley, whose atheism was traced, by an Eton headmaster, to the difficulty which he found in reconciling the existence of God with the existence of Eton. In short, Swinburne was perpetually talking shop: the bookish spirit in which he looked on nature and mankind, with his head full of his own trade, is essentially the same as the spirit in which *The Tailor and Cutter* annually criticises the portraits in the Royal Academy, interested, not in the artist, not in the subject, but in the cut of the subject's clothes.

I have been speaking of the themes of his *lyrical* poetry, because it is only as a lyrist that Swinburne is important. The themes of his

281

dramatic and narrative works were not ill chosen, and the unsatis-
factoriness of those poems was not due to their subject but to
Swinburne's lack of talent for narrative and the drama. His plays
have a certain empty dignity, but he was not a dramatist nor even,
like Browning, a psychologist: his characters are talking masks. In
his only considerable narrative poem, *Tristram of Lyonesse*, the
prologue, which in essence is lyric, is worth all the rest of the book
put together; just as *Atalanta in Calydon* is raised far above his other
dramas by the brilliant beauty of its very undramatic lyrics. It is of
his lyrical poetry that I am speaking when I say that after the first
series of *Poems and Ballads* he was chiefly occupied with bad subjects
or with subjects not suited to his genius.

But it has long been a commonplace that the strong side of
Swinburne's poetry was not its matter but its manner; and though
the matter of *Poems and Ballads* had much to do with the celebrity of
the book, it is to its diction and versification that it will mainly owe
its place in literature. Of these it is very difficult to speak adequately
and justly; to keep the balance between admiration for their extra-
ordinary merit and originality, and due recognition of the fact that
they belong essentially to the second order, not to the first.

If a man does not hear the melody of Swinburne's verse, he must
be deaf; he would not hear the melody of any verse. But if, as many
do, he thinks its melody the best, he must have a gross ear. The man
who now calls Swinburne the most musical of poets would, if he
had been born one hundred and fifty years earlier, have said the
same of Pope. To the ears of his contemporaries Pope's verse was
perfection: the inferiority of Milton's and Shakespeare's was not a
thing to be disputed about but to be explained and excused. The
melody of Pope and of Swinburne have this in common, and owed
their acceptation to this, that they address themselves frankly and
almost exclusively to what may be called the external ear. This, in
different ways and by different methods, they fill and delight: it is a
pleasure to hear them, and a pleasure to read them aloud. But there,
in that very fact, you can tell that their music is only of the second
order. To read aloud poets whose music is of the first, poets so
much unlike one another as Blake and Milton, is not a pleasure but
an embarrassment, because no reader can hope to do them justice.
Their melody is addressed to the inner chambers of the sense of
hearing, to the junction between the ear and the brain; and you

should either hire an angel from heaven to read them to you, or let them read themselves in silence. None better understood their superiority than Swinburne himself, the finest of whose critical qualities was his capacity to admire excellence unlike his own. His devotees might call him the most melodious of English poets, but he thought that the most melodious lines in English were the first five lines of *Lycidas*; he acknowledged in the Border Ballads a strain of music which no later poetry could reproduce; and he recognised that the best versification of modern times is to be found in the irregular and simple-seeming measures of the *Ancient Mariner*.

Among Swinburne's technical achievements the most conspicuous, if not the greatest, was his development of anapaestic verse. It was he who first made the anapaest fit for serious poetry. Before his time it had been used with some success for the lightest purposes, but when used for purposes other than the lightest it had seldom been managed with skill. At its best it had a simple and rather shallow music:

> The blackbird has fled to another retreat
> Where the hazels afford him a screen from the heat,
> And the scene where his melody charmed me before
> Resounds with his sweet-flowing ditty no more.

But it was notably unsure of foot, and seldom went without stumbling for more than four lines at a time: it was for ever collapsing into such meanness as this:

> There is mercy in every place,
> And mercy, encouraging thought!
> Gives even affliction a grace
> And reconciles man to his lot.

Yet this is almost the very stanza which Swinburne dignified and strengthened till it yielded a combination of speed and magnificence which nothing in English had possessed before.

> Out of Dindymus heavily laden
> Her lions draw bound and unfed
> A mother, a mortal, a maiden,
> A queen over death and the dead.

She is cold, and her habit is lowly,
    Her temple of branches and sods;
Most fruitful and virginal, holy,
    A mother of gods.

She hath wasted with fire thine high places,
    She hath hidden and marred and made sad
The fair limbs of the Loves, the fair faces
    Of gods that were goodly and glad.
She slays, and her hands are not bloody;
    She moves as a moon in the wane,
White-robed, and thy raiment is ruddy,
    Our Lady of Pain.

Other stanzas he invented for it, to display its capacities.

In the darkening and whitening
    Abysses adored,
With dayspring and lightning
    For lamp and for sword,
God thunders in heaven, and his angels are red with the wrath
    of the Lord.

There lived a singer in France of old
    By the tideless dolorous midland sea.
In a land of sand and ruin and gold
    There shone one woman, and none but she.
And finding life for her love's sake fail,
Being fain to see her, he bade set sail,
Touched land, and saw her as life grew cold,
    And praised God, seeing; and so died he.

True, the anapaestic rhythm, even when invested by a master with these alluring splendours, is not, in English, the best vehicle for poetry. Better poetry has been written in iambics and trochaics than will ever be written in anapaests; but still it is an unparalleled achievement, at so late a period of the literature, to have added this new and resonant string to the lyre.

In the second place, not only did he create new metres but he recreated old; and in particular he resuscitated the heroic couplet. It might have been thought, after all the practitioners through whose hands this measure had passed, that nothing remained for it but decent burial. The valley was full of bones; and behold, there were very many in the open valley; and lo, they were very dry. The form which the couplet had taken in the seventeenth century it retained to the nineteenth; and the innovations or reactions of Leigh Hunt and Keats were not improvements. Upon these dry bones Swinburne brought up new flesh and breathed into them a new spirit. In the hands of the last considerable poet who had used it, the metre still went to the tune of Pope and Dryden:

> Night wanes – the vapours round the mountains curled
> Melt into morn, and Light awakes the world.
> Man has another day to swell the past,
> And lead him near to little, but his last;
> But mighty Nature bounds as from her birth,
> The sun is in the heaven, and life on earth;
> Flowers in the valley, splendour in the beam,
> Health on the gale, and freshness in the stream.
> Immortal man! behold her glories shine,
> And cry, exulting inly, they are thine.
> Gaze on, while yet thy gladdened eye may see;
> A morrow comes when they are not for thee:
> And grieve what may above thy senseless bier,
> Nor earth nor sky will yield a single tear;
> Nor cloud shall gather more, nor leaf shall fall,
> Nor gale breathe forth one sigh for thee, for all;
> But creeping things shall revel in their spoil,
> And fit thy clay to fertilise the soil.

These lines are much above Byron's average; they say something worth saying, and they say it capably and with emotion; but their structure is still formal, and their vocabulary a trifle poor. Now take Swinburne:

> Thee too the years shall cover; thou shalt be
> As the rose born of one same blood with thee,
> As a song sung, as a word said, and fall
> Flower-wise, and be not any more at all,
> Nor any memory of thee anywhere;
> For never Muse has bound above thine hair
> The high Pierian flower whose graft outgrows

>   All summer kinship of the mortal rose
>   And colour of deciduous days, nor shed
>   Reflex and flush of heaven about thine head,
>   Nor reddened brows made pale by floral grief
>   With splendid shadow from that lordlier leaf.

It is hardly recognisable as the same metre. You are free to like it less: it is less brisk and forthright, but its fulness and richness and variety are qualities of which one would never have supposed the couplet to be capable.

In the third place he possessed an altogether unexampled command of rhyme, the chief enrichment of modern verse. The English language is comparatively poor in rhymes, and most English poets, when they have to rhyme more than two or three words together, betray their embarrassment. They betray it, for instance, when they write sonnets after the strict Petrarchan rule: the poetical inferiority of most English sonnets, if compared with what their own authors have achieved in other forms of verse, is largely though not entirely the result of this difficulty. Milton is embarrassed by it; Wordsworth, though probably the best of our sonneteers, is pitiably embarrassed, and driven to end the noblest of his sonnets with a wretched tag about 'titles manifold;' Rossetti, our most determined workman in this line, dissimulates his embarrassment by inventing, for the purpose of sonnet-writing, a jargon in which every word is so unnatural that the words which form the rhymes are no more unnatural than the rest and so give rise to no special wonder. To Swinburne a sonnet was child's play: the task of providing four rhymes was not hard enough, and he wrote long poems in which each stanza demanded eight or ten rhymes, and wrote them so that he never seemed to be saying anything for the rhyme's sake. His pre-eminence was most remarkable in the mastery of feminine rhymes, as we call them, rhymes of two syllables. Before Swinburne, few English poets had used them much, and few without doing themselves an injury. They would start swimmingly enough:

>   How delicious is the winning
>   Of a kiss at love's beginning,
>   When two mutual hearts are sighing
>   For the knot there's no untying.

But unless they made up their mind to desert the scheme it would generally entice them to use words which they would rather not have used:

> Yet remember, 'midst your wooing,
> Love has bliss, but love has ruing,
> Other smiles may make you fickle,
> Tears for other charms may trickle.

The word *trickle*, in that verse, is not preferred to the word *flow* because of its intrinsic merit, but for quite another reason. Swinburne's language, no doubt, is often wanting in clearness and aptness, but that defect is never caused by any difficulty in finding feminine rhymes: they come at call as readily as the others. I will mention one significant detail. The ordinary versifier, if he employs feminine rhymes, makes great use of words ending with *ing*: they are the largest class of these rhymes, and they form his mainstay. Swinburne, so plentiful and ready to hand were his stores, almost disdains this expedient: in all the four hundred and forty lines of *Dolores*, for example, he only twice resorts to it.

The ornament of verse especially associated with the name of Swinburne is alliteration. This of course was no invention of his. Not to speak of the old poetry extinguished by Chaucer and his rhymes, whose very base was alliteration, this artifice had been used, and even used to excess, by many earlier writers than Swinburne. The greatest of our poets did not largely avail themselves of its aid; in Milton, for instance, its appearance is sporadic and sometimes even, one would say, unintentional: we are arrested and surprised at encountering now and then such lines as these:

> Fairer than feigned of old or fabled since
> Of fairy damsels met in forest wide
> By Knights of Logres or of Lyones,
> Lancelot, or Pelleas, or Pellenore.

The first English poet to employ alliteration methodically and scientifically was Gray, and after Gray it was most systematically practised by Tennyson: in Gray it is perhaps less effective than one might expect, and in Tennyson, though very effective, it is rather too prominent and ubiquitous. Swinburne, in much of his writing, employed the artifice so profusely, so wastefully, and indeed so ignorantly, that in the end he brought it into disrepute and sent it out of fashion. The proper function of alliteration is to add speed and force to the motion of verse. How it should be applied, if it is to compass these ends, is a matter on which I might say a good deal; but that belongs rather to a paper on the artifice of versification than to a paper on Swinburne. From Swinburne I will take one example, and I might take hundreds, of how it should not be applied.

> Many a long blithe wave
> Buoyed their blithe bark between the bare bald rocks,
> Deep, steep, and still, save for the swift free flocks . . .

but that is enough. Those verses make on the ear and mind two immediate impressions: they are cumbrous and they are artificial; and if they are analysed it will be found that their unskilful artifice is the chief cause of their cumbrousness. They are the work of a craftsman who has forgotten his trade; who has lost sight of the end proposed, and who actually defeats the end by mechanically hammering away at the means. This is mere bungling; but in the celebrated stanza about the lilies and languors of virtue and the raptures and roses of vice, though the artifice is rather crude and obvious, the effect is nevertheless attained: the verse, though it pays a price for them, does gain force and rapidity. In his best time he used alliteration, never indeed with perfect art, but still with some rectitude of instinct: this he lost in his later years, as he lost almost everything else. He had deafened himself with his own noise, till his verse became downright unpleasant to ears which were still open. His growing obtuseness of perception showed itself most clearly in his employment of trochaic rhythms. This metre he had never written so skilfully as iambics or anapaests, and in the end he may be said to have written it worse than anyone had ever written it before. The parody of Laura Matilda in the *Rejected Addresses* is not exactly good verse; but it is better verse than Swinburne's poem on Grace Darling.

If you turn from his versification to his diction, the case is much the same, though it cannot be examined in the same detail. The first impression produced by his style, as it was in 1866, is one of great and even overpowering richness. He seemed to have ransacked all the treasuries of the language and melted the whole plunder into a new and gorgeous amalgam. In the poems of his later life his style was threadbare. It had not become austere: it was as voluble and diffuse as ever, but it had ceased to be rich and various. The torrent streamed on, but it streamed from an impoverished vocabulary, and consisted of a dwindled stock of words repeated again and again. A few favourite epithets were conferred on all manner of different things, instead of different and truly descriptive epithets. If he admired something very much he would not wait to find a word indicative of its quality, but he would call it 'god-like;' upon which one of his critics observed that, in view of Mr Swinburne's theological opinions, to call a thing god-like must be very much the same as calling it devilish good. If an epithet struck him as pretty in itself he would work it to death by associating it with objects to which it had no special appropriateness; and it would be interesting to draw up a list of the various unlike things which he has called 'sun-bright' or 'flower-soft,' or 'deep as the sea.' This is a fashion of speaking which attains its legitimate culmination in the conversational style of the British workman, who thinks that no noun should be without an adjective, and that one adjective is suitable to every noun.

But even in the days of its early freshness and abundance his diction had the fault that amidst all its magnificence it did not ring quite true: it would not sustain comparison even with the best contemporary poetry, the best of Tennyson's and Matthew Arnold's, no, nor the best of Coventry Patmore's and Christina Rossetti's. Speaking broadly, it was a diction of the same cast as Pope's. The differences between the two are evident and striking; but their differences are less essential than their resemblance in this point – that they both run in a groove. They impose upon all thought and feeling a set mode of speech: they are mannerisms, and consequently they are imitable. Pope's diction was long imitated successfully; Swinburne's was imitated successfully, but not long, because those who were clever enough to imitate it were also clever enough to see that it was not well worth imitating.

In fact, what Swinburne wrote, and what Pope and Dryden wrote, was not, in the very strictest sense of the word, poetry. It was often capital stuff, and to the taste of many of their contemporaries it was better than the best poetry. But time went on, and the power of its spell was found to wane; its appeal was not to the core of the human mind and the unalterable element in its constitution. I suppose that most people, while admitting that Swinburne's poetry is less poetical than Milton's or even than Tennyson's, would maintain that on the other hand it is much more poetical than Pope's or even Dryden's. Well, I think so too; but I cannot feel sure that I am right in thinking so. The atmosphere of taste in which Swinburne's poetry grew up is not yet altogether dispersed: we ourselves grew up in it, and we have not all grown out of it. But if permanency is any test of merit, then we must remark that the poetry inaugurated by Dryden was supreme for a century and a half, while the influence of Swinburne spent itself within five and twenty years. It began in 1865, it reached its height before 1880, by 1890 there was not much left of it. Here of course it must be borne in mind that Pope and Dryden had two strings to their bow and Swinburne had only one. If Pope's and Dryden's verse were not poetry at all, they still would be very great men of letters and representatives of their age. Their sense, their wit, their knowledge of life and men, and their eminence in those merits which poetry shares with prose, would still preserve for their verse a high place in literature. But if Swinburne's verse had not poetical merit, it would have no merit at all.

Poetry, which in itself is simply a tone of the voice, a particular way of saying things, is mainly concerned with three great provinces. First, with human affection, and those emotions which we assign to the heart: no one could say that Swinburne succeeded or excelled in this province. The next province is the world of thought; the contemplation of life and the universe: in this province Swinburne's ideas and reflections are not indeed identical with those of Mrs Hemans, but they belong to the same intellectual order as hers: unwound from their cocoon of words they are either superficial or second-hand. Last, there is the province of external nature as perceived by our senses; and on this I must dwell for a little, because there is one department of external nature which Swinburne is supposed to have made his own: the sea.

The sea, to be sure, is a large department; and that is how it succeeded in attracting Swinburne's attention; for he seldom noticed any object of external nature unless it was very large, very brilliant, or very violently coloured. But the sea as a subject of poetry is somewhat barren. Those poets who have a true eye for nature and a sure pen for describing it, spend few words on describing the sea; and their few words describe it better than Swinburne's thousands. It is historically certain that he had seen the sea, but if it were not, it could not with certainty have been inferred from his descriptions: they might have been written by a man who had never been outside Warwickshire. Descriptions of nature equally accurate, though not equally eloquent, have actually been composed by persons blind from their birth, merely by combining anew the words and phrases which they have had read to them from books. When Swinburne writes thus –

And the night was alive and anhungered of life as a tiger from
    toils cast free:
And a rapture of rage made joyous the spirit and strength of the
    soul of the sea.
All the weight of the wind bore down on it, freighted with
    death for fraught:
And the keen waves kindled and quickened as things
    transfigured or things distraught.
And madness fell on them laughing and leaping; and madness
    came on the wind:
And the might and the light and the darkness of storm were as
    storm in the heart of Ind.
Such glory, such terror, such passion, as lighten and harrow the
    far fierce East,
Rang, shone, spake, shuddered around us: the night was an altar
    with death for priest –

it would be cruel to set against such a passage a single line of Tennyson's or a single epithet of Shakespeare's: I take instead a snatch of verse whose author few of you know and most of you never heard of:

> Hurry me, Nymphs, O, hurry me
> Far above the grovelling sea,
> Which, with blind weakness and bass roar
> Casting his white age on the shore,
> Wallows along that slimy floor;
> With his wide-spread webbèd hands
> Seeking to climb the level sands,
> But rejected still to rave
> Alive in his uncovered grave.

Admirers of the sea may call that a lampoon or a caricature, but they cannot deny that it is life-like: the man who wrote it had seen the sea, and the man who reads it sees the sea again.

If even so bare and simple an object as the sea was too elusive and delicate for Swinburne's observation and description, you would not expect him to have much success with anything so various and manifold as the face of the earth. And I am downright aghast at the dullness of perception and the lack of self-knowledge and self-criticism which permitted him to deposit his prodigious quantity of descriptive writing in the field of English literature. That field is rich beyond example in descriptions of nature from the hands of unequalled masters, for in the rendering of nature English poetry has outdone all poetry: and here, after five centuries, comes Swinburne covering the grass with his cartload of words and filling the air with the noise of the shooting of rubbish. It is a clear morning towards the end of winter: snow has fallen in the night, and still lies on the branches of the trees under brilliant sunshine. Tennyson could have surveyed the scene with his trained eye, made search among his treasury of choice words, sorted and sifted and condensed them, till he had framed three lines of verse, to be introduced some day in a narrative or a simile, and there to flash upon the reader's eye the very picture of a snowy and sunshiny morning. Keats or Shakespeare would have walked between the trees thinking of whatever came uppermost and letting their senses commune with their souls; and there the morning would have transmuted itself into half a line or so which, occurring in some chance passage of their poetry, would have set the reader walking between the same trees again. Swinburne picks up the sausage-machine into which he crammed anything and everything; round goes the handle, and out at the other end comes this noise:

Ere frost-flower and snow-blossom faded and fell, and the
    splendour of winter had passed out of sight,
The ways of the woodlands were fairer and stranger than
    dreams that fulfil us in sleep with delight;
The breaths of the mouths of the winds had hardened on
    tree-tops and branches that glittered and swayed
Such wonders and glories of blossom-like snow or of frost that
    outlightens all flowers till it fade

That the sea was not lovelier than here was the land, nor the
   night than the day, nor the day than the night,
Nor the winter sublimer with storm than the spring: such mirth
   had the madness and might in thee made,
March, master of winds, bright minstrel and marshal of storms
   that enkindle the season they smite.

That is not all, it clatters on for fifty lines or so; but that is enough
and too much. It shows what nature was to Swinburne: just
something to write verse about, a material for making a particular
kind of sausage.

This inattention or insensibility betrays itself very plainly in his
imagery, which is at once profuse and meagre. It is profuse, for he
constantly uses metaphors and similes where they are not wanted
and do not help the thought; and yet it is meagre, for the same
metaphors and similes are perpetually repeated. They are derived
from the few natural objects which he had noticed: the sea, the stars,
sunset, fire, and flowers, generally of a red colour, such as the rose
and the poppy. However, the worst that can be said of them is that
they are monotonous, perfunctory, and ineffective. But much
worse can be said of another kind of simile, which grows common
in his later writings. When a poet says that hatred is hot as fire or
chastity white as snow, we can only object that we have often heard
this before and that, considered as ornament, it is rather trite and
cheap. But when he inverts his comparisons and says that fire is hot
as hatred and snow white as chastity, he is a fool for his pains. The
heat of fire and the whiteness of snow are so much more sharply
perceived than those qualities of hatred and chastity which have
heat and whiteness for courtesy titles, that these similes actually
blur the image and dilute the force of what is said. But with such
similes Swinburne's later works abound: similes to him were part
of the convention of poetry, and he mechanically used them
when they no longer served, and even when they frustrated, the
only purpose which can justify their introduction. In fact he came
to write like an automaton, without so much as knowing the
meaning of what he said. Here are four lines from the *Tale of
Balen*:

> A table of all clear gold thereby
> Stood stately, fair as morning's eye,

– the beauty of a table is not more clearly apprehended when compared to the beauty of morning's eye: that is the perfunctory simile, poor and useless; but let that pass, and proceed –

> With four strong silver pillars, high
> And firm as faith and hope may be.

These four pillars are the four legs of the table: they were possibly five feet in height, probably less, certainly not much more; and they were high as hope may be. Now therefore we know the maximum height of hope: five feet and a few odd inches.

It is not then for mastery nor even for competent handling of any of the three great provinces of poetry that Swinburne will be known to posterity. And not only so, but he was deficient in some of the qualities which go to constitute excellence on the formal side of poetry: he had little power of construction and little power of condensation. His nearest approach to a good short poem is the *Garden of Proserpine*, and that contains 96 lines, though it is true that they are short ones: *Ilicet* has about 150, *The Triumph of Time* nearly 400, *Dolores* more than 400. Of course in this defect Swinburne does not stand alone among eminent poets: he stands with Chaucer and Spenser, whose shorter pieces give hardly a hint of their true powers and excellences. But the defect was a worse misfortune to him than to them, because they in the main were narrative poets, and he was a lyrist. Gray writing to Mason on January 13, 1758, has these words: 'Extreme conciseness of expression, yet pure, perspicuous and musical, is one of the grand beauties of lyric poetry. This I have always aimed at, and never could attain.' Much less did Swinburne ever attain, what he never even recognised as a mark to aim at, this grand beauty of lyric poetry. Again, the virtue of construction and orderly evolution is almost absent from his lyrics. To take three of his most impressive and characteristic poems, the three which I mentioned last, *Dolores*, and *Ilicet* and *The Triumph of Time*: there is no reason why they should begin where they do or end where they do; there is no reason why the middle should be in the middle; there is hardly a reason why, having once begun, they should ever end at all; and it would be possible to rearrange the stanzas which compose them in several different orders without lessening their coherency or impairing their effect. Almost the only piece which satisfies in this respect is the last good poem he ever wrote, the elegy on the death of Baudelaire, which indeed, if it has not all the fresh and luxuriant beauty of his earlier writing, may yet perhaps be reckoned his very best poem, in virtue of its dignity, and its unusual and uncharacteristic merit of structure and design.

It is therefore by two things mainly, his verse and his language, in the vigour and magnificence which at his best period they possessed, that Swinburne must stand or fall; and by those two things he will not fall but stand. I have said that neither is of the first order; but there is no need that they should be: to things so novel and original it suffices that they should be good; you cannot demand that they should be the best. Henry the Seventh's chapel is not the most beautiful part of Westminster Abbey; but it is beautiful, and the fabric is more enriched by the addition of that new and different beauty than if the chapel had been built in the purer style of the choir and transepts. Who is the greatest English poet of the nineteenth century it is difficult, gloriously difficult, to say; assuredly not Swinburne; but its two most original poets are Wordsworth, who began the age, and Swinburne, who ended it. And when Swinburne died last year, thirty years later than he would have died if the gods had loved him, and my memory took me back to the heart of that movement in literature which he created and survived, I thought that Wordsworth had pronounced his fittest epitaph in the sonnet on the extinction of the Venetian Republic:

> And what if she had seen those glories fade,
> Those titles vanish, and that strength decay;
> Yet shall some tribute of regret be paid
> When her long life hath reached its final day:
> Men are we, and must grieve when even the shade
> Of that which once was great is passed away.

Cambridge Inaugural Lecture (1911)

Three hundred years ago, when Bacon, in his treatise on *The Advancement of Learning*, set out to enumerate and classify the causes which hindered that advancement and brought learning into discredit, he professed to find the chief cause in the errors and imperfections of learned men themselves. Not, he explains, in their poverty and the meanness of their employments – for example, that the government of youth is commonly allotted to them; nor again in their manners – 'that they do many times fail to observe decency and discretion in their behaviour and carriage;' but in 'those errors and vanities which have intervened amongst the studies themselves of the learned,' and which make them go the wrong way to work.

Whatever the advance of learning since Bacon's day, it has not yet progressed beyond the reach of errors and imperfections; and vigilance over the mode in which we conduct our studies has not ceased to be advisable. An inaugural address is a fitting occasion for taking stock of our vanities, or at least for looking the worst of them in the face and forming resolutions for their amendment. I propose today to consider two current errors, as it seems to me, of some magnitude and of opposite nature. The study of Latin is a science conversant with literature: there are therefore two ways in which it ought not to be pursued. It ought not to be pursued as if it were a science conversant with the operations of nature or with the properties of number and space, nor yet as if it were itself a branch of literature, and no science at all.

It so happens that the consideration of this subject can easily be interwoven with another theme on which it is natural and proper that I should speak today. As Horace's father, desiring to exhort his son to virtue, would set before him a pattern for imitation in flesh and blood – *unum ex iudicibus selectis obiciebat* – so I can bring in example to the aid of precept, and combine a discussion of some width and generality with the commemoration of the names of individuals. This commemoration therefore, to which I now digress, is not in all aspects a digression, but has on the contrary a near relationship to one at least of the matters which I have chosen for consideration.

The Chair of Latin in this University was founded, by his friends and disciples, to the honour of the greatest classical teacher of his century, Benjamin Hall Kennedy, on his retirement, after thirty years' service, from his memorable Headmastership of Shrewsbury School. It was held in succession by two of his pupils, and indeed it has now fallen, I might almost say, to a third, though a pupil who never saw him and whom he never saw. What first turned my mind to these studies and implanted in me a genuine liking for Greek and Latin was the gift, when I was seventeen years old, of the most delightful, at any rate to me, of all volumes of translated verse – the third edition of *Sabrinae Corolla*, having Kennedy for its chief editor and chief contributor.

The practice of translation into Greek and Latin verse is often commended, in England, upon rather unsubstantial grounds, and has an efficacy imputed to it which it does not really possess. It is no doubt one way of learning prosody, but it is certainly not the only way, and possibly not even the best; while to suppose that it will confer on its practitioners any peculiar insight into the principles of ancient metre, or even any sufficient knowledge of its laws, is a delusion, and a delusion which ought by this time to have been dispelled by the facts of history. Skill to imitate the verse of the Greeks and Romans, and skill to explore its secrets and discover its rules, have both been conspicuous features of English scholarship. But they have not been conspicuous at the same time, nor in the same persons. Of the many and important additions to our knowledge of Greek and Latin metre which were made in the eighteenth century the great majority were made by English scholars: but they were made by scholars who did not themselves write Greek and Latin verse, or who did not excel in writing it.

In the nineteenth century Greek and Latin verse was written in England, and especially in Cambridge, better than it had been written anywhere in Europe since classical antiquity itself; but meanwhile the most important additions of the nineteenth century to our knowledge of Greek and Latin were made, not in England, but in Germany. That is what history has to say about the fabulous virtues of the exercise; and indeed, quite apart from history, it stands to reason that you are not likely to discover laws of metre by composing verses in which you occasionally break those laws because you have not yet discovered them. But there was the less need for fable, because verse-translation has other titles to honour which are not simply legendary. In the first place, it has intrinsic value as a fine art. It is not one of the great arts, but it is no mere handicraft either; it is an art of the same worth and dignity as the art of engraving.

As engraving to the great art of painting, so is translation to the great art of poetry; and, like the great arts, it is itself an act of creation. And here lies its chief utility in the process of educating a scholar. Learning is in the main a passive and receptive function; but the human mind, from infancy upward, feels the impulse to create; and to indulge that impulse, however slight the value of the creation, promotes the happiness of the creator, and so enhances his powers and enlarges his capacities. The schoolboy who is put to his books, whether those books are accidence and syntax or Virgil and Homer, is further off from heaven in one regard than the child of a few years past who sat on the ground and made mud pies. To make mud pies is to follow at a distance and share in modest measure the activities of the demiurge: let the boy, as well as the child, evoke a small world out of a small chaos; let him also behold the work of his hands and pronounce it, if he can, to be pretty good. A desire to create and a pleasure in creating are often alive and ardent in minds whose true business later is to be not creation but criticism; and even if the things created have small intrinsic merit, the intellectual stir and transport which produced them is not therefore vain, and has other results than these.

The elixir of life and the philosopher's stone are not yet discovered, but alchemy in its pursuit of them found much treasure by the way and laid the foundation of a science; so that 'it may be compared' says Bacon 'to the husbandman whereof Aesop makes the fable; that, when he died, told his sons that he had left unto them gold buried underground in his vineyard; and they digged over all the ground, and gold they found none; but by reason of their stirring and digging the mould about the roots of their vines, they had a great vintage the year following.' I could take no better example of what I mean than the early Greek hexameters of Richard Dawes. In themselves they are almost worthless, and they swarm with errors unsparingly exposed and censured by himself. But this, till he was nearly thirty years old, was evidently, in alternation with bell-ringing at St Mary's, his favourite occupation, and its true fruits are to be found elsewhere. It set up a propitious ferment in the mind, by which its faculties were enlivened, invigorated and developed; and these compositions, no monuments to his fame, are yet stepping-stones, by which he advanced to his unique achievement and celebrity in his own proper province.

When, in 1869, this chair was first constituted, there could be no question who its first occupant should rightly be; for one man was at the same time the most eminent of Kennedy's pupils, the greatest scholar in Cambridge, and the foremost English Latinist of the century. A hundred years ago the continent learnt Greek from England, and Godfrey Hermann, Porson's chief antagonist, was also Porson's chief disciple. Half a century later the English learnt Latin from the continent, and the Prometheus who fetched us the new fire from the altars of Lachmann and Madvig and Ritschl was Hugh Munro. I do not know if the affectionate admiration felt for that name in my time is still as warm as ever among those who are addressing themselves to the study of Latin; but the history of scholarship in England must be forgotten before English Latinists can cease to remember him with gratitude and reverence, *for we are also his offspring*: every one of us may make salutation to him in the words pronounced by the senate and people over the grave of Romulus,

> O pater, o genitor, o sanguen dis oriundum,
> tu produxisti nos intra luminis oras.

Munro was not primarily himself a discoverer and inventor; it is neither on the establishment of canons nor on the purification of texts nor on the illumination of obscurities that his fame is founded. But the definition of a scholar is *vir bonus discendi peritus*, and that conception was personified in Munro. In his Lucretius he produced a work more compact of excellence than any edition of any classic which has ever been produced in England. None of our great original critics, neither Bentley nor Markland, Porson nor Elmsley, has left behind him a work making any pretence to such complete-ness: no author of any work to be compared in completeness with Munro's has observed the same austerity in selection, eschewed so scrupulously the inessential, and applied himself with such strict attention to the proper concerns of the interpreter and critic. Nor was he only a scholar: he wrote English so well that most scholars do not know how well he wrote it; and he was surely the most entertaining controversialist that ever redeemed these studies from the reproach of dullness and dustiness. It will be a long time before England or the world beholds again the same powers in the same harmony, so much sterling stuff knit together so well, such a union of solidity and accuracy, keenness and sobriety, manly taste, exhilarating humour, and engaging pugnacity. I speak, I suppose, in the presence of some to whom he was personally known: myself I never saw him, and the Cambridge photographers either did not possess his likeness or did not think proper to sell it to an Oxford undergraduate; but I did in those days molest him with letters, and I still preserve his patient and amiable replies to the young man who never even in the dreams of youth imagined that he was one day to be the successor of his illustrious correspondent.

Most good scholars are much fonder of learning than of teaching, and to Munro the duties of his office proved uncongenial and irksome. He resigned the Chair after a tenure of three years, and in 1872 it passed to the venerable man who left it vacant only last December; a scholar who in learning, if that word is taken to mean range and thoroughness of reading, had no equal in England and no superior in Europe. To dwell on the erudition of John Mayor is not merely superfluous but presumptuous; and I will now speak rather of a characteristic on which speech perhaps is not unnecessary. It is well known and sometimes lamented that for all his amplitude of knowledge he left behind him no complete work and no work having even the air of completeness. This regret I do not share; I am much more disposed to recommend for imitation the example of one who recognised his own bent and followed it, and whose inclinations were exactly in harmony with his talents. Many a good piece of work has been spoilt by the vain passion for completeness. A scholar designs to edit a certain author, a complete edition of whom would involve the treatment of matters to whose study the editor has not been led by his own tastes and interests, and in which he therefore is not at home. The author discourses of philosophy, and the editor is no philosopher; or the author writes in complex metres, and the editor's metrical education stopped short at Porson's canon of the final cretic. It then sometimes happens that the editor, having neither the humility to acknowledge his deficiency nor the industry or capacity to repair it, scrapes a perfunctory acquaintance with the unfamiliar subject, and treats it incompetently rather than not treat it at all; so that his work, for the sake of ostensible completeness, is disfigured with puerile errors, and he himself is detected, not merely in ignorance, but in imposture.

It is the absence of any such vanity, the abstention from all misdirected effort, which redeems and even converts into merit what might else appear defective in the works of Mayor. The establishment and the interpretation of an author's text were not matters in which he took the liveliest interest nor tasks for which he felt in himself a special aptitude: his likings pointed the same way as his abilities, to the collection of illustrative material. I said while he was alive, and I shall not unsay it because he is dead, that this labour is labour bestowed upon the circumference and not the centre of the subject. But this also is work which must be done, and which no other could have done so thoroughly. 'If a man read Richardson for the story,' said Johnson, 'he would hang himself;' and much the same may be said not only of Mayor's *Juvenal* but of a still more celebrated book, Lobeck's *Ajax of Sophocles*. When you have finished Lobeck's commentary you have imbibed a vast deal of information, but your knowledge and understanding of the Ajax has not proportionally increased. Lobeck himself in his preface admits that this is so: τὸ μὲν πάρεργον ἔργον ὡς ποιούμεθα. He in his commentary is not principally the critic nor the interpreter, but the grammarian; and Mayor in his is principally the antiquarian and the lexicographer: his main concern is not with what the author wrote or meant, but with the words he used and the things he mentioned. These he carried in his mind through the whole width of his incomparable reading, and brought back from the limits of the literature all the parallels and imitations and echoes which it contained. What he has bequeathed us is less an edition than a treasure of subsidies: there he saw his true business, and to that business he stuck: and 'it is an uncontrolled truth,' says Swift, 'that no man ever made an ill figure who understood his own talents, nor a good one who mistook them.'

These three scholars, Kennedy, Munro, and Mayor, were typical examples of what was known in the middle of the nineteenth century as Cambridge scholarship. The distinction which then existed between scholarship of the Cambridge and the Oxford type was one which did not arise till the century was in its second quarter; for scholarship meant to Elmsley what it meant to Dobree. By the fourth quarter of the century the distinction was fading away, and it cannot be said to exist at present. But while it existed it was this: Cambridge scholarship simply meant scholarship with no nonsense about it; Oxford scholarship embodied one of those erroneous tendencies against which I take up my parable to-day. It was never confined to Oxford, and if now it has ceased to be regnant there it is not therefore extinct, but has gained in diffusion what it has lost in concentration.

Scholarship, that study of the ancient literatures for which chairs of Greek and Latin are founded, is itself a department (as I said before) not of literature but of science; and science ought to be scientific and ought not to be literary. The science, though it has works of literature for its subject, does not make its appeal to the same portion of the mind as do those works themselves. Scholarship, in short, is not literary criticism; and of the duties of a Latin Chair literary criticism forms no part.

And Professors of Latin may thank their stars that it does not; for a scholar, unless by accident, is not a literary critic. Whether the faculty of literary criticism is the best gift that heaven has in its treasuries I cannot say, but heaven seems to think so, for assuredly it is the gift most charily bestowed. Orators and poets, sages and saints and heroes, if rare in comparison with blackberries, are yet commoner than the appearance of Halley's comet; literary critics are less common. And when, once in a century, or once in two centuries, the literary critic does appear – will someone in this home of mathematics tell me what are the chances that his appearance will be made among that small number of people who possess a considerable knowledge of the Latin language? It may be said that Latin scholarship and literary criticism were united in the person of Lessing. Lessing, to be sure, was a great critic, and, though not a great scholar, was a good one; but if this purely accidental conjunction occurred so lately as the eighteenth century, it ought to be thousands of years before it occurs again. If, in spite of the doctrine of probabilities, the twentieth century is also to behold a Latin scholar who is a literary critic, all I know is that I am not he.

By a literary critic I understand a man who has things to say about literature which are both true and new. Appreciation of literature, and the ability to say things about it which are true but not new, is a much commoner endowment. That a scholar should appreciate literature is good for his own pleasure and profit; but it is none of his business to communicate that appreciation to his audience. Appreciation of literature is just as likely to be found in his audience as in him, for it has no connexion with scholarship. He has no right to presume that his own aesthetic perceptions are superior to those of anyone whom he addresses, or that in this respect he is better qualified to teach them than they to teach him. It is unfortunately true that audiences in general are fond of being told what they know already, and that the desire of most readers and hearers is not to be given thoughts which are new and true, but thoughts whicn, whether true or false, are their own thoughts, and which they rejoice to recognise dressed up in the current variety of academic journalese, and tricked out with an assortment of popular adjectives. Present to them the literary opinions which they already hold, couched in the dialect which they believe to be good English, and sprinkled over with epithets like *delicate*, *sympathetic*, and *vital*, and you will easily persuade the great majority that they are listening to literary criticism. But not quite all: there are a few, nay in some places there are not a few, who know better; and if my tastes and talents invited me in that direction I might yet be deterred by remembering what manner of men have been accustomed to frequent this seat of learning. I do not relish the prospect of standing up and pretending to be a literary critic, when in truth I am none, before audiences which may for aught I know contain such persons as Mr Thomas Gray of Peterhouse, Mr Alfred Tennyson of Trinity, or Mr John Milton of Christ's.

Why is it that the scholar is the only man of science of whom it is ever demanded that he should display taste and feeling? Literature, the subject of his science, is surely not alone among the subjects of science in possessing aesthetic qualities and in making appeal to the emotions. The botanist and the astronomer have for their provinces two worlds of beauty and magnificence not inferior in their way to literature; but no one expects the botanist to throw up his hands and say 'how beautiful,' nor the astronomer to fall down flat and say 'how magnificient:' no one would praise their taste if they did perform these ceremonies, and no one calls them unappreciative pedants because they do not. Why should the scholar alone indulge in public ecstasy? why from him rather than from them is aesthetic comment to be demanded? why may not he stick to his last as well as they? To be sure, we are all told in our childhood a story of Linnaeus – how, coming suddenly on a heath covered with gorse in blossom, he fell upon his knees and gave thanks to the creator. But when Linnaeus behaved in that way, he was out for a holiday: during office hours he attended to business. If Linnaeus had spent his life in genuflexions before flowering shrubs, the classification of the vegetable kingdom would have been carried out by someone else, and neither Linnaeus himself nor this popular and edifying anecdote would ever have been heard of.

Or take astronomy. If there is one sight more than another which man has been wont to regard with admiration and awe, it is the starry heavens; and these emotions are natural, just, and wholesome. If therefore you like to go out on a clear night and lift up your eyes to the stars, surrender yourself to the sentiment or meditation which they inspire, and repeat, as your choice may determine, the poetry which they have evoked from Homer or David, from Milton or Leopardi – do so by all means. But don't call it astronomy. Call it what it really is: recreation. The largest and brightest orbs of those same heavens form the subject of the third book of Newton's *Principia*; and the tenour of Newton's discourse is after this fashion:

Let S represent the sun, T the earth, P the moon, CADB the moon's orbit. In SP take SK equal to ST, and let SL be to SK in the duplicate proportion of SK to SP; draw LM parallel to PT; and if ST or SK is supposed to represent the *accelerated* force of gravity of the *earth* towards the sun, SL will represent the *accelerative* force of gravity of the *moon* towards the sun.

That is how scholars should write about literature. If the botanist and the astronomer can go soberly about their business, unseduced by the beauties of the field and unbewildered by the glories of the firmament, let the scholar amidst the masterpieces of literature maintain the same coolness of head, and let his hearers and readers allow him to exhibit the same propriety of demeanour.

In saying this, I do not depreciate the literary faculty: on the contrary, I wish to see it indulged in a sphere where it will not encounter hindrance. If you are literary, produce literature: pour the stream along its proper channel, and do not let it soak into the surrounding soil, where it will only create a quagmire. Literature is so alien from science that the literary temper in himself is a peril against which the scholar must stand on his guard. The aim of science is the discovery of the truth, while the aim of literature is the production of pleasure; and the two aims are not merely distinct but often incompatible, so that large departments of literature are also departments of lying. Not only so, but man is generally more of a pleasure-seeker than a truth-seeker, and the literary spirit, if once admitted to communication with the scientific, will ever tend to encroach upon its domain. I will give a single and signal example of this usurpation.

Among Shelley's poems of the year 1821 there is a famous and beautiful lyric, entitled *A Lament*, which was printed, and is known by heart to hundreds of thousands, in this form.

> O world! O life! O time!
> On whose last steps I climb,
> Trembling at that where I had stood before, –
> When will return the glory of your prime?
> No more, oh never more!
>
> Out of the day and night
> A joy has taken flight:
> Fresh Spring, and Summer, and Winter hoar
> Move my faint heart with grief, – but with delight
> No more, oh never more.

Against the third line of the second stanza there lie two objections, which you may call, as you please, scientific or pedantic: it has nine syllables instead of ten, and it mentions three seasons instead of four. To repair these deficiencies Mr William Rossetti in his edition of 1870(?) substituted *Autumn* for the second *and*:

> Fresh Spring and Summer, Autumn, Winter hoar.

I may say in passing that I do not think Mr Rossetti's verse a good verse, nor worthy of Shelley; and I suppose that when Mr Swinburne in his *Essays and Studies* spoke of Mr Rossetti's deaf and desperate daring, he was expressing, in nobler language, the same opinion. But that is not the present point: the point is that Mr Swinburne took up the defence of the traditional text as follows:

If there is one verse in Shelley or in English of more divine and sovereign sweetness than any other, it is that in the *Lament*,

> Fresh Spring, and Summer, and Winter hoar.

The music of this line taken with its context – the melodious effect of its exquisite inequality – I should have thought was a thing to thrill the veins and draw tears to the eyes of all men whose ears were not closed against all harmony by some denser and less removable obstruction than shut out the song of the Sirens from the hearing of the crew of Ulysses.

Now suppose the story ended there. How confidently, with what a depth and warmth of inward conviction, would Shelley's countrymen believe that Shelley wrote and designed to write the defective verse. How eagerly, with the sanction and encouragement of another poet so eminent as Mr Swinburne, would they give the rein to their natural inclinations and revel in the melodious effect of its exquisite inequality. But Shelley's MS exists; and the inequality, though exquisite, does not exist in Shelley's MS. Shelley wrote with his own hand

> Fresh Spring and Autumn, Summer and Winter hoar
> Move my faint heart with grief.

The one verse, in Shelley and in English, of more divine and sovereign sweetness than any other is the verse, not of Shelley, but of a compositor. Mr Swinburne's veins were thrilled, and tears were drawn to Mr Swinburne's eyes, by a misprint.

These are the performances of the literary mind when, with its facile emotions and its incapacity for self-examination, it invades the province of science, and allows mere prejudice in favour of the familiar to put on the air of an aesthetic judgment. And if these things are done in the green tree, what shall be done in the dry? Mr Swinburne was Shelley's compatriot, not fifty years removed from him in date, like him a poet, like him a lyrist, and indeed, in the general estimation, the authentic heir and successor of Shelley in that field of poetry. What value shall we attach to similar judgments pronounced by men who are not themselves men of letters, but merely scholars with a literary taint, on disputed passages in books written hundreds and thousands of years ago by an alien race amidst an alien culture?

When Horace is reported to have said *seu mobilibus ueris inhorruit adventus foliis*, and when pedants like Bentley and Munro object that the phrase is unsuitable to its context, of what avail is it to be assured by persons of taste – that is to say persons of British taste, Victorian taste, and sub-Tennysonian taste – that these are exquisite lines? Exquisite to whom? Consider the mutations of opinion, the reversals of literary judgment, which this one small island has witnessed in the last 150 years: what is the likelihood that your notions or your contemporaries' notions of the exquisite are those of a foreigner who wrote for foreigners two millenniums ago? And for what foreigners? For the Romans, for men whose religion you disbelieve, whose chief institution you abominate, whose manners you do not like to talk about, but whose literary tastes, you flatter yourself, were identical with yours. No: in this aspect we must learn to say of our tastes what Isaiah says of our righteousnesses: they are as filthy rags.

Our first task is to get rid of them, and to acquire, if we can, by humility and self-repression, the tastes of the classics; not to come stamping into the library of Apollo on the Palatine without so much as wiping our shoes on the doormat, and cover the floor with the print of feet which have waded through the miry clay of the nineteenth century into the horrible pit of the twentieth. It is not to be supposed that this age, because it happens to be ours, has been specially endowed with a gift denied to all other modern ages; that we, by nature or by miracle, have mental affinity with the ancients, or that we can lightly acquire it, or that we can even acquire it at all. Communion with the ancients is purchasable at no cheaper rate than the kingdom of heaven; we must be born again. But to be born again is a process exceedingly repugnant to all right-minded Englishmen. I believe they think it improper, and they have a strong and well-grounded suspicion that it is arduous. They would much rather retain the prevalent opinion that the secret of the classical spirit is open to anyone who has a fervent admiration for the second-best parts of Tennyson.

But if in England the scholar's besetting sin is the literary attitude, or the attitude which passes for literary, the case is different in that other country, whose name can never be omitted from a survey of the condition of learning. For the past hundred years the study of the classics has had its centre in Germany, and in most departments of that study it was to Germany that Europe still looked for leadership some thirty or forty years ago. That Europe looks thither no longer is one of the many fruits of the diplomacy of Bismarck. On the battlefield of Sedan you may set up the gravestone not of one empire but of two; for where the military predominance of France fell down and perished, there also the intellectual predominance of Germany received a wound of which it bled slowly to death. It is not in classical study alone, but I hear the same tale from all quarters: that Germany, throughout the circle of the sciences, is losing or has lost her place, because her best brains are no longer employed upon the pursuit of knowledge. The Germany which led the thought of Europe was Germany disunited and poor; her union and power and wealth now provide great careers in politics, arms, and commerce; and German capabilities – these are not my words but the words of a Chancellor of the Empire – 'German capabilities,' said Prince Bülow four years ago, 'have taken refuge in our industry and our army.' The superiority which Germany now retains in classical scholarship is not one of quality but of quantity.

Students of Greek and Latin are by far more numerous in Germany than in any other country, and their studies are also far more completely and efficiently organised; but the students themselves are not pre-eminent, as once they were, in the power or the will to perform intellectual operations. In those periodicals which review work upon the classics you may note a perpetual recurrence of two favourite adjectives, one the conventional sign of approval, and the other of disapprobation. The one is the German word which means *methodical*, the other is the German word which means *arbitrary*. Whenever you see a writer's practice praised as *methodisch*, you find upon investigation that he has laid down a hard and fast rule and has stuck to it through thick and thin. Whenever you see a writer's practice blamed as *willkürlich*, you find upon investigation that he has been guilty of the high crime and misdemeanour of reasoning. Now the cause of this labelling, and its purpose, are equally evident. The cause may be expressed in the words of the greatest of Germans. 'Thinking is hard,' says Goethe, 'and acting according to thought is irksome' (*Denken ist schwer, nach dem*

Gedachten handeln unbequem). The purpose is to lighten this labour for minds unable to cope with it, and to make the editing of a classic as simple a matter as consulting a table of logarithms. In short, while the English fault is to confuse this study with literature, the German fault is to pretend that it is mathematics.

Aristotle, near the beginning of his *Ethics*, cautions his readers against expecting or seeking, in any department of knowledge or inquiry, a greater degree of exactness than the subject admits: πεπαιδευμένου γάρ ἐστιν ἐπὶ τοσοῦτον τἀκριβὲς ἐπιζητεῖν καθ' ἕκαστον γένος, ἐφ' ὅσον ἡ τοῦ πράγματος φύσις ἐπιδέχεται. To require demonstration from a pleader, he says, is no less absurd than to accept mere plausibility from a mathematician: the just measure of precision is that which is conformable to the subject-matter, κατὰ τὴν ὑποκειμένην ὕλην. Now the criticism and interpretation of the classical texts is not an exact science; and to treat it as if it were is falsification. Its subject-matter is a series of phenomena which are the results of the play of the human mind; and if you want to piece these phenomena together, and reconstruct the past conditions which produced them, the last person you should send for is a formulist; you had much better send for a rat-catcher. To deal with the mutable and the evasive you want no cut and dried method; and rigid rules for a fluid matter are false rules. In fact, so soon as ever we quit the abstractions of mathematics, general rules, and indeed all generalisations whatsoever, are only feasible at the cost of some sacrifice of truth.

No two particular things are exactly alike, and the better we know them the less alike we find them: perfect knowledge, if we possessed it, would render generalisation impossible. Nothing therefore is more foolish, nothing combines pedantry and thought-lessness in a more untoward union, than solemn prating about the laws of criticism, and pious horror at their violation. A man who never violates the laws of criticism is no critic. The laws of criticism are nothing but a string of generalisations, necessarily inaccurate, which have been framed by the benevolent for the guidance, the support, and the restraint, of three classes of persons. They are leading strings for infants, they are crutches for cripples and they are strait-waistcoats for maniacs. To those three large divisions of mankind they may be unreservedly recommended; but they concern nobody else, and least of all the critic, for the critic is himself the source from which they have derived whatever validity they possess. Just as poets are said to be the fountains of grammar, so the laws of criticism are merely representations, imperfect and inadequate representations, of the practice of critics; and for a critic to set about obeying them is as if a man should try to make himself look like his own reflexion in the bowl of a spoon. The critic keeps the laws of criticism nine times out of ten, because they ought to be kept: the tenth time he breaks them, because they ought to be broken. What Diderot in his third conversation on the *Fils Naturel* says of dramatic composition is no less true and salutary here: 'Especially remember,' says he, 'that there is no general principle: I do not know a single one of those that I have indicated which a man of genius cannot infringe with success.'

But to the common acceptance of this truth there is a very formidable obstacle: nothing less than the nature of man himself. 'The nature of man,' says Bacon, 'doth extremely covet to have somewhat in his understanding fixed and unmovable, and as a rest and support of the mind.' Men hate to feel insecure; and a sense of security depends much less on the correctness of our opinions than on the firmness with which we hold them; so that by excluding intelligence we can often exclude discomfort. The first thing wanted is a canon of orthodoxy, and the next thing is a pope. The disciple resorts to the teacher, and the request he makes of him is not *tell me how to get rid of error* but *tell me how to get rid of doubt*. In this there is nothing new: 'as knowledges are now delivered,' said Bacon 300 years ago, 'there is a kind of contract of error between the deliverer and the receiver. For he that delivereth knowledge desireth to deliver it in such form as may be best believed, and not as may be best examined; and he that receiveth knowledge desireth rather present satisfaction than expectant enquiry.' Blind followers of rules will be blind followers of masters: a pupil who has got out of the habit of thinking will take his teacher's word for gospel, and will be delighted with a state of things in which intellectual scrutiny not only ceases to be a duty but becomes an act of insubordination. How this nonsense of orthodoxy and this propensity to servitude at the present time impede the advance of learning and even set it back I will show by one simple example.

Who was the first and chief Latin writer to use the Greek word for a cat, αἴλουρος? The answer to this question can be found in many

Latin dictionaries, but not in the latest and most elaborate. The five greatest universities of Germany have combined their resources to produce a *thesaurus linguae Latinae*, whose instalments, published during the last twelve years, run to 6,000 pages, and have brought it down to the letter D. The part containing *aelurus* appeared in 1902; it cites the word from Gellius, from Pelagius, and from the so-called Hyginus; but it does not cite it from the fifteenth satire of Juvenal. Here we find illustrated a theme on which historians and economists have often dwelt, the disadvantage of employing slave-labour.

In Germany in 1902 the inspired text of Juvenal was the text of Buecheler's second edition. That edition was published in the last decade of the nineteenth century, when the tide of obscurantism, now much abated, was at its height, and when the cheapest way to win applause was to reject emendations which everyone had hitherto accepted and to adopt lections from the MSS which no one had yet been able to endure. Buecheler, riding on the crest of the wave, had expelled from the text the conjecture, as it then was, *aeluros*, and restored the *caeruleos* of the MSS. That was enough for the chaingangs working at the dictionary in the ergastulum at Munich: theirs not to reason why. That every other editor for the last three centuries, and that Buecheler himself in his former edition, had printed *aeluros*, they consigned to oblivion; they provided this vast and expensive lexicon with an article on *aelurus* in which Juvenal's name did not occur.

Nine years, only nine, have elapsed. *Aeluros* in Juvenal's fifteenth satire is now no longer a conjecture but the reading of an important MS. Buecheler is dead, his Juvenal has been re-edited by his most eminent pupil, who happens to be an independent thinker, and *aeluros* is back again in the text. The *thesaurus linguae Latinae*, not yet arrived at the letter E, is thus already antiquated. Now it is the common lot of such works of reference that they begin to be obsolete the day after they are published; but that damage, inflicted by the mere progress of knowledge, is inevitable: what is not inevitable is this additional and superabundant damage, inflicted by the mental habits of the slave.

Everyone can figure to himself the mild inward glow of pleasure and pride which the author of this unlucky article felt while he was writing it, and the peace of mind with which he said to himself, when he went to bed that night, 'Well done, thou good and faithful servant.' This is the felicity of the house of bondage, and of the soul which is so fast in prison that it cannot get forth; which commands no outlook upon the past or the future, but believes that the fashion of the present, unlike all fashions heretofore, will endure perpetually, and that its own flimsy tabernacle of second-hand opinions is a habitation for everlasting. And not content with believing these improbable things it despises those who do not believe them, and displays to the world that stiff and self-righteous arrogance of the unthinking man which ages ago provoked this sentence from Solomon: 'the sluggard is wiser in his own conceit than seven men that can render a reason.'

Well, I have now spoken of two diverse evils, as I consider them, which you and I should do our best to avoid. But if you ask me how we are to avoid them, I must answer that I do not altogether know, and that perhaps after all we cannot. It is well enough to inculcate the duty of self-examination, but then we must also bear in mind its difficulty, and the easiness of self-deception. For self-examination the will, however sincere, is not sufficient: there needs also the faculty, and that is neither universal nor even commonly found. The mind of man, as Bacon says, 'is far from the nature of a clear and equal glass, wherein the beams of things should reflect according to their true incidence; nay, it is rather like an enchanted glass, full of superstition and imposture, if it be not delivered and reduced.' But one clue I think I can commend to you which will lead in the right direction, though not all the way. I spoke just now of servility shown towards the living; and I think it significant that this is so often found in company with lack of due veneration towards the dead. My counsel is to invert this attitude, and to think more of the dead than of the living. The dead have at any rate endured a test to which the living have not yet been subjected. If a man, fifty or a hundred years after his death, is still remembered and accounted a great man, there is a presumption in his favour which no living man can claim; and experience has taught me that it is no mere presumption. It is the dead and not the living who have most advanced our learning and science; and though their knowledge may have been superseded, there is no supersession of reason and intelligence. Clear wits and right thinking are essentially neither of to-day nor yesterday, but historically they are rather of yesterday than of to-day: and to study the greatest of the scholars of the past is to enjoy intercourse with superior minds. If our conception of scholarship and our methods of procedure are at variance with theirs, it is not indeed a certainty or a necessity that we are wrong, but it is a good working hypothesis; and we had better not abandon it till it proves untenable. Do not let us disregard our contemporaries, but let us regard our predecessors more; let us be most encouraged by their agreement, and most disquieted by their dissent.

The Period of the French Revolution: A Review of *The Cambridge History of English Literature*. Vol. XI

It is to be supposed that when the people of England demanded, as apparently they did, a new history of its literature, their desire was not so much for a history which should issue from the Cambridge Press as for a better account of the matter than they had already. In this eleventh volume they will find 100 pages of bibliography, presumably full and accurate; a table of principal dates which would be nearer perfection if it recorded Gray's death instead of Hogarth's, and Macaulay's birth instead of Balzac's or Charles Darwin's; and chapters written with knowledge and sobriety on Burke, Cowper, Crabbe, Blake, Burns, Wordsworth, Coleridge, the lesser poets and lesser novelists of the period, the utilitarian philosophers, the political writers, the drama, prosody, and blue-stockings of the Georgian age, the production and distribution of books from 1625 onward, and the writing of books for children down to 1889. But yet one could wish that this history of English literature were rather more literary and rather more historical.

History need not adhere to chronology, and such anachronisms as the inclusion of Peacock in this volume and the postponement of Scott till the next are shifts of expediency which have no historical importance. But the order of date should be kept where nothing is gained by inverting it. Nothing is gained, nay much is lost, by an inversion which places Wordsworth on p. 93, Crabbe on p. 140, and Blake and Burns on still later pages; for this is an inversion not simply of chronological but of historical sequence. Historically considered, Wordsworth is the pivot of the epoch, and indeed the chief figure in English poetry after Chaucer, if redemption ranks next to creation. No poet later born, not even Campbell, entirely escaped his influence; and 1798 is in the literature of England what 1789 is in the polity of France. But Burns was dead when the *Lyrical Ballads* were published, and Crabbe might have been dead too for all the good or harm they did him. Blake, it may be said, belongs to no age, and is a star that might have shot from heaven at any hour of the night; but, appearing when he did, he was the morning star, the harbinger of Wordsworth, and that is his place, not indeed in literature, but in its history. Again, it is not an historical arrangement which entrusts the treatment of Wordsworth and Coleridge to different hands: the achievements of Castor and Pollux should not be recounted separately, but in one article, *Dioscuri*.

These are faults of design and disposition: the literary shortcomings of the work are diffused, though unequally, among the contributors. The contributors are twelve, and their number does not include the two critics whom one would most have hoped and expected to find here, Mr Andrew Bradley and Sir Walter Raleigh. Expectation, if not hope, is gratified by the presence of Professor Saintsbury, whose abundant knowledge, immense gusto, and general soundness of judgment make him readable even when he is discussing Southey and Peacock for the third or fourth time, airing prejudices neither new nor relevant, and using the barbarous language to which we are now inured. *Gryll Grange* 'has a wonderful absence of glaring Rip-van-Winkleism.' Traces of Coleridge's hand in a book of Southey's are 'Estesian proofs.' If this adjective sends any readers on a wild-goose chase, first to the New English Dictionary and then to the ducal annals of Modena and Ferrara, Mr Saintsbury will feel that it has not been coined in vain; and a reviewer who guided the wanderers to Coleridge's poem beginning *A bird, who for his other sins*, would be regarded by Mr Saintsbury as a spoil-sport. The best writers among the contributors write upon subjects of no great literary moment. The most lucid and graceful chapter is Dr Sorley's on Bentham and the Utilitarians; next comes Mr Routh's on the Georgian drama. But not one of the chapters dealing with the principal figures gives any lively or continuous pleasure by its style or diction, and the account of the greatest prose-writer is written in the worst prose. The estimate conveyed is sound, the reflexions just – 'Burke's political aphorisms are so pregnant that they distend the mind with the same sense of fulness with which Shakespeare's lines affect the student of the passions and movements of the human heart' – and the expression sometimes pointed – 'the speech *On Conciliation* . . . remains some compensation to English literature for the dismemberment of the British empire;' but progress through its clumsy and invertebrate sentences is like plodding over a ploughed field of clay. It opens thus:

Edmund Burke, the greatest of English orators, if we measure greatness not by immediate effect alone but by the durability and the diffusive power of that effect, and one of the profoundest, most suggestive and most illuminating of political thinkers, if we may not call a philosopher one who did not elaborate any system and who refrained on principle from the discussion of purely theoretical issues, was an Irishman . . . ;

and there is worse to follow.

It might be contended that, fleeing from one abstraction, he drew near to another, and consecrated prescription, inherited right, when judged and condemned by that expediency which is the sanction of prescription:

the reader discovers in process of time that *consecrated* is one part of speech and *inherited* another.

Whatever be now our judgment on the questions of a bygone age with which he was concerned, the importance of the principles to which his mind always gravitated, his preoccupation at every juncture with the fundamental issues of wise government, and the splendour of the eloquence in which he set forth these principles, an eloquence in which the wisdom of his thought and the felicity of his language and imagery seem inseparable from one another, an eloquence that is wisdom (not 'seeming wisdom' as Hobbes defined eloquence), have made his speeches and pamphlets a source of perennial freshness and interest:

importance, *preoccupation*, and *splendour* are not, like *questions*, governed by the preposition *on*, but are subjects of the verb *have made*, which the reader finds waiting for him on the further side of the anaphora and the parenthesis: then he must start again at the other end of the alligator and retrace the whole length of its dislocated spine. In the last sentence of the chapter the writer has tried to say that Johnson differed from Burke in party politics: what he has succeeded in saying is that Johnson, Goldsmith, and Reynolds differed from one another.

In this chapter it is the form which is not literary: in others it is the attitude and the writers' conception of their subject. Every figure of the first order in this volume, excepting Burke, is a poet. Now the centre of interest in a poet is his poetry: not his themes, his doctrines, his opinions, his life or conduct, but the poetical quality of the works he has bequeathed to us. Therefore a chapter on Wordsworth ought not to begin like this:

Wordsworth's surprise and resentment would surely have been provoked had he been told that, at half a century's distance and from an European point of view, his work would seem, on the whole, though with several omissions and additions, to be a continuation of the movement initiated by Rousseau. It is, nevertheless, certain that it might be described as an English variety of Rousseauism, revised and corrected, in some parts, by the opposite influence of Edmund Burke

The European view of a poet is not of much importance unless the poet writes in Esperanto. Wordsworth wrote in English; from a European point of view the three great English poets are Shakespeare, Byron, and the late Mr Wilde; and it is no cause for surprise or resentment that Wordsworth, from the same point of view, should seem on the whole to be a continuator of a French or Genevan prose-writer. Then we hear of his 'fundamental tenets,' his 'faith in the goodness of nature as well as in the excellence of the child,' his 'ideas on education,' his 'diffidence in respect of the merely intellectual processes of the mind,' his 'trust in the good that may accrue to man from the cultivation of his senses and feelings.' Poetry is no matter of fundamental tenets; faith in the goodness of nature is no more poetical than faith in Jupiter and Juno; and that quality in Wordsworth which alone preserves from oblivion his faith and tenets is one which he did not derive from Burke or Rousseau and could not derive from any writer of prose. There are poets whose poetry is not their chief title to fame: Chaucer and Burns, if all poetical quality were taken away from them, would keep more than they lost and would still be great men of letters, because they are rich in merits which are not poetical. Wordsworth is a much greater poet than either; but if the poetical element were withdrawn from his works he would be only a mediocre man of letters. And the mediocre man of letters is the main theme of this chapter on Wordsworth. There is talk of his moral doctrine, his realism, his attitude to nature, none of them poetical in essence; there is much talk of his optimism, which is downright unpoetical: of his poetry there is less talk, and the fact seems to be that the writer does not feel Wordsworth's poetry. True, he selects for especial praise the two very best and most characteristic stanzas, *Will no one tell me what she sings*, and *No motion has she now, no force*; but these have so often been selected for praise already that he would have proved his competency better by choosing some other stanzas of the same inimitable virtue, *My eyes are dim with childish tears*, or *And I can listen to thee yet*. His favourite piece, which he mentions four times over, is *The Ruined Cottage*, embodied in the first book of *The*

Excursion, 'a perfect poem, such as Wordsworth never surpassed,' 'he never outdid that pastoral and, indeed, only once or twice again reached such perfection.' Now *The Ruined Cottage* is a simple and pathetic story of misfortune, told in pure English and good verse; but the heavenly alchemy is absent. 'The tale,' says the critic, 'is most distressing and desolate,' and he innocently adds 'Wordsworth's usual optimism is not to be found in it.' For that relief much thanks; but if *The Ruined Cottage* were 'a perfect poem,' it would be exalting and not distressing. The fourteenth chapter of Job is not distressing, nor the *Antigone*, nor even *King Lear*. And at such a sentence as 'these instances tend to prove that his poetry is not identical with his habitual teaching, that it sometimes revolts against it, that it may here and there go beyond it,' one asks oneself what the writer can possibly mean by poetry. How can any poetry be identical with any teaching? It would not however be fair to quit this chapter without acknowledging that it contains true things well said: 'his undisputed sovereignty (as a poet of nature) . . . lies in his extraordinary faculty of giving utterance to some of the most elementary and at the same time obscure sensations of man confronted by natural phenomena;' 'if he thought like others, he always thought by himself. He gives us the impression that, had he lived alone on a bookless earth, he would have reached the same conclusions.'

The volume conveys plenty of information, and especially in the chapters on the Georgian drama and the production and distribution of books it collects information which is not collected elsewhere. Its estimates of the principal authors are generally the accepted estimates, and accepted estimates of literature more than a hundred years old are likely to be somewhere near the truth. What it lacks is quality. If one tries to picture a reader cherishing this volume, the image does not come at call.

A Georgian History of Victorian Literature: A Review of *The Cambridge History of English Literature*. Vols. XIII and XIV

These two volumes complete the Cambridge history of English literature and embrace that period which is commonly and almost accurately entitled the Victorian age. The names included range from Carlyle, who was born before Keats and began to write under George IV, to Meredith and Swinburne, who lived on, and, alas, wrote on, through most of King Edward's reign; but all the chief names are those of men who did their chief work between 1837 and 1901. Newman is not here, but has probably found an earlier place in some chapter sacred to religion: the living also are excluded, and the youngest writer of note who receives notice is Francis Thompson, born in 1859.

The Victorian age of literature has been disparaged, as the manner is, by 'ces enfants drus et forts d'un bon lait qu'ils ont sucé, qui battent leur nourrice,' and, like most other ages, it was assiduously depreciated by some of its own chief ornaments. 'It is odd that the last 25 years,' wrote Macaulay in 1850, 'should have produced hardly a volume that will be remembered in 1900;' and in 1855 'the general sterility, the miserably enervated state of literature' was still prevailing. But it is now safe to say that the Queen's reign was a great age of English letters, the more remarkable because it followed almost without pause upon a greater. France in the same years produced perhaps as good a crop as England, but that field had lain fallow for a whole generation. One great age of literature exhausted Germany; one age of literature less than great has exhausted America; but never since the defeat of the Armada has great literature ceased to flourish and renew itself in the island home of inefficiency.

Whether the time has yet come to weigh one Victorian author against another, or one work against another of the same author's, is not so sure.

The tuneful quartos of Southey are already little better than lumber: – and the rich melodies of Keats and Shelley, – and the fantastical emphasis of Wordsworth, – and the plebeian pathos of Crabbe, are melting fast from the field of our vision. The novels of Scott have put out his poetry. Even the splendid strains of Moore are fading into distance and dimness, except where they have been married to immortal music; and the blazing star of Byron himself is receding from its place of pride . . . The two who have the longest withstood this rapid withering of the laurel, and with the least marks of decay on their branches, are Rogers and Campbell.

So wrote the first professional critic of his time when the greatest age of English literature had just reached its close; and this judgment he reprinted in 1843, and again in 1846, more than twenty years from the end of that age and nearly fifty from its beginning. But there is reason to hope that we can now judge Victorian writers less perversely than Jeffrey is seen to have judged their predecessors. Jeffrey was little younger than Wordsworth, and had formed his taste before the year 1798, when the Lord created a new thing in the earth. All the critics who contribute to these volumes were bred in the Victorian tradition, and most of them were born much later than the authors committed to them for criticism. The Victorian age, moreover, introduced no great and disconcerting change; it did but develop and modify existing tendencies, with some progress and some relapse. The pause after 1824 was nothing but a momentary dearth of great writers, no prelude to any tide of revolution rolling under the breath of a Wordsworth or carrying a Dryden on its crest. The more salient novelties of Victorian literature were not durable and have now lost their vogue; except that for some few years a novelist or two will still sport the suit of buckram which Meredith ordered at his tailor's to disguise the failure of his genius. No author of the time has exercised the permanent influence of Keats or Scott. Browning had no following, Tennyson had no following that mattered, and Carlyle's endeavour to naturalise in England the style of Jean Paul Richter is a long way further from accomplishment than his wish to substitute a Hindenburg for the British constitution. In the sixties it seemed indeed as if there had arisen a band of writers to launch poetry on a new career; but time showed that they were cruising in a backwater, not finding a channel for the main stream, and in twenty years all heart had gone out of the enterprise. The fashions of that interlude are already so antique that Mr Gilbert Murray can adopt them for his rendering of Euripides; and there they now receive academic approbation, which is the second death.

It is probable that these volumes reflect with due fidelity the current estimate of Victorian authors and their works. If posterity is surprised to find ten pages about William Morris and less than two about Coventry Patmore, it will also be instructed; for this scale unquestionably corresponds to the prevalent opinion of 1916 and even 1917. But a list of 'Lesser Poets' comprising Dobell and Francis Thompson as well as Patmore may provoke some wonder even now, if it is borne in mind that 'lesser' means lesser than Clough, James Thomson, and O'Shaughnessy. That Carlyle should have twenty-two pages to Macaulay's eight reflects perhaps rather the estimate of three years since, Carlyle's repute being now a trifle damaged by our temporal relations with his spiritual home. And posterity will probably be wrong if it infers that most of us thought two pages enough for Stevenson in a work where George Gissing has more than seven, or a page and a quarter enough for Pater, a true man of letters though not a great one, in a work where Froude, who was base metal all through, has three and a half.

The criticism of the twenty-four contributors is sober and for the most part competent, but not every subject is judiciously allotted. For example, a writer who is qualified to treat of Thackeray may yet be ill sorted with 'The Rossettis, William Morris, Swinburne and others.' The chapter on Tennyson, though rather clumsily written, is perhaps the best, and does justice alike to the greatness and the pettiness of its theme. The worst chapter, without any perhaps, is that on Anglo-Irish literature, in which the thinking is as flaccid as the writing.

But it now seems fairly certain, in the opinion of Windisch and other Celtic scholars, including Quiggin, that some of the Welsh rhapsodists apparently served a kind of apprenticeship with their Irish brethren.

On the same page it is suggested that Shakespeare may have got what Matthew Arnold calls his note of Celtic magic 'at second hand, through Edmund Spenser, or his friend Dowland the luten-ist, who, if not an Irishman, had an Irish association.' Let us all seek the society of Mr A. P. Graves and then perhaps we too shall write things like *daffodils That come before the swallow dares, and take The winds of March with beauty*; though it is true that Mr Graves himself, like Dowland and Spenser, does not.

In an interesting chapter on 'changes in the language since Shakespeare's time' it is said that the fear of degeneration expressed by Johnson in the preface to his dictionary has not yet been justified. But it has; and these volumes are one small part of the justification. 'In prose,' wrote Coleridge a hundred years ago, 'I doubt whether it be even possible to preserve our style wholly unalloyed by the vicious phraseology which meets us everywhere. Our chains rattle, even while we are complaining of them.' And the English language, since Coleridge wrote, has continued to deteriorate in fibre. Is there, can there be, such a word as *purposive*? There is: it was invented by a surgeon in 1855; and instead of being kept on the top shelf of an anatomical museum it is exhibited in both these volumes. And the decline is not only in our language but in our skill to use it. Before the middle of the eighteenth century the writing of good English had ceased to come by nature, but it was widely and successfully practised as an art. The common stock of words was already both impoverished and contaminated, but there was a high and strict tradition of comeliness in style. This is extinct, and our bricklaying is no better than our bricks. It is now possible, nay usual, to spend a lifetime in the study of literature without ever learning the knack of it, and no reader opening this book will even expect to find the dyer's hand subdued to what it works in. Two hundred years ago John Dennis was reckoned a dunce; but no chapter here can compare with his *Remarks upon Cato* for race and flavour of diction or for spring and terseness of style. Soame Jenyns was an old woman and his vocabulary was as trite as could be; and yet, because he wrote in the eighteenth century, he put his poor words and thoughts into shipshape sentences. But written English is now inert and inorganic: not stem and leaf and flower, not even trim and well-joined masonry, but a daub of untempered mortar. The following extracts, it is fair to say, are not typical examples of the work; but that they should make their appearance in a history of literature is noteworthy and significant.

There was, however, never so much difference in his case between the public and, at first, a few, but, latterly, nearly all, critics as occurred in the case of Lewis Morris, who, also, was later knighted.

The somewhat epicene touch (acknowledged long after it had been recognised by some under the for a long time well-kept pseudonym Fiona Macleod) by William Sharp can receive no extended notice here.

The editor of the nearly finished (fourth) volume left behind him by Gairdner of his *Lollardy and the Reformation* considers that, in writing the section on *The History of the English Church*, of which Gairdner's later work was an unfinished enlargement, he (though already at an advanced age) believed himself to be fulfilling a duty; and he, certainly, had the cause of truth at heart.

Since, in 1786, he had (though matters of finance were never much to his taste) in an admired maiden speech attacked Pitt's commercial treatises, he never faltered, either in the days of the eclipse of the whig party, or in those of catholic emancipation (in which he delivered a speech which Stanley (Derby) said he would rather have made than four of Brougham's) and of reform.

Nor does it mend matters to stick in sprigs of ornament.

All . . . pay unconstrained honour to Swinburne's celebration of his ideals of liberty and justice, clothed in music which is borne upon the wings of the wind and wails and rejoices, now loud with delight in its beauty and strength and now threatening or plaintive in its anger or sadness, like the voice of the sea.

As rhetoric this is puerile, as criticism it is null. It is like what the *Daily Chronicle* said when Matthew Arnold died; and that is worth communicating to those who do not know it already.

His music mounted upward with bright thoughts, as the skylark shakes dewdrops from its wing as it carols at 'Heaven's Gate,' or, like a mountain brooklet carrying many a wild flower on its wavelets, his melody flowed cheerily on. Sometimes too his music rises like that of the mysterious ocean casting up pearls as it rolls.

The value of the work as a repertory of information is not affected by lumpish writing nor even by disputable judgments, and it is certainly an ample and probably a trustworthy collection of facts. There is however one department of which so much cannot be said. Upon what principle, and from what materials, the bibliography has been compiled, is far from clear; but it does not seem that either the *Dictionary of National Biography* or the general catalogue of the University Library has been consulted. Completeness was not to be expected or even desired in a book of this compass; but the information supplied is in many cases neither adequate nor accurate, and even the memory of a reader conversant with the period will enable him to correct mistakes and repair omissions. Here are three entries in the 'Table of Principal Dates,' vol. XIII, p. 576.

'1863 Lear's *Book of Nonsense*': its date was 1846. '1877 Palgrave's *Golden Treasury*': its date was 1861. '1908 Thompson's *The Hound of Heaven*': its date was 1893, and Thompson died in 1907.

The Application of Thought to
Textual Criticism

In beginning to speak about the application of thought to textual criticism, I do not intend to define the term *thought*, because I hope that the sense which I attach to the word will emerge from what I say. But it is necessary at the outset to define *textual criticism*, because many people, and even some people who profess to teach it to others, do not know what it is. One sees books calling themselves introductions to textual criticism which contain nothing about textual criticism from beginning to end; which are all about palaeography and manuscripts and collation, and have no more to do with textual criticism than if they were all about accidence and syntax. Palaeography is one of the things with which a textual critic needs to acquaint himself, but grammar is another, and equally indispensable; and no amount either of grammar or of palaeography will teach a man one scrap of textual criticism.

Textual criticism is a science, and, since it comprises recension and emendation, it is also an art. It is the science of discovering error in texts and the art of removing it. That is its definition, that is what the name *denotes*. But I must also say something about what it does and does not *connote*, what attributes it does and does not imply; because here also there are false impressions abroad.

First, then, it is not a sacred mystery. It is purely a matter of reason and of common sense. We exercise textual criticism whenever we notice and correct a misprint. A man who possesses common sense and the use of reason must not expect to learn from treatises or lectures on textual criticism anything that he could not, with leisure and industry, find out for himself. What the lectures and treatises can do for him is to save him time and trouble by presenting to him immediately considerations which would in any case occur to him sooner or later. And whatever he reads about textual criticism in books, or hears at lectures, he should test by reason and common sense, and reject everything which conflicts with either as mere hocus-pocus.

Secondly, textual criticism is not a branch of mathematics, nor indeed an exact science at all. It deals with a matter not rigid and constant, like lines and numbers, but fluid and variable; namely the frailties and aberrations of the human mind, and of its insubordinate servants, the human fingers. It therefore is not susceptible of hard-and-fast rules. It would be much easier if it were; and that is why people try to pretend that it is, or at least behave as if they thought so. Of course you can have hard-and-fast rules if you like, but then you will have false rules, and they will lead you wrong; because their simplicity will render them inapplicable to problems which are not simple, but complicated by the play of personality. A textual critic engaged upon his business is not at all like Newton investigating the motions of the planets: he is much more like a dog hunting for fleas. If a dog hunted for fleas on mathematical principles, basing his researches on statistics of area and population, he would never catch a flea except by accident. They require to be treated as individuals; and every problem which presents itself to the textual critic must be regarded as possibly unique.

Textual criticism therefore is neither mystery nor mathematics: it cannot be learnt either like the catechism or like the multiplication table. This science and this art require more in the learner than a simply receptive mind; and indeed the truth is that they cannot be taught at all: *criticus nascitur, non fit.* If a dog is to hunt for fleas successfully he must be quick and he must be sensitive. It is no good for a rhinoceros to hunt for fleas: he does not know where they are, and could not catch them if he did. It has sometimes been said that textual criticism is the crown and summit of all scholarship. This is not evidently or necessarily true; but it is true that the qualities which make a critic, whether they are thus transcendent or no, are rare, and that a good critic is a much less common thing than for instance a good grammarian. I have in my mind a paper by a well-known scholar on a certain Latin writer, half of which was concerned with grammar and half with criticism. The grammatical part was excellent; it showed wide reading and accurate observation, and contributed matter which was both new and valuable. In the textual part the author was like nothing so much as an ill-bred child interrupting the conversation of grown men. If it was possible to mistake the question at issue, he mistook it. If an opponent's arguments were contained in some book which was not at hand, he did not try to find the book, but he tried to guess the arguments; and he never succeeded. If the book was at hand, and he had read the arguments, he did not understand them; and represented his opponents as saying the opposite of what they had said. If another scholar had already removed a corruption by slightly altering the text, he proposed to remove it by altering the text violently. So possible is it to be a learned man, and admirable in other departments, and yet to have in you not even the makings of a critic.

But the application of thought to textual criticism is an action which ought to be within the power of anyone who can apply thought to anything. It is not, like the talent for textual criticism, a gift of nature, but it is a habit: and, like other habits, it can be formed. And, when formed, although it cannot fill the place of an absent talent, it can modify and minimise the ill effects of the talent's absence. Because a man is not a born critic, he need not therefore act like a born fool; but when he engages in textual criticism he often does. There are reasons for everything, and there are reasons for this; and I will now set forth the chief of them. The *fact* that thought is not sufficiently applied to the subject I shall show hereafter by examples; but at present I consider the causes which bring that result about.

First, then, not only is a natural aptitude for the study rare, but so also is a genuine interest in it. Most people, and many scholars among them, find it rather dry and rather dull. Now if a subject bores us, we are apt to avoid the trouble of thinking about it; but if we do that, we had better go further and avoid also the trouble of writing about it. And that is what English scholars often did in the middle of the nineteenth century, when nobody in England wanted to hear about textual criticism. This was not an ideal condition of affairs, but it had its compensation. The less one says about a subject which one does not understand, the less one will say about it which is foolish; and on this subject editors were allowed by public opinion to be silent if they chose. But public opinion is now aware that textual criticism, however repulsive, is nevertheless indispensable, and editors find that some pretence of dealing with the subject is obligatory; and in these circumstances they apply, not thought, but words, to textual criticism. They get rules by rote without grasping the realities of which those rules are merely emblems, and recite them on inappropriate occasions instead of seriously thinking out each problem as it arises.

Secondly, it is only a minority of those who engage in this study who are sincerely bent upon the discovery of truth. We all know that the discovery of truth is seldom the sole object of political writers; and the world believes, justly or unjustly, that it is not always the sole object of theologians: but the amount of sub-conscious dishonesty which pervades the textual criticism of the Greek and Latin classics is little suspected except by those who have had occasion to analyse it. People come upon this field bringing with them prepossessions and preferences; they are not willing to look all facts in the face, nor to draw the most probable conclusion unless it is also the most agreeable conclusion. Most men are rather stupid, and most of those who are not stupid are, consequently, rather vain; and it is hardly possible to step aside from the pursuit of truth without falling a victim either to your stupidity or else to your vanity. Stupidity will then attach you to received opinions, and you will stick in the mud; or vanity will set you hunting for novelty, and you will find mare's-nests. Added to these snares and hindrances there are the various forms of partisanship: sectarianism, which handcuffs you to your own school and teachers and associates, and patriotism, which handcuffs you to your own country. Patriotism has a great name as a virtue, and in civic matters, at the present stage of the world's history, it possibly still does more good than harm; but in the sphere of intellect it is an unmitigated nuisance. I do not know which cuts the worse figure: a German scholar encouraging his countrymen to believe that 'wir Deutsche' have nothing to learn from foreigners, or an Englishman demonstrating the unity of Homer by sneers at 'Teutonic professors,' who are supposed by his audience to have goggle eyes behind large spectacles, and ragged moustaches saturated in lager beer, and consequently to be incapable of forming literary judgments.

Thirdly, these internal causes of error and folly are subject to very little counteraction or correction from outside. The average reader knows hardly anything about textual criticism, and therefore cannot exercise a vigilant control over the writer: the addle-pate is at liberty to maunder and the impostor is at liberty to lie. And, what is worse, the reader often shares the writer's prejudices, and is far too well pleased with his conclusions to examine either his premises or his reasoning. Stand on a barrel in the streets of Bagdad, and say in a loud voice, 'Twice two is four, and ginger is hot in the mouth, therefore Mohammed is the prophet of God,' and your logic will probably escape criticism; or, if anyone by chance should criticise it, you could easily silence him by calling him a Christian dog.

Fourthly, the things which the textual critic has to talk about are not things which present themselves clearly and sharply to the mind; and it is easy to say, and to fancy that you think, what you really do not think, and even what, if you seriously tried to think it, you would find to be unthinkable. Mistakes are therefore made which could not be made if the matter under discussion were any corporeal object, having qualities perceptible to the senses. The human senses have had a much longer history than the human intellect, and have been brought much nearer to perfection: they are far more acute, far less easy to deceive. The difference between an icicle and a red-hot poker is really much slighter than the difference between truth and falsehood or sense and nonsense; yet it is much more immediately noticeable and much more universally noticed, because the body is more sensitive than the mind. I find therefore that a good way of exposing the falsehood of a statement or the absurdity of an argument in textual criticism is to transpose it into sensuous terms and see what it looks like then. If the nouns which we use are the names of things which can be handled or tasted, differing from one another in being hot or cold, sweet or sour, then we realise what we are saying and take care what we say. But the terms of textual criticism are deplorably intellectual; and probably in no other field do men tell so many falsehoods in the idle hope that they are telling the truth, or talk so much nonsense in the vague belief that they are talking sense.

This is particularly unfortunate and particularly reprehensible, because there is no science in which it is more necessary to take precautions against error arising from internal causes. Those who follow the physical sciences enjoy the great advantage that they can constantly bring their opinions to the test of fact, and verify or falsify their theories by experiment. When a chemist has mixed sulphur and saltpetre and charcoal in certain proportions and wishes to ascertain if the mixture is explosive, he need only apply a match. When a doctor has compounded a new drug and desires to find out what diseases, if any, it is good for, he has only to give it to his patients all round and notice which die and which recover. Our conclusions regarding the truth or falsehood of a MS reading can never be confirmed or corrected by an equally decisive test; for the only equally decisive test would be the production of the author's autograph. The discovery merely of better and older MSS than were previously known to us is *not* equally decisive; and even this inadequate verification is not to be expected often, or on a large scale. It is therefore a matter of common prudence and common decency that we should neglect no safeguard lying within our reach; that we should look sharp after ourselves; that we should narrowly scrutinise our own proceedings and rigorously analyse our springs of action. How far these elementary requirements are satisfied, we will now learn from examples.

At the very beginning, to see what pure irrelevancy, what almost incredible foolishness, finds its way into print, take this instance. It had been supposed for several centuries that Plautus' name was *M. Accius Plautus*, when Ritschl in 1845 pointed out that in the Ambrosian palimpsest discovered by Mai in 1815, written in the fourth or fifth century, and much the oldest of Plautus' MSS, the name appears in the genitive as *T. Macci Plauti*, so that he was really called *Titus Maccius* (or *Maccus*) *Plautus*. An Italian scholar, one Vallauri, objected to this innovation on the ground that in all printed editions from the sixteenth to the nineteenth century the name was *M. Accius*. He went to Milan to look at the palimpsest, and there, to be sure, he found *T. Macci* quite legibly written. But he observed that many *other* pages of the MS were quite illegible, and that the whole book was very much tattered and battered; whereupon he said that he could not sufficiently wonder at anyone attaching any weight to a MS which was in such a condition. Is there any other science, anything calling itself a science, into which such intellects intrude and conduct such operations in public? But you may think that Mr Vallauri is a unique phenomenon. No: if you engage in textual criticism you may come upon a second Mr Vallauri at any turn. The MSS of Catullus, none of them older than the fourteenth century, present at 64 23 the verse:

heroes saluete, deum genus! o bona mater!

The Veronese scholia on Vergil, a palimpsest of the fifth or sixth century, at *Aen.* V 80, 'salue sancte parens,' have the note: 'Catullus: saluete, deum *gens*, o bona *matrum* | progenies, saluete iter[um]' – giving *gens* for *genus*, *matrum* for *mater*, and adding a half-verse absent from Catullus' MSS; and scholars have naturally preferred an authority so much more ancient. But one editor is found to object: 'the weight of the Veronese scholia, imperfect and full of lacunae as they are, is not to be set against our MSS.' There is Mr Vallauri over again: because the palimpsest has large holes else-where and because much of it has perished, therefore what remains, though written as early as the sixth century, has less authority than MSS written in the fourteenth. If however anyone gets hold of these fourteenth-century MSS, destroys pages of them and tears holes in the pages he does not destroy, the authority of those parts which he allows to survive will presumably deteriorate, and may even sink as low as that of the palimpsest.

Again. There are two MSS of a certain author, which we will call A and B. Of these two it is recognised that A is the more correct but the less sincere, and that B is the more corrupt but the less interpo-lated. It is desired to know which MS, if either, is better than the other, or whether both are equal. One scholar tries to determine this question by the collection and comparison of examples. But another thinks that he knows a shorter way than that; and it consists in saying 'the more sincere MS is and must be for any critic who understands his business the better MS.'

This I cite as a specimen of the things which people may say if they do not think about the meaning of what they are saying, and especially as an example of the danger of dealing in generalisations. The best way to treat such pretentious inanities is to transfer them from the sphere of textual criticism, where the difference between truth and falsehood or between sense and nonsense is little regarded and seldom even perceived, into some sphere where men are obliged to use concrete and sensuous terms, which force them, however reluctantly, to think.

I ask this scholar, this critic who knows his business, and who says that the more sincere of two MSS is and must be the better – I ask him to tell me which weighs most, a tall man or a fat man. He cannot answer; nobody can; everybody sees in a moment that the question is absurd. *Tall* and *fat* are adjectives which transport even a textual critic from the world of humbug into the world of reality, a world inhabited by comparatively thoughtful people, such as butchers and grocers, who depend on their brains for their bread. There he begins to understand that to such general questions any answer must be false; that judgment can only be pronounced on individual specimens; that everything depends on the degree of tallness and the degree of fatness. It may well be that an inch of girth adds more weight than an inch of height, or vice versa; but that altitude is incomparably more ponderous than obesity, or obesity than altitude, and that an inch of one depresses the scale more than a yard of the other, has never been maintained. The way to find out whether this tall man weighs more or less than that fat man is to weigh them; and the way to find out whether this corrupt MS is better or worse than that interpolated MS is to collect and compare their readings; not to ride easily off on the false and ridiculous generalisation that the more sincere MS is and must be the better.

When you call a MS *sincere* you instantly engage on its behalf the moral sympathy of the thoughtless: moral sympathy is a line in which they are very strong. I do not desire to exclude morality from textual criticism; I wish indeed that some moral qualities were commoner in textual criticism than they are; but let us not indulge our moral emotions out of season. It may be that a scribe who interpolates, who makes changes deliberately, is guilty of wickedness, while a scribe who makes changes accidentally, because he is sleepy or illiterate or drunk, is guilty of none; but that is a question which will be determined by a competent authority at the Day of Judgment, and is no concern of ours. Our concern is not with the eternal destiny of the scribe, but with the temporal utility of the MS; and a MS is useful or the reverse in proportion to the amount of truth which it discloses or conceals, no matter what may be the causes of the disclosure or concealment. It is a mistake to suppose that deliberate change is always or necessarily more destructive of truth than accidental change; and even if it were, the main question, as I have said already, is one of degree. A MS in which 1 per cent of the words have been viciously and intentionally altered and 99 per cent are right is not so bad as a MS in which only 1 per cent are right and 99 per cent have been altered virtuously and unintentionally; and if you go to a critic with any such vague inquiry as the question whether the 'more sincere' or the 'more correct' of two MSS is the better, he will reply, 'If I am to answer that question, you must show me the two MSS first; for aught that I know at present, from the terms of your query, either may be better than the other, or both may be equal.' But that is what the incompetent intruders into criticism can never admit. They *must* have a better MS, whether it exists or no; because they could never get along without one. If Providence permitted two MSS to be equal, the editor would have to choose between their readings by considerations of intrinsic merit, and in order to do that he would need to acquire intelligence and impartiality and willingness to take pains, and all sorts of things which he neither has nor wishes for; and he feels sure that God, who tempers the wind to the shorn lamb, can never have meant to lay upon his shoulders such a burden as this.

This is thoughtlessness in the sphere of recension: come now to the sphere of emendation. There is one foolish sort of conjecture which seems to be commoner in the British Isles than anywhere else, though it is also practised abroad, and of late years especially at Munich. The practice is, if you have persuaded yourself that a text is corrupt, to alter a letter or two and see what happens. If what happens is anything which the warmest good-will can mistake for sense and grammar, you call it an emendation; and you call this silly game the palaeographical method.

The palaeographical method has always been the delight of tiros and the scorn of critics. Haupt, for example, used to warn his pupils against mistaking this sort of thing for emendation. 'The prime requisite of a good emendation,' said he, 'is that it should start from the thought; it is only afterwards that other considerations, such as those of metre, or possibilities, such as the interchange of letters, are taken into account.' And again: 'If the sense requires it, I am prepared to write *Constantinopolitanus* where the MSS have the monosyllabic interjection *o*.' And again: 'From the requirement that one should always begin with the thought, there results, as if self-evident, the negative aspect of the case, that one should not, at the outset, consider what exchange of letters may possibly have brought about the corruption of the passage one is dealing with.' And further, in his oration on Lachmann as a critic: 'Some people, if they see that anything in an ancient text wants correcting, immediately betake themselves to the art of palaeography, investigate the shapes of letters and the forms of abbreviation, and try one dodge after another, as if it were a game, until they hit upon something which they think they can substitute for the corruption; as if forsooth truth were generally discovered by shots of that sort, or as if emendation could take its rise from anything but a careful consideration of the thought.'

But even when palaeography is kept in her proper place, as handmaid, and not allowed to give herself the airs of mistress, she is apt to be overworked. There is a preference for conjectures which call in the aid of palaeography, and which assume, as the cause of error, the accidental interchange of similar letters or similar words, although other causes of error are known to exist. One is presented, for instance, with the following maxim: 'Interpolation is, speaking generally, comparatively an uncommon source of alteration, and we should therefore be loth to assume it in a given case.'

Every case is a given case; so what this maxim really means is that we should always be loth to assume interpolation as a source of alteration. But it is certain, and admitted by this writer when he uses the phrase 'comparatively uncommon,' that interpolation does occur; so he is telling us that we should be loth to assume interpolation even when that assumption is true. And the reason why we are to behave in this ridiculous manner is that interpolation is, speaking generally, comparatively an uncommon source of alteration.

Now to detect a *non sequitur*, unless it leads to an unwelcome conclusion, is as much beyond the power of the average reader as it is beyond the power of the average writer to attach ideas to his own words when those words are terms of textual criticism. I will therefore substitute other terms, terms to which ideas must be attached; and I invite consideration of this maxim and this ratiocination:

A bullet-wound is, speaking generally, comparatively an uncommon cause of death, and we should therefore be loth to assume it in a given case.

Should we? Should we be loth to assume a bullet-wound as the cause of death if the given case were death on a battlefield? and should we be loth to do so for the reason alleged, that a bullet-wound is, speaking generally, comparatively an uncommon cause of death? Ought we to assume instead the commonest cause of death, and assign death on a battlefield to tuberculosis? What would be thought of a counsellor who enjoined that method of procedure? Well, it would probably be thought that he was a textual critic strayed from home.

Why is interpolation comparatively uncommon? For the same reason that bullet-wounds are: because the opportunity for it is comparatively uncommon. Interpolation is provoked by real or supposed difficulties, and is not frequently volunteered where all is plain sailing; whereas accidental alteration may happen anywhere. Every letter of every word lies exposed to it, and that is the sole reason why accidental alteration is more common. In a given case where either assumption is possible, the assumption of interpolation is equally probable, nay more probable; because action with a motive is more probable than action without a motive. The truth therefore is that in such a case we should be loth to assume accident and should rather assume interpolation; and the circumstance that such cases are comparatively uncommon is no reason for behaving irrationally when they occur.

There is one special province of textual criticism, a large and important province, which is concerned with the establishment of rules of grammar and of metre. Those rules are in part traditional, and given us by the ancient grammarians; but in part they are formed by our own induction from what we find in the MSS of Greek and Latin authors; and even the traditional rules must of course be tested by comparison with the witness of the MSS. But every rule, whether traditional or framed from induction, is sometimes broken by the MSS; it may be by few, it may be by many; it may be seldom, it may be often; and critics may then say that the MSS are wrong, and may correct them in accordance with the rule. This state of affairs is apparently, nay evidently, paradoxical. The MSS are the material upon which we base our rule, and then, when we have got our rule, we turn round upon the MSS and say that the rule, based upon them, convicts them of error. We are thus working in a circle, that is a fact which there is no denying; but, as Lachmann says, the task of the critic is just this, to tread that circle deftly and warily; and that is precisely what elevates the critic's business above mere mechanical labour. The difficulty is one which lies in the nature of the case, and is inevitable; and the only way to surmount it is just to be a critic.

The paradox is more formidable in appearance than in reality, and has plenty of analogies in daily life. In a trial or lawsuit the jury's verdict is mainly based upon the evidence of the witnesses; but that does not prevent the jury from making up its mind, from the evidence in general, that one or more witnesses have been guilty of perjury and that their evidence is to be disregarded. It is quite possible to elicit from the general testimony of MSS a rule of sufficient certainty to convict of falsehood their exceptional testimony, or of sufficient probability to throw doubt upon it. But that exceptional testimony must in each case be considered. It must be recognised that there are two hypotheses between which we have to decide: the question is whether the exceptions come from the author, and so break down the rule, or whether they come from the scribe, and are to be corrected by it: and in order to decide this we must keep our eyes open for any peculiarity which may happen to characterise them.

One of the forms which lack of thought has assumed in textual criticism is the tendency now prevailing, especially among some Continental scholars, to try to break down accepted rules of grammar or metre by the mere collection and enumeration of exceptions presented by the MSS. Now that can never break down a rule: the mere number of exceptions is nothing; what matters is their weight, and that can only be ascertained by classification and scrutiny. If I had noted down every example which I have met, I should now have a large collection of places in Latin MSS where the substantive *orbis*, which our grammars and dictionaries declare to be masculine, has a feminine adjective attached to it. But I do not therefore propose to revise that rule of syntax, for examination would show that these examples, though numerous, have no force. Most of them are places where the sense and context show that *orbis*, in whatever case or number it may be, is merely a corruption of the corresponding case and number of *urbs*; and in the remaining places it is natural to suppose that the scribe has been influenced and confused by the great likeness of the one word to the other. Or again, read Madvig, *Adu. Crit.*, vol. I, book I, chap. IV, where he sifts the evidence for the opinion that the aorist infinitive can be used in Greek after verbs of saying and thinking in the sense of the future infinitive or of the aorist infinitive with ἄν. The list of examples in the MSS is very long indeed; but the moment you begin to sort them and examine them you are less struck by their number than by the restriction of their extent. Almost all of them are such as δέξασθαι used for δέξεσθαι, where the two forms differ by one letter only; a smaller number are such as ποιῆσαι for ποιήσειν, where the difference, though greater, is still slight; others are examples like ἥκιστα ἀναγκασθῆναι for ἥκιστ' ἂν ἀναγκασθῆναι, where again the difference is next to nothing. Now if the MSS are right in these cases, and the Greek authors did use this construction, how are we to explain this extraordinary limitation of the use? There is no syntactical difference between the first and second aorist: why then did they use the 1st aorist so often for the future and the 2nd aorist so seldom? why did they say δέξασθαι for δέξεσθαι dozens of times and λαβεῖν for λήψεσθαι never? The mere asking of that question is enough to show the true state of the case. The bare fact that the aorists thus used in the MSS are aorists of similar *form* to the future, while aorists of dissimilar form are not thus used, proves that the phenomenon has its cause in the copyist's eye and not in the author's mind, that it is not a variation in grammatical usage but an error in transcription. The number of examples is nothing; all depends upon their character; and a single example of λαβεῖν in a future sense would have more weight than a hundred of δέξασθαι.

In particular, scribes will alter a less familiar form to a more familiar, if they see nothing to prevent them. If metre allows, or if they do not know that metre forbids, they will alter ἐλεινός to ἐλεεινός, οἰστός to ὀϊστός, *nil* to *nihil*, *deprendo* to *deprehendo*. Since metre convicts them of infidelity in some places, they forfeit the right to be trusted in any place; if we choose to trust them we are credulous, and if we build structures on our trust we are no critics. Even if metre does not convict them, reason sometimes can. Take the statement, repeatedly made in grammars and editions, that the Latins sometimes used the pluperfect for the imperfect and the perfect. They did use it for the imperfect; they used it also for the preterite or past aorist; but for the perfect they did not use it; and that is proved by the very examples of its use as perfect which are found in MSS. All those examples are of the 3rd person plural. Why? We must choose between the two following hypotheses:

(*a*) That the Latins used the pluperfect for the perfect in the 3rd person plural only.

(*b*) That they did not use the pluperfect for the perfect, and that these examples are corrupt.

If anyone adopted the former, he would have to explain what syntactical property, inviting the author to use pluperfect for perfect, is possessed by the 3rd person plural and not by the two other plural or the three singular persons: and I should like to see some one set about it.

If we adopt the latter, we must show what *external* feature, inviting the *scribe* to write pluperfect for perfect, is possessed by the 3rd person plural exclusively: and that is quite easy. The 3rd person plural is the only person in which the perfect and the pluperfect differ merely by one letter. Moreover in verse the perfect termination -*ĕrunt*, being comparatively unfamiliar to scribes, is altered by them to the nearest familiar form with the same scansion, sometimes -*erint*, sometimes -*erant*: in Ovid's *Heroides* there are four places where the best MS gives *praebuĕrunt, stetĕrunt, excidĕrunt, expulĕrunt*, and the other MSS give -*erant* or -*erint* or both. Accordingly, when the much inferior MSS of Propertius present pluperfect for perfect in four places, *fuerant* once, *steterant* once, *exciderant* twice, Scaliger corrects to *fuĕrunt, stetĕrunt, excidĕrunt*. Thereupon an editor of this enlightened age takes up his pen and writes as follows: 'It is quite erroneous to remove the pluperfects where it can be done without great expenditure of conjectural sagacity (*steterunt* for *steterant* and the like), and not to trouble oneself about the phenomenon elsewhere.' I ask, how is it possible to trouble oneself about the phenomenon elsewhere? It does not exist elsewhere. There is no place where the MSS give *steteram* in the sense of the perfect *steti*, nor *steteras* in the sense of the perfect *stetisti*. Wherever they give examples of the pluperfect which cannot be removed by the change of one letter – such as *pararat* in I 8 36 or *fueram* in I 12 11 – those are examples where it has sometimes the sense of the imperfect, sometimes of the preterite, but never of the perfect. And the inference is plain: the Latins did not use the pluperfect for the perfect.

Scaliger knew that in the sixteenth century: Mr Rothstein, in the nineteenth and twentieth, does not know it; he has found a form of words to prevent him from knowing it, and he thinks himself in advance of Scaliger. It is supposed that there has been progress in the science of textual criticism, and the most frivolous pretender has learnt to talk superciliously about 'the old unscientific days.' The old unscientific days are everlasting; they are here and now; they are renewed perennially by the ear which takes formulas in, and the tongue which gives them out again, and the mind which meanwhile is empty of reflexion and stuffed with self-complacency. Progress there has been, but where? In superior intellects: the rabble do not share it. Such a man as Scaliger, living in our time, would be a better critic than Scaliger was; but we shall not be better critics than Scaliger by the simple act of living in our own time. Textual criticism, like most other sciences, is an aristocratic affair, not communicable to all men, nor to most men. Not to be a textual critic is no reproach to anyone, unless he pretends to be what he is not. To *be* a textual critic requires aptitude for thinking and willingness to think; and though it also requires other things, those things are supplements and cannot be substitutes. Knowledge is good, method is good, but one thing beyond all others is necessary; and that is to have a head, not a pumpkin, on your shoulders, and brains, not pudding, in your head.

Napoleon III: A Review of *Louis Napoleon and the Recovery of France*

Fourteen years ago there was published by a country curate a study of the third Napoleon's ascent from the cradle to the Presidency of the Republic which placed its author among the best living historians. *The Rise of Louis Napoleon* is now followed by *Louis Napoleon and the Recovery of France*, continuing the story from 1848 to 1856 and confirming Mr Simpson's reputation. The same virtues reappear: originality, integrity, sobriety, research, a sprightly and engaging style, a strong turn for epigram, and a great deal of pleasant malice expended upon such objects as most invite it and deserve it – historians, republicans, the British nation, and the human race. The writing is not so easy and equable as in the earlier volume, and the epigrams, though more brilliant and abundant, are not always so naturally or artfully introduced as epigrams should be; but the style has yet so much grace and vigour that one wishes the diction were purer than it is. It would be pedantry in a history of 1851 to eschew *coup d'état*; but who can imagine *sotto voce* or παρεργον on a page of Macaulay? The slang with which Mr Simpson now and then defiles his pen is probably slang which he heard in his cradle and believed in his innocence to be English: 'a settlement *of sorts*' for example on p. 362, which does not mean what Shakespeare would suppose, but only that Mr Simpson has no high opinion of the settlement. Here too, as everywhere, are the daisies and dandelions of contemporary metaphor. Till I read p. 241 I did not know that a storm could have an aftermath nor that an aftermath could reach a throne; but I have since found the same blend of meteorology and agriculture in a novel of Mr Hugh Walpole's – though the aftermath is there a 'faint' one and so no throne is threatened. The illustrations, which are more numerous and less apposite than comports with the dignity of history, may be imputed to the publishers, for publishers seek to attract readers whom authors would wish to repel; but it is to be feared that the page-headings – 'Cruel habitations,' 'If winter comes,' and so forth – are the historian's.

These eight years of Louis Napoleon's life were so much fuller of events than the preceding forty that the second volume is a good deal longer than the first. Yet it might with advantage have been longer still. For an historian of this reign Mr Simpson spends perhaps too much time abroad but certainly too little at home. The Crimea, where Napoleon, to humour the English Government, did not appear in person, and the Europe of diplomacy, fill most of the pages after once the Emperor is seated on his throne. But the chief event of the time was what Mr Simpson calls in his title 'the recovery of France.' Social reforms and a wise internal administration were the Empire's best gifts to the country, and were not cancelled by its fall; and though Mr Simpson duly mentions and briefly enumerates these measures, they deserve to be explained in detail and shown in the working. It was the French people's gratitude to their tyrant which enabled him to wage unpopular wars in the interests of foreigners. His friendship for England and his sentimental affection for Italy and Germany were injurious and finally disastrous to his subjects: not so his compassion for the poor and his endeavours to alleviate the common lot of man. Henry IV had earned a name for benevolence by the inexpensive wish that every peasant should have a fowl in his pot: Napoleon III did his best to put it there.

The task of a fair and temperate historian, in treating of one who attracted so much spite and calumny, is a task of rehabilitation; and Mr Simpson, without resorting to advocacy, dispels much malevolent fiction by contrasting it with reality. Every new fact, every substitution of truth for falsehood, redounds to Napoleon's credit. For instance, it has been repeated, oftener than anything true is ever repeated, that he manoeuvred England into the Crimean war to be revenged on Nicholas I for a personal slight, to obtain admission on equal terms among European sovereigns, and to distract his enslaved countrymen from the contemplation of their chains. His countrymen were contented and pacific, and the war endangered his popularity; he made many efforts and some sacrifice of dignity to avert it; and it was forced upon Europe by the intrigues of a British ambassador, the stiffness of the Czar, and the bellicose temper of the English people and especially of their radical journalists.

It is fitting that amends should thus be made by an English historian to this ruler of France, for those amends are a national debt. That the Emperor should have enemies among the French was inevitable: he had deprived many professional politicians of their livelihood, and bereaved many orators of the sound of their own voice; and he was to this extent a tyrant, that he strictly repressed the minority opposed to his rule, – a minority comprising many who approved both his aims and his measures, but nevertheless were bound to oppose him because he was Count neither of Chambord nor of Paris. There was no such cause or excuse for the detestation of his person and government which was felt and expressed in our own happy, constitutional, and censorious country. Queen Victoria had ascended her throne without saying by your leave or with your leave; one house of Parliament was hereditary, and five-sixths of the adult male population had no voice in electing the other. These were the people who talked about despotism when a neighbouring nation, by universal suffrage and enormous majorities, had settled its own form of government. Though in truth it was not the English people but the enlightened English Liberals, then at the beginning of their long ascendancy, to whom the Emperor was odious; and the reason why they called him a despot was that he had put a despotism down, and had delivered France from the tyranny of Paris. The divine right of 2,000,000 Radicals to govern 30,000,000 Conservatives had been trampled underfoot; and Napoleon's chief offence in our country was this great service which he had rendered to his own. He left France diminished in territory and weakened in the face of Europe; but the eighteen years of his rule had at least cut the claws of the capital. When in 1871 Paris tried her last struggle with France, it was no longer dominion that she claimed, but only independence, and even independence was denied her; and those who had prated about the blood-stained origin of the Second Empire, and had dignified with the name of massacre the street-accident of Dec. 4, 1851, were taught what a massacre really is, and how much more blood it takes to found a republic than an empire.

One count in the British indictment against him was his private life, which was certainly dissolute; perhaps as dissolute as the Duke of Wellington's. I have been told by those who remembered his first visit to Windsor, in 1855, that the public was agitated, more furiously than the newspapers record, by the knowledge or belief that sovereigns embrace when they meet, and by rage and horror at the notion that 'those lips' should be allowed to sully the pure cheek of England's Queen. England's Queen, who had been kissed by her uncles, did not turn a hair; and a few months later, when Victor Emmanuel was the visitor and nobody made any fuss, the exemplary matron must have been pained to discover that her subjects' solicitude for the purity of her cheek was not sincere.

In this volume Mr Simpson has to deal with the two matters which supplied the Emperor's adversaries with their favourite themes: his broken oath to the Republic, and the famous massacre. On the former he has some excellent casuistry (in the proper sense of a word which Pascal and the Jesuits between them have brought into undeserved discredit), which may be cited here because it is also a characteristic piece of writing: pp. 170 f.

Oath-breaking is bad. But it is an altogether fortunate thing that oaths of allegiance have no worse effect than to exclude from political life a few abnormally honest men. Else all constitutional change would long ago have been rendered universally impossible, by the simple device of confining political life to the oath-bound. From this fate men's readiness to break oaths, and not their reluctance to impose them, has saved the world. Even though it knows them frangible few governments can resist the desire for the fictitious sense of security attained by the imposition of oaths of allegiance. But were such oaths really unbreakable no government could be deterred from what would then be a frantic eagerness to extort a genuine pledge of immortality. That there may never be lacking a supply of men willing at a pinch to break such oaths is the humiliating but manifest interest of mankind.

As for the affair of December 4, when the soldiery lost their heads and fired among the sight-seers, Mr Simpson condemns Napoleon because he profited by it, which is doubtful, and because he did not punish it; and he finds a parallel in William III's relation to the massacre of Glencoe. But the sight-seers had been warned by proclamation to stay at home; and from that point of view Napoleon may be held less responsible for their fate, not only than William III for the slaughter of the Macdonalds, but than William IV for the lamented death of Huskisson; for William IV had issued no proclamation advising ex-Presidents of the Board of Trade not to stand in front of railway trains.

Preface to *Nine Essays* by Arthur Platt

The author of the papers collected in this volume was one whose published writings, though they show the rare quality of his mind, do not portray the range of his studies and the variety of his accomplishments. Nor do these papers themselves complete the picture; but they have been recovered and put together that the world may know a little more of an uncommonly gifted man who was not much before its eye, and whose reputation was highest within the narrower circle which knew him well enough to admire him rightly.

It is not certain that he would have consented to their publication, for he must have felt that they bear some traces of the circumstances which called them forth. University College London, like many other colleges, is the abode of a Minotaur. This monster does not devour youths and maidens: it consists of them, and it preys for choice on the Professors within its reach. It is called a Literary Society, and in hopes of deserving the name it exacts a periodical tribute from those whom it supposes to be literate. Studious men who might be settling *Hoti*'s business and properly basing *Oun* are expected to provide amusing discourses on subjects of which they have no official knowledge and upon which they may not be entitled even to open their mouths. Platt, whose temper made him accessible, whose pen ran easily, and whose mind was richly stored, paid more of this blackmail than most of his colleagues, and grudged it less; but the fact is not to be concealed that these unconstrained and even exuberant essays were written to order. The only one which he allowed to be printed, and that only in a college magazine, is *Aristophanes*. Two however have a different origin and were composed with more deliberation. *Science and Arts among the Ancients* is an address delivered before the Faculties of Arts and Science in University College on a ceremonial occasion, the opening of the Session in October 1899; and the Prelection is one of those read in public by the candidates for the Cambridge Chair of Greek when it fell vacant in 1921.

John Arthur, eldest of the fourteen children of Francis Thomas Platt, was born in London on the 11th of July 1860 and died at

Bournemouth on the 16th of March 1925. He was sent to school at Harrow, whence he went up to Cambridge in 1879, winning a scholarship at Trinity College. In the first part of the Classical Tripos of 1882 he was placed in the second division of the first class, a position which may have disappointed himself but did not surprise those friends who, whenever they went into his rooms, had found him deep in books which had no bearing on the examination. In the second part a year later he obtained a first class in Literature and Criticism and also in Ancient Philosophy. In 1884, like his father and grandfather before him, he was elected a Fellow of Trinity. This Fellowship he lost under the old statutes by his marriage in 1885 with Mildred Barham, daughter of Sir Edward Bond, K C B, sometime Librarian of the British Museum, and granddaughter of R.H. Barham, the author of the *Ingoldsby Legends*. Their children were one son and one daughter. For the next eight years he taught at the coaching establishment of Wren and Gurney in Bayswater; in 1894 he was chosen to succeed his friend William Wyse as Professor of Greek in University College London, and soon after took up his residence about a mile away on the edge of Regent's Park. He held his Professorship more than 30 years. In 1921, when Henry Jackson died, he was persuaded to become a candidate for the Chair of Greek at Cambridge, to which few or none of the competitors had a juster claim; but he was relieved when he was not elected, and it is certain that Cambridge would have been less to his taste than London as a place to live in. He would have vacated his office at University College by reason of age in July 1925, but in 1924 he was attacked by illness, and did not live to complete his term.

At the time of his appointment some feared that they were yoking a racehorse to the plough and that his duties might be irksome to him because they could hardly be interesting. Much of the teaching which he was required to give was elementary, and he seldom had pupils who possessed a native aptitude for classical studies or intended to pursue them far. But he proved assiduous, patient, and effective: only an oaf could help learning from him and liking him; and with his best students he formed enduring ties, and would inveigle them into reading Dante or Cervantes with him at his house of an evening after they had taken their degrees. Outside his own class-room he was a centre and fount of the general life of the College, most of all in the Musical Society and among his colleagues in the smoking-room after luncheon. Nearer to his house he made another circle of friends. He was a Fellow of the Zoological Society, frequented its Gardens, and inspired a romantic passion in their resident population. There was a leopard which at Platt's approach would almost ooze through the bars of its cage to establish contact with the beloved object; the gnu, if it saw him on the opposite side of its broad enclosure, would walk all the way across to have its forelock pulled; and a credible witness reports the following scene.

I remember going to the giraffe-house and seeing a crowd of children watching a man who had removed his hat while the giraffe, its neck stretched to the fullest capacity, was rubbing its head backwards and forwards upon the bald crown. When the object of this somewhat embarrassing affection turned his head, Platt's features were revealed.

In youth he had poetical ambitions, and his first book was a volume of verse; a smaller one on a personal theme was printed privately, and so was a collection, made after his death, of sonnets, very personal indeed, with which he had entertained and striven to ameliorate his colleagues. He early produced recensions of the *Odyssey* and the *Iliad*, in which it was his aim to restore, so far as might be, the original language of the poet or poets, and thus to pursue further that special line of Homeric study which began with Bentley and his digamma, engaged the acute but undisciplined minds of Payne Knight and Brandreth, and has left as memorials of its progress the editions of Bekker and of Nauck. Nothing could be more different, or could better display his versatility, than his other chief work, the translation of Aristotle's *De generatione animalium* with its multifarious notes on matters zoological. A slighter performance was a free rendering of the *Agamemnon* of Aeschylus into the prose of King James's Bible.

Among the Greek scholars of his country Platt belonged to that company of explorers whose leading figures, after the universal genius of Bentley, are Dawes, Porson, and Elmsley. Minute and refined observation for the ascertainment of grammatical and metrical usage was his chosen province; and his early investigations of Homeric practice were his most characteristic work, and probably surpass in value his later and more various contributions to interpretation and textual criticism. Metrical science, upon the death of Elmsley, had deserted its native isle and taken flight to the Continent: Platt was one of the very few Englishmen who in the last hundred years have advanced the study, and among those few he was the foremost. In conjectural emendation, like Dawes and Elmsley, he was shrewd and dexterous enough, but not, like Bentley and Porson, eminent. In literary comment he did not expatiate, although, or rather because, he was the most lettered scholar of his time. He stuck to business, as a scholar should, and preferred, as a man of letters will, the dry to the watery. He knew better than to conceive himself that rarest of all the great works of God, a literary critic; but such remarks on literature as he did let fall were very different stuff from the usual flummery of the cobbler who is ambitious to go beyond his last.

If his contemporaries rated him, both comparatively and absolutely, below his true position in the world of learning, the loss was chiefly theirs, but the blame was partly his. He had much of the boy in his composition, and something even of the schoolboy. His conversation in mixed company was apt to be flighty, and his writing, though it was not so, carried jauntiness of manner to some little excess. Those who judge weight by heaviness were perplexed and deceived by a colloquial gaiety, much less unseemly indeed than the frolic sallies of Dawes, but striking more sharply on the sense because not draped like them in the Latin toga; and it was disturbing to meet with a scholar who carried his levity, where others carry their gravity, on the surface, and was austere, where he might without offence or detection have been frivolous, in conducting the operations of his mind.

That he wrote little was the direct and natural consequence of his extraordinary capacity and the variety of his interests and attainments. He would rather improve himself than instruct others. He wrote on subjects where he could make definite and original contributions to the advancement of learning: otherwise he preferred to read. Greek was his trade, but the home in which he dwelt was great literature, whether its language were Greek, Latin, English, French, Italian, Spanish, German, or Persian. The best authors were his study, but his reading ran far beyond them; his curiosity invaded holes and corners, and his taste ranged from the *Divine Comedy* to *Jorrocks's Jaunts*. He followed his inclinations and

347

read for his own delight, with a keen and natural relish, not a dutiful and obedient admiration of the things which are admired by the wise and good. Nor were his studies warped and narrowed by ambition. A scholar who means to build himself a monument must spend much of his life in acquiring knowledge which for its own sake is not worth having and in reading books which do not in themselves deserve to be read; *at illa iacent multa et praeclara relicta*.

Music was a rival of literature in his affections, and his knowledge of the art and its history was almost an expert's. He followed with interest and understanding the progress of discovery in the natural sciences, and his acquaintance with zoology in particular was such as few laymen can boast. In conclusion it is proper to mention his vices. He was addicted to tobacco and indifferent to wine, and he would squander long summer days on watching the game of cricket.

His happy and useful life is over, and now begins the steady encroachment of oblivion, as those who remember him are in their turn summoned away. This record will not preserve, perhaps none could preserve, more than an indistinct and lifeless image of the friend who is lost to us: good, kind, bright, unselfish, and as honest as the day; versatile without shallowness, accomplished without ostentation, a treasury of hidden knowledge which only accident brought to light, but which accident brought to light perpetually, and which astonished us so often that astonishment lost its nature and we should have wondered more if wonders had failed. Yet what most eludes description is not the excellence of his gifts but the singularity of his essential being, his utter unlikeness to any other creature in the world.

The Name and Nature of Poetry

It is my first duty to acknowledge the honour done me by those
who have in their hands the appointment of the Leslie Stephen
Lecturer, and to thank them for this token of their good will. My
second duty is to say that I condemn their judgment and deplore
their choice. It is twenty-two years to-day since I last, and first,
spoke in this Senate-House; and in delivering my inaugural lecture,
and telling this University what it was *not* to expect from me, I used
these words.

Whether the faculty of literary criticism is the best gift that Heaven has
in its treasuries I cannot say; but Heaven seems to think so, for assuredly it
is the gift most charily bestowed. Orators and poets, sages and saints and
heroes, if rare in comparison with blackberries, are commoner than
returns of Halley's comet: literary critics are less common. And when,
once in a century, or once in two centuries, the literary critic does appear –
will some one in this home of mathematics tell me what are the chances
that his appearance will be made among that small number of people who
are called classical scholars? If this purely accidental conjunction occurred
so lately as the eighteenth century in the person of Lessing, it ought to be a
long while before it occurs again; and if so early a century as the twentieth
is to witness it in another person, all I know is that I am not he.

In these twenty-two years I have improved in some respects and
deteriorated in others; but I have not so much improved as to
become a literary critic, nor so much deteriorated as to fancy that I
have become one. Therefore you are not about to be addressed in
that tone of authority which is appropriate to those who are, and is
assumed by some of those who conceive themselves to be, literary
critics. In order to hear Jehovah thundering out of Zion, or Little
Bethel, you must go elsewhere.

But all my life long the best literature of several languages has
been my favourite recreation; and good literature continually read

for pleasure must, let us hope, do some good to the reader: must quicken his perception though dull, and sharpen his discrimination though blunt, and mellow the rawness of his personal opinions. But personal opinions they remain, not truths to be imparted as such with the sureness of superior insight and knowledge. I hope however that for brevity's sake, and your own, you will accept the disclaimer once for all, and that when hereafter I may say that things are thus or thus, you will not insist on my saying instead that I humbly venture to conceive them so or that I diffidently offer the suggestion to your better judgment.

There is indeed one literary subject on which I think I could discourse with profit, because it is also scientific, so that a man of science can handle it without presumption, and indeed is fitter for the task than most men of letters. The Artifice of Versification, which I first thought of taking for my theme to-day, has underlying it a set of facts which are unknown to most of those who practise it; and their success, when they succeed, is owing to instinctive tact and a natural goodness of ear. This latent base, comprising natural laws by which all versification is conditioned, and the secret springs of the pleasure which good versification can give, is little explored by critics: a few pages of Coventry Patmore and a few of Frederic Myers contain all, so far as I know, or all of value, which has been written on such matters;[1] and to these pages I could add a few more. But they would not make a good lecture: first, because of their fewness; secondly, because of their dryness; and thirdly, because they might not be easy for listeners to follow, and what I had to say would be more clearly communicated by writing than by speech. For these reasons I renounced my first intention, and chose instead a subject much less precise, and therefore less suitable to my capacity, and yet one which may be treated, as I hope to treat it, with some degree of precision.

[1] I mean such matters as these: the existence in some metres, not in others, of an inherent alternation of stresses, stronger and weaker; the presence in verse of silent and invisible feet, like rests in music; the reason why some lines of different length will combine harmoniously while others can only be so combined by great skill or good luck; why, while blank verse can be written in lines of ten or six syllables, a series of octosyllables ceases to be verse if they are not rhymed; how Coleridge, in applying the new principle which he announced in the preface to *Christabel*, has fallen between two stools; the necessary limit to inversion of stress, which Milton understood and Bridges overstepped; why, of two pairs of rhymes, equally correct and both consisting of the same vowels and consonants, one is richer to the mental ear and the other poorer; the office of alliteration in verse, and how its definition must be narrowed if it is to be something which can perform that office and not fail of its effect or actually defeat its purpose.

When one begins to discuss the nature of poetry, the first impediment in the way is the inherent vagueness of the name, and the number of its legitimate senses. It is not bad English to speak of 'prose and poetry' in the sense of 'prose and verse.' But it is wasteful; it squanders a valuable word by stretching it to fit a meaning which is accurately expressed by a wider term. Verse may be, like the Tale of Sir Thopas in the judgment of Our Host of the Tabard, 'rym dogerel;' and the name of poetry is generally restricted to verse which can at least be called literature, though it may differ from prose only in its metrical form, and be superior to prose only in the superior comeliness of that form itself, and the superior terseness which usually goes along with it. Then further there is verse which gives a positive and lively pleasure arising from the talent and accomplishment of its author.

> Now Gilpin had a pleasant wit
>   And loved a timely joke,
> And thus unto the Callender
>   In merry guise he spoke:
>
> I came because your horse would come;
>   And, if I well forbode,
> My hat and wig will soon be here:
>   They are upon the road.

Capital: but no one, if asked for a typical example of poetry, would recite those verses in reply. A typical example need not be any less plain and simple and straightforward, but it would be a little raised.

> Come, worthy Greek, Ulysses, come,
>   Possess these shores with me:
> The winds and seas are troublesome,
>   And here we may be free.
> Here may we sit and view their toil
>   That travail in the deep,
> And joy the day in mirth the while,
>   And spend the night in sleep.

There we are ceasing to gallop with the Callender's horse and beginning to fly with Pegasus. Indeed a promising young poetaster could not do better than lay up that stanza in his memory, not necessarily as a pattern to set before him, but as a touchstone to keep at his side. Diction and movement alike, it is perfect. It is made out of the most ordinary words, yet it is pure from the least alloy of prose; and however much nearer heaven the art of poetry may have mounted, it has never flown on a surer or a lighter wing.

It is perfect, I say; and nothing more than perfection can be demanded of anything: yet poetry is capable of more than this, and more therefore is expected from it. There is a conception of poetry which is not fulfilled by pure language and liquid versification, with the simple and so to speak colourless pleasure which they afford, but involves the presence in them of something which moves and touches in a special and recognisable way. Set beside that stanza of Daniel's these lines from Bruce's or Logan's Cuckoo:

> Sweet bird, thy bower is ever green,
>   Thy sky is ever clear;
> Thou hast no sorrow in thy song,
>   No winter in thy year.

There a new element has stolen in, a tinge of emotion. And I think that to transfuse emotion – not to transmit thought but to set up in the reader's sense a vibration corresponding to what was felt by the writer – is the peculiar function of poetry. Even where the verse is not thus beautiful and engaging in its external form, as in Johnson's lines,

> His virtues walked their narrow round,
>   Nor made a pause, nor left a void;
> And sure the Eternal Master found
>   The single talent well employed,

it may yet possess the same virtue and elicit a like response.

Further than this I will not now ascend the stair of poetry. I have chosen these two examples because they may almost be called humble, and contain hardly more than the promise of what poetry attains to be. Here it is not lofty or magnificent or intense; it does not transport with rapture nor overwhelm with awe; it does not stab the heart nor shake the soul nor take the breath away. But it is

poetry, though not in the highest, yet in the highest definable
sense.

> Duncan is in his grave;
> After life's fitful fever he sleeps well.

Even for that poetry there is no other name.

I said that the legitimate meanings of the word poetry were
themselves so many as to embarrass the discussion of its nature. All
the more reason why we should not confound confusion worse by
wresting the term to licentious use and affixing it either to dissimilar
things already provided with names of their own, or to new things
for which new names should be invented.

There was a whole age of English in which the place of poetry
was usurped by something very different which possessed the
proper and specific name of wit: wit not in its modern sense, but as
defined by Johnson, 'a combination of dissimilar images, or dis-
covery of occult resemblances in things apparently unlike.' Such
discoveries are no more poetical than anagrams; such pleasure as
they give is purely intellectual and is intellectually frivolous; but this
was the pleasure principally sought and found in poems by the
intelligentsia of fifty years and more of the seventeenth century.
Some of the writers who purveyed it to their contemporaries were,
by accident, considerable poets; and though their verse was gener-
ally inharmonious, and apparently cut into lengths and tied into
faggots by deaf mathematicians, some little of their poetry was
beautiful and even superb. But it was not by this that they capti-
vated and sought to captivate. Simile and metaphor, things inessen-
tial to poetry, were their great engrossing pre-occupation, and were
prized the more in proportion as they were further fetched. They
did not mean these accessories to be helpful, to make their sense
clearer or their conceptions more vivid; they hardly even meant
them for ornament, or cared whether an image had any indepen-
dent power to please: their object was to startle by novelty and
amuse by ingenuity a public whose one wish was to be so startled
and amused. The pleasure, however luxurious, of hearing St Mary
Magdalene's eyes described as

> Two walking baths, two weeping motions,
> Portable and compendious oceans,

was not a poetic pleasure; and poetry, as a label for this particular commodity, is not appropriate.

Appropriateness is even more carefully to be considered when the thing which we so much admire that we wish to give it the noblest name we can lay our tongue to is a new thing. We should beware of treating the word poetry as chemists have treated the word salt. Salt is a crystalline substance recognised by its taste; its name is as old as the English language and is the possession of the English people, who know what it means: it is not the private property of a science less than three hundred years old, which, being in want of a term to embody a new conception, 'an acid having the whole or part of its hydrogen replaced by a metal,' has lazily helped itself to the old and unsuitable word salt, instead of excogitating a new and therefore to that extent an apt one. The right model for imitation is that chemist who, when he encountered, or thought he had encountered, a hitherto nameless form of matter, did not purloin for it the name of something else, but invented out of his own head a name which should be proper to it, and enriched the vocabulary of modern man with the useful word *gas*. If we apply the word poetry to an object which does not resemble, either in form or content, anything which has heretofore been so called, not only are we maltreating and corrupting language, but we may be guilty of disrespect and blasphemy. Poetry may be too mean a name for the object in question: the object, being certainly something different, may possibly be something superior. When the Lord rained bread from heaven so that man did eat angels' food, and the children of Israel saw upon the face of the wilderness a small round thing, as small as the hoar frost on the ground, they did not call it quails: they rose to the occasion and said to one another 'it is manna.'

There is also such a thing as sham poetry, a counterfeit deliberately manufactured and offered as a substitute. In English the great historical example is certain verse produced abundantly and applauded by high and low in what for literary purposes is loosely called the eighteenth century: not a hundred years accidentally begun and ended by chronology, but a longer period which is a unity and a reality; the period lying between *Samson Agonistes* in 1671 and the *Lyrical Ballads* in 1798, and including as an integral part and indeed as its most potent influence the mature work of Dryden.

Matthew Arnold more than fifty years ago, in speaking of Wordsworth's and Coleridge's low estimate of the poetry of the eighteenth century, issued the warning 'there are many signs to show that the eighteenth century and its judgments are coming into favour again.' I remember thinking to myself that surely this could never be; but there you see what it is to be a literary critic. There has now for a good many years been a strong disposition to revise the verdict pronounced by the nineteenth century on the poetry of the eighteenth and to represent that its disparaging judgment was no more than an expression of distaste for a sort of poetry unlike its own. That is a misconception. It set a low value on the poetry of the eighteenth century, not because it differed in kind from its own, but because, even at its best, it differed in quality, as its own best poetry did not differ, from the poetry of all those ages, whether modern or ancient, English or foreign, which are acknowledged as the great ages of poetry. Tried by that standard the poetry of the eighteenth century, even when not vicious, even when sound and good, fell short.

The literature of the eighteenth century in England is an admirable and most enjoyable thing. It has a greater solidity of excellence than any before or after; and although the special task and characteristic achievement of the age was the invention and establishment of a healthy, workmanlike, athletic prose, to supersede the cumbrous and decorated and self-admiring prose of a Milton or a Jeremy Taylor, and to become a trustworthy implement for accurate thinking and the serious pursuit of truth, yet in verse also it created masterpieces, and perhaps no English poem of greater than lyric length, not even *The Nonne's Priest's Tale* or *The Ancient Mariner*, is quite so perfect as *The Rape of the Lock*. But the human faculty which dominated the eighteenth century and informed its literature was the intelligence, and that involved, as Arnold says, 'some repressing and silencing of poetry,' 'some touch of frost to the imaginative life of the soul.' Man had ceased to live from the depths of his nature; he occupied himself for choice with thoughts which do not range beyond the sphere of the understanding; he lighted the candles and drew down the blind to shut out that patroness of poets, the moon. The writing of poetry proceeded, and much of the poetry written was excellent literature; but excellent literature which is also poetry is not therefore excellent poetry, and the poetry of the eighteenth century was most satisfactory when it did not try to be poetical. Eighteenth-century poetry is in fact a name for two different things, which ought to be kept distinct. There was a good sound workaday article, efficiently discharging a worthy and honourable though not an exalted duty. Satire, controversy, and burlesque, to which the eighteenth century was drawn by the character of its genius, and in which its achievement was unrivalled, are forms of art in which high poetry is not at home, and to which, unless introduced with great parsimony and tact, it would be actually injurious and disfiguring. The conclusion of *The Dunciad* may fairly be called sublime; but such a tone was wisely reserved for the conclusion. The modicum of the poetical element which satire can easily accommodate is rather what we find in lines like these:

> Riches, like insects, when conceal'd they lie,
> Wait but for wings, and in their season fly.
> Who sees pale Mammon pine amidst his store
> Sees but a backward steward for the poor:
>
> This year a reservoir, to keep and spare;
> The next, a fountain, spouting through his heir,
> In lavish streams to quench a country's thirst,
> And men and dogs shall drink him till they burst.

And what sterling stuff they are! But such writing, which was their true glory and should have been their proper pride, did not content its writers. They felt that this, after all, did not rank as equal with the poetry of other ages, nor fulfil the conception of poetry which was obscurely present in their minds; and they aspired to something which should be less pedestrian. It was as though the ostrich should attempt to fly. The ostrich on her own element is the swiftest of created things; she scorneth the horse and his rider; and although we are also told that God hath deprived her of wisdom, neither hath he imparted to her understanding, he has at any rate given her sense enough to know that she is not a lark or an eagle. To poets of the eighteenth century high and impassioned poetry did not come spontaneously, because the feelings which foster its birth were not then abundant and urgent in the inner man; but they girt up their loins and essayed a lofty strain at the bidding of ambition. The way to write real poetry, they thought, must be to write something as little like prose as possible; they devised for the purpose what was called a 'correct and splendid diction,' which consisted in always using the wrong word instead of the right, and plastered it as ornament, with no thought of propriety, on whatever they desired to dignify. It commanded notice and was not easy to mistake; so the public mind soon connected it with the notion of poetry and came in course of time to regard it as alone poetical.[1]

It was in truth at once pompous and poverty-stricken. It had a very limited, because supposedly choice, vocabulary, and was consequently unequal to the multitude and refinement of its duties. It could not describe natural objects with sensitive fidelity to nature; it could not express human feelings with a variety and delicacy answering to their own. A thick, stiff, unaccommodating medium was interposed between the writer and his work. And this deadening of language had a consequence beyond its own sphere: its effect worked inward, and deadened perception. That which could no longer be described was no longer noticed.

The features and formation of the style can be studied under a cruel light in Dryden's translations from Chaucer. The Knight's *Tale of Palamon and Arcite* is not one of Chaucer's most characteristic and successful poems: he is not perfectly at home, as in the *Prologue* and the *Tale of Chauntecleer and Pertelote*, and his movement is a trifle languid. Dryden's translation shows Dryden in the maturity of his power and accomplishment, and much of it can be honestly and

---

[1] It is now customary to say that the nineteenth century had a similar lingo of its own. A lingo it had, or came to have, and in the seventies and eighties the minor poets and poetasters were all using the same supposedly poetic diction. It was imitative and sapless, but not preposterous: its leading characteristic was a stale and faded prettiness.

> As one that for a weary space has lain
>   Lull'd by the song of Circe and her wine
>   In gardens near the pale of Proserpine,
> Where that Æean isle forgets the main,
> And only the low lutes of love complain,
>   And only shadows of wan lovers pine –
>   As such an one were glad to know the brine
> Salt on his lips, and the large air again . . .

The atmosphere of the eighteenth century made much better poets write much worse.

> Lo! where the rosy-bosom'd Hours,
>   Fair Venus' train, appear,
> Disclose the long-expecting flowers
>   And wake the purple year!
> The Attic warbler pours her throat

and so forth.

soberly admired. Nor was he insensible to all the peculiar excellence of Chaucer: he had the wit to keep unchanged such lines as 'Up rose the sun and up rose Emily' or 'The slayer of himself yet saw I there;' he understood that neither he nor anyone else could better them. But much too often in a like case he would try to improve, because he thought that he could. He believed, as he says himself, that he was 'turning some of *The Canterbury Tales* into our language, as it is now refined;' 'the words' he says again 'are given up as a post not to be defended in our poet, because he wanted the modern art of fortifying;' 'in some places' he tells us 'I have added somewhat of my own where I thought my author was deficient, and had not given his thoughts their true lustre, for want of words in the beginning of our language.'

Let us look at the consequences. Chaucer's vivid and memorable line

> The smiler with the knife under the cloke

becomes these three:

> Next stood Hypocrisy, with holy leer,
> Soft smiling and demurely looking down,
> But hid the dagger underneath the gown.

Again:

> Alas, quod he, that day that I was bore.

So Chaucer, for want of words in the beginning of our language. Dryden comes to his assistance and gives his thoughts their true lustre thus:

> Cursed be the day when first I did appear;
> Let it be blotted from the calendar,
> Lest it pollute the month and poison all the year.

Or yet again:

> The queen anon for very womanhead
> Gan for to weep, and so did Emily
> And all the ladies in the company.

If Homer or Dante had the same thing to say, would he wish to say it otherwise? But to Dryden Chaucer wanted the modern art of fortifying, which he thus applies:

358

He said; dumb sorrow seized the standers-by.
The queen, above the rest, by nature good
(The pattern formed of perfect womanhood)
For tender pity wept: when she began
Through the bright quire the infectious virtue ran.
All dropped their tears, even the contended maid.

Had there not fallen upon England the curse out of Isaiah, 'make the heart of this people fat, and make their ears heavy, and shut their eyes'? That there should ever have existed an obtuseness which could mistake this impure verbiage for a correct and splendid diction is a dreadful thought. More dreadful is the experience of seeing it poured profusely, continually, and with evident exultation, from the pen of a great and deservedly illustrious author. But most dreadful of all is the reflexion that he was himself its principal origin. The correctness of calling Emily 'the contended maid' is his correctness, and the splendour of 'through the bright quire the infectious virtue ran' is his own infectious vice. His disciple Pope admired this line so much that he put it twice into his *Iliad*.

Through all her train the soft infection ran.

The infectious softness through the heroes ran.

This same Dryden, when his self-corrupted taste and the false guidance of ambition would let him, could write in verse even better than he wrote in prose, dipping his bucket in the same well of pure, wholesome, racy English. What a joy it is to whistle correctness and splendour down the wind, and hear him speak out straight in the vernacular.

Till frowning skies began to change their cheer,
And time turned up the wrong side of the year.

Bare benting times and moulting months may come,
When lagging late they cannot reach their home.

Your benefices twinkled from afar;
They found the new Messiah by the star.

And not only in his domestic sphere of satire and controversy but in this very book of *Fables*, where he is venturing abroad. To his translation of *The Flower and the Leaf* he prefixed these nineteen lines of his own.

359

Now, turning from the wintry signs, the Sun
His course exalted through the Ram had run,
And whirling up the skies his chariot drove
Through Taurus and the lightsome realms of Love,
Where Venus from her orb descends in showers
To glad the ground and paint the fields with flowers:
When first the tender blades of grass appear
And buds that yet the blast of Eurus fear
Stand at the door of life and doubt to clothe the year,
Till gentle heat and soft repeated rains
Make the green blood to dance within their veins.
Then at their call emboldened out they come
And swell the gems and burst the narrow room,
Broader and broader yet their blooms display,
Salute the welcome sun and entertain the day.
Then from their breathing souls the sweets repair
To scent the skies and purge the unwholesome air:
Joy spreads the heart, and with a general song
Spring issues out and leads the jolly months along.

What exuberant beauty and vigour! and what nature! I believe that I
admire that passage more heartily and relish it more keenly than
Pope or Johnson or Dryden's own contemporaries could, because I
live outside their dungeon, the dungeon in which Dryden himself
had shut them up; because my ears are not contentedly attuned to
the choir of captives singing hymns in the prison chapel, but can
listen to the wild music that burdens every bough in the free world
outside the wall.

Not that even this passage will quite sustain that comparison.
When I am drinking *Barolo stravecchio* in Turin, I am not disturbed,
nor even visited, by the reflexion that there is better wine in Dijon.
But yet there is; and there was better poetry, not reckoning
Milton's, even in the perverse and crooked generation preceding
Dryden. Thinly scattered on that huge dross-heap, the Caroline
Parnassus, there were tiny gems of purer ray; and the most genuine
of Dryden's own poetry is to be found, never more than four lines
at once, seldom more than two, in his early, unshapely, and
wearisome poem the *Annus Mirabilis*.

His great successor, whose *Iliad* was a more dazzling and seductive example of the false manner than any work of Dryden's own, and became, as Coleridge said, 'the main source of our pseudo-poetic diction' – Pope, though he threw open to others the wide gate, did not long keep them company on the broad way, which led them to destruction. He came to recognise, and for the last twenty years of his life he steadily followed, the true bent of his genius, in satire or disputation: into these he put no larger quantity and no rarer quality of poetry than they would assimilate, and he made no more ascents in the balloon. Pope had less of the poetic gift than Dryden; in common with his contemporaries he drew from a poorer vocabulary; and his versification, though more evenly good, did not reach the buoyant excellence of Dryden's at its best. What lifts him nearest to true poetry is sincere inward ardour. Pope had a soul in his body, an aery and fiery particle, when Dryden had nothing but a lump of clay, and he can be nobler than Dryden can. But not even in the *Elegy to the Memory of an Unfortunate Lady* does the fire burn clear of smoke, and truth of emotion do itself full justice in naturalness and purity of diction.

Nuns fret not at their convent's narrow room, and the eighteenth century, except for a few malcontents, was satisfied with what its leading poets provided. 'It is surely superfluous' says Johnson 'to answer the question that has once been asked, whether Pope was a poet, otherwise than by asking in return, if Pope be not a poet, where is poetry to be found?' It is to be found, Dr Johnson, in Dr Watts.

> Soft and easy is thy cradle;
> Coarse and hard thy Saviour lay,
> When his birthplace was a stable
> And his softest bed was hay.

That simple verse, bad rhyme and all, is poetry beyond Pope. It is to be found again, Samuel, in your namesake Benjamin, as tough a piece of timber as yourself.

> What gentle ghost, besprent with April dew,
> Hails me so solemnly to yonder yew,
> And beckoning woos me, from the fatal tree,
> To pluck a garland for herself or me?

When Pope imitated that, he got no nearer than this:

> What beck'ning ghost along the moon–light shade
> Invites my steps and points to yonder glade?
> 'Tis she! – but why that bleeding bosom gor'd, etc.

When I hear anyone say, with defiant emphasis, that Pope was a poet, I suspect him of calling in ambiguity of language to promote confusion of thought. That Pope was a poet is true; but it is one of those truths which are beloved of liars, because they serve so well the cause of falsehood. That Pope was not a poet is false; but a righteous man, standing in awe of the last judgment and the lake which burneth with fire and brimstone, might well prefer to say it.

It is impossible to admire such poetry as Pope's so whole-heartedly as Johnson did, and to rest in it with such perfect contentment, without losing the power to appreciate finer poetry or even to recognise it when met. Johnson's unlucky frankness in letting the world know how he was affected by *Lycidas* has earned his critical judgment discredit enough; but consider also his response to poetry which, though somehow written in the eighteenth century, is of an alien strain and worthy of other ages; consider his attitude to Collins. For Collins himself he felt esteem and liking, and his kind heart must have made him wish to speak well of his friend's poetry; but he was an honest man, and could not.

The first impediment, I said, to dealing with the subject of poetry is the native ambiguity of the term. But the course of these remarks has now brought us to a point where another and perhaps greater difficulty awaits us in determining the competence or incompetence of the judge, that is the sensibility or insensibility of the percipient. Am I capable of recognising poetry if I come across it? Do I possess the organ by which poetry is perceived? The majority of civilised mankind notoriously and indisputably do not; who has certified me that I am one of the minority who do? I may know what I like and admire, I may like and admire it intensely; but what makes me think that it is poetry? Is my reason for thinking so anything more than this: that poetry is generally esteemed the highest form of literature, and that my opinion of myself forbids me to believe that what I most like and admire is anything short of the highest? Yet why be unwilling to admit that perhaps you cannot perceive poetry? Why think it necessary to your self-respect that you should? How many of the good and great, how many saints and heroes have possessed this faculty? Can you hear the shriek of the bat? Probably not; but do you think the less of yourself on that account? do you pretend to others, or even try to persuade yourself, that you can? Is it an unbearable thing, and crushing to self-conceit, to be in the majority?

If a man is insensible to poetry, it does not follow that he gets no pleasure from poems. Poems very seldom consist of poetry and nothing else; and pleasure can be derived also from their other ingredients. I am convinced that most readers, when they think that they are admiring poetry, are deceived by inability to analyse their sensations, and that they are really admiring, not the poetry of the passage before them, but something else in it, which they like better than poetry.

To begin with a very obvious instance. I have been told by devout women that to them the most beautiful poetry is Keble's. Keble is a poet; there are things in *The Christian Year* which can be admired by atheists; but what devout women most prize in it, as Keble himself would have wished, is not its poetry; and I much doubt whether any of them, if asked to pick out the best poem in the book, would turn at once to the *Second Sunday after Easter*. Good religious poetry, whether in Keble or Dante or Job, is likely to be most justly appreciated and most discriminatingly relished by the undevout.

Again, there existed in the last century a great body of Wordsworthians, as they were called. It is now much smaller; but true appreciation of Wordsworth's poetry has not diminished in proportion: I suspect that it has much increased. The Wordsworthians, as Matthew Arnold told them, were apt to praise their poet for the wrong things. They were most attracted by what may be called his philosophy; they accepted his belief in the morality of the universe and the tendency of events to good; they were even willing to entertain his conception of nature as a living and sentient and benignant being, a conception as purely mythological as the Dryads and the Naiads. To that thrilling utterance which pierces the heart and brings tears to the eyes of thousands who care nothing for his opinions and beliefs they were not noticeably sensitive; and however justly they admired the depth of his insight into human nature and the nobility of his moral ideas, these things, with which his poetry was in close and harmonious alliance, are distinct from poetry itself.

When I examine my mind and try to discern clearly in the matter, I cannot satisfy myself that there are any such things as poetical ideas. No truth, it seems to me, is too precious, no observation too profound, and no sentiment too exalted to be expressed in prose. The utmost that I could admit is that some ideas do, while others do not, lend themselves kindly to poetical expression; and that these receive from poetry an enhancement which glorifies and almost transfigures them, and which is not perceived to be a separate thing except by analysis.

'Whosoever will save his life shall lose it, and whosoever will lose his life shall find it.' That is the most important truth which has ever been uttered, and the greatest discovery ever made in the moral world; but I do not find in it anything which I should call poetical. On the other hand, when Wisdom says in the Proverbs 'He that sinneth against me wrongeth his own soul; all they that hate me, love death,' that is to me poetry, because of the words in which the idea is clothed; and as for the seventh verse of the forty-ninth Psalm in the Book of Common Prayer, 'But no man may deliver his brother, nor make agreement unto God for him,' that is to me poetry so moving that I can hardly keep my voice steady in reading it. And that this is the effect of language I can ascertain by experiment: the same thought in the bible version, 'None of them can by any means redeem his brother, nor give to God a ransom for him,' I can read without emotion.

Poetry is not the thing said but a way of saying it. Can it then be isolated and studied by itself? for the combination of language with its intellectual content, its meaning, is as close a union as can well be imagined. Is there such a thing as pure unmingled poetry, poetry independent of meaning?

Even when poetry has a meaning, as it usually has, it may be inadvisable to draw it out. 'Poetry gives most pleasure' said Coleridge 'when only generally and not perfectly understood;' and perfect understanding will sometimes almost extinguish pleasure. *The Haunted Palace* is one of Poe's best poems so long as we are content to swim in the sensations it evokes and only vaguely to apprehend the allegory. We are roused to discomfort, at least I am, when we begin to perceive how exact in detail the allegory is; when it dawns upon us that the fair palace door is Roderick Usher's mouth, the pearl and ruby his teeth and lips, the yellow banners his hair, the ramparts plumed and pallid his forehead, and when we are reduced to hoping, for it is no more than a hope, that the wingèd odours have no connexion with hair-oil.

Meaning is of the intellect, poetry is not. If it were, the eighteenth century would have been able to write it better. As matters actually stand, who are the English poets of that age in whom pre-eminently one can hear and recognise the true poetic accent emerging clearly from the contemporary dialect? These four: Collins, Christopher Smart, Cowper, and Blake. And what other characteristic had these four in common? They were mad. Remember Plato: 'He who without the Muses' madness in his soul comes knocking at the door of poesy and thinks that art will make him anything fit to be called a poet, finds that the poetry which he indites in his sober senses is beaten hollow by the poetry of madmen.'

That the intellect is not the fount of poetry, that it may actually hinder its production, and that it cannot even be trusted to recognise poetry when produced, is best seen in the case of Smart. Neither the prize founded in this University by the Rev. Thomas Seaton nor the successive contemplation of five several attributes of the Supreme Being could incite him to good poetry while he was sane. The only poem by which he is remembered, a poem which came to its own in the kinder climate of the nineteenth century and has inspired one of the best poems of the twentieth, was written, if not, as tradition says, in actual confinement, at any rate very soon after release; and when the eighteenth century, the age of sanity and intelligence, collected his poetical works, it excluded this piece as 'bearing melancholy proofs of the recent estrangement of his mind.'

Collins and Cowper, though they saw the inside of mad-houses, are not supposed to have written any of their poetry there; and Blake was never mad enough to be locked up. But elements of their nature were more or less insurgent against the centralised tyranny of the intellect, and their brains were not thrones on which the great usurper could sit secure. And so it strangely came to pass that in the eighteenth century, the age of prose and of unsound or unsatisfying poetry, there sprang up one well of the purest inspiration. For me the most poetical of all poets is Blake. I find his lyrical note as beautiful as Shakespeare's and more beautiful than anyone else's;

and I call him more poetical than Shakespeare, even though Shakespeare has so much more poetry, because poetry in him preponderates more than in Shakespeare over everything else, and instead of being confounded in a great river can be drunk pure from a slender channel of its own. Shakespeare is rich in thought, and his meaning has power of itself to move us, even if the poetry were not there: Blake's meaning is often unimportant or virtually non-existent, so we can listen with all our hearing to his celestial tune.

Even Shakespeare, who had so much to say, would sometimes pour out his loveliest poetry in saying nothing.

> Take O take those lips away
>   That so sweetly were forsworn,
> And those eyes, the break of day,
>   Lights that do mislead the morn;
> But my kisses bring again,
>   bring again,
> Seals of love, but seal'd in vain,
>   seal'd in vain.

That is nonsense; but it is ravishing poetry. When Shakespeare fills such poetry with thought, and thought which is worthy of it, as in *Fear no more the heat o' the sun* or *O mistress mine, where are you roaming?*, those songs, the very summits of lyrical achievement, are indeed greater and more moving poems, but I hardly know how to call them more poetical.

Now Blake again and again, as Shakespeare now and then, gives us poetry neat, or adulterated with so little meaning that nothing except poetic emotion is perceived and matters.

> Hear the voice of the Bard,
>   Who present, past, and future sees;
> Whose ears have heard
> The Holy Word
>   That walk'd among the ancient trees,
>
> Calling the lapsèd soul
>   And weeping in the evening dew;
> That might control
> The starry pole,
>   And fallen, fallen light renew.

'O Earth, O Earth, return!
  Arise from out the dewy grass;
Night is worn,
And the morn
  Rises from the slumberous mass.

'Turn away no more;
  Why wilt thou turn away?
The starry floor,
The watery shore
  Is giv'n thee till the break of day.'

That mysterious grandeur would be less grand if it were less mysterious; if the embryo ideas which are all that it contains should endue form and outline, and suggestion condense itself into thought.

Memory, hither come
  And tune your merry notes;
And while upon the wind
  Your music floats
I'll pore upon the stream
Where sighing lovers dream,
And fish for fancies as they pass
Within the watery glass.

That answers to nothing real; memory's merry notes and the rest are empty phrases, not things to be imagined; the stanza does but entangle the reader in a net of thoughtless delight. The verses which I am now going to read probably possessed for Blake a meaning, and his students think that they have found it; but the meaning is a poor foolish disappointing thing in comparison with the verses themselves.

My Spectre around me night and day
Like a wild beast guards my way;
My Emanation far within
Weeps incessantly for my sin.

A fathomless and boundless deep,
There we wander, there we weep;
On the hungry craving wind
My Spectre follows thee behind.

He scents thy footsteps in the snow
Wheresoever thou dost go:
Through the wintry hail and rain
When wilt thou return again?

Dost thou not in pride and scorn
Fill with tempests all my morn,
And with jealousies and fears
Fill my pleasant nights with tears?

Seven of my sweet loves thy knife
Has bereavèd of their life.
Their marble tombs I built with tears
And with cold and shuddering fears.

Seven more loves weep night and day
Round the tombs where my loves lay,
And seven more loves attend each night
Around my couch with torches bright.

And seven more loves in my bed
Crown with wine my mournful head,
Pitying and forgiving all
Thy transgressions great and small.

When wilt thou return and view
My loves, and them to life renew?
When wilt thou return and live?
When wilt thou pity as I forgive?

I am not equal to framing definite ideas which would match that
magnificent versification and correspond to the strong tremor of
unreasonable excitement which those words set up in some region
deeper than the mind. Lastly take this stanza, addressed 'to the
Accuser who is the God of this World'.

Tho' thou art worship'd by the names divine
Of Jesus and Jehovah, thou art still
The Son of Morn in weary Night's decline,
The lost traveller's dream under the hill.

It purports to be theology: what theological sense, if any, it may
have, I cannot imagine and feel no wish to learn: it is pure and

368

self-existent poetry, which leaves no room in me for anything besides.

In most poets, as I said, poetry is less often found thus disengaged from its usual concomitants, from certain things with which it naturally unites itself and seems to blend indistinguishably. For instance:

> Sorrow, that is not sorrow, but delight;
> And miserable love, that is not pain
> To hear of, for the glory that redounds
> Therefrom to human kind, and what we are.

The feeling with which those lines are read is composite, for one constituent is supplied by the depth and penetrating truth of the thought. Again:

> Though love repine and reason chafe,
>   There came a voice without reply, –
> ''Tis man's perdition to be safe,
>   When for the truth he ought to die.'

Much of the emotion kindled by that verse can be referred to the nobility of the sentiment. But in these six simple words of Milton –

> Nymphs and shepherds, dance no more –

what is it that can draw tears, as I know it can, to the eyes of more readers than one? What in the world is there to cry about? Why have the mere words the physical effect of pathos when the sense of the passage is blithe and gay? I can only say, because they are poetry, and find their way to something in man which is obscure and latent, something older than the present organisation of his nature, like the patches of fen which still linger here and there in the drained lands of Cambridgeshire.

Poetry indeed seems to me more physical than intellectual. A year or two ago, in common with others, I received from America a request that I would define poetry. I replied that I could no more define poetry than a terrier can define a rat, but that I thought we both recognised the object by the symptoms which it provokes in us. One of these symptoms was described in connexion with another object by Eliphaz the Temanite: 'A spirit passed before my face: the hair of my flesh stood up.' Experience has taught me, when

369

I am shaving of a morning, to keep watch over my thoughts, because, if a line of poetry strays into my memory, my skin bristles so that the razor ceases to act. This particular symptom is accompanied by a shiver down the spine; there is another which consists in a constriction of the throat and a precipitation of water to the eyes; and there is a third which I can only describe by borrowing a phrase from one of Keats's last letters, where he says, speaking of Fanny Brawne, 'everything that reminds me of her goes through me like a spear.' The seat of this sensation is the pit of the stomach.

My opinions on poetry are necessarily tinged, perhaps I should say tainted, by the circumstance that I have come into contact with it on two sides. We were saying a while ago that poetry is a very wide term, and inconveniently comprehensive: so comprehensive is it that it embraces two books, fortunately not large ones, of my own. I know how this stuff came into existence; and though I have no right to assume that any other poetry came into existence in the same way, yet I find reason to believe that some poetry, and quite good poetry, did. Wordsworth for instance says that poetry is the spontaneous overflow of powerful feelings, and Burns has left us this confession, 'I have two or three times in my life composed from the wish rather than the impulse, but I never succeeded to any purpose.' In short I think that the production of poetry, in its first stage, is less an active than a passive and involuntary process; and if I were obliged, not to define poetry, but to name the class of things to which it belongs, I should call it a secretion; whether a natural secretion, like turpentine in the fir, or a morbid secretion, like the pearl in the oyster. I think that my own case, though I may not deal with the material so cleverly as the oyster does, is the latter; because I have seldom written poetry unless I was rather out of health, and the experience, though pleasurable, was generally agitating and exhausting. If only that you may know what to avoid, I will give some account of the process.

Having drunk a pint of beer at luncheon – beer is a sedative to the brain, and my afternoons are the least intellectual portion of my life – I would go out for a walk of two or three hours. As I went along, thinking of nothing in particular, only looking at things around me and following the progress of the seasons, there would flow into my mind, with sudden and unaccountable emotion, sometimes a line or two of verse, sometimes a whole stanza at once, accompanied, not preceded, by a vague notion of the poem which they were destined to form part of. Then there would usually be a lull of an hour or so, then perhaps the spring would bubble up again. I say bubble up, because, so far as I could make out, the source of the suggestions thus proffered to the brain was an abyss which I have already had occasion to mention, the pit of the stomach. When I got home I wrote them down, leaving gaps, and hoping that further inspiration might be forthcoming another day. Sometimes it was, if I took my walks in a receptive and expectant frame of mind; but sometimes the poem had to be taken in hand and completed by the brain, which was apt to be a matter of trouble and anxiety, involving trial and disappointment, and sometimes ending in failure. I happen to remember distinctly the genesis of the piece which stands last in my first volume. Two of the stanzas, I do not say which, came into my head, just as they are printed, while I was crossing the corner of Hampstead Heath between the Spaniard's Inn and the footpath to Temple Fortune. A third stanza came with a little coaxing after tea. One more was needed, but it did not come: I had to turn to and compose it myself, and that was a laborious business. I wrote it thirteen times, and it was more than a twelvemonth before I got it right.

By this time you must be sated with anatomy, pathology, and autobiography, and willing to let me retire from my incursion into the foreign territory of literary criticism. Farewell for ever. I will not say with Coleridge that I recentre my immortal mind in the deep sabbath of meek self-content; but I shall go back with relief and thankfulness to my proper job.

FROM THE CLASSICAL EDITIONS

===

The Editing of Manilius

Perhaps no critic has ever effected so great and permanent a change in any author's text as Scaliger in Manilius'. Except the *Emendatio Temporum*, which is too dissimilar for comparison, this is his greatest work; and its virtues, if they had fewer vices to keep them company, are such that it is almost importunate to praise them. True, there is luck as well as merit in the achievement: many of his emendations required no Scaliger to make them, and were made by Scaliger only because Manilius hitherto, instead of finding a Beroaldus or Marullus to befriend him, had fallen, as he was destined often to fall again, into the hands of dullards. To write *tum di* for *timidi* in I 422 was a feat of easy brilliancy, and such corrections are less of an honour to Scaliger than a shame to his predecessors; but after all deductions there remains enough to make a dozen editors illustrious. The commentary is the one commentary on Manilius, without forerunner and without successor; to-day, after the passage of three hundred years, it is the only avenue to a study of the poem. He seems to have read everything, Greek and Latin, published and unpublished, which could explain or illustrate his author; and his vast learning is carried lightly and imparted simply in terse notes of moderate compass. Discursive he often is, and sometimes vagrant, but even in digressions he neither fatigues his readers like Casaubon nor bewilders them like Salmasius. His style has not the ease and grace and Latinity of Lambinus', but no commentary is brisker reading or better entertainment than these abrupt and pithy notes, with their spurts of mockery at unnamed detractors, and their frequent and significant stress upon the difference between Scaliger and a jackass.

There is a reverse to the medal, and I give it in the words of his most intelligent enemy, Huet p. 87.

[. . .]

In particular he will often propound interpretations which have no bearing either on his own text of Manilius or on any other, but pertain to things which he has read elsewhere, and which hang like mists in his memory and veil from his eyes the verses which he thinks he is explaining.

Huet was a critic of uncommon exactness, sobriety, and malevolence, whose naturally keen wits were sharpened to a finer edge by his dislike of Scaliger. He frankly owns in chapter V of the Huetiana 'je n'ai écrit sur Manile que pour faire voir que dans les trois éditions de ce Poëte il (Scaliger) a entassé fautes sur fautes et ignorances sur ignorances.' Hence it happens, in the irony of human affairs, that he, the shrewd and accomplished Huet, is now excessively admired by the dull, who cherish a timid enmity for great and victorious innovators, and delight to see them rapped over the knuckles by Huet or anyone else who has the requisite address. His services to Manilius are not so many and great as to estrange the affection of these admirers; indeed it would be hard to find 300 verses in a row for which Scaliger has not done more than Huet did for all five books together. Perhaps if he had been less bent on harming Scaliger he might have helped Manilius more: at any rate it is matter for some surprise and disappointment that so competent a critic should after all have done so little where there was so much to do. But the fact is that his mind had keenness without force, and was not a trenchant instrument. His corrections, deft as they are, touch only the surface of the text; his precise and lucid explanations are seldom explanations of difficulties, but only dispel perverse misunderstandings of things which hardly any one but Scaliger can ever have misunderstood. When a real obscurity had baffled Scaliger, it baffled Huet, and was reprieved till the advent of Bentley.

Lucida tela diei: these are the words that come into one's mind when one has halted at some stubborn perplexity of reading or interpretation, has witnessed Scaliger and Gronouius and Huetius fumble at it one after another, and then turns to Bentley and sees Bentley strike his finger on the place and say *thou ailest here, and here.*

★

Great as was Scaliger's achievement it is yet surpassed and far surpassed by Bentley's: Scaliger at the side of Bentley is no more than a marvellous boy. In mere quantity indeed the corrections of the critic who came first may be the more imposing, but it is significant that Scaliger accomplished most in the easiest parts of the poem and Bentley in the hardest. The firm strength and piercing edge and arrowy swiftness of his intellect, his matchless facility and adroitness and resource, were never so triumphant as where defeat seemed sure; and yet it is other virtues that one most admires and welcomes as one turns from the smoky fire of Scaliger's genius to the sky and air of Bentley's: his lucidity, his sanity, his just and simple and straightforward fashion of thought. His emendations are only a part, though the most conspicuous part, of his services to Manilius; for here, as in Horace, there are many passages which he was the first to vindicate from mistaken conjecture by discovering their true interpretation. He had furnished himself too with fresh and efficacious tools: he had procured not only the use of G but collations of L and also, more important, of V, which first revealed in a clear form the tradition of the second family; and from II 684, where V begins, to the end of the poem, his incomparable skill and judgment in the use of MSS have left but little in this department for his successors to do, provided they have the wit, or in default of that the modesty, to follow his example.

The faults of this edition, which are abundant, are the faults of Bentley's other critical works. He was impatient, he was tyrannical, and he was too sure of himself. Hence he corrupts sound verses which he will not wait to understand, alters what offends his taste without staying to ask about the taste of Manilius, plies his desperate hook upon corruptions which do not yield at once to gentler measures, and treats the MSS much as if they were fellows of Trinity. Nay more: though Bentley's faculty for discovering truth has no equal in the history of learning, his wish to discover it was not so strong. Critics like Porson and Lachmann, inferior in εὐστοχία and ἀγχίνοια, put him to shame by their serious and disinterested purpose and the honesty of their dealings with themselves. His buoyant mind, elated by the exercise of its powers, too often forgot the nature of its business, and turned from work to play; and many a time when he feigned and half fancied that he was correcting the scribe, he knew in his heart (and of his *Paradise Lost* they tell us he confessed it) that he was revising the author.

*

It was one of Bentley's chief services to the text that he first detected the presence there of spurious verses. But this discovery, like Scaliger's discovery of transpositions in Propertius, was misused and perverted by its own author till its utility was well-nigh cancelled and its credit annulled. When a genuine verse was so corrupt that no meaning glimmered through it, and even Bentley's divination was baffled at the first assault, then the impatient critic, who had no turn for tiresome blockades, chastised its recalcitrancy by proclaiming it counterfeit. He forgot that counterfeit verses are not wont to be meaningless unless they are corrupt as well, and that the aim of interpolators is not to make difficulties but to remove them. The best prize that Bentley missed, and the richest province left for his successors, is the correction of those verses of Manilius which he precipitately and despotically expelled.

*

If a man will comprehend the richness and variety of the universe, and inspire his mind with a due measure of wonder and of awe, he must contemplate the human intellect not only on its heights of genius but in its abysses of ineptitude; and it might be fruitlessly debated to the end of time whether Richard Bentley or Elias Stoeber was the more marvellous work of the Creator: Elias Stoeber, whose reprint of Bentley's text, with a commentary intended to confute it, saw the light in 1767 at Strasburg, a city still famous for its geese. This commentary is a performance in comparison with which the *Aetna* of Mr S. Sudhaus is a work of science and of genius. Stoeber's mind, though that is no name to call it by, was one which turned as unswervingly to the false, the meaningless, the unmetrical, and the ungrammatical, as the needle to the pole.

*

Bentley is first, and Scaliger second, among the conjectural emendators of Manilius, and there is no third; but if there were a third it would be Jacob. Say what you will, he has contributed to the *Astronomica*, as to the *Aetna* twenty years before, a body of corrections not only considerable in number but often of the most arresting ingenuity and penetration. Yet the virtues of his work are quenched and smothered by the multitude and monstrosity of its vices. They say that he was born of human parentage; but if so he must have been suckled by Caucasian tigers. His false quantities, *quāter, octŏtopos, sūb hoc, cónōr ét, numerabīs ordine, scorpiŏn* nom., *fēmina* neut. plur., are the least and fewest of the horrors here amassed upon Manilius. Not only had Jacob no sense for grammar, no sense for coherency, no sense for sense, but being himself possessed by a passion for the clumsy and the hispid he imputed this disgusting taste to all the authors whom he edited; and Manilius, the one Latin poet who excels even Ovid in verbal point and smartness, is accordingly constrained to write the sort of poetry which might have been composed by Nebuchadnezzar when he was driven from men and did eat grass as oxen.

*

In the notes with which he now and again supports his corruptions and misinterpretations of the text he seems to stick at no falsehood and no absurdity which the pen will consent to trace on paper. In short his book, if only its vices are considered, is a scarce less woful piece of work than Stoeber's: the difference is that, while Stoeber never reminds one of a rational animal, the fog of Jacob's intellect is shot through, and that not seldom, by flashes of conspicuous and startling brilliancy. They are Capricorn and Sagittarius: pars huic hominis, sed nulla priori.

*

Some ancient authors have descended to modern times in one MS only, or in a few MSS derived immediately or with little interval from one. Such are Lucretius, Catullus, Valerius Flaccus, and Statius in his *siluae*. Others there are whose text, though in the main reposing on a single copy, can be corrected here and there from others, inferior indeed, but still independent and indispensable. Such are Juvenal, Ovid in his *Heroides*, Seneca in his tragedies, and Statius in his *Thebais* and *Achilleis*. There is a third class whose text comes down from a remote original through separate channels, and is preserved by MSS of unlike character but like fidelity, each serving in its turn to correct the faults of others. Such are Persius, Lucan, Martial, and Manilius.

If I had no judgment, and knew it, and were nevertheless immutably resolved to edit a classic, I would single out my victim from the first of these three classes: that would be best for the victim and best for me. Authors surviving in a solitary MS are by far the easiest to edit, because their editor is relieved from one of the most exacting offices of criticism, from the balancing of evidence and the choice of variants. They are the easiest, and for a fool they are the safest. One field at least for the display of folly is denied him: others are open, and in defending, correcting, and explaining the written text he may yet aspire to make a scarecrow of the author and a byword of himself; but with no variants to afford him scope for choice and judgment he cannot exhibit his impotence to judge and choose.

But the worst of having no judgment is that one never misses it, and buoyantly embarks without it upon enterprises in which it is not so much a convenience as a necessity. Hence incompetent editors are not found flocking to texts like Valerius Flaccus' and leaving texts like Manilius' alone. They essay to edit the latter no less promptly than the former; and then comes the pinch. They find themselves unexpectedly committed to a business which demands not only the possession, but the constant exercise, of intellectual faculties. An editor of no judgment, perpetually confronted with a couple of MSS to choose from, cannot but feel in every fibre of his being that he is a donkey between two bundles of hay. What shall he do now? Leave criticism to critics, you may say, and betake himself to any honest trade for which he is less unfit. But he prefers a more flattering solution: he confusedly imagines that if one bundle of hay is removed he will cease to be a donkey.

So he removes it. Are the two MSS equal, and do they bewilder him with their rival merit and exact from him at every other moment the novel and distressing effort of using his brains? Then he pretends that they are not equal: he calls one of them 'the best MS,' and to this he resigns the editorial functions which he is himself unable to discharge. He adopts its readings when they are better than its fellow's, adopts them when they are no better, adopts them when they are worse: only when they are impossible, or rather when he perceives their impossibility, is he dislodged from his refuge and driven by stress of weather to the other port.

This method answers the purpose for which it was devised: it saves lazy editors from working and stupid editors from thinking. But somebody has to pay for these luxuries, and that somebody is the author; since it must follow, as the night the day, that this method should falsify his text. Suppose, if you will, that the editor's 'best MS' is in truth the best: his way of using it is none the less ridiculous. To believe that wherever a best MS gives possible readings it gives true readings, and that only where it gives impossible readings does it give false readings, is to believe that an incompetent editor is the darling of Providence, which has given its angels charge over him lest at any time his sloth and folly should produce their natural results and incur their appropriate penalty. Chance and the common course of nature will not bring it to pass that the readings of a MS are right wherever they are possible and impossible wherever they are wrong: that needs divine intervention; and when one considers the history of man and the spectacle of the universe I hope one may say without impiety that divine intervention might have been better employed elsewhere. How the world is managed, and why it was created, I cannot tell; but it is no feather-bed for the repose of sluggards.

Apart from its damage to the author, it might perhaps be thought that this way of editing would bring open scorn upon the editors, and that the whole reading public would rise up and tax them, as I tax them now, with ignorance of their trade and dereliction of their duty. But the public is soon disarmed. This planet is largely inhabited by parrots, and it is easy to disguise folly by giving it a fine name. Those who live and move and have their being in the world of words and not of things, and employ language less as a vehicle than as a substitute for thought, are readily duped by the assertion that this stolid adherence to a favourite MS, instead of being, as it is, a private and personal necessity imposed on certain editors by their congenital defects, is a principle; and that its name is 'scientific criticism' or 'critical method.' This imposture is helped by the fact that there really are such things as scientific methods and principles of criticism, and that the 19th century was specially distinguished by a special application of these methods and principles which is easily confused, by parrots, with the unprincipled and unmethodical practice now in question. Till 1800 and later no attempt was made by scholars to determine the genealogy and affiliation of MSS: science and method, applied to this end by the generation of Bekker and Lachmann, Madvig and Cobet, have cast hundreds of MSS, once deemed authorities, on the dust-heap, have narrowed the circle of witnesses by excluding those who merely repeat what they have heard from others, and have proved that the text of certain authors reposes on a single document from which all other extant MSS are copied. Hence it is no hard task to diffuse among parrots the notion that an editor who assigns preponderant authority to any single MS is following the principles of critical science, since the question whether the MS really possesses that authority is one which does not suggest itself to the creature of which Pliny has written 'capiti eius duritia eadem quae rostro.' Nay more: the public is predisposed in favour of the falsehood, and has reasons for wishing to believe it true. Tell the average man that inert adhesion to one authority is methodical criticism, and you tell him good news: I too, thinks he, have the makings of a methodical critic about me. 'Man kann nur etwas aussprechen,' said Goethe, 'was dem Eigendünkel und der Bequemlichkeit schmeichelt, um eines grossen Anhanges in der mittelmässigen Menge gewiss zu sein.'

But still there is a hitch. Competent editors exist; and side by side with those who have embraced 'the principles of criticism,' there are those who follow the practice of critics: who possess intellects, and employ them on their work. Consequently their work is better done, and the contrast is mortifying. This is not as it should be. As the wise man dieth, so dieth the fool: why then should we allow them to edit the classics differently? If nature, with flagitious partiality, has given judgment and industry to some men and left other men without them, it is our evident duty to amend her blind caprice; and those who are able and willing to think must be deprived of their unfair advantage by stringent prohibitions. In Association football you must not use your hands, and similarly in textual criticism you must not use your brains. Since we cannot make fools behave like wise men, we will insist that wise men should behave like fools: by these means only can we redress the injustice of nature and anticipate the equality of the grave.

To this end, not only has the simple process of opening one's mouth and shutting one's eyes been dignified by the title of 'eine streng wissenschaftliche Methode,' but rational criticism has been branded with a term of formal reprobation. 'Butter and honey shall he eat,' says Isaiah of Immanuel, *'that he may know to refuse the evil and choose the good.'* This is a very bad system of education: to refuse the evil and choose the good is 'der reinste Eclecticismus.'

By this use of tickets it is rendered possible, in a world where names are mistaken for things, not only to be thoughtless and idle without discredit, but even to be vain of your vices and to reprove your neighbour for his lack of them. It is rendered possible to pamper self-complacency while indulging laziness; and the 'scientific critic,' unlike the rest of mankind, contrives to enjoy in combination the usually incompatible luxuries of shirking his work and despising his superiors.

Thus are good MSS converted into implements of destruction. In books like Manilius and Lucan, preserved in various copies of equal merit, the editor cloaks his frailty by feigning that their merit is not equal: in books like Juvenal and Ovid's *Heroides*, where one MS far excels the rest, he feigns that it excels them further, and tries hard to treat it not merely as the best but as the sole authority. The poet is brought low that the MS may be exalted.

*

But it is in books where there is no best MS at all, and the editor, in order to escape the duty of editing, is compelled to feign one, that the worst mischief ensues; and those authors whose text the kindness of fortune has transmitted from a remote original through separate channels of equal purity are now deprived of their advantage and mechanically consigned to depravation for fear a sluggish brain should be required to work: butchered to make a German holiday, or an English one.

*

But no more dismal example of an author corrupted through and through by the very means which fortune has ordained for his preservation and restitution is anywhere to be found than the two last editions of Manilius. To elude what Byron calls 'the blight of life – the demon Thought,' Messrs Jacob and Bechert have committed themselves respectively to the Vossianus and the Gemblacensis, the devil and the deep sea. Having small literary culture they are not revolted by illiteracy, having slight knowledge of grammar they are not revolted by solecism, having no sequence of ideas they are not revolted by incoherency, having nebulous thoughts they are not revolted by nonsense: on the contrary the illiterate and ungrammatical and inconsecutive and meaningless things with which both

MSS abound are supposed by their respective votaries to be 'Manilian,' and each believes himself a connoisseur of the poet's peculiar style. Strange to say, their conception of that style is identical; and the two texts, though based on opposite authorities and diverging in innumerable details, have in their general aspect a conspicuous and frightful similarity. The Manilian peculiarities of v are just like the Manilian peculiarities of G, for the simple reason that they are neither Manilian nor peculiar. They are ordinary corruptions; and Jacob can see that this is so in G, and Bechert can see it in v. And after all, though they may mount their hobbies, they cannot stick in the saddle. Again and again their favourites offer readings which they are forced to abandon, and to accept the readings of the rival MSS; but these lessons they hasten to forget, and are no wiser next time.

Thus far of the places where our MSS dissent, and the reading of their archetype is to be regained by choice and comparison. Where they agree, there the text of the archetype is before us, an archetype, like themselves, corrupt and interpolated; and now begins the business of correcting this. But first, in every place where the tradition is thus clearly ascertained, comes the question whether this be not itself the truth; and it is no simple question. The Romans are foreigners and write to please themselves, not us; Latin poets compose Latin poetry, which is very unlike English or German poetry; and each writer has his own peculiarities and the peculiarities of his generation and his school, which must be learnt by observation and cannot be divined by taste. In Manilius, an author both corrupt and difficult, who since the revival of learning has had few competent students, it is no cause for wonder that even after Scaliger and Bentley there remains as much to explain as to emend, and that these toiling giants, amidst loads of rubbish, have carted away some fragments of the fabric. A properly informed and properly attentive reader will find that many verses hastily altered by some editors and absurdly defended by others can be made to yield a just sense without either changing the text or inventing a new Latinity; and I think that I have often vindicated the MSS by a reasonable explanation in passages where my betters had assailed them.

But those who can understand what Scaliger and Bentley and

Gronouius and Heinsius and Lachmann could not understand are now so numerous, and their daily exploits in hermeneutics are so repulsive and deterrent, that I have avoided nothing so anxiously as this particular mode of being ridiculous; and it is likely enough that my dread of seeming to march with the times has led me here and there to err on the side of caution, and timidly to alter what I might without rashness have defended.

*

   The art of explaining corrupt passages instead of correcting them is imagined by those who now practise it to be something new, a discovery of these last twenty years. But man is not thus tardy in devising follies. Wakefield's Lucretius, to go no further back, is a stately monument of the craft; Goerenz plied it busily in Cicero and Fickert in Seneca before ever Mr Buecheler wrote a word, and in Alschefski's Livy the style produced a masterpiece as yet unrivalled by Mr Sudhaus himself. What stamps the last twenty years with their special character is not the presence of such scholars as these but the absence of great scholars. During the other part of the 19th century, before the North-German school had entered on its decline, critics of this order were no less plentiful than now, – *the poor shall never cease out of the land* says the scripture, – but they were cowed and kept under by critics of another order. To-day this tyranny is overpast: the Lachmanns and Madvigs are gone, the Mosers and Forbigers remain; and now they lift up their heads and rejoice aloud at the emancipation of human incapacity. History repeats itself, and we now witness in Germany pretty much what happened in England after 1825, when our own great age of scholarship, begun in 1691 by Bentley's *Epistola ad Millium*, was ended by the successive strokes of doom which consigned Dobree and Elmsley to the grave and Blomfield to the bishopric of Chester. England disappeared from the fellowship of nations for the next forty years: Badham, the one English scholar of the mid-century whose reputation crossed the Channel, received from abroad the praises of Duebner and Nauck and Cobet, but at home was excluded from academical preferment, set to teach boys at Birmingham, and finally transported to the antipodes: his country-men, having turned their backs on Europe and science and the past, sat down to banquet on mutual approbation, to produce the

Classical Museum and the Bibliotheca Classica, and to perish without a name.

★

The average man, if he meddles with criticism at all, is a conservative critic. His opinions are determined not by his reason, – 'the bulk of mankind' says Swift 'is as well qualified for flying as for thinking,' – but by his passions; and the faintest of all human passions is the love of truth. He believes that the text of ancient authors is generally sound, not because he has acquainted himself with the elements of the problem, but because he would feel uncomfortable if he did not believe it; just as he believes, on the same cogent evidence, that he is a fine fellow, and that he will rise again from the dead. And since the classical public, like all other publics, is chiefly composed of average men, he is encouraged to hold this belief and to express it. But beside this general cause there are peculiar circumstances which explain and even excuse the present return to superstition. At the end of the great age, in the sixties and seventies, conjecture was employed, and that by very eminent men, irrationally. Ritschl's dealings with Plautus and Nauck's with the Attic tragedians were violent and arbitrary beyond all bounds; and their methods were transferred to the sphere of dactylic poetry by Baehrens, a man of vast energy and vigorous intelligence but of unripe judgment and faulty scholarship, who with one hand conferred on the Latin poets more benefits than any critic since Lachmann and with the other imported ten times as many corruptions as he removed.

This could not last, and a student of the world's history might have predicted what has now ensued. Error, if allowed to run its course, secures its own downfall, and is sooner or later overthrown, not by the truth, but by error of an opposite kind. When this misuse of conjecture had disgusted not only the judicious but the greater number of the injudicious, there followed a recoil, and it now became the fashion, instead of correcting the handiwork of poets, to interpret the handiwork of scribes. The conservative reaction was chiefly fostered by the teaching and example of Messrs Vahlen and Buecheler: men of wide learning and no mean acuteness, but without simplicity of judgment. Once set going by critics of repute, the movement, commended by its very nature to the general public, has prospered as downhill movements do; and its original leaders, as usually happens to those who instruct mankind in easy and agreeable vices, are far outdone by their disciples. In racing back to the feet of Alschefski Messrs Buecheler and Vahlen are hampered by two grave encumbrances: they know too much Latin, and they are not sufficiently obtuse. Among their pupils are several who comprehend neither Latin nor any other language, and whom nature has prodigally endowed at birth with that hebetude of intellect which Messrs Vahlen and Buecheler, despite their assiduous and protracted efforts, have not yet succeeded in acquiring. Thus equipped, the apprentices proceed to exegetical achievements of which their masters are incapable, and which perhaps inspire those masters less with envy than with fright: indeed I imagine that Mr Buecheler, when he first perused Mr Sudhaus' edition of the *Aetna*, must have felt something like Sin when she gave birth to Death.

*

The promptness with which these scholars defend the corrupt and the ease with which they explain the inexplicable are at first sight a strange contrast to the embarrassment they suffer where the text is sound and the difficulty they find in understanding Latin. Indeed it may almost be said of them that if they are to construe a passage fluently the passage must be corrupted first. But the one phenomenon is only the result of the other. If a man is acquainted with the Latin tongue and with the speech of poets, he is sharply warned of corruption in a Latin poet's text by finding that he can make neither head nor tail of it. But Mr Vollmer and his fellows receive no such admonitory shock; for all Latin poets, even where the text is flawless, abound in passages of which they can make neither head nor tail. Thus they gradually come to regard Latin poetry as having absurdity for its main characteristic; and when they encounter in a corrupt passage the bad grammar or nonsense which they habitually impute to an author by misunderstanding what he has written, they encounter nothing unexpected.

*

By this time it has become apparent what the modern conservative critic really is: a creature moving about in worlds not realised. His trade is one which requires, that it may be practised in perfection, two qualifications only: ignorance of language and abstinence from thought. The tenacity with which he adheres to the testimony of scribes has no relation to the trustworthiness of that testimony, but is dictated wholly by his inability to stand alone. If one cannot discriminate between grammar and solecism, sequence and incoherency, sense and nonsense, one has no protection against falsehood, and believes all the lies one is told. And critics who treat MS evidence as rational men treat all evidence, and test it by reason and by the knowledge which they have acquired, these are blamed for rashness and capriciousness by gentlemen who use MSS as drunkards use lamp-posts, – not to light them on their way but to dissimulate their instability.

I hope and believe then that my numerous defences and explanations of passages attacked and altered by Scaliger and Bentley are not such as would have occurred to Mr Vollmer or Mr Sudhaus, and that I have nowhere encroached on the ample field which Manilius' text affords them for the exercise of their favourite industry and the display of their peculiar prowess.

*

When a passage is apparently inexplicable and probably corrupt, then comes the question, by what means shall we correct it? and here, first of all, we must have no favourite method. An emendator with one method is as foolish a sight as a doctor with one drug. The scribes knew and cared no more about us and our tastes than diseases care about the taste of doctors; they made mistakes not of one sort but of all sorts, and the remedies must be of all sorts too. Haase in Seneca, for ever assuming lacunas, and Bake in Cicero, for ever assuming glosses, are examples of editors maimed by their own whims: criticism requires a mind as various as its matter, nimble, flexible, empty of prepossessions and alert for every hint. It is neither my business nor my purpose to rehearse and classify here the modes of emendation; but I shall mention two, because some readers will perhaps suppose them to be favourites of my own. I do not think so myself: I think that the reason why I have to use them so often is that my predecessors have not used them often enough. They are the antidotes of two particular sorts of corruption whose ease and frequency are not yet fully understood.

*

It is no reproach to Scaliger and Bentley that they, amidst the dust of their labours and the blaze of their discoveries, left much undone which was easy to do and overlooked many things which were plain to see. But it is a heavy reproach to the other editors, whose discoveries are not dazzling and whose labours are not Titanic, that they have let slip so many obvious and trivial blunders whose detection required neither genius nor effort but only common attention and ordinary acquaintance with Latin. It is not decent that I, in the 20th century after Christ, should have to remark that Pyrrhus (I 786) was not defeated by Papirius; that 'intra Capricorni sidus et mundum imo axe subnixum' (I 375 sq.) is not Latin for inter; and that Phryxaei (III 304) is not the way to spell Phrixei.

[ADDENDA]

The succeeding editors Breiter and van Wageningen learnt from me how to spell Phrixei; but I did not tell them how to spell Tydiden or Arachnaeo, so they never knew.

*

When Breiter, to whom I sent a copy of my first volume, had read the information I gave on these pages about the two codd. Vrbinates, he set off post-haste for Rome, discovered them himself, and published his discovery in the Woch. f. klass. Phil. 1904 pp. 669–72. There are therefore now in Germany two sects of opinion concerning these M S S: some hold that they are of value and were brought to light by Breiter, others that they are of no value and were brought to light by me. Because I had called them U and R, Breiter called them u^2 and u^1; for his statement in vol. I p. vi that he followed Bechert in this notation is false. Because I had said that they were mutually independent, he said that R might be regarded as a copy of U.

*

I did not praise Bechert's accuracy, because accuracy is a duty and not a virtue; but if I could have foreseen the shameful carelessness of Breiter and van Wageningen I should have said with emphasis, as I do now, that he was very accurate indeed.

*

I have chosen this sentence for preservation as a specimen of the arts which it was thought permissible and advisable to employ against me when I made my unwelcome appearance. 'Le mensonge' said Voltaire 'n'est un vice que quand il fait du mal; c'est une très grande vertu quand il fait du bien;' and my detractors were of his opinion. I enjoy the unfair advantage of being able to say disagreeable things about them without any departure from the truth.

★

The first volume of the edition of Manilius now completed was published in 1903, the second in 1912, the third in 1916, and the fourth in 1920. All were produced at my own expense and offered to the public at much less than cost price; but this unscrupulous artifice did not overcome the natural disrelish of mankind for the combination of a tedious author with an odious editor. Of each volume there were printed 400 copies: only the first is yet sold out, and that took 23 years; and the reason why it took no longer is that it found purchasers among the unlearned, who had heard that it contained a scurrilous preface and hoped to extract from it a low enjoyment.

★

Breiter's papers in Fleckeisen's *Neue Jahrbuecher*, vol. 139 (1889) and vol. 147 (1893), were the most estimable contribution made to the study of Manilius after Jacob's edition. The corrections of Ellis were rather more numerous, and one or two of them were very pretty, but his readers were in perpetual contact with the intellect of an idiot child: in Breiter's articles the good preponderated, and he thought and wrote like a sane man and a grown man. His edition therefore, when at last it came, was a severe disappointment; and on a general view it detracts from his merit. It was not senile, but it showed that an edition was an undertaking beyond his powers.

His recension is to be commended in so far as it maintains a fairly just balance between the rival MSS and avoids the bias of Bechert on one side and of Jacob on the other; but his use and choice of emendation was haphazard, and his own new conjectures, extorted by the task of editing, were without exception worthless. In his apparatus criticus he persisted in retaining the cod. Cusanus, because he was much too old to take example by me; he wantonly

387

deceived the less wary of his readers with an inaccurate collation of G, which others had collated accurately; and his collation of L, which should have been a boon and a blessing, because much fuller and more minute than Bechert's, was an insidious peril and a pernicious nuisance. His eyesight was evidently feeble, and did not serve him well in collating MSS or correcting proofs; but that is not enough to account for the bucketfuls of falsehood which he discharged on an ignorant and confiding public. In book III, which is much the shortest book, his apparatus, consisting of fewer than 350 lines, contains more than 110 definitely false statements: I do not reckon its frequent and deceitful omissions, nor the equally deceitful consequences of the editor's ignorance of his trade.

*

Mr Garrod brought to his task activity and energy, a brisk intelligence, and a strong desire to shine. His book, unlike the work of a later editor, was the fruit of independent investigation, diversified reading, and genuine industry. The most valuable part of its contents was the new and enlarged knowledge of the cod. Venetus provided by his discovery of Gronouius' collation in the margin of a book of Bentley's. There is one passage, 681 sq., which Mr Garrod, though not the first to understand it, was the first to explain, because the interpreters had not understood it; but I do not think that any other of his interpretations is both new and true. His conjectures were singularly cheap and shallow, and his impatience of more circumspect emendators, such as Bentley, broke out at 689 in insolence. The apparatus criticus is neither skilful nor careful, often defective and sometimes visibly so; I have counted more than 60 positive misstatements, of which only a minority can be laid at Breiter's door. The translation is dexterous and serviceable, but has an average of more than three false renderings to the page, not counting the suppression of inconvenient words and the insertion of convenient ones. Some of his interpretations were so little pondered that he changed them in the course of his work without perceiving it: there are more than a dozen places where translation and commentary contradict one another, and at 409 discrepancy is not confined to them. An astrological figure on p. 146, borrowed from others, is false in four particulars to the editor's own text. The commentary, which is full and mainly original, contains much more truth than error, but it contains so much error that the only readers who can use it with safety are those whose knowledge extends beyond Mr Garrod's; though even a student quite ignorant of the subject must discover, if intelligent and attentive, that some things which the editor tells him, for instance at 361–70, cannot possibly be true. What is taken at second hand is not always verified, and Bouché-Leclercq's prodigious blunder (*astr. Gr.* p. 374) about Hor. *carm.* I 12 50 *orte Saturno* is introduced at 509 as if original. Unconscious ignorance here and there exults too merrily, and it cannot be said that Mr Garrod's attainment in scholarship corresponds to his pretensions. Few will listen to a lecture at 747 sq. on elision in Latin poetry from a metrist who has not found time to read even his own text of one book of Manilius, and does not know what he has printed at 3 and 275 and 341 and 385 and 542 and 860. Few at 740, in a note which is to supersede the authority of Lachmann, will want to read further than the words '*fluuii* in *Aen.* III 702 = *fluuji,* cf. *Georg.* I 482 *fluujorum.*' But this seems to be a sort of English book which Germans admire, as they once admired Wakefield's Lucretius, and it was greeted as 'Garrods trefflicher Kommentar,' 'das herrliche Werk,' 'das vortreffliche Buch.' There were no such bouquets for me; and perhaps the reader will do well to consider how far my judgment of Mr Garrod's performance may have been warped by the passion of envy.

It is comprehensible that Breiter and Mr Garrod should aspire to edit Manilius, or a book of Manilius, and should attempt the enterprise; but why Jakob van Wageningen took it into his head that the world would be the better for an edition from him, and fetched his paste and scissors to this particular spot, I cannot imagine.

*

The Latin commentary was separately published in 1921 with no small magnificence by the royal academy of sciences at Amsterdam. What it most resembles is a magpie's nest. With the rarest exceptions, all that it contains of any value, whether interpretation or illustration, is taken from others, and usually without acknowledgment. A reader new to the author and the editor might mistake van Wageningen for a man of learning; but with my knowledge of both I can trace every stolen penny to the pouch it came from. On p. 41 the note of seventeen lines upon verses 149–66 may seem to indicate a considerable amount of reading, and so it does, for it is from Ed. Mueller de Pos. Man. auct. p. 2. On pp. 43 sq. thirty-three consecutive lines, equally impressive, are a mosaic put together from pp. 3 and 4 and 7 of the same treatise and from F. Malchin de auct. quib. qui Pos. libr. met. adhib. pp. 15 sq. P. 178 consists of thirty-seven lines: seventeen of them are mine. From those of his predecessors who wrote in Latin he copies many whole sentences word for word, especially from Fayus and me. I am his chief resource in books I and III; my fourth volume appeared when his compilation was nearing completion and is therefore plundered less; in book II his wants were so abundantly supplied by the ampler and more elementary commentary of Mr Garrod that he left mine unread, only dipping into it here and there.

★

Some of his thefts he took measures to dissemble. Sextus empiricus, whose polemical treatise is the best introduction to Greek astrology, he had never read, and almost every word of that author which appears in his notes has been taken from mine. But he had enough originality to alter my references, and if I wrote πρὸς ἀστρ. 70 he substituted 'adu. math. 70,' which he supposed to mean the same thing. It does not even mean anything: 'adu. math.,' if the poor pilferer did but know it, is a work in six books, of which πρὸς ἀστρ. is the fifth. But envy rather than shame is his usual motive for disguise, and he will name a false source to conceal the true. At I 424 *non posse timens* I had noted that *non posse* meant *ne non posset* and had remarked upon this rarer sense, neglected by grammarians and lexicographers, of the infinitive after *timere*. Thereupon he wrote '*non posse timens* pro *ne non posset*, cf. Kühner L.G. II^2 i 667 a,' where of course there is not a word on the subject. At I 871 I said '*modo, postmodo,*' citing parallels, unknown to the dictionaries and grammars, from Lucr. II 1133–5 and other classical poets. Eight years later Mr Loefstedt explained the word in Lucretius similarly, citing no parallel from any classical author. This enabled van Wageningen to write '*modo, postmodo,* Lucr. II 1133–5 (Löfst. Per. 242).' At III 257 his inapposite references to Bouché-Leclercq and Boll are means of diverting attention from the fact that his note is a reproduction of mine.

In adorning her humble home with extraneous objects the

magpie is not more helped by her freedom from scruple than she is hindered by her defects of taste and judgment. Diamonds and broken glass are all one to her, and she picks up and carries off what a discriminating thief would leave in the gutter. At II 1 Mr Garrod had made the irrelevant and unhappy remark that Homer was held by some to be ἀστρπλόγος: a fact which Manilius, if it occurred to him, took good care not to mention. Van Wageningen, having read this note and forgotten his own text, said '1–11 Homerus laudatur primus uates et astrologus.' At II 31 sq. the devoted daughter of Icarius is described as *pietate ad sidera ductam* | *Erigonen*, on which Mr Garrod wrote '*pietate*: because Erigone = Virgo = Iustitia.' This is a mistake which can never have been made before, but van Wageningen hastens to make it again, '*Erigonen* = Virginem = Iustitiam.'

*

His opinions, not being his own, were not permanently held, but picked up and dropped again, and he lived from hand to mouth on the borrowed beliefs of the moment.

*

The apparatus criticus is embedded in the commentary and the two are closely interwoven; and that is as it should be. The usual separation of inseparable things, interpretation and criticism, is injurious to both but especially to the latter. It is the expedient of editors who wish to shirk discussion of their text because they fear that they could not defend it. Criticism apart from interpretation does not exist; and 'critical edition' is the most inappropriate of all names for the thing to which custom applies it, an edition in which the editor is allowed to fling his opinions in the reader's face without being called to account and asked for his reasons.

*

There is another set of facts which I am almost alone in commemorating, for it is desired to suppress them. Many a reading discovered by conjecture has afterwards been confirmed by the authority of MSS; and I record the occurrence, as instructive, instead of concealing it, as deplorable. The resistance of conservatives to true emendation is perpetual, and to enjoy credit in the future they must obliterate their past. When therefore a conjecture has turned out to be a manuscript reading, and they have gnashed their teeth and accepted it as such, they try to make the world forget that they formerly condemned it on its merits. Its author, who bore the blame of its supposed falsehood, is denied mention after the establishment of its truth; and the history of scholarship is mutilated to save the face of those who have impeded progress.

There is an industriously propagated legend that many of my own corrections are 'violent' or 'palaeographically improbable,' by which it is merely meant that they alter a good number of letters. Violence and palaeographical improbability do not consist in that: they consist in ignoring the habits of copyists; and the terms should not be used by those to whom the habits of copyists are imperfectly known. A conjecture which alters only a single letter may be more improbable palaeographically than one which leaves no letter unaltered. The greatest change which I have admitted is none of my own but Breiter's *quaeue* (*iacent*) for *contra* (*iacet*) in II 253, which is what Manilius must have written. It is less violent, presumes less unwonted behaviour in the scribes, than the universally accepted conjecture *quorum* for *quarum* in III 300; and *quorum* has worse features than violence. If I had to name three of my own conjectures which I judge to be quite certain, I should be inclined to choose I 423 *eguit Ioue* for *esurcione*, IV 800 *ubi ab his ope sumpta* for *ubi pisce suruptor*, and V 461 *uix una trium* for *atri luxum*; two of which, I can well believe, will make the hair stand up on many uninstructed heads.

The first virtue of an emendation is to be true; but the best emendations of all are those which are both true and difficult, emendations which no fool could find. It is humiliating to reflect how many of the type commonly called brilliant, – neat and pretty changes of a letter or two –, have been lighted upon, almost fortuitously, by scholars whose intellectual powers were beneath the ordinary. Textual criticism would indeed be a paradise if scribes had confined themselves to making mistakes which Isaac Voss and Robinson Ellis could correct. But we know by comparing one MS with another that they also made mistakes of a different character; and it is these that put a good emendator on his mettle. First he must recognise them, then he must deal with them suitably. Anxious adherence to the ductus litterarum is the fruitful parent of false conjectures. It seduced even such men as Scaliger and Porson: it led

Scaliger to write *ultimus ex solido tetrans* in IV 757; it made Porson spoil his famous correction of Eur. *Ion* 1115 by omitting a necessary particle. The merits essential to a correction are those without which it cannot be true, and closeness to the MSS is not one of them; the indispensable things are fitness to the context and propriety to the genius of the author. The question whether the error presupposed was great or small is indeed a question to be asked, but it is the last question. With vulgar judges it is the first, though usually the last as well. This detail is their favourite criterion, because it can be discerned, or they think it can, by a bodily sense, without disturbing the slumbers of the intellect.

It surprises me that so many people should feel themselves qualified to weigh conjectures in their balance and to pronounce them good or bad, probable or improbable. Judging an emendation requires in some measure the same qualities as emendation itself, and the requirement is formidable. To read attentively, think correctly, omit no relevant consideration, and repress self-will, are not ordinary accomplishments; yet an emendator needs much besides: just literary perception, congenial intimacy with the author, experience which must have been won by study, and mother wit which he must have brought from his mother's womb.

It may be asked whether I think that I myself possess this outfit, or even most of it; and if I answer yes, that will be a new example of my notorious arrogance. I had rather be arrogant than impudent. I should not have undertaken to edit Manilius unless I had believed that I was fit for the task; and in particular I think myself a better judge of emendation, both when to emend and how to emend, than most others.

The following stanza of Mr de la Mare's 'Fare Well' first met my eyes, thus printed, in a newspaper review.

> Oh, when this my dust surrenders
> Hand, foot, lip, to dust again,
> May these loved and loving faces
>   Please other men!
> May the rustling harvest hedgerow
> Still the Traveller's Joy entwine,
> And as happy children gather
>   Posies once mine.

I knew in a moment that Mr de la Mare had not written *rustling*, and in another moment I had found the true word. But if the book of poems had perished and the verse survived only in the review, who would have believed me rather than the compositor? The bulk of the reading public would have been perfectly content with *rustling*, nay they would sincerely have preferred it to the epithet which the poet chose. If I had been so ill-advised as to publish my emendation, I should have been told that *rustling* was exquisitely apt and poetical, because hedgerows do rustle, especially in autumn, when the leaves are dry, and when straws and ears from the passing harvest-wain (to which 'harvest' is so plain an allusion that only a pedant like me could miss it) are hanging caught in the twigs; and I should have been recommended to quit my dusty (or musty) books and make a belated acquaintance with the sights and sounds of the English countryside. And the only possible answer would have been *ugh!*

My first reception was not worse than I expected. I provoked less enmity and insolence than Scaliger or Bentley in proportion as my merits were less eminent and unbearable than theirs. But my disregard of established opinions and my disrespect for contemporary fashions in scholarship made the ignorant feel sure that I was greatly and presumptuously in error and could be put down without much difficulty; and critiques were accordingly published which I do not suppose that their authors would now wish to rescue from oblivion. Not by paying any attention to any of them, not by swerving an inch from my original principles and practice, but by the mere act of living on and continuing to be the same, I have changed that state of things; and the deaf adder, though I can hardly say that she has unstopped her own ears, has begun to stifle her hisses for fear that they should reach the ears of posterity. Perhaps there will be no long posterity for learning; but the reader whose good opinion I desire and have done my utmost to secure is the next Bentley or Scaliger who may chance to occupy himself with Manilius.

The Editing of Juvenal

PREFACE OF MDCCCCV

A year ago I had no design of publishing or composing any such work as this. I knew indeed that the current texts of Juvenal, though praised in reviews and seemingly acceptable to readers, were neither well founded nor well constructed, and that this classic, like many more, had suffered some hurt from the reigning fashion of the hour, the fashion of leaning on one manuscript like Hope on her anchor and trusting to heaven that no harm will come of it. But I neither realised the extent of this injury nor fully understood its causes. I ascribed it first to the sloth and distaste for thinking which are the common inheritance of humanity, and secondly to that habit of treading in ruts and trooping in companies which men share with sheep. I did not know that it had also a third source, sheer ignorance of facts, and that the editors had left undone the first of all their duties and neglected to provide the author with an apparatus criticus.

*

What here follows, on pp. xi–xvi, is meant for one only of the three classes into whose hands this book will come. It is not for those who are critics: they know it already and will find it nothing but a string of truisms. It is not for those who never will be critics: they cannot grasp it and will find it nothing but a string of paradoxes. It is for beginners; for those who are not critics yet, but are neither too dull to learn nor too self-satisfied to wish to learn.

Open a modern recension of a classic, turn to the preface, and there you may almost count on finding, in Latin or German or English, some words like these: 'I have made it my rule to follow *a* wherever possible, and only where its readings are patently erroneous have I had recourse to *b* or *c* or *d*.' No scholar of eminence, even in the present age, has ever enunciated such a principle. Some, to be sure, like Mr Buecheler in his Juvenal, have virtually assumed it in their practice, as a convenient substitute for mental exertion; but to blurt it out as a maxim is an indiscretion which they leave to their unreflecting imitators, who formulate the rule without misgiving and practise it with conscious pride.

Either *a* is the source of *b* and *c* and *d* or it is not. If it is, then never in any case should recourse be had to *b* or *c* or *d*. If it is not, then the rule is irrational; for it involves the assumption that wherever *a*'s scribes made a mistake they produced an impossible reading. Three minutes' thought would suffice to find this out; but thought is irksome and three minutes is a long time.

How, you may ask, did the mind of man ever excogitate anything so false and foolish? The answer is that the mind of man had nothing to do with it. What the mind sets up the mind can pull down, and fancies based on false reasons can be overthrown by true reasons. But if true reasons could overthrow this fancy it would have been overthrown long before our time; by Madvig for instance in *opusc.* II pp. 298–319. Its strength is that it has no reasons, only causes. Its root is not in the mind but in the soul; and it partakes the solidity of its indestructible foundations, the sloth and vanity of man.

The task of editing the classics is continually attempted by scholars who have neither enough intellect nor enough literature. Unless a false reading chances to be unmetrical or ungrammatical they have no means of knowing that it is false. Show them these variants,

$$\text{molliaque} \left\{ \begin{matrix} \text{inmittens} \\ \text{inmites} \end{matrix} \right\} \text{fixit in ora manus,}$$

and they cannot tell which is right and which is wrong; and, what is worse, they honestly believe that nobody else can tell. If you suppose yourself able to distinguish a true reading from a false one, – suppose yourself, that is, to be a critic, a man capable of doing what the Greeks called ϰρίνειν, – they are aghast at your assurance. I am aghast at theirs: at the assurance of men who do not even imagine themselves to be critics, and yet presume to meddle with criticism.

What a critic is, and what advantage he has over those who are not critics, can easily be shown by one example. Cicero's oration *pro rege Deiotaro* was edited between 1830 and 1840 by Klotz, Soldan, and Benecke. The best MS then known was the Erfurtensis, and all three editors pounced on this authority and clung to it, believing themselves safe. Madvig in 1841, maintaining reason against superstition in Cicero's text as I now maintain it in Juvenal's, impugned

17 readings adopted from the Erfurtensis by these editors, and upheld the readings of inferior MSS. We now possess MSS still better than the Erfurtensis, and in 12 of the 17 places they contradict it; they confirm the inferior MSS and the superior critic. Authority itself has crossed over to the side of reason and left superstition in the lurch.

But there are editors destitute of this discriminating faculty, so destitute that they cannot even conceive it to exist; and these are entangled in a task for which nature has neglected to equip them. What are they now to do? Set to and try to learn their trade? that is forbidden by sloth. Stand back and leave room for their superiors? that is forbidden by vanity. They must have a rule, a machine to do their thinking for them. If the rule is true, so much the better; if false, that cannot be helped: but one thing is necessary, a rule.

A hundred years ago it was their rule to count the MSS and trust the majority. But this pillow was snatched from under them by the great critics of the 19th century, and the truth that MSS must be weighed, not counted, is now too widely known to be ignored. The sluggard has lost his pillow, but he has kept his nature, and must needs find something else to loll on; so he fabricates, to suit the change of season, his precious precept of following one MS wherever possible. Engendered by infirmity and designed for comfort, no wonder if it misses the truth at which it was never aimed. Its aim was purely humanitarian: to rescue incompetent editors alike from the toil of editing and from the shame of acknowledging that they cannot edit.

Frailty of understanding is in itself no proper target for scorn and mockery: 'nihil in eo odio dignum, misericordia digna multa.' But the unintelligent forfeit their claim to compassion when they begin to indulge in self-complacent airs, and to call themselves sane critics, meaning that they are mechanics. And when, relying upon their numbers, they pass from self-complacency to insolence, and reprove their betters for using the brains which God has not denied them, they dry up the fount of pity. 'D'où vient' asks Pascal 'qu'un boiteux ne nous irrite pas, et qu'un esprit boiteux nous irrite? C'est à cause qu'un boiteux reconnoit que nous allons droit, et qu'un esprit boiteux dit que c'est nous qui boitons; sans cela nous en aurions plus de pitié que de colère.' If a hale man walks along the street upon two sound legs, he is not liable to be chased by crowds of cripples

397

vociferating 'Go home and fetch your crutch.' If a reasoning man edits a classic rationally, he is.

When the Pithoeanus has one reading and other MSS another, and it is sought to determine which reading, if either, is true, then, if a critic attempts to settle the question, as critics will, by pertinent considerations, considerations of sense or usage or palaeography, he is exposed to a form of molestation from which the students of other sciences are probably exempt. He is pretty sure to be told that the judgment of critics is fallible, which he knew already, and that he ought to follow the authority of the best MS P. Now ask the intermeddler a question which he has never asked himself. Whence comes authority? In what does the goodness of a MS consist, and upon what does our belief in its goodness repose? If any one has heard a voice from heaven saying 'P is the best MS of Juvenal,' let him take example by M. Caedicius and carry his tale to the magistrates. But if not, then the goodness of a MS consists simply and solely in the goodness of the readings which it proffers; and our belief in its goodness, that is to say in the goodness of its readings, reposes simply and solely upon our judgment: upon that same judgment which we are now forbidden to exercise. When you invoke the authority of a MS against the exercise of the judgment, you are inciting the creature to rebel against the creator, and you are sapping the very ground on which you stand. If nobody can tell a true reading from a false reading, it follows of necessity that nobody can tell a truthful MS from a lying MS. Continue then, if you like, to urge that the judgment of critics is fallible, as indeed it is; but desist from talking in the same breath about the superiority of one MS to another; for this phrase either means nothing at all, or else it means that the one MS has been placed above the other by the fallible judgment of critics.

Take another aspect of the case. If a student, desiring to find out whether Pindar was stupid or no, should begin to read him, would any one touch him on the shoulder and say 'Shut that book: Boeotians were stupid, Pindar was a Boeotian, therefore Pindar was stupid'? No, not even a 'sane critic:' even he reserves such reasoning for his own ghostly realm of make-believe, and does not carry it into the waking world where men pursue their business in the daylight and detect *petitio principii*. Whether Boeotians were stupid, and to what extent, can only be settled by considering on its intrinsic merits the case of every known Boeotian, and Pindar's case among the rest. And whether P is the best MS of Juvenal, and to what extent, can only be settled by considering on its intrinsic merits every discrepancy between P and the other MSS. If, while we are engaged in so considering one of these discrepancies, you interrupt us with the assertion, possibly quite true, that P is the best MS and far the best, we shall reply: 'That is the question which we are now investigating at a preliminary stage. When we have made up our minds about this passage, then we will add it either to the evidence in favour of P or else to the evidence in favour of Ψ. To warp our choice in this particular instance by assuming as proved the general conclusion for which we are now collecting materials is, in the full sense of the term, preposterous.'

The truth is that when these gentlemen talk about the authority of better MSS they are repeating at second hand a phrase which they have caught up and run away with. They have overheard critics using it, but what the critics meant by it they do not understand. There is a sphere, a narrow sphere, within which the authority of better MSS is properly and usefully invoked, not indeed as a good means of arriving at the truth, but as the best means available. I 2 'rauci Theseide *Cordi*' P, *Codri* Ψ: the man's name is unknown. I 21 'si uacat *ac* placidi rationem admittitis' P, *et* Ψ: there is not a pin to choose. I 134 '*caulis* miseris atque ignis emendus' P, *caules* Ψ: the singular is no better than the plural nor the plural than the singular. To decide what Juvenal wrote in these places the judgment is helpless: here then we avail ourselves of an instrument which the judgment has forged and put into our hands: our knowledge or opinion of the relative merits of the MSS. Since we have found P the most trustworthy MS in places where its fidelity can be tested, we infer that it is also the most trustworthy in places where no test can be applied; and we read *Cordi, ac, caulis*. In thus committing ourselves to the guidance of the best MS we cherish no hope that it will always lead us right: we know that it will often lead us wrong; but we know that any other MS would lead us wrong still oftener. By following any other MS we shall only be right in the minority of cases; by following P we shall be right in the majority: that is all we look for. A critic therefore, when he employs this method of trusting the best MS, employs it in the same spirit of gloomy resignation with which a man lies down on a stretcher when he has broken both his legs. But far other is the spirit in which it is hailed by the reciter of formulas. He is not dejected by its inadequacy, but captivated by its ease. 'Here' says he 'is a method, sanctioned by critics, employed in scientific enquiry, and yet involving not the slightest expenditure of intellectual effort: this is the method for me;' and he espouses it for ever. In places where critics rise up and walk, where judgment has scope and authority is superseded, he remains supine and marvels at the vagaries of pedestrians: presumptuous beings who expect to reach their goal by the capricious and arbitrary method of putting forward first one foot, and then, with strange inconsistency, the other.

Misfortunes never come single, and the prattlers about P's authority are afflicted not only with lack of understanding but with loss of memory. They forget that they themselves repeatedly do what they say that we ought not to do; repeatedly prefer their own judgment to the authority of the Pithoeanus. The Pithoeanus at I 35 omits the word *palpat*, but they will not omit it; at I 38 it reads *non tibi*, but they will read *noctibus*: they will follow the worse MSS instead of the best. For deserting the Pithoeanus then they cannot blame us, since in that action we agree with them: they must blame us for the feature in which our conduct differs from theirs. Our offence is that we do not desert the Pithoeanus in the proper spirit, the spirit of rats leaving a sinking ship. We quit the best MS in search of truth: we ought only to quit it, as they do, in search of shelter. In enquiring whether a given reading of P's is right, we behave as if we really wanted to know, and we ask whether it is probable: they ask only whether it is possible, and unless it is impossible they believe it to be right: much as if you should believe that every Irishman is a Roman Catholic unless he knocks you down for looking as if you thought so.

How often the Pithoeanus is abandoned perforce, even by those who love it far better than truth and reason, appears to be little known; so let me render a brief statement of the facts. It omits five whole verses which the editors accept as genuine; it further omits one phrase of five words, three phrases of three words, two phrases of two words, and sixteen single words not counting monosyllables, which the editors admit into their text from other MSS; and, leaving out of count a vast number of errors too trivial for record in an 'apparatus uere criticus,' there are more than a hundred places where the editors reject its readings and take the readings of other MSS instead.

That there is no hope of resolving particular questions by the general proposition that P is the best MS, would be clearly perceived if men used language to clothe their thoughts and not to muffle them, and took care to have in their minds ideas accurately corresponding to the phrases which stream from their tongues and pens.

★

This is no way to earn applause. But to the common sort of reviewers I say with Seneca *laudari me a uobis, nisi laudaretis etiam malos, uellem*: you should be welcome to praise me if you did not praise one another. If applause were what I wanted, applause I would have; for I know the way, and it is easy. Applause is to be earned by outdoing the last editor in partiality for P and adopting false readings which the last editor was shrewd enough to reject. To echo the vaunt of Priam, ἔτλην οἷ᾽ οὔ πώ τιο ἐπιχθόνιος βροτὸς ἄλλος, 'I have tolerated such things as nobody in the world ever tolerated before,' has now for years been the chief ambition of each fresh editor of Juvenal. The progress of depravation is not however rapid, nor the sum of damage considerable; for each fresh editor, while importing his own corruptions, expels a certain number of the corruptions imported by his predecessor: the bloom of novelty is evanescent and does not long disguise the native badness of the goods. P has two besetting sins: it adds or subtracts the letter *s* at the end of a word, especially if the next word begins with *s* or *f*; and it makes mistakes in the tense, the person, the number, and especially the mood, of verbs. In the interest of those who wish to receive praise without deserving it I have taken the trouble to make a pretty complete list of these blunders; and I trust that my humble diligence may smooth the next editor's path to glory.

★

I have placed in the text not only conjectures which I think certain, such as *ferendis* at VI 195, but also others, such as *ac similis* at XIV 269, which I think doubtful. This I do to arrest attention and challenge opposition. What is important is not that I should correct and explain Juvenal but that Juvenal should be corrected and explained: if the text is right, and I have missed the sense, let others trace it; if the text is wrong, and I have failed to right it, let others try. The conjecture of which I expect to hear most evil is *ramitis* at XI 168. That conjecture will entice its adversaries to do what they have never done before, to read the passage with attention. If they can then attempt a defence of *diuitis*, let them attempt it by all means: if it succeeds, I shall claim half the credit.

★

Forty years ago it was the fashion to be suspicious; and scholars ejected from the text of Juvenal every verse that could be spared, and judged themselves acute for doing so. Now it is the fashion to be insensible; and scholars lay claim to the merit of caution when they accept as genuine every verse which the text of Juvenal contains. For steering a middle course I claim no merit at all, except the slight and negative merit of setting fashion at naught and of taking warning by terrible examples. Truth and wisdom have never been the fashion, no more than virtue; and for the same reason, because they are not easy to attain. The question whether Juvenal's text contains spurious verses, and, if so, which those verses are, is a question demanding more thought than any large number of men at any one period are either willing or able to bestow upon it. But all can follow the fashion, for that needs no pains and no brains.

★

These misadventures happen, and must happen, even to eminent scholars, when they have taken a line and assumed an attitude, and consider rather what is required by their position and expected by their admirers than what is true or probable or credible.

★

I call attention to these shortcomings, but I make no apology for them. Neither the purveyors nor the consumers of the 'apparatus critici' now on sale are in any position to throw stones at the first production which has ever deserved that name. This work, as I said before, is not meant for a model; it is an enterprise undertaken in haste and in humane concern for the relief of a people sitting in darkness.

★

When this book was first published, a quarter of a century ago, there were few who could reproduce the title as it was printed: it generally became 'editorum in usum (!)' or 'editorum [sic!] in usum.' Twenty years later I published an edition of Lucan which professed the same benevolent purpose, and its title was everywhere transcribed without exclamation. The injurious opinion that editors are past helping would therefore appear to be on the wane. Indeed the phrase has now passed into currency, and I have seen Mr Marx's *Rudens*, for instance, described, perhaps not very aptly, as an 'editio in usum editorum.'

The book has now been three years out of print, and booksellers are beginning to call it 'scarce' and to ask more than the original price for it; so I have accepted the liberal offer of the Syndics of the Cambridge University Press to bring out a new edition. Its novelty is almost confined to this second preface, and consists much more in additions than in corrections; but every considerable change is set forth in these pages, where no error of any moment is passed over in silence, and no change of opinion is dissimulated. In the reprinted parts I have amended a few errors of the press and slips of the pen, chiefly in numerals; modified a few reports from MSS on the authority of recent collators; added one or two testimonia and subtracted a larger number of the less ancient; inserted a few new examples; and that is all. For the purpose of the work, as I said in the original preface, was to meet the needs and remedy the ailments of the time; and its actual contribution to learning or criticism is of less interest than its historical character as the memorial of an epoch.

After Buecheler's death in 1908 the task of revising his Juvenal, from which he had himself hung back, was assigned to the most eminent of his pupils; and Leo's revision was a new book. He threw overboard, in accordance with my injunction, the superfluities which composed the greater portion of the notes, and substituted a proper apparatus criticus partly derived from mine. He brought Buecheler's text into agreement with mine in fifty or sixty places, and altered it on his own initiative about as often. He produced five-and-twenty original conjectures and placed eight of them in the text, all in my judgment false, and mostly destitute even of superficial attractions. Neither in penetration nor in skill was he an emendator of the first rank: he could restore with ease and felicity a new-found remnant of Menander which had only been edited by a Frenchman, but a much-laboured field like the text of Juvenal would yield no harvest to his husbandry; and he was hampered in addition by peculiarly awkward circumstances. Where I had pointed out a fault and proposed a remedy, it was necessary for him, after recognising the fault, to propose a remedy different from mine; and this compulsion may partly explain, though it can hardly excuse, the poor quality of much which he proposed.

*

But when I in my Lucan comport myself towards Mr Hosius with strict integrity and anxious fairness, then there is protest. I must admit that the truths which I have told about Mr Hosius are much more damaging than any fibs which he has told about me.

*

VI O 13. I published the emendation *has* (my predecessors had retained *as* or proposed *aes*) in the *Athenaeum* of May 13th 1899; but as it was afterwards proposed independently by Mr Owen in June and by Buecheler in July or August, I added in my note 'item Owenus et Buechelerus.' Messrs Labriolle and Villeneuve, who had never heard of a classical scholar behaving in this way, inferred that I was a half-witted pickpocket without skill enough to hide a theft; and their note accordingly is '*has* Owen et Bücheler.' If I had not been the first corrector I should not have mentioned myself at all, and if anyone else had been the first I should have mentioned no second, much less a third.

The Editing of Lucan

Now I do not insist on the fact that in one of the two manuscripts which contain the subscriptio it is not in this place, and that in neither of them does it accompany the *ancient* scholia: I only say, look at the logic. Because an ancestor of P's had here suffered loss, therefore the lost portion contained something which Buecheler wished it to have contained.

We arrive at evening upon a field of battle, where lie 200 corpses. 197 of them have no beards; the 198th has a beard on the chin; the 199th has a false beard slewed round under the left ear; the 200th has been decapitated and the head is nowhere to be found. Problem: Had it a beard, a false beard, or no beard at all? Buecheler can tell you: it had a beard, a beard on the chin.

This belief was accepted by scholars whose analytical faculty did not enable them to detect any error in this reasoning. But Mr Duff in 1898 quietly ignored the whole fuss, and I in 1905 dismissed it in a few derisive words (p. xxviii) which echo for ever in the memory of Mr W.M. Lindsay. Four years passed, and the imposture collapsed in the land of its origin. Buecheler died in 1908, and the troop of little dogs which trotted at his heels was scattered abroad in quest of other heels to trot at. These were soon found: in the very next year (*Hermes* XLIV p. 617) Leo, who undertook the fourth edition of Jahn, gave Buecheler's theory up: 'Die Handschriften des Nicaeus und Epicarpius waren keine Ausgaben (so verbreitet auch dieser Irrtum immer noch ist), sondern "emendirte" Exemplare.' Everybody turned like one weathercock.

★

Here we pass from recension to emendation; and that is a thing which encounters much ill will. Any attempt to demonstrate and correct an error is likely to evoke the irrelevant proposition that the text of Lucan is good. The text of Lucan contains about 48,000 words; and an editor who sees cause to alter only 60 or so, 1 in 800, professes thereby that he thinks it good. But even folk who are willing to acknowledge in general terms that there are and must be corruptions in the text, are ready to take up arms in defence of any particular reading which incurs suspicion. The fact that it is suspected enlists them on its side; and one is left to infer that the only corrupt readings are those which show no sign of being wrong.

It would not be true to say that all conservative scholars are stupid, but it is very near the truth to say that all stupid scholars are conservative. Defenders of corruptions are therefore assured beforehand of wide approval; and this is demoralising. They need not seriously consider what they say, because they are addressing an audience whose intelligence is despicable and whose hearts are won already; and they use pretexts which nobody would venture to put forward in any other case. Emendators should thank their stars that they have the multitude against them and must address the judicious few, and that moral integrity and intellectual vigilance are for them not merely duties but necessities.

★

At least a dozen emendations in the text of Lucan have been afterwards confirmed by the discovery or collation of manuscripts: II 13 *habet* Cortius and Bentley, 556 *en* Heinsius, III 410 *ulli* . . . *aurae* Dorville, 510 *maris* Dorville and Bentley, 564 *percussae* Rutgersius, IV 562 *iuguli* . . . *manum* Gronouius, V 210 *locutae* Burman, 372 *tenet* Bentley, VI 293 *Hennaeis* Heinsius, 330 *condixit* Heinsius, VII 780 *desisset* Grotius, VIII 311 *fallent* Heinsius. But nothing of this will be learnt from conservative editors. They reject emendation as long as they can, and when they can reject it no longer they take their revenge upon the emendator by concealing his good action, lest it should breed others. The most annoying of all conjectures is the true conjecture which cannot any more be called false.

★

For the emendation of Lucan Bentley did much more than any one else, but less than he ought to have done. The characteristic which Napoleon so much admired in Turenne, that he grew bolder as he grew older, was not for Bentley a fortunate endowment. His judgment ripened early and reached perfection before he was forty: from that time onward the vices of his temper began to invade his intellect, and confidence usurped the place of consideration. Already in the Horace of 1711 he is seen aiming in haste at wrong targets; and by the time he came to Lucan he had acquired the worst habits of deity,

> ut in deserta recedens
> saeuiat exercens telum quod saepe nocentes
> praeterit exanimatque indignos inque merentes.

He conceived the design of expelling from the text those repetitions of the same word at a brief interval which are commoner in this poet than in any other; and, though he did his worst and waded knee-deep in carnage, he failed. They were too many for him; more than he could remove, more even than he could detect. I think it pertinent to add that there are modern editors who understand this matter no better than Bentley, and who defend repetitions, as he assailed them, without discrimination. Each author has his own principles and practice. Horace was as sensitive to iteration as any modern; and those who choose to believe that he wrote *tutus bos etenim rura perambulat, nutrit rura Ceres*, which not even Lucan could have written, are as blind to truth as to beauty. Virgil was less sensitive, Ovid much less; Lucan was almost insensible, but not, like the scholars I speak of, quite. Some repetitions have been expelled from his text, not by the conjectures of Bentley, but by the collation of better manuscripts; and if we had better manuscripts still, more still would be expelled.

I pass over C.F. Weber's perfectly useless edition of 1821 and come to the handy text and notes produced in 1835 by C.H. Weise.

*

The text is the sort of text which satisfies the general reader, and therefore is not good. A certain number of true or probable readings neglected by earlier editors are introduced from those manuscripts which Mr Hosius regards with most favour; but these are balanced by an equal number of new false readings admitted with no less hospitality from the same source. Corruptions are usually preferred to corrections, and the punctuation lays bare so many misunderstandings that many more must be supposed to lie concealed. All the good that Mr Hosius has done to the text – not only any improvement in punctuation, but the introduction of new truth from the manuscripts where the gain is anything appreciable, – I have recorded in my notes with scrupulous care. This is more than any editor of any author has ever done before for any of his predecessors; and yet complaint will be made of my injustice.

The recension of Lucan by Mr W.E. Heitland which appeared in 1900 as part of Postgate's *corpus poetarum Latinorum* is mainly founded on Mr Hosius' first edition and adheres to it with undue fidelity: where he asserts independence he is usually right.

An elaborate edition with apparatus criticus and commentary was produced in 1896 and 1897 by C.M. Francken. Hardly a page of it can be read without anger and disgust. Francken was a born blunderer, marked cross from the womb and perverse; and he had not the shrewdness or modesty to suspect that others saw clearer than he did, nor the prudence and decency to acquaint himself with what he might have learnt from those whom he preferred to contradict. IV 52 '*non . . . pruinae* continent ampliationem subiecti,' VI 304 '*maiorem* quam qui Thessalico arcu configi possit,' IX 653 '*angues* in uniuersum, non Gorgonis,' 1105 'fletus talia fatus (sic) inuenit comitem': he would rather advertise such errors by the score and the hundred than take any steps to be rid of them. I often comment in my notes on the mistakes of other editors; but Francken's are too many to mention and too naked to need exposure. The width and variety of his ignorance are wonderful; it embraces mythology, palaeography, prosody, and astronomy, and he cannot keep it to himself: III 205 'Marsyae fabula cum Pallade nihil commune habet,' VI 712 '*aiâm = aliquam*,' VIII 229 *Persĭs* 'quam Persae,' X 212 'sol est in Sirio 1° Iulio, in Cancro 1° Augusti.' His text is full of things which have got there without his knowledge, because what he sent to his printer was a copy of Weise corrected, of course inefficiently, by his own helpless hand. For stupidity of plan and slovenliness of execution his apparatus criticus is worse than Breiter's apparatus to Manilius; and I never saw another of which that could be said. And yet he has rendered more service to Lucan than Mr Hosius. He had a sincere desire, not always frustrate, to find out what Lucan really wrote; and his perception of the difference between one Latin word and another, *consertus* and *confertus* for instance, was such as enabled him to choose the more appropriate of two variants instead of having to print whichever might happen to be given by M.

From the Classical Papers

1 Euripides

The heroes who undertake the defence of the text say that we have here an aposiopesis. Aposiopesis is a comforting word; but the sphere of the figure so named is limited by conditions which here preclude it. In cases of aposiopesis it is requisite that we should be able to form a notion how the speaker was about to complete the sentence which he breaks off: this is obviously necessary to the understanding of the situation, because it is the thought of the suppressed words which causes to arise in his mind the emotion which restrains him from uttering them. But here the spoken part of the sentence consists only of three words, and we cannot tell the meaning of the first or the construction of the second: we cannot tell whether ὅθεν means *since which time* or *for which reason*; we cannot tell whether the inflexion of νόμοισι means *with* or *by* or *in* or *for* or *to* or *because of*: much less then can we guess how the sentence would proceed.

2 Aeschylus

But there remains a far heavier, a fatal objection. It is entirely permissible to say, with impressive exaggeration, οὐδέπω κακῶν κρηπὶς ὕπεστιν, that is, *calamity is as yet not even begun*. Precisely thus does Prometheus say in *P. V.* 767 [741] οὓς γὰρ νῦν ἀκήκοας λόγους | εἶναι δόκει σοι μηδέπω 'ν προοιμίοις. But, having said so much, there you must stop: you cannot proceed to say ἀλλ' ἔτ' ἐκπιδύεται, *but it is still going on*. Begin by saying that a thing is not yet *finished*, then you may proceed to say, with such pleonasm as poets love, that it is still going on: οὐδέπω κακῶν | ἔπεστι θριγκός, ἀλλ' ἔτ' ἐκπιδύεται, for instance, would be the writing, not indeed of a decent stylist, but still the writing of a sane man. But to say that a thing *is not yet begun but is still going on* is such nonsense as not one of us can conceive himself uttering in the loosest negligence of conversation; only when centuries of transcription by barbarians have

409

imputed it to an incomparable poet, then we accept it as a matter of course.

3 Aeschylus

Thanks to Wecklein it is at length possible to study Aeschylus in comfort. Next to an accurate collation of the cardinal MSS, a complete register of the conjectures of critics is the student's prime requisite. Nothing short of a complete register will serve: no man can be trusted to sift good from bad: some editors do not know a correction when they see one, others through childish jealousy of this scholar or that ignore his discoveries, the most candid and the soundest judgment is human and errs. The time lost, the tissues wasted, in doing anew the brainwork done before by others, and all for lack of a book like Wecklein's *Appendix*, are in our brief irreparable life disheartening to think of.

4 Aeschylus

This edition gives proof of many virtues: common sense, alert perception, lucidity of thought, impatience of absurdity, a rational distrust of MS tradition, and a masculine taste in things poetical. The learner who attacks the play with this commentary will find unfailing help by the way and acquire much information before his journey's end. The old miserable experiences of the classical student who wants to understand what he reads, his lonely fights with difficulties whose presence the editor has never apprehended, his fruitless quest of a meaning in notes where the editor has rendered Greek nonsense into English nonsense and gone on his way rejoicing, are not repeated here. Here on the contrary is a commentator who shares the reader's difficulties, rescues him from some of them, warns him of some existing unperceived, and to tell the truth invents a good many where none exist.

5 Aeschylus

When Mr Tucker's conjectures are not palaeographically improbable they are apt to be causeless and even detrimental. Among the axioms assumed in the preface are the following: 'the reading in the text must hold its place until such cause to the contrary can be shewn as will satisfy a rigidly impartial tribunal. The *onus probandi* lies entirely with the impugner of the text.' 'The conditions of dispossession are these. It must either be proved that the reading is an impossibility, or else that in point of grammar it is so abnormal, or in point of relevance so manifestly inappropriate, as to produce a thorough conviction that the MS is in error.' I for my part should call this much too strict; but these are Mr Tucker's principles. His practice is something quite different: in practice no word, however good, is safe if Mr Tucker can think of a similar word which is not much worse.

6 Aeschylus

The emendations of scholars fare no better than the readings of the MS if their place is wanted for a conjecture of the editor's own. Again and again in passages which we all thought had been corrected long ago Mr Tucker proffers another solution, not better but newer, and promotes it, with rigid partiality, to the text.

7 Euripides

The introduction, which covers fifty pages, is a full and interesting account of the legend, plot, artistic structure, and metres of the play. Mr Flagg calls this 'negatively considered, the most faultless of Euripides' extant tragedies,' and thinks that 'there remains not another one that is marred by so few of those grave lapses from dramatic propriety and universal good taste to which the poet's mind was subject.' Even negatively considered I should have thought the *Hippolytus* by far the most faultless tragedy of Euripides, if not indeed the most faultless of all tragedies except the *Antigone* alone: what lapses mar it, apart from a certain artificiality in the altercation of Theseus with the hero, I do not know; assuredly none to compare with the see-saw of divine intervention in the ἔξοδος of our play. Mr Flagg defends this machinery as the only way to rescue the chorus, which is one of those excuses which

Aristotle calls ridiculous; the poet, as he says, should take care from the outset not to construct his play in such a manner. And when Mr Flagg says that 'the modern reader cannot adequately reproduce the feelings stirred by this final scene in the Athenian spectator's breast,' this is to arraign Euripides, not to defend him. It means that he wrote for an age and not for all time: he defaced his drama that he might gladden the eyes of the vulgar with the resplendent stage-properties of their beloved goddess: a trap to catch applause which does not differ in kind from the traditional sentiment, always welcome to the gallery of our own theatres, that the man who lays his hand upon a woman, save in the way of kindness, is unworthy of the name of a British sailor.

8 Horace

This passage is well known as a supposed example of 'uereor ut' = 'uereor ne.' The use is absolutely unique – Mr Palmer disposes of certain irrelevant passages cited as parallel – and, to me as to him, absolutely incredible. A language in which one phrase possesses two diametrically opposite senses and can be employed indifferently in either without anything to tell which is meant, is not a language in which man can make himself intelligible to his fellow man. Explanations of a familiar sort are forthcoming: Horace is dead and cannot protect himself, so we are told that 'ut' coming first makes a difference: his intellect was not equal to the strain of remembering from one verse to another how he had opened the sentence: when he began to write he thought he was going to say 'uerisimile non est' and so wrote 'nam ut ferula caedas': when he reached the next line he fancied he had written 'nam ne ferula caedas' and so wrote 'non uereor': what philtre, what hippomanes it was that produced this 'animi caligo et magna obliuio rerum quas modo gessit' we do not learn.

9 Sophocles

This, too, I fear must be a long discussion, and through no fault of mine. The scholars whose names follow have earned a title to respect which is not forfeited even by such notes as they have written on this passage. But of the notes themselves it would be hard to speak too severely. They are vicious to a degree which well-nigh protects them from refutation. So intricate is the tangle of error that I scarce know where to begin the task of unravelling it and half despair of making all its convolutions clear: the spectacle of such confusion almost dizzies the brain. If the argument proves tedious, I ask the reader to lay the blame on the right shoulders and remember that making mistakes is much quicker and easier work than showing that mistakes have been made. The comments to be considered can have given little trouble to those who wrote them, but for that very reason they impose the more labour on him whose duty it is to examine them.

10 Propertius

I have the greatest difficulty in setting before my mind's eye a conception of these scribes, who first invent for themselves, with no motive and on no foundation and against the metre of the verse they are transcribing, a false scansion of a word, and then adhere with such tenacity to this causeless, baseless and embarrassing fiction that instead of reforming their pronunciation as the verse suggests they deform the verse to keep their pronunciation unreformed.

11 Catullus

He has abandoned then the basis of Lachmann's conjecture, but to the conjecture he adheres; and why not? its merit is not that he thinks it has a basis but that he knows it is Lachmann's. Again, when Lachmann has amended a passage, Mr Schulze allows no one to improve Lachmann's emendation, because he does not know whether the improvement is an improvement and he does know that it is not Lachmann's.

12 Catullus

True, the reader would never guess this, for Mr Schulze only notes the agreement of other MSS in about a third of his examples, and leaves you to draw the false inference that in the other two thirds, where he does not note their agreement, they do not agree: in another writer this suppression of facts would argue fraud, but no such hypothesis is necessary in the case of Mr Schulze.

13 Propertius

To conclude: I design this treatise for a defence of eclecticism, but of eclecticism within scientific bounds. The student of an ancient text has two enemies. There is the devotee of system who prefers simplicity to truth, and who having half learnt from Madvig and Bekker the great lesson of our century, *magnam et inconditam testium turbam ad paucos et certos esse redigendam, a quibus ceteri rem acceperint*, selects his few witnesses without ascertaining if they were really the informants of the rest, constructs a neat apparatus at whatever cost to the text of his hapless author, and seeks to overawe the timid by sonorous talk about 'sanae artis praecepta omnia;' and there is the born hater of science who ransacks Europe for waste paper that he may fill his pages to half their height with the lees of the Italian renascence, and then by appeals to the reader's superstition would persuade him to hope without reason and against likelihood that he will gather grapes of thorns and figs of thistles. Here is my attempt to fortify against delusion on either hand the student of at least one Latin author.

14 Propertius

My name is scattered through the treatise, and I hasten to acknowledge the invariable benignity with which Dr Postgate reproves me, sometimes for doing what I have not done, and sometimes for doing what it was my bounden duty to do.

15 Propertius

Thus much I have written to adjust Dr Postgate's partial estimate of his new codex L. But on pp. 61–74 he discusses the relations and comparative value of Propertius' MSS in general. I hoped I had done with this matter for a long time to come; for after all, Propertius' MSS are not the only things in the world. But apparently, like Nehemiah's builders, one must carry the sword to protect the labours of the trowel. When Baehrens Leo Solbisky and I with some thought and pains have got this rather uninteresting garden of the Muses into decent order, here is Dr Postgate hacking at the fence for no discoverable reason unless it is the hope of boasting 'liquidis immisi fontibus apros.' I feel it a hardship, but I suppose it is a duty, to withstand this inroad. Dr Postgate makes his mistakes with a tranquil air of being in the right which is likely enough to satisfy students not possessing my weary familiarity with the subject; so here I put it at their service.

In confusing anew the relations of the MSS Dr Postgate has two principal aims: to exalt N and to disparage D V. It was easy to foresee that the next writer on Propertius' MSS would disparage D V: Baehrens had disparaged N, Mr Leo had disparaged O, Mr Solbisky had disparaged A F, I had defended one and all; so to disparage D V was the only way left of being original. Idolatry of N, on the other hand, is nothing new.

'It is in his treatment of the Neapolitanus' says Dr Postgate (p. 63) 'that I find Mr Housman least satisfactory;' and he proceeds to explain why: 'though not the enemy of N, he is its most discriminating friend.' I had said, in my discriminating and unsatisfactory way, that there is no best MS of Propertius. 'The critics of the future' writes Dr Postgate (p. 73) 'will, unless I am much mistaken, pronounce on the contrary that the Neapolitanus *is* the best MS of Propertius, best as being the oldest of our witnesses' – but age is no merit. Age is merely a promise of merit, which experience may ratify or annul. The hoary head is a crown of glory, says Solomon, *if it be found in the way of righteousness*. Till we have examined two rival MSS, we presume that the older is the better. When we have examined them, we judge them by their contents. Till we have examined the Ambrosian fragment of Seneca's tragedies (saec. V) and the codex Etruscus (saec. XI–XII) we presume that the former has the purer text. When we have examined them we find that it has not. Just so in the first decade of Livy: the MS which is by five or six centuries the oldest is not the best. The worst texts of Euripides yet known to man were written in classical antiquity itself. Useless then to call the Neapolitanus 'best as being the oldest of our witnesses,' unless you can keep it out of our reach. But Dr Postgate continues 'best again as the one that presents the greatest amount of truth with the smallest amount of falsehood.' Then if I set a clerk to copy out the Teubner text the result will be in Dr Postgate's opinion a still better MS than the Neapolitanus, because it will present a great amount of truth with a smaller amount of falsehood. How often must I repeat that the legitimate glory of a MS is not correctness but integrity, and that a MS which adulterates its text, as N does, forfeits integrity in direct proportion as it achieves correctness? Give us our ingredients pure: we will mix the salad: we will not take it ready made from other cooks if we can help it.

16 Propertius

In short, every word that Dr Postgate says against Baehrens' account of the relation between N and Δ can be turned against his own account of the relation between N and Φ. All the tools he employs are two-edged, though to be sure both edges are quite blunt.

But Dr Postgate further engages to show that DV are more interpolated (interpolated by conjecture, that is) than N. His method is the good old rule, the simple plan, of 'heads I win, tails you lose.' N and DV commit just the same offences: he extenuates them in N and denounces them in DV. His divers weights and divers measures may escape the eye in his pamphlet because they are there arranged on separate pages; but I shall bring them together, and in juxtaposition I fancy they will astonish even their owner.

17 Propertius

This ends what I have to say on Dr Postgate's spirited attempt (pp. 61–74) to re-establish chaos amongst Propertius' MSS. He calls it (p. 74) 'a toilsome though necessary examination of the past in Propertian criticism.' The attempt to find grounds for groundless opinions is likely to be toilsome; but the necessity seems to have been purely subjective.

If it were not for the humour of the situation I might well resent the tone of placid assurance in which I, who think before I write and blot before I print, am continually admonished by the author of this pamphlet.

18 Ovid

Mr Riese is saved by common sense and a comparative purity of taste from the most grotesque excesses of the two Teubner editors, but he is fully their accomplice in their worst offence. It is not that they afford so little illumination themselves: it is that they stand between us and the light. In the 17th and 18th centuries Ovid was as lucky as he is unlucky now. He was intently studied and brilliantly emended by the two greatest of all critics of Latin poetry. The discoveries of those critics are uncongenial to our modern editors, who treat them accordingly. They steadfastly ignore the work of Bentley, and they diligently undo the work of Heinsius.

19 Ovid

Now will it be believed that this necessary and certain emendation was made long before me by Richard Bentley; that it was published three-quarters of a century ago; and that not one editor of Ovid has accepted it, and only one has even mentioned it? Bentley's emendations are the most important contribution to the criticism of Ovid which has been made since Heinsius. Since they were published in the Oxford edition of 1825–6, many MSS of Ovid have been collated with the utmost diligence; but no collation of any MS since 1826, or indeed since 1661, has helped so much towards purifying the text as Bentley's emendations might have helped. Haupt again and again called attention to their value; but who was Haupt, that an editor of Ovid should listen to him? It is hard to write without bitterness of the loss of time inflicted on an intelligent student by editors who cannot even be trusted to hand down the discoveries which their betters have made.

Here and everywhere I substitute Lachmann's number for Mr Brieger's. Munro did a little and Bernays did more to hinder the student from finding his place; but Mr Brieger has quite eclipsed their puny efforts, and the numeration of Lucretius is now as trackless a jungle as that of Aeschylus or Propertius themselves. Mr Brieger's first victim, I rejoice to see, is Mr Brieger, whose introduction contains more mistakes in figures than I ever yet beheld in the same compass: *they have digged a pit before me, and are fallen into the midst of it themselves.*

21 Ovid

His [Palmer's] inspiration was fitful, and when it failed him he lacked the mental force and rightness which should have filled its place. His was a nimble but not a steady wit: it could ill sustain the labour of severe and continuous thinking; so he habitually shunned that labour. He had no ungovernable passion for knowing the truth about things: he kept a very blind eye for unwelcome facts and a very deaf ear for unwelcome argument, and often mistook a wish for a reason. No one could defend more stubbornly a plain corruption, or advocate more confidently an incredible conjecture, than Palmer when the fancy took him. He had much natural elegance of taste, but it was often nullified by caprice and wilfulness, so that hardly Merkel himself has proposed uncouther emendations. Moreover Palmer was not, even for his own age and country, a learned man. He read too little, and he attended too little to what he read; and with all his genius he remained to the end of his days an amateur. And these defects he crowned with an amazing and calamitous propensity to reckless assertion.

22 Ovid

XXI 205 '*si mihi lingua foret*, if I had a tongue to speak out. The reading is universally condemned, but it seems a proverbial expression.' If you ask a man what o'clock it is, and he replies that a bird in the hand is worth two in the bush, that is a proverbial expression; and yet there is something strange about it.

23 Ovid

His chief fault here is the fault which most editors now commit and plume themselves upon committing: he treats the best MS as if it were better than it is, and sometimes prefers its authority to the thing on which authority is founded, reason.

24 Ovid

To settle this case by appeals to the relative worth of MSS is to stand upon one's head: cases like this are the things by which the relative worth of MSS is settled.

25 Ovid

For the worst of Palmer's work is this: it contains indeed much which is true, but no assertion of his can be believed until it is verified. When, as often happens, he knows nothing about a thing, he does not try to find out something about it, nor even hold his peace, but he says anything he pleases.

26 Classical Metres

Southey's and Longfellow's hexameters are often very bad verses, and they differ from Homer's in the important particular that they are written in triple while Homer's are written in quadruple time; but still verses they are of a sort. Mr Stone's hexameters are verses of no sort, but prose in ribands.

It is true that Mr Stone himself believes a number of things by believing which he is enabled to avoid this conclusion. He is conscious, he says on p. 44, that his language 'suffers heavily from the phrase *I believe* and its synonyms;' and he calls this unavoidable, 'from the unfortunate fact that the opinions expressed are such as no one else thinks or believes.' Another fact, equally unfortunate though very likely unavoidable, is this: that Mr Stone never makes the faintest attempt to substantiate his beliefs. His method of pursuing truth may be studied in little on p. 35. It is well known that under certain conditions the metrical accent in Plautus shortens adjacent long syllables. Mr Stone 'believes,' p. 4, that the verses of the ancients did not 'read themselves,' i.e. had little if any metrical accent, and he therefore imputes these shortenings to the grammatical accent. 'I was a little upset,' says he, 'to find some scholars declare that the metrical accent as well as the natural accent may account for such shortening; but' – now comes his answer – 'I am convinced that this is not so, and' – what do you expect? Plautus is extant and accessible, and to read him would dispel this conviction; so Mr Stone resorts instead to a kindred spirit – 'Mr –, whom I consulted on the point, believes that Plautus always made the two coincide, which the great roughness of his metrical system enabled him to do.' It is a scene to remember: these two gentlemen putting their heads together and believing things, and Plautus standing shut upon the shelf.

27 Classical Metres

Since Mr Stone has nothing to say for any of his beliefs he propitiates us from time to time by observing that he feels sure we do not agree with them; and on this same page 32 he remarks 'I know I shall be looked upon as insane.' He will not be looked upon as insane; he will be looked upon as having a whim. Whims govern men as Dionysius never governed Syracuse: sentinels patrol the frontier with orders that no bad news from abroad is to reach the sovereign; and a stress-accent arriving at the portals of the sense is translated into a pitch-accent before transmission to the seat of government.

These beliefs do half the work: they prevent Mr Stone from hearing the overpowering noise with which the ironshod English accent tramples his versification to nought. But this merciful deliverance leaves his verses without any rhythm at all; so half the work remains undone. This half the reader is to do: p. 50, 'Now what do I require of my readers? I ask them to read my verses slowly, with the natural accent unimpaired', – we have seen what that means – *'and with such stress as they think right on the long syllables by way of ictus.'* The stress-accent, having been conjured out at the door, now comes back down the chimney and falls where it has no business to fall. If we pronounce our mother tongue correctly, Mr Stone's verses will be prose; so we are asked to pronounce it incorrectly.

I suppose we could all write verses if we were allowed to have our own way with the language. For instance: I propose to make English poetry on French principles. What do I require of my readers? not near so much as Mr Stone: I only ask them to weaken the English accent till it is no stronger than the French, and to count accurately up to twelve. Here are four alexandrines:

> Why does not the lobster ever climb trees or fly?
> Can he not? or does he think it would look silly?
> I have made these verses as well as I am able:
> You must be to blame if they sound disagreeable.

Observe the *rime riche*.

There is something novel to me not only in Mr Stone's dealings with his native tongue but in his attitude towards his customers: it opens a vista of new relations between the producers and consumers of commodities. He says of his readers, p. 50, 'If they cannot have the ordinary accent emphasising the metre, they pine at least for unquestionably long syllables. This desire is quite unreasonable, because the gradations of quantity are infinite.' He means to have monosyllabic endings, and he tells us on pp. 41–2 that 'if we do not like them at first, we must get used to them.' Perhaps one might take this firm tone in other trades. Say I am erecting houses, and I propose in future to use gingerbread as a building material. I address my tenants thus: 'If you cannot have a tiled roof, you pine at least for a roof which does not let the rain through. This desire is quite unreasonable, because gingerbread is a porous substance. As to falling through the floor, if you do not like it at first, you must get used to it.' Or is it only on readers of verse, *animis natum inuentumque poema iuuandis*, that these exhortations to fortitude will take effect?

The long and short of the matter is this. We now regulate English verse by the strong and determinate element of stress: its management is what distinguishes verse from prose. The weak and indeterminate element of quantity we subordinate: its management is one of the many things which distinguish, not verse from prose, but good verse from bad. Mr Stone proposes that we should put the weak to the work of the strong, and subject the strong to the predominance of the weak. Summer is come, and cricket is playing everywhere. If Mr Stone will accost the next eleven he sees in the field, and advise them to run after the ball on their hands and pick it up with their feet, he will hear some very good criticism of his quantitative hexameters.

28 Germanicus

Such examples destroy any presumption that o will be right and z be wrong when the two are found to differ: each difference must be tried on its merits, and only when reason professes itself unable to decide can resort be had to the pis-aller of authority. Those who cannot reason may wish that it were not so, but so it is.

29 Propertius

'Scholars will pardon an attempt, however bald, to render into English these exquisite love-poems.' Why? Those who have no Latin may pardon such an attempt, if they like bad verses better than silence; but I do not know why bald renderings of exquisite love-poems should be pardoned by those who want no renderings at all. One who cannot read or understand

> omniaque ingrato largibar munera somno,
> munera de prono saepe uoluta sinu,

may perhaps pardon the translation

> Ungrateful sleep! Give all I could,
> Roll from your lap my presents would!

But who else? only the personage of whom Heine tells us 'c'est son métier.' Some bald renderings there are which even scholars will pardon: when Mr Paley sings 'It is present to me to feel the chill, the very severe chill, of a hostile public executioner,' or Mr Buckley 'They cut off his ears and nostrils with the sharp brass; but he, injured in his feelings, went about, enduring that calamity with a frantic mind,' scholars are as grateful as other folk; but Mr Tremenheere never rejoices the heart like this, though he does write 'To eclipse your honoured uncle strive' and ask 'Is yours the spirit that can brave The hard bunk and the howling wave?'

The chief merit of his version is its admirable and even surprising conciseness: he has chosen his metre ill, for our octosyllabic couplet is not only as much unlike the elegiac as one couplet can be unlike another, but also affords very little room; yet nothing essential is omitted, except now and then the definite article. The phrasing too is often pointed; but it mostly wants grace and finish and is sometimes ugly: 'When, Gallus, stuttering and agasp, You languished in the damsel's clasp,' 'And, by Hylaeus bludgeoned well, Lay groaning on the Arcadian fell.' Where everything else is sacrificed to smartness and 'illa suis uerbis cogat amare Iouem' is rendered 'She'd coax the devil to her feet,' some will admire; but there is nothing smart about slang terms like 'cut' and 'wig': they misrepresent Propertius, who is not a colloquial writer but literary to a fault, and they are repulsive. Misrepresentation of Propertius is indeed the capital defect of this performance: good or bad, in movement, in diction, in spirit, it is unlike the original. I will quote some verses from the second poem, which is much the best translated:

> Life of my life, why court applause
> In fluttering folds of Coan gauze,
> With Syrian scent on plaits and curls
> And all the gauds of foreign girls?
>
> . . .
>
> What beauties e'er with Nature's vied?
> Wild ivy, meadows gaily pied,
> Lone dells with beauteous berries fraught,
> Clear streams that find their way untaught,
> Bright shores with native gems self-strewn,
> And birds that never learnt a tune!

'Twas not their toilets that did win
Leucippus' daughters each her Twin:
It was not for a powdered face
That Pelops came so far to race;
Nor Idas with Apollo vied
To bear Marpessa off a bride.

Excellent: the rendering is close and deft, the English is pure, the phrasing neat, the lines run well; but what was the Latin? elegiacs by Propertius or hendecasyllables by Martial?

A text is printed opposite the translation, and there are notes at the end.

30 Lucretius

Mr Bailey says in his preface that he has been sparing of original conjectures because he does not wish to inflict new wounds upon the text. This estimate of his own talent in that department is certainly modest and seemingly correct. He prints only one emendation, and it is *intust*. Better one than two.

31 *Corpus Poetarum Latinorum*

I have spent most of my time in finding faults, because finding faults, if they are real and not imaginary, is the most useful sort of criticism. Now I will find one more. The first instalment of this work appeared in 1893, the second in 1894; for the third, which is much the slimmest, we have waited six years; and there is no news of the fourth. W.E. Weber finished his *Corpus* single-handed in the four years 1828–32, and equipped it not only with an apparatus criticus, which in his day, true enough, was easier to compile than now, but with brief explanatory notes which often help the reader greatly. So let it not be six years more before we see the completion of a work so long required and so signally useful.

32 Lucan

On Lucan I 463 '*bellis* arcere Caycos | oppositi' I gave my reasons for accepting Bentley's *Belgis*. 'But it should be added' says Mr

Heitland 'that he proposed to rewrite lines 460–72 in an astounding manner.' Why should it be added? Because Mr Heitland cannot afford to rely upon the merits of his case, and must import this foreign matter to create prejudice. The rightness or wrongness of *Belgis* has no dependence on anything else that Bentley ever did; but because he annoys us very much by his bad conjectures, therefore we will refuse his good conjectures, for revenge is sweet. I avoided this irrelevancy; so it is said that I 'do not always manage to state the case fairly.' Then Mr Heitland, who shrinks from the conjectural emendation of Lucan, proceeds to the conjectural emendation of me; though I have not been dead nearly so long, nor do nine centuries of transcription intervene between my autograph and last December's *Classical Review*. To show that the Romans had no wish to restrain the Chauci from war, but only from war on Roman subjects, I adduced Tac. Germ. 33, where the Romans are seen exulting in the wars of Germans upon other Germans and praying to heaven for their continuance. Mr Heitland alters my '33' to '35', because the word *Chauci* occurs in that chapter: consequently at this point his argument runs off the rails and ceases to pertain to me. He then suggests that *bellis* may mean 'campaigns carried on, when necessary, beyond the Rhine,' and asks if Caesar did not twice cross the Rhine to impress the Germans. Yes, he did, in imposing strength; but that is not what frontier garrisons are for. Last, he enquires 'Are not the Chauci a rather ill-chosen *pars pro toto*?' I think that they are very well chosen, and that they are not a *pars pro toto*; but to whom, and with what design, is this question addressed? it is Mr Heitland's own business to answer it. *Caycos* is his reading and the M S reading, not a conjecture of Bentley's or mine.

33 Lucan

Mr Heitland says 'a good deal here and elsewhere depends on the value to be assigned to the codex Vossianus primus (v),' and he wishes me to settle this question finally. I have plenty else to do, but perhaps I can enable him to settle it. Nothing here, and not much elsewhere, depends on the value to be assigned to v. That v has some value is admitted: the way to find the amount of that value is to collect the passages, including this III 276, where its reading is intrinsically more probable than that of the 'Pauline' MSS, to confront these passages with those where its reading is intrinsically less probable, and to see which class is the larger and more important, and by how much. Having thus ascertained the value of v, dismiss it from your mind: never think of it again except in places where the intrinsic probability of v's readings and the 'Pauline' readings is exactly equal. In these places your knowledge of the relative value of v and the 'Paulines' will serve to guide your choice a little better than the method of drawing lots or spinning a coin: not much better, but a little. Such are the precepts of common sense and the practice of my masters Bentley and Madvig. But in Germany they have now adopted another plan, which is very different and much easier. You assume (and if you have luck you may be right in assuming) that one MS is better than another; and you then proceed to settle, in accordance with this assumption, the intrinsic probability of their readings, endeavouring above all to persuade yourself that the other MS is as nearly valueless as possible. This is scientific criticism; though liberal shepherds give it the grosser name of putting the cart before the horse.

34 Lucan

For scholars to argue against me as Mr Heitland argues is just the way to foster in me that arrogant temper to which I owe my deplorable reputation.

35 Lucan

This fabulous narrative is a specimen of the 'sympathetic exegesis' which is supposed to have arisen in the last twenty years of the 19th century; though in point of fact it flourished high at the century's beginning in Cicero's philosophical works, amidst great though temporary applause, under the auspices of Goerenz. The engine was invented to protect corrupt passages from correction: let a text be impeached as bad grammar or nonsense, and the commentator instantly overflows with fictitious details of the disorder which he alleges to have existed in the author's mind: they may seem incredible, they may lack all confirmation, but he is a sympathetic interpreter and you disbelieve him at your peril. This practice of concocting fictions at a moment's notice, instead of stopping and thinking, or trying to think, is naturally attended with a certain amount of moral and intellectual damage; and often when the sympathetic interpreter arrives at a passage which is not corrupt, but only difficult, and which really wants interpreting, the event proves that his bad habit has crippled his powers of interpretation. Instead of probing the difficulty to find its solution, he resorts to the easier and more familiar expedient of smothering it under a cascade of figments; and the office of interpreter devolves upon the unsympathetic.

36 Virgil

It amends the language, but the sense it does not amend. 'The morning's milk is made into cheese at night': so far so good. 'The evening's milk' – now we are going to hear that the evening's milk is made into cheese at some other time, or that it is not made into cheese – 'the evening's milk is either carried to town at daybreak in baskets or else salted and put by for the winter.' But the stuff men carry in baskets and salt for the winter is cheese, not milk; so it appears that the evening's milk as well as the morning's (they do not get much sleep in this dairy) is made into cheese at night. Was it then simply in order to turn round and laugh at us that you led us to suppose the contrary? But to proceed: you have now told us that the cheese from the evening's milk is sold or salted: what are we to infer about the cheese from the morning's milk? The natural inference is that something else becomes of it; and if so we should like to know what. But you are so playful to-day that we dare not draw the natural inference, for fear you should turn round and laugh at us again: perhaps we had best assume that there is no difference in destination, as there seemingly was none in manufacture, between these two batches of cheese which you so carefully distinguish. This is didactic poetry: 'the morning's milk is made into cheese at night (never mind what afterwards becomes of it); the evening's milk (never mind what happens in the interval) is carried to town next morning in cheese-baskets or salted for winter eating.' 'The horse has four legs; the mare has two ears and a tail.'

37 The *Culex*

The authors of the *Culex* and *Ciris* and *Aetna* were mediocre poets, and worse; and the gods and men and booksellers whom they affronted by existing allotted them for transcription to worse than mediocre scribes. The *Ciris* was indited by a twaddler, and the *Culex* and *Aetna* by stutterers: but what they stuttered and twaddled was Latin, not double-Dutch; and great part of it is now double-Dutch, and Latin no more. The deep corruption of the MSS is certified not merely by the jargon which they offer us, but by other and external proofs.

38 The *Culex*

Just as it is hard to tell, in Statius or Valerius Flaccus, whether this or that absurd expression is due to miscopying or to the divine afflatus of the bard, so in the *Culex* and *Ciris* and *Aetna* it is for ever to be borne in mind that they are the work of poetasters. Many a time it is impossible to say for certain where the badness of the author ends and the badness of the scribe begins. And many a time, when the guilt is firmly saddled on the copyist, there is no more to be done except sit down and sigh; because in such corruptions as *metuenda* for *Zanclaea* all vestige of the truth has vanished: etiam periere ruinae.

Here then, between poets capable of much and copyists capable of anything, is a promising field for the exercise of tact and caution: a prudent editor will be slow to emend the text and slow to defend it, and his page will bristle with the obelus. But alas, it is not for specimens of tact and caution that one resorts to the editors of the *Culex*; it is rather to fill one's bosom with sheaves of improbable corrections and impossible explanations. In particular the editions of Baehrens in 1880 and of Leo in 1891 are patterns of insobriety.

39 Ovid

There you see the modern editor of Ovid: unacquainted with textual criticism, and content to remain so; unwilling to learn, unwilling to think. He has not heard that glosses are written in margins and find their way into texts, and he has no desire to hear it. If he chances upon critics who have learnt their trade and practise it, the spectacle does not arouse his curiosity nor induce him to reflect; it only sets him exclaiming in blank astonishment at the existence of human beings so unlike himself.

40 Ovid

Many of the conjectures which he has to report are the conjectures of thoughtful persons: Mr Ehwald is not thoughtful, and must expect to be puzzled by the proceedings of those who are.

41 Persius and Juvenal

There is a strange notion abroad in the world that close adherence to one MS or family of MSS is scientific. It was lately the fashion among editors of Persius to overestimate AB: Mr J. Bieger in a dissertation published in 1890 set the example of underestimating them, and of overestimating P; and Mr Buecheler in his edition of 1893 proceeded as far in this direction as his intelligence would allow. Mr Owen proceeds a trifle further.

42 Persius and Juvenal

The lazy habit of preferring P to other MSS even where its readings are inferior to theirs is now not only in fashion but in honour; and I spend no words on the passages where Mr Owen merely follows in the steps of his contemporaries: XIV 215 sq. for instance, where we are grown familiar with this wretched spectacle –

> parcendum est teneris, nondum impleuere medullas:
> naturae mala nequitia est, –

in lieu of the admirable sentence which our fathers saw there and our sons will see there again.

43 Persius and Juvenal

Yet Mr Owen has still left something to be done, or suffered shall I say, by future critics of superior insensibility. He can feel, for instance, that at XIII 208 the 'has patitur poenas peccandi *sola uoluntas*' of other MSS is right and that the *saeua uoluptas* of P is wrong. But probably there are people in the world who cannot feel it; and if one of these worthies edits Juvenal to-morrow he will be congratulated on having produced a text as much purer than Mr Owen's as Mr Owen's is purer than Mr Buecheler's. In this race it is neither the hare nor the tortoise that wins, but the limpet.

44 Persius and Juvenal

With this exception Mr Owen's innovations, so far as I can see, have only one merit, which certainly, in view of their character, is a merit of some magnitude: they are few.

45 Persius and Juvenal

If theories of this sort are to be published at all, which is highly undesirable, it is best not to preface them with comments on the *securitas* and the *ignorantia* of other folk, who do not publish such theories.

46 Juvenal

Crispinus airs a light summer ring on his sweating fingers, unable to sustain the weight of a heavier one.

[. . .]

Instead of which Messrs Gercke and Duff and Wilson, following Haeckermann, declare that *aestiuum* does not imply a special ring, but is adverbial and only signifies 'in summer;' and from the next verse they extort the meaning that Crispinus wears a very heavy ring, so heavy that he could not bear a heavier. And why this stern

430

endeavour to dodge the plain sense of the words? Because there is no evidence that the Romans wore lighter rings in summer than in winter! Of course the Romans did not: it was a single Egyptian who did. The foppery was insufferable precisely because it was unparalleled. An early device of Mr Disraeli's for attracting notice was to have two canes in use, one for the morning, one for the afternoon. Suppose someone contested the truth of this story 'because there is no evidence that the English used different canes for afternoon and morning:' what would be said of him? That he argued like a classical scholar.

47 Persius and Juvenal

Here I should stop, but for one circumstance, of which I think it right that readers should be warned. Mr Owen has an unfortunate habit of saying things which he believes to be true. He says on p. 126*a* –

'Whereas Mr Housman (*Journal of Philology* xxi 101 ff, xxii 84 ff) depreciated the Neapolitanus of Propertius and appreciated four late MSS of the 15th century or thereabouts, and denied the supremacy of the Neapolitanus, which he wished to assign to the 15th century, this house of cards has been lately overthrown, since Mr Montague James has proved (*Classical Review* xvii 462) that the Neapolitanus was written in the 12th century, as Keil long ago maintained, and is consequently by far our earliest MS of Propertius.'

The reader needs to be told that when Mr Owen says I depreciated the Neapolitanus he is attempting to state the fact that I made the most elaborate defence of the Neapolitanus which is anywhere extant; that when he says I appreciated four late MSS he is attempting to state the fact that I pulled down those four MSS from the elevation on which they had been placed by Baehrens; and that when he says I wished to assign the Neapolitanus to the fifteenth century he is attempting to state the fact that I declared myself totally indifferent to the question whether the Neapolitanus belonged to the fifteenth century or the twelfth. I think I am right in supposing that an incautious student might be misled by Mr Owen's phraseology.

If Lachmann, having no good MSS, used a bad one, is that a reason
why Lachmann's disciples, having two good MSS, should use it
still? Parisians ate rats in the siege, when they had nothing better to
eat: must admirers of Parisian cookery eat rats for ever?

49 Virgil

The difference in look between *Hesperiam* and *expectat*, though
slight compared with the difference in sense between *expectat* and
moratur, is nevertheless, I daresay, more quickly and sharply per-
ceived. Our bodies are much superior to our minds; and the human
eye, though severely criticised by Helmholtz, is at any rate an
instrument of greater precision than the average human brain.

50 Propertius

The mixture of mirth and horror with which such notes as this
would have been read by critics in the past, and are likely to be read
by critics in the future, is an emotion of which we in these times are
fast ceasing to be capable. 'Direness, familiar to our slaughterous
thoughts, Cannot once start us.' And notes of this sort, common
almost everywhere, are common in Mr Butler's Propertius. It is
true that he often revolts against the fashion, and says of the MS
lections defended by his contemporaries that they are impossible or
that they possess no meaning; and he adopts conjectures such as II
30 8 *ipsa*, III 2 16 *nec defessa*, IV 8 48 *totus*, whose merit and
probability would be invisible to a dull man. But when one reads
on, and comes to some other emendations which he rejects, and to
some other MS lections which in his eyes possess a meaning and are
possible, one attributes his occasional recalcitrancy less to any
virtue of his own than to the sudden and violent intervention of his
guardian angel.

51 Propertius

I 8 27 hic erat! 'She was here all the time!' Of course she was, or
not a word of lines 1–26 could have been written. If a man who had

been talking to Mr Butler for the last five minutes should suddenly burst out 'you were here all the time,' it would surprise him; because the only people who say such things are live madmen and dead classics.

52 Propertius

At I 21 6–10 he writes 'ne soror . . . sentiat . . . Gallum . . . effugere . . . non potuisse . . . ; | nec (et MSS) quaecumque super dispersa inuenerit ossa | montibus Etruscis, haec sciat esse mea.' These are the words of a dying soldier whose last thought is of his sister, and Mr Butler thus translates them: 'nor let her ever know that whatever bones she may find on the Tuscan hills are mine.' Certainly the discovery that her brother had 1000 skulls, 2000 femora, and 26,000 vertebrae, would be at once a painful shock to her affections and an overwhelming addition to her knowledge of anatomy.

53 Propertius

I suppose that this is hardly what would be called a favourable review; and I feel the compunction which must often assail a reviewer who is neither incompetent nor partial, when he considers how many books, inferior to the book he is criticising, are elsewhere receiving that vague and conventional laudation which is distributed at large, like the rain of heaven, by reviewers who do not know the truth and consequently cannot tell it. But after all, a portion of the universal shower is doubtless now descending, or will soon descend, upon Mr Butler himself; and indeed, unless some unusual accident has happened, he must long ere this have received the punctual praises of the *Scotsman*.

54 Lucilius

Both works deserve praise, both deserve thanks, and both deserve more thanks than praise; for while gratitude is earned simply by the element of good which a book presents to us, admiration must depend on the greater or less predominance of the good element over the bad.

55 Lucilius

It is therefore no praise of an editor of Lucilius to say that he is conservative, and it is false to say that any editor of Lucilius is cautious. Cautious men do not edit Lucilius; they leave him to be edited by bold and devoted men, whose heroism they admire with that mixture of pity and self-congratulation which a Roman may be supposed to have felt as he saw Curtius descend into the gulf, or an Israelite as he watched the departure of the scapegoat into the wilderness.

56 Lucilius

Anyone who looks at this verse can see that there are three possible ways of amending it, all equally probable. The alternative Turnebus chose was *uident*, and everyone followed him till Baehrens in 1886 was egotistical enough to substitute the second alternative, *uocans*. The third alternative, *uocat*, was now left lying on the ground for anyone who was not too proud to take it: Mr Marx stoops down and picks it up, and his touch transmutes it to pure gold. Conjectures, to his eyes, are arranged in this threefold order of merit: 1st the conjectures of Mr Marx, 2nd the conjectures of mankind in general, 3rd the conjectures of certain odious persons. Conformably to this classification he sets *uocat* in the text, because it is his own; relegates *uident* to the note, because it is another man's; suppresses *uocans* altogether, because it is Baehrens's.

57 Lucilius

Mr Marx will not condescend to learn the road by reading the signposts: he prefers to domineer and err. It is his will and pleasure that *narcessibai* should be altered into something scarce less

monstrous than itself, *narce, saeua i*; and *uomitum* he declares to
be a neuter substantive, which has kindly consented to appear, by
special request, for this occasion only.

58 Lucilius

In short, this is a country where Mr Marx is not at home.

And there is another: Latium. For the office of editing Lucilius
Mr Marx is not sufficiently acquainted with the language which
Lucilius spoke.

59 Lucilius

If Mr Marx had cared to know what this rule was worth, he had
three ways of finding out. He might have thought about it, and then
he would have discovered that it was absurd in essence: there is no
imaginable reason why the corruption of a word should upset the
metre of a verse. He might have put it to the test, and then he would
have discovered that it was false in fact: Nonius p. 120 [172 Lindsay]
quotes from Horace (*serm.* II 4 73) 'ego faecem primus et allec |
miscui,' which is quite metrical (for cretic words occur in Horace's
hexameters) but very far removed from what Horace wrote. He
might have read his own edition of Lucilius, and then he would
have discovered that he had broken his precious rule about once in
every ten lines: 401 *scalprorum* for *scalptorum*, 408 *sternendam* for
sternenda, 420 *dare* for *da*, 429 *fisco* for *pisco*, 434 *decolaui* for *decollaui*,
442 *extructa* for *extructam*, 451 *quorsum* for *cursum*, 454 *aula mollis* for
ala molis, 472 *horae* for *hora et*, 474 *aegre* for *aegri*, 489 *fictorum* for
pictorum, 491 *aetati*' for *aetate*, 494 *pus* for *plus*, and so on. Three
ways, and he took none of them. Why should he? Why should a
classical scholar care what he says, so long as everyone knows that
his heart is in the right place? In no single line of human activity
except our own, – not in politics, not in religion, not in the
advertisement of patent medicines, – would a man venture to stand
forward and utter words so evidently irreconcilable with reason,
with reality, and with his own behaviour. But Mr Marx knew well

that he had nothing to fear. He knew that he was addressing an audience less thoughtful, less truth-loving, and less able to take care of itself, than the audiences addressed by demagogues and dervishes and quacks. He looked round Europe and saw a ring of classical scholars sitting waiting to have their prejudices flattered and their intellects affronted, and he obliged them.

60 Lucilius

But the most arresting feature in Mr Marx's edition is neither the resolution with which he defends Lucilius' fragments against other folk's alterations, nor the faintheartedness with which he surrenders them to his own, but the facility, the confidence, and the boundless knowledge with which he explains their relation to one another and to their lost and unforthcoming context. For interpreting those words and sentences which we possess in black and white, his aptitude, as we have already seen, is not remarkable; but in the invisible world he is quite at home. Apion, unless he was the liar Iosephus thought him, called up the spirit of Homer from the dead, and ascertained from his own melodious lips the true city and parentage of that widely born and many-fathered man. But the information thus elicited he kept secret in the deep of his heart, and the world was none the wiser. Mr Marx, like Apion, is an adept in the black art, but he is not, like Apion, a dog in the manger. He is brimful of knowledge which he can only have acquired by necromancy, and he puts it all at our disposal.

61 Lucilius

Mr Marx should write a novel. Nay, he may almost be said to have written one; for his notes on book III (Lucilius' journey to Sicily) are not so much a commentary on the surviving fragments as an original narrative of travel and adventure.

'Audacia' is the chief crime which Mr Marx (I p. cxv) imputes to Mueller; to Mueller, who on p. xliii of his preface has these sober observations, 'fragmentis explicandis uel copulandis nihil facilius

436

esse, si uulgi plausum spectes, neque difficilius quidquam, si peri-
torum, pridem sanxit auctoritas prudentium.' But when Mr Marx
and his school talk about 'audacia' they do not mean audacity, they
mean alteration of the text; and they would be surprised to hear that
the fabrication of imaginary contexts has any audacity about it. Just
as murder is murder no longer if perpetrated by white men on black
men or by patriots on kings; just as immorality exists in the
relations of the sexes and nowhere else throughout the whole field
of human conduct; so a conjecture is audacious when it is based on
the letters preserved in a MS, and ceases to be audacious, ceases
even to be called a conjecture, when, like these conjectural sup-
plements of Mr Marx's, it is based on nothing at all. No editor of
these fragments, neither Mueller nor Baehrens, has been so rash and
venturesome as Mr Marx; none has such cause to wish that the earth
may lie heavy on Herculaneum and that no roll of Lucilius may ever
emerge into the light of day.

62 Dorotheus

Is it a rule of etiquette, or pure vanity, or irrepressible originality
of genius, which ordains that each successive editor of a collection
of fragments shall complicate our studies by changing the sequence
and numeration established by his predecessor?

63 The *Culex*

The fact is that Mr Ellis does not collate MSS: he transcribes from
them, without reference to any particular text, such things as attract
his attention.

64 *Appendix Vergiliana*

Mr Némethy, like Mr Curcio, provides his recension with a
commentary, and fully half of it is devoted to the collection of
verbal parallels. These are very numerous, and some of them, I
suppose, have never been adduced before: certainly some should
never be adduced again.

Works of this sort are little better than interruptions to our studies, and Mr Némethy was ill-advised in attempting a task so much beyond his powers. It appears from his preface that he is an ardent and even flamboyant Hungarian patriot; so to Germans and Croats his book may possibly afford a pleasure whose Croatian name I do not know, but whose German name is *Schadenfreude*.

66 Juvenal

It was a fine August morning which placed in Monsignore Ratti's hand the envelope containing this fragment, and he gives us leave to imagine the trepidation with which he opened it and the joy with which he discovered that the parchment was in two pieces instead of one. When a scholar is so literary as all this, it would be strange if he were quite accurate: accordingly his transcript of the text has three misprints in its second line; he quotes from the *Classical Review* of 1809; he has discovered, and frequently cites, an edition of Juvenal by J. P. Postgate; Friedlaender's edition he provides with *Aumer Kungen*, and confers on Mr Chatelain the baptismal name of Hemilius.

67 Propertius

When they enquired of Solon why he had provided in his code no penalty for parricide, he answered that he thought nobody would ever do such a thing; and there prevails a tacit assumption, no truer than Solon's, that transpositions of this nature do not occur. They do occur, as anyone can ascertain who cares to know; but their occurrence is disquieting, so they are noticed with reluctance and rapidly forgotten. I will here hand over two specimens of the offence to be dealt with *more maiorum*: sew them up together in the usual sack and drown them according to precedent in Lethe.

68 The Forming of Adjectives

The *thes. ling. Lat.* has not yet arrived at CYD-, so we lose the guidance of a will-o'-the-wisp.

Little in this volume is new, for seven-eighths of it consist of the *ex Ponto*, which Mr Owen has edited once already, and the *Tristia*, which he has edited twice. His first edition of the *Tristia* had value, which it still retains, as furnishing full collations of the principal manuscripts; but its reader was repeatedly jolted out of his chair by collision with obstacles in the text. Picking himself up from the hearthrug, and feeling his neck to make sure it was not broken, he would find that what he had encountered was either a lection which no other editor had ever admitted or a conjecture which no other editor could easily have made. The disfigurement inflicted upon Ovid's text by Mr Owen's recension is not a matter of dispute, for it is tacitly acknowledged by its author, whose labours on the *Tristia* for the last quarter of a century have chiefly consisted in removing his own corruptions and reinstating the comparatively pure text of his predecessors. For example, of more than thirty original conjectures which he printed in 1889, only eight remain in 1915. That is six or seven too many; but Augeas failed to clean out his own stables, and it is no wonder if Mr Owen's similar task is even yet unfinished and will need a fourth edition to complete it.

70 Ovid

There has been some dispute in the past about the authorship of this fragment, but that is now happily set at rest, for Mr Owen assures us that the genuineness of the work is fully established by the testimony of Pliny. He says this once on p. iii and twice on p. xi, so that no further doubt is possible; for, in the words of another Student of Christ Church, 'What I tell you three times is true.'

Another poem, more than 600 lines long, was written by Ovid in his exile and has come down to our own times. Its name is not upon Mr Owen's title-page, but under cover of this silence it has been slipped into the middle of the book, – *medio tutissimus Ibis*, as its author himself observed, – apparently in the hope that it may escape notice. Well, so it shall.

71 Ovid

When these scholars ask me these questions, they are not beseeching me to lighten their darkness; nothing is further from their desire. They hope and believe that they are asking me awkward questions, questions which I in my precipitancy have forgotten to ask myself; and accordingly, like Pilate of old, they do not stay for an answer. They assume without more ado that there is no answer, and that my conjecture is therefore wrong.

72 Varius

One day towards the end of the eighth century the scribe of cod. Paris. Lat. 7530, a miscellany to which we owe the *carmen de figuris* (anth. Lat. Ries. 485, P.L.M. Baehr. III pp. 273–85), began to copy out for us, on the 28th leaf of the MS, the *Thyestes* of Varius. He transcribed the title and the prefatory note, which run thus: *INCIPIT THVESTA VARII. Lucius Varius cognomento Rufus Thyesten tragoediam (traged . . . cod.) magna cura absolutam (absoluto cod.) post Actiacam uictoriam Augusti (aug . . . cod.) ludis eius in scaena edidit, pro qua fabula sestertium deciens accepit.* Then he changed his mind: he proceeded with a list of the *notae* employed by Probus and Aristarchus, and the masterpiece of Roman tragedy has rejoined its author in the shades.

This testimony is cited, though not always fully or accurately, in the ordinary books of reference; and if for any reason I wished to confer the *Thyestes* on another than L. Varius, my first business would be to impugn the credit of this testimony. If I could not, I must renounce my design. Simply to say nothing about it, and hope that nobody else would say anything either, is an alternative which would not occur to me.

73 Varius

My present concern however is not with his arithmetic but with the phrasing by which he has obscured the true state of affairs. The state of affairs, in Brummer's collection, and with little difference in

Diehl's, is this. *Varus* occurs in 14 places, and only once does any MS corrupt it to *Varius*. *Varius* occurs in 15 places, and in every one of them it is corrupted to *Varus* by some or most or all of the MSS.

The reader wonders, and Mr Garrod, whom I should not judge to be skilled in self-analysis, must also wonder, why he has huddled away this salient contrast, so material to the question at issue, under a counterpane of indeterminate language. But I have long dwelt among men and I see the reason plain enough. It is because coming events cast their shadows before. Mr Garrod is going to say on the next page, in support of his thesis, 'Bear in mind . . . how much greater for a scribe was the temptation to change *Varum* to *Varium* than to make the inverse change;' and if he now allows himself to notice how scribes really behaved, he will be unable to cherish this delusion or to bid us bear it in mind. Instinct, more sensitive to danger than the conscious intellect, takes alarm betimes; and the pen automatically glides into a form of words which will help the truth to escape detection.

After some inexact observations on Quintilian and Martial he adds that 'the MSS of Horace tell a like tale.' They tell a tale like mine and unlike Mr Garrod's.

74 Varius

This fifth eclogue, in common with the rest, is generally thought to have been published about 39 B.C. Mr Garrod, for reasons which he sets forth on p. 217, assigns it a date 'in or after 35 B.C.' If 'after' means six years after, when Virgil is usually supposed to have finished the *georgics*, I have no remark to make on that. But 'in' perplexes me; because, if Varus was dead, 'extinctus crudeli funere,' in the year 35 B.C., I do not see how he could produce the *Thyestes* in the year 29.

Yes, perhaps I do see. Mr Garrod has not given a full and consecutive account of Varus' career, but has left something to the intelligence of his readers. By putting together his scattered utterances, dotting his *i*'s and crossing his *t*'s, I think I have constructed what is surely the most eventful history in the annals of literature: the life, death, and resurrection of Alfenus Varus.

441

Varus was living when Virgil wrote *buc.* VI and IX, and also when he wrote VIII (pp. 212 sq.), which was in 35 B.C. (p. 217). He was living, in old age and unreverend profligacy (his mother, who according to Virgil *buc.* V 23 survived him, must have been a venerable figure), when Horace wrote *epod.* 5 (p. 214), to which no precise date is assigned. But when Virgil wrote *buc.* V, that is 'in or after 35 B.C.' (p. 217), he was dead (pp. 215 sq.). Then there is silence for a while; and then in the August of 29 B.C. is produced the *Thyestes*, which was no posthumous work, for its author was rewarded with a gift of a million sesterces.

The explanation of this seeming inconsistency will be found in a passage already cited by Mr Garrod, *laud. Pis.* 238 sq.

> Maecenas tragico quatientem pulpita gestu
> erexit Varum.

Mr Garrod did not translate these words, but I now see how he understands them: 'Maecenas erexit Varum' means that Maecenas raised Varus from the dead. And no public man of the time was more competent to do so. Eques Etrusco de sanguine regum, imbued with the traditions of an ancient and religious folk much given to the worship of infernal deities, he possessed the further and exceptional advantage of a house on the Esquiline. There, from the *turris Maecenatiana*, most likely built for the purpose, he commanded a view of the adjacent graveyard and could observe the nocturnal sorceries of Canidia. If the moon blushed and withdrew, as would sometimes happen, he sent out Horace as a spy. The zeal with which the grateful poet discharged his mission has left its literary record in *serm.* I 8, and his inquisitorial supervision of her rites provoked Canidia to describe him as 'Esquilini pontifex uenefici.' 'crematos excitare mortuos' was one of the accomplishments on which this good lady prided herself, and we may believe that she practised it often; Maecenas was an apt though furtive pupil; and never did the black art subserve a better end than when, no doubt at Virgil's request, he resuscitated Alfenus Varus, enriching the literature of Rome with its loftiest tragedy and the late deceased with more than £10,000.

'It is the moderns,' says Mr Garrod on p. 217, 'who rush into print.' Well, perhaps some of them do.

The following remarks are occasioned by Mr S.G. Owen's paper on 'The Phillipps manuscripts of Juvenal' in the last number of this Journal, pp. 238–64, and more especially by the six paragraphs in which my name occurs. The particular questions at issue are mostly trifles and mostly incapable of decision; but their discussion will have a more general interest as showing how differently it is possible for two scholars to conduct their mental operations. The causes which render me unintelligible to Mr Owen and Mr Owen unintelligible to me are probably many and various, but perhaps it is not difficult to distinguish and isolate one. I am accustomed to reach conclusions by reasoning and to commend them by argument. How Mr Owen reaches conclusions I have no means of knowing except by observing how he commends them; and I observe that argument is not his favourite method. His favourite method is simple affirmation, which he applies to the settlement of disputed questions with the utmost freedom and confidence. For this confidence I see so little ground that I infer it has some ground which I cannot see; and the less evidence of reason I find in Mr Owen's writing the more am I forced to the hypothesis that he has access to a higher and purer source of illumination.

76 Juvenal

But Mr Owen says that 'there are two insuperable objections to the conjecture;' and they are these. '(1) it leaves Neptune unmentioned in this full catalogue of the gods.' This full catalogue of the gods already omits Apollo, Diana, Mercury, Mars, Venus, Vesta, Ceres, and Minerva, not to mention Amphitrite; but if it also omitted Neptune it would cease to be a full catalogue; and this is an insuperable objection. Mr Owen and I do not even speak the same language: he uses the word 'full' to express the idea which I express by the word 'defective.' Pass to the second insuperable objection: '(2) it assigns to *profundum* the meaning of "hell," a meaning which as far as I know is unparalleled.' It assigns to *profundum* its proper meaning, 'the deep;' and *imum profundum* is what Milton calls 'the lowest deep.' There are half a dozen verses in the *Aetna* alone where *profundum* signifies the subterranean world; for example 578 'septemque duces raptumque profundo' (Amphiaraum). So 'insuperable' is another of the English words to which Mr Owen and I attach different notions. But even after surmounting two insuperable objections I cannot escape defeat, for Mr Owen now brings up his 42 centimetre gun: '*aliquis* is unquestionably right.' Nil ultra quaero plebeius.

77 Juvenal

> pone Tigellinum, taeda lucebis in illa
> qua stantes ardent qui fixo pectore fumant.

pectore PBAO, *gutture* most MSS.

'The reading *gutture* is absurd. It is defended by Mr Housman on the ground that to fasten a victim by the throat would involve less trouble.' It was defended by me on four grounds; but this is the only one of them which Mr Owen can remember. 'As if the object of torturers was to save themselves trouble! Such people are prepared to take infinite trouble.' If necessary. I had better quote what I actually said: '*gutture* . . . is on every count superior: superior palaeographically, as the less common word, and superior in sense, because to fasten a victim by the throat involves less trouble, consumes less material, *and causes more discomfort*, than to fasten him by the chest.' Mr Owen however dissents: 'And consider what the result of fastening the victim by the throat would be. The swift result would be throttling and consequent death, the last thing desired by the torturer, whose object is to prolong the pain.' If the torturer were so misguided as to use a slipknot, throttling, I imagine, would indeed be the result; but not otherwise: we do not hear that throttling was of frequent occurrence in the pillory. *fixo* moreover, properly 'nailed,' implies nothing so loose as a slipknot, and will indicate rather a collar clamped to the stake. But the torturer's object, says Mr Owen, 'would be better attained by fastening by the chest: then the victim while being roasted could not struggle, so far from stopping his anguish by throttling himself he could not even show it.' I cannot struggle either: I feel like the queen of Sheba when she had seen all Solomon's wisdom and there was no more spirit in her. Is there in all the wide world a single person except Mr Owen who conceives that to fasten a man by the chest will prevent him from moving his arms and legs? Does Mr Owen himself conceive it? Does his mind know that this is the meaning of the words which his hand has written?

His final stroke is now impending. 'So the scholiast understood it: "ut lucerent spectatoribus, cum fixa essent illis guttura, ne se curuarent."' The dispute is whether Juvenal wrote *fixo pectore* or *fixo gutture*; and when the scholiast says 'cum *fixa* essent illis *guttura, ne se curuarent*', Mr Owen quotes those words as showing how the scholiast understood *fixo pectore*. Am I awake or asleep?

78 Ovid

One of the causes why any proposal to correct a verse or sentence alarms and distresses the natural man is that it makes an unusual demand upon his intellect and entails the weary work of reading and considering the context. That form of correction which consists in transferring a verse or sentence from one place to another is in consequence doubly discomposing, because the mental fatigue which it involves is twice as heavy. There are two contexts to be read and considered, not only one.

Disrelish for excessive and unwonted labour will often put on disguises, and much is sometimes said on these occasions about the respect due to the authority of MSS. But that is a cloak which does not always fit; and whatever may be the reason why Ovid's editors, in the passage which I shall first examine, maintain the arrangement of verses which I propose to disturb, it cannot be their respect for MS authority. MS authority is here divided, and the weight of it is adverse.

79 Ovid

Before I edit a work, I read it; and a quarter of a century ago I read the *Ibis* and consequently noticed this discrepancy. I am the first editor who ever did read the *Ibis*, and down to this year 1916 I am the last; but it may have been read by some persons other than its editors, and this passage at any rate was read by one scholar before me.

445

But who will convey an apprehension of such matters as these to the mind of Mr Ehwald or Mr Owen? They find three editors in succession, Guethling, Merkel, and me, arrested by the same invisible obstacle; and our behaviour inspires them, not with curiosity, not with a wish to read the passage instead of skimming it, but with the impatient wonder of Balaam when his ass persisted in seeing the angel of the Lord. If transposition is proposed, they must of course resist it, but they resist in the dark and have nothing more apposite to urge than the automatic objection, always ready to be reached down from the shelf, that the verses to be separated are inseparable.

81 Phaedrus

To handle a text of this sort is a business which calls for diffidence and flexibility: Dr Postgate is both sanguine and stubborn, and if once he gets hold of the stick by the wrong end he does not soon let go.

82 Phaedrus

An orderly and intelligible apparatus criticus, as several volumes of this series have shown, is a gift not always to be expected from an English editor. Dr Postgate's notes on I 19 7, 28 5, IV 9 5, 17 8 and 10, 18 14, 20 15, V 5 1, *app.* 13 25, 14 10, 15 10, appear to have been written before he knew what his text was going to be, or after he had forgotten what it was.

83 Ovid

This of course is not what he was trying to say, but the pen is mightier than the wrist.

84 Ovid

Dr Postgate's willingness to teach is great and obvious, yet I do not find him very instructive. An air of ripe and penetrating judgment is never absent from anything that he writes, but I sometimes miss the substance, and I cannot reconcile the strength of his anxiety to seem superior with the faintness of his endeavour to be so.

85 Ovid

Who was Ibis? Nobody. He is much too good to be true. If one's enemies are of flesh and blood, they do not carry complaisance so far as to choose the dies Alliensis for their birthday and the most ineligible spot in Africa for their birthplace. Such order and harmony exist only in worlds of our own creation, not in the jerry-built edifice of the demiurge. Nor does man assail a real enemy, the object of his sincere and lively hatred, with an interminable and inconsistent series of execrations which can neither be read nor written seriously. To be starved to death and killed by lightning, to be brayed in a mortar as you plunge into a gulf on horseback, to be devoured by dogs, serpents, a lioness, and your own father in the brazen bull of Phalaris, are calamities too awful to be probable and too improbable to be awful. And when I say that Ibis was nobody I am repeating Ovid's own words. In the last book that he wrote, several years after the *Ibis*, he said, *ex Pont.* IV 14 44, 'extat adhuc nemo saucius ore meo.'

86 Manilius

Professor J. van Wageningen has sent me a review of my fourth volume of Manilius which he has published in *Museum* vol. 28 pp. 173–7. I never contradict the taradiddles usual in reviews, because, if the reader thinks it worth his while, he can find out for himself whether they are true or no, and if he chooses to believe them without enquiry, it serves him right. But when he is fed with false information about a MS which is out of his reach, he can do nothing to help himself, and may fairly claim to be protected.

87 Manilius

If Mr van Wageningen wishes to know of errors in my writings he had better address enquiry to me. I am more interested in discovering them than anyone else can possibly be, and consequently I discover more of them. Here are two: II 79 'minusque GLM' should be 'minusque GL, mimusque M,' and II 394 'adsumpto L^2, assumpto L' should be 'adsumpto L, assumpto L^2.'

88 Catullus

But his main purpose in withholding indispensable information and deceiving the reader by silence is to find room for a long record of conjectures which dishonour the human intellect.

89 *Fragmenta Poetarum Latinorum*

I should have written less harshly if Mr Morel had not taken measures to secure favourable reviews from his own countrymen. By duly disparaging Baehrens (in bad Latin) on his first page, and by ritual homage to Leo and Cichorius and other acceptable names, he has done his best to create a friendly atmosphere and obtain commendation irrespective of desert; and he must not be surprised if smoke ascending from domestic altars draws in a current of cold air from abroad.

90 Ovid

Encounters between Ovid and the French Academy have not always been happy, and Anatole France's amended text of *trist.* IV 10 42 is dropped by common consent into the neighbouring stream of Lethe when the two authors sit down together in Elysium for a chat about the art of love.

91 Martial

The printers have indulged immoderately in their favourite sport of dropping letters on the floor and then leaving them to lie there or else putting them back in wrong places; and at the top of p. 113 of the text their merriment transgresses the bounds of decorum.

If unthinking critics could know how much ashamed one is to answer what they write, they would begin to be a little ashamed of writing it.

93 Statius

The sum total of original conjectures which Mr Klotz has introduced into the text appears to be seventeen, half-a-dozen of which are merely orthographical; but he contrives to see his name in print at seventeen other places by attaching it to readings which are no conjectures of his. For instance at I 22 he says *'teque o'* Klotzius,' but immediately divulges that this is the reading of P; and Mueller had told us that it was also the conjecture of Gronouius. Apparently he thus lays claim to honour for printing any MS lection which has not been printed by another editor. Suppose that all of us wooed fame so strenuously! When Mueller and Kohlmann similarly introduced, as they often did from P, a novel reading, they did not add 'Muellerus' or 'Kohlmannus;' and Mr Klotz does not extricate them from the dank shade of modesty by supplying *their* names.

94 Juvenal

I have made no search for faults in the other satires, but so many have caught my eye that the total must be very great, and some are very grave. The note at VI 614 on p. 92 is an assemblage of almost all imaginable blunders. That at III 109, though so chaotic that it must bewilder everybody, is so incredible that it can deceive nobody.

FROM THE LETTERS

To his stepmother, Lucy Housman, 29 November 1877

This afternoon Ruskin gave us a great outburst against modern times. He had got a picture of Turner's, framed and glassed, representing Leicester and the Abbey in the distance at sunset, over a river. He read the account of Wolsey's death out of *Henry VIII*. Then he pointed to the picture as representing Leicester when Turner had drawn it. Then he said, 'You, if you like, may go to Leicester to see what it is like now. I never shall. But I can make a pretty good guess.' Then he caught up a paintbrush. 'These stepping-stones of course have been done away with, and are replaced by a be-au-ti-ful iron bridge.' Then he dashed in the iron bridge on the glass of the picture. 'The colour of the stream is supplied on one side by the indigo factory.' Forthwith one side of the stream became indigo. 'On the other side by the soap factory.' Soap dashed in. 'They mix in the middle – like curds,' he said, working them together with a sort of malicious deliberation. 'This field, over which you see the sun setting behind the abbey, is now occupied in a *proper* manner.' Then there went a flame of scarlet across the picture, which developed itself into windows and roofs and red brick, and rushed up into a chimney. 'The atmosphere is supplied – thus!' A puff and cloud of smoke all over Turner's sky: and then the brush thrown down, and Ruskin confronting modern civilisation amidst a tempest of applause, which he always elicits now, as he has this term become immensely popular, his lectures being crowded, whereas of old he used to prophesy to empty benches.

How he confuted the geological survey, and science in general, by the help of the college cook I have no time to tell you, but remain, with love to father and all, your affectionate son

ALFRED E. HOUSMAN

To his brother, Laurence Housman, 14 December 1894

What makes many of your poems more obscure than they need be is that you do not put yourself in the reader's place and consider how, and at what stage, that man of sorrows is to find out what it is all about. You are behind the scenes and know all the data; but he knows only what you tell him. It appears from the alternative titles 'Heart's Bane' and 'Little Death' that in writing that precious croon you had in your head some meaning of which you did not suffer a single drop to escape into what you wrote: you treat us as Nebuchadnezzar did the Chaldeans, and expect us to find out the dream as well as the interpretation. That is the worst instance; but there are others where throughout the first half of a poem the hapless reader is clawing the air for a clue and has not enough breath in his body to admire anything you show him. Take 'The Stolen Mermaid': I was some time in discovering who was talking, whether it was the stolen mermaid or the robbed merman. There matters might be made clearer by altering the crabbed lines 'O, heart to captive be,' etc., into something like 'This land-bound heart of me Hears sound its mother-sea,' only better expressed I hope. In 'The Great Ride', to begin with, you had better add place as well as date to the title, or the allusion may easily be missed. You start off 'Where the merciful waters *rolled*': the reader sees the past tense, and instead of thinking of the heavenly Jordan, as you want him to, he is off to Abana and Pharphar, rivers of Damascus, and expects to hear you tell him about some historical crossing of a river where a lot of people were killed: all which you would avoid by saying '*roll*.' Further: how soon do you imagine your victim will find out that you are talking about horses? Not until the thirteenth of these long lines, unless he is such a prodigy of intelligence and good will as I am: there you mention 'hoofs,' and he has to read the thirteen lines over again. 'Flank' in line six is not enough: Swinburne's women have flanks. And as line six is at present a foot too short I advise you to introduce hoofs into it; or tails?

To Laurence Housman, 27 April 1896

Kate writes to say that she likes the verse better than the sentiments. The sentiments, she then goes on to say, appear to be taken from the book of Ecclesiastes. To prefer my versification to the sentiments of the Holy Ghost is decidedly flattering, but strikes me as a trifle impious.

To Laurence Housman, 5 October 1896

I was in Bridgnorth for several hours. In the churchyard there I remembered having heard our mother describe it and the steps up to it, which I had absolutely forgotten for more than 25 years.

I ascertained by looking down from Wenlock Edge that Hughley Church could not have much of a steeple. But as I had already composed the poem and could not invent another name that sounded so nice, I could only deplore that the church at Hughley should follow the bad example of the church at Brou, which persists in standing on a plain after Matthew Arnold has said that it stands among mountains. I thought of putting a note to say that Hughley was only a name, but then I thought that would merely disturb the reader. I did not apprehend that the faithful would be making pilgrimages to these holy places.

Morris dead! now Swinburne will have something to write about. He wrote 12 epicediums on P.B. Marston, so Morris ought to be good for at least 144.

Reading your poems in print I was a good deal struck by 'Gammer Garu,' which I don't remember noticing much in manuscript. The last stanza is really quite beautiful.

A new firm of publishers has written to me proposing to publish 'the successor' of *A.S.L.* But as they don't also offer to write it, I have had to put them off.

To Laurence Housman, 4 December 1896

I am extremely anxious that you should spend a happy Christmas; and as I have it in my power, – here goes. Last night at dinner I was sitting next to Rendall, Principal of University College Liverpool and Professor of Greek there, a very nice fellow and a great student of Marcus Aurelius and modern poetry. He was interested to hear that you were my brother: he said that he had got *Green Arras*, and then he proceeded, 'I think it is the best volume by him that I have seen: the *Shropshire Lad* had a pretty cover.'

I remain

Your affectionate brother (what a thing is fraternal affection, that it will stand these tests!)

A.E. HOUSMAN

P.S. After all, it was I who designed that pretty cover; and he did not say that the cover of *Green Arras* was pretty. (*Nor is it.*)
P.P.S. I was just licking the envelope, when I thought of the following venomed dart: I had far, far rather that people should attribute my verses to you than yours to me.

To the publisher Grant Richards, 21 February 1898

My dear Sir,

My brother Laurence has sent me a proposal from you to take over the remaining copies of *A Shropshire Lad* and publish a second edition at your own risk.

I suppose no author is averse to see his works in a second edition, or slow to take advantage of an infatuated publisher; and it is impossible not to be touched by the engaging form which your infatuation takes. But there are two points to consider at the outset.

I should not like the second edition to differ from the first in form, nor to be sold at a higher price. But, so far as I can judge from the finances of the first edition, unless it were produced cheaper or sold dearer, the sale of an entire edition of 500 copies would not pay for the printing and binding and advertising; and so, apart from the royalty, which I do not care about, you would be out of pocket.

Also I should have to ask Kegan Paul if their feelings would be lacerated by the transfer. I do not think very much of them as men of business, but their manager has been nice to me and takes a sentimental interest in the book, like you.

At the present moment I can think of nothing else to damp your ardour.

I am yours very truly A. E. HOUSMAN

To Grant Richards, 24 July 1898

Dear Sir,

I think it best not to make any alterations, even the slightest, after one has once printed a thing. It was Shelley's plan, and is much wiser than Wordsworth's perpetual tinkering, as it makes the public fancy one is inspired. But after the book is set up I should like to have the sheets to correct, as I don't trust printers or proof-readers in matters of punctuation.

3/6 is perhaps the largest sum which can be called moderate, but I suppose it deserves the name.

I am yours very truly   A.E. HOUSMAN

To the book-collector Paul Lemperly, 11 December 1899

Dear Sir,

The second edition contains nothing new except a few misprints. I have not published any other book.

I am much obliged by your letter and bookplate. I think yours is the only letter containing no nonsense that I have ever received from a stranger, and certainly it is the only letter containing an English stamp that I have ever received from an American. Your countrymen generally enclose the stamps of your great and free republic.

I am yours faithfully   A.E. HOUSMAN

To the classical scholar Gilbert Murray, 23 April 1900

I rather doubt if man really has much to gain by substituting peace for strife, as you and Jesus Christ recommend. Sic notus Ulixes? do you think you can outwit the resourceful malevolence of Nature? God is not mocked, as St Paul long ago warned the Galatians. When man gets rid of a great trouble he is easier for a little while, but not for long: Nature instantly sets to work to weaken his power of sustaining trouble, and very soon seven pounds is as heavy as fourteen pounds used to be. Last Easter Monday a young woman threw herself into the Lea because her dress looked so shabby amongst the holiday crowd: in other times and countries women have been ravished by half-a-dozen dragoons and taken it less to heart. It looks to me as if the state of mankind always had been and always would be a state of just tolerable discomfort.

To the poet Witter Bynner, 3 June 1903

My dear Sir,

You seem to admire my poems even more than I admire them myself, which is very noble of you, but will most likely be difficult to keep up for any great length of time.

However it is not for me to find fault with you; and naturally there is a pleasure in receiving such ardent letters as yours.

As to your inquiries: I wrote the book when I was thirty-five, and I expect to write another when I am seventy, by which time your enthusiasm will have had time to cool. My trade is that of professor of Latin in this college: I suppose that my classical training has been of some use to me in furnishing good models, and making me fastidious, and telling me what to leave out. My chief object in publishing my verses was to give pleasure to a few young men here and there, and I am glad if they have given pleasure to you.

I am yours very truly

A. E. HOUSMAN

To Grant Richards, 22 June 1903

Dear Richards,

I have no objection to Mr Ettrick setting the verses to music; but I have not exacted fees from other people who have set other pieces, so I don't want to begin now. Vanity, not avarice, is my ruling passion; and so long as young men write to me from America saying that they would rather part with their hair than with their copy of my book, I do not feel the need of food and drink.

Yours sincerely

A. E. HOUSMAN

To Grant Richards, 11 August 1903

The Duchess of Sutherland is under the impression that I not only gave her my consent to print some verses of mine in a novel of hers, but also wrote her a kind letter about it; neither of which things did I ever do. I have no doubt that you gave her my consent, as you have given it to other people; and I have no particular objection: but when it comes to writing kind letters to Duchesses I think it is time to protest.

To Gilbert Murray, 22 September 1903

Radicalism in textual criticism is just as bad as conservatism; but it is not now rampant, and conservatism is. Radicalism was rampant thirty or forty years ago, and it was then rebuked by Madvig and Haupt: now it is conservatism that wants rebuking. Similarly in social morality, puritanism is a pest; but if I were writing an Epistle to the Parisians I should not dwell on this truth, because it is not a truth which the Parisians need to consider: the pest they suffer from is quite different.

To Grant Richards, 27 July 1904

I enclose a copy of our joint work. The results of your collaboration are noted on pages 4, 22, 45, 55, 71, 77, 78, 92, 116 (this last occurred also in the previous edition, where I overlooked it). I don't mark details of punctuation.

I am bound to say however that the leather binding makes a very pretty book.

To Grant Richards, 1 March 1905

The applicant may publish the songs so far as I am concerned, but I had rather you should tell her so, as I do not want to write letters to a lady whose name is Birdie.

To the publishers Messrs Alexander Moring, 17 August 1906

Dear Sirs,

Mr Grant Richards included my book *A Shropshire Lad* in his series of *The Smaller Classics* without consulting me, and to my annoyance. I contented myself with remonstrating, and did not demand its withdrawal; but now that I have the chance, I take it, and I refuse to allow the book to be any longer included in the series. I hope that you will not be very much aggrieved; but I think it unbecoming that the work of a living writer should appear under such a title.

I am yours faithfully   A. E. HOUSMAN

To Grant Richards, 29 June 1907

My dear Richards,

Pray who gave Mr E. Thomas leave to print two of my inspired lays in his and your *Pocket Book of Poems and Songs*? I didn't, though he thanks me in the preface. Just the same thing happened in the case of Lucas' *Open Road*, issued by the same nefarious publisher. You must not treat my immortal works as quarries to be used at will by the various hacks whom you may employ to compile anthologies. It is a matter which affects my moral reputation: for six years back I have been refusing to allow the inclusion of my verses in the books of a number of anthologists who, unlike Mr Thomas, wrote to ask my permission; and I have excused myself by saying that I had an inflexible rule which I could not transgress in one case rather than another. Now these gentlemen, from Quiller-Couch downward, will think I am a liar.

Mr Thomas thanks me for 'a poem,' and prints two: which is the one he doesn't thank me for?

My temper, as you are well aware, is perfectly angelic, so I remain yours sincerely   A. E. HOUSMAN

To Grant Richards, 2 July 1907

My dear Richards,

Thanks for your letter. What you have got in your head is the fact that I allow composers to set my music to words without any restriction. I never hear the music, so I do not suffer; but that is a very different thing from being included in an anthology with W. E. Henley or Walter de la Mare.

I did not remonstrate about *The Open Road*: I was speechless with surprise and indignation.

Yours sincerely   A. E. HOUSMAN

To Grant Richards, 16 May 1908

Mr I. B. Gurney (who resides in Gloucester Cathedral along with St Peter and Almighty God) must not print the words of my poems in full on concert programmes (a course which I am sure his fellow-lodgers would disapprove of); but he is quite welcome to set them to music, and to have them sung, and to print their titles on programmes when they are sung.

To Grant Richards, 15 January 1909

Miss or Mrs Jewell may be told that she can set and publish to her heart's content. If you like to add that she displays an honourable scrupulousness which is doubly remarkable inasmuch as it makes its appearance in a woman and an American; or if you like to quote the opinion of a doctor which I see in to-day's paper, that there are more people with unbalanced minds in Boston than anywhere else, do so: but don't say that I put you up to it.

To Gilbert Murray, 9 December 1909

Dear Murray,
I have read Mrs Taylor's poems, that you were kind enough to give me, with a good deal of pleasure and interest. There are phrases and lines that are quite beautiful, and she has not only technical skill but impulse; and yet there is a curious indistinctness about the general impression, and hardly a poem that rings clear. She is rather like the second Lord Lytton; susceptible to the beauty of other people's poetry, and giving out an answering note, beautiful in its way; and she is not so terribly fluent as he was, not such a bare-faced thief. The appeal to the optic nerve is almost shameless, and becomes monotonous. I like best some of the short pieces, like 'The Young Martyrs.' The poem on the Magi, as you said, is also good.
Will it be possible to break female poets of using such words as 'passional' and feeling proud of it?
Yours sincerely   A. E. HOUSMAN

To Witter Bynner, 17 May 1911

It is true that I am now professor of Latin here, and I thank you for your congratulations. Of course it is nonsense when they talk about my 'steadily refusing to write any more poetry': poetry does not even *steadily* refuse to be written by me; but there is not yet enough to make even a small book.

To Grant Richards, 28 August 1911

4. The type-written text contains the letters:

      J (cap.)   j (l.c.)   v (l.c.)

These are everywhere to be changed to

      I   i   u.

The compositor's simplest way to avoid error will be to put lids on the receptacles containing the types of the forbidden forms, so that his hand cannot get into them; but no doubt he is too proud to take advice from me.

5. As to errors of the press. On former occasions the proofs have come to me full of the usual blunders, – numerals wrong, letters upside-down, stops missing, and so on. I have then, at the cost of much labour, removed all these errors. Then, when the last proof has left my hands, the corrector for the press has been turned on to it, and has found nothing to correct; whereupon, for fear his employers should think he is not earning his pay, he has set to work meddling with what I have written, – altering my English spelling into Webster's American spelling, my use of capitals into his own misuse of capitals, my scientific punctuation into the punctuation he learnt from his grandmother. What ought to be done is the reverse of this. The errors which are introduced by the printer should be removed by the press corrector, who will do it more easily and rapidly, though not more efficiently, than I; then and not till then the proofs should come to me, and after that no corrections should be made except by me.

I am yours sincerely   A.E. HOUSMAN

P.S. Because my hand is particularly good and clear, printers misread it whenever they can; but there is only one letter which they can misread, and that is the letter *r*. At the end of a word they pretend they think it is *s*, and in other positions they pretend they think it is *v*. If they would just notice how I write it, and not expect to find *ʒ*, it would save trouble.

To Grant Richards, 5 December 1916

I do not make any particular complaint about your doubling the price of my book, but of course it diminishes the sale and therefore diminishes my chances of the advertisement to which I am always looking forward: a soldier is to receive a bullet in the breast, and it is to be turned aside from his heart by a copy of *A Shropshire Lad* which he is carrying there. Hitherto it is only the Bible that has performed this trick.

To the Poet Laureate Robert Bridges, 30 December 1918

My dear Bridges,
    I must send you my thanks for the poems of G.M. Hopkins. I value the book as your gift, and also for some good condensed lines and an engaging attitude of mind which now and again shines through. But the faults which you very fairly and judicially set forth thrust themselves more upon my notice; and also another. Sprung Rhythm, as he calls it in his sober and sensible preface, is just as easy to write as other forms of verse; and many a humble scribbler of words for music-hall songs has written it well. But he does not: he does not make it audible; he puts light syllables in the stress and heavy syllables in the slack, and has to be helped out with typographical signs explaining that things are to be understood as being what in fact they are not. Also the English language is a thing which I respect very much, and I resent even the violence Keats did to it; and here is a lesser than Keats doing much more. Moreover his early poems are the promise of something better, if less original; and originality is not nearly so good as goodness, even when it is good. His manner strikes me as deliberately adopted to compensate by strangeness for the lack of pure merit, like the manner which Carlyle took up after he was thirty. Well, the paper warns me I must

not run on, and perhaps you will not think this a very grateful letter.

I am yours sincerely

A. E. HOUSMAN

To the Vice-Master of Trinity College, Cambridge,
3 January 1920

My dear Parry,

I must begin with grateful acknowledgment to you and my other friends, because I could not read your letter without feelings which had some pure pleasure in them; but this was swallowed up in surprise, and surprise itself was engulfed in horror.

Not if the stipend were £150,000 instead of £150 would I be Public Orator. I could not discharge the duties of the office without abandoning all other duties and bidding farewell to such peace of mind as I possess. You none of you have any notion what a slow and barren mind I have, nor what a trouble composition is to me (in prose, I mean: poetry is either easy or impossible). When the job is done, it may have a certain amount of form and finish and perhaps a false air of ease; but there is an awful history behind it. The letter to Jackson last year laid waste three whole mornings: the first, I sat staring in front of me and wishing for death; the second, I wrote down disjointed phrases and sentences which looked loathsome; the third, after a night in which I suppose my subliminal self had been busy, I had some relief in fitting them together and finding they could be improved into something respectable. I can stand this once in a way; but to be doing it often, and have it always hanging over one, and in connexion with subjects much less congenial than Jackson, I could not bear.

The University has been very good to me, and has given me a post in which I have duties which are not disagreeable, and opportunity for studies which I enjoy and in which I can hope to do the University credit; and I should not really be doing it a good turn if I sacrificed that work, as I must, to the performance, even if more efficient than mine would be, of the duties of the Orator.

Do not think this an unkind reply to a kind letter. I have also written to Jackson, as an interview would be useless, and distressing to both of us.

Yours sincerely

A. E. HOUSMAN

To his friend Percy Withers, 4 May 1920

Sciatica is one of the few ailments I sympathise with, as I used to have it myself, no doubt in a mild form, twenty years ago, till I learnt to change my things when I had got into a sweat. Cancer is worse, they say, and being shot through the palm of the hand makes one scream louder.

To Grant Richards, 21 August 1920

Revenge is a valuable passion, and the only sure pillar on which justice rests, so I do not want to hinder your pursuit of Constable if it can be conducted without making me seem to be the pursuer. But have you also a vendetta against James Agate? From reading your serial in the *Literary Supplement* I supposed that he was one of your pets.

To Grant Richards, 28 September 1920

As to Rothenstein, his portraits are of 15 years ago, and one of them, the one he shows in exhibitions, is a venomous libel, to which he adds fresh strokes whenever he feels nasty. This is full face; the other one, more side face, he reserves for his private delectation.

To Grant Richards, 20 December 1920

I return Lovat Fraser's designs, most of which I do not like at all, though the landscapes are generally pleasing. The trouble with book-illustrators, as with composers who set poems to music, is not merely that they are completely wrapped up in their own art and their precious selves, and regard the author merely as a peg to hang things on, but that they seem to have less than the ordinary human allowance of sense and feeling. To transpose into the 18th century a book which begins with Queen Victoria's jubilee is the act of a rhinoceros. I should look a fool if I allowed the book to appear with these decorations.

This reminds me. I am told that composers in some cases have mutilated my poems, – that Vaughan Williams cut two verses out of 'Is my team ploughing' (I wonder how he would like me to cut two bars out of his music), and that a lady whose name I forget has set one verse of 'The New Mistress,' omitting the others. So I am afraid I must ask you, when giving consent to composers, to exact the condition that these pranks are not to be played.

To Grant Richards, 27 September 1921

Tell him that the wish to include a glimpse of my personality in a literary article is low, unworthy, and American. Tell him that some men are more interesting than their books but my book is more interesting than its man. Tell him that Frank Harris found me rude and Wilfrid Blunt found me dull. Tell him anything else that you think will put him off. Of course if he did nevertheless persist in coming to see me I should not turn him out, as I only do that to newspaper reporters.

To Percy Withers, 12 June 1922

The photograph is not quite true to my own notion of my gentleness and sweetness of nature, but neither perhaps is my external appearance.

To Grant Richards, 4 May 1923

My old, dear, and intimate friend Princess Marie Louise, who is furnishing the Queen's doll's-house, asked me some months ago to let 12 poems of mine be copied small to form one volume in the library; and I selected the 12 shortest and simplest and least likely to fatigue the attention of dolls or members of the illustrious House of Hanover. Now she says that there is to be printed a book describing or reproducing the contents of this library, and asks me to allow these poems to be included in it: and I have consented. So do not send a solicitor's letter to the Queen (for the book is to be hers) when it appears. The issue is to be 2000 copies in this country and 500 for America, and the Queen is to do what she likes with the proceeds. As I say, the poems are my shortest, and the 12 together are 96 lines.

To the journalist F.C. Owlett, 18 March 1924

It is very unreasonable for people to be depressed by unfavourable reviews: they should say to themselves 'do I write better than Wordsworth and Shelley and Keats? am I worse treated than they were?'

To Robert Bridges, 25 September 1924

My dear Bridges,
   I adjure you not to waste your time on Manilius. He writes on astronomy and astrology without knowing either. My interest in him is purely technical. His best poetry you will find in I 483–531, where he appeals to the regularity of the heavenly motions as evidence of the divinity and eternity of the universe. He has nothing else so good, and little that is nearly so good.
   Yours sincerely   A. E. HOUSMAN

To the publishers Messrs Macmillan and Company, 16 November 1924

Dear Sirs,
   In the last twenty years I have produced several editions of Latin classics, which are printed at my expense, offered to the public at less than cost price, and sold for me by a publisher on commission.
   I am just completing an edition of Lucan, which I wish to produce in the same way. The printers of my last three books, Messrs Robert Maclehose and Co. of the Glasgow University Press, are prepared to undertake the work; and Mr Charles Whibley has

suggested to me that you may be willing to act as publishers for me on the usual terms, and to be the channel of my communications with the printers. As in 1895 you refused to publish another book of mine, *A Shropshire Lad*, under similar conditions, I did not think this likely; but he assures me you are now less haughty.

If so, I will send you the text and notes, which are already complete and constitute the bulk of the work, that you may transmit them to Messrs Maclehose and obtain an estimate of the cost.

     I am yours faithfully

A. E. HOUSMAN

To the Master of Trinity College, Cambridge, J.J. Thomson, 22 February 1925

My dear Master,

I take up my pen in a rather sorrowful mood, because I recognise the compliment implied in the Council's offer of the Clark Lectureship, and am grateful for their friendliness and for yours, and therefore I cannot help feeling ungracious in making the answer which nevertheless is the only answer possible.

I do regard myself as a connoisseur; I think I can tell good from bad in literature. But literary criticism, referring opinions to principles and setting them forth so as to command assent, is a high and rare accomplishment and quite beyond me. I remember Walter Raleigh's Clark lecture on Landor: it was unpretending, and not adorned or even polished, but I was thinking all the while that I could never have hit the nail on the head like that. And not only have I no talent for producing the genuine article, but no taste or inclination for producing a substitute. If I devoted a whole year (and it would not take less) to the composition of six lectures on literature, the result would be nothing which could give me, I do not say satisfaction, but consolation for the wasted time; and the year would be one of anxiety and depression, the more vexatious because it would be subtracted from those minute and pedantic studies in which I am fitted to excel and which give me pleasure.

I am sorry if this explanation is tedious, but I would rather be tedious than seem thankless and churlish.

     I am yours sincerely

A. E. HOUSMAN

To the publisher Sir Frederick Macmillan, 27 December 1926

Dear Sir Frederick Macmillan,
I am much obliged by your amiable letter. The Lucan however was published last January, and is now nearly sold out, which testifies to such efficiency in the publisher as even you could hardly surpass.
     I am yours sincerely   A. E. HOUSMAN

To an unidentified correspondent, 23 January 1928

Dear Sir,
French is the only tongue of which I know enough to keep my translators in order; in other languages I generally give permission and hope for the best, and I have no reason to hope for less than the best from you.
     I am yours faithfully   A. E. HOUSMAN

To Grant Richards, 9 October 1928

My dear Richards,
If Mr Symons will consider, he will see that to do as he wishes would be a shabby act towards the generations of anthologists whom I have repelled by saying that I have an invariable rule. He may be consoled, and also amused, if you tell him that to include me in an anthology of the Nineties would be just as technically correct, and just as essentially inappropriate, as to include Lot in a book on Sodomites; in saying which I am not saying a word against sodomy, nor implying that intoxication and incest are in any way preferable.
Thanks for the handbook on hanging, though the author seems to be rather a buffoon.
     Yours sincerely   A. E. HOUSMAN

If Mr Symons ever feels sad, he ought to be able to cheer himself up by contemplating his handwriting.

To the Editor of *The Times*, about 13 December 1928

Shelley's Skylark

Sir,

Although this ode is not one of Shelley's best poems and enjoys more fame than it deserves, it is good enough to be worth interpreting. Quintilian says that you will never understand the poets unless you learn astronomy; and as this subject is not now much studied in girls' schools it was only to be expected that Mr Moore's 'Egeria' should darken with misinformation the ignorance of Mr Eliot. In the stanza

> Keen as are the arrows
>   Of that silver sphere
> Whose intense lamp narrows
>   In the white dawn clear
> Until we hardly see – we feel that it is there,

the silver sphere is the Morning Star, the planet Venus; and Shelley is giving a true description of her disappearance and using an apt comparison. The moon, when her intense lamp narrows in the white dawn clear, is not a sphere but a sickle: when she is a sphere at sunrise she is near the western horizon, visible in broad daylight and disappearing only when she sets; so that nothing could be less like the vanishing of the skylark.

A.E.H.

To Grant Richards, 19 August 1929

I am deserting the air on this occasion because my life, until my Manilius is quite finished, is too precious to be exposed to a $\frac{1}{186,000}$ risk of destruction; even though they have already killed their proper quota for this year.

To Charles Wilson, 4 June 1931

My feelings are much the same as Huxley's; but in my case school is not the cause, for I was quite uninfluenced by my school, which was a small one. I think the cause is in the home. Class is a real thing: we may wish that it were not, and we may pretend that it is not, but I find that it is.

To Laurence Housman, 1 March 1932

Your generous offer to pass on Coventry Patmore to me has its allurements, for I have often idly thought of writing an essay on him and have even been inclined sometimes to regard it, as you say, in the light of a duty, because nobody admires his best poetry enough, though the stupid papists may fancy they do. But it would give me more trouble than you can imagine, whereas I want peace in my declining years; and the result would not be good enough to yield me pride or even satisfaction. I should say as little as possible about his nasty mixture of piety and concupiscence; but his essay on English metre is the best thing ever written on the subject, though spoilt by one great mistake.

To Maurice Pollet, 5 February 1933

Dear M. Pollet,

As some of the questions which you ask in your flattering curiosity may be asked by future generations, and as many of them can only be answered by me, I make this reply.

I was born in Worcestershire, not Shropshire, where I have never spent much time. My father's family was Lancashire and my mother's Cornish. I had a sentimental feeling for Shropshire because its hills were our western horizon. I know Ludlow and Wenlock, but my topographical details – Hughley, Abdon under Clee – are sometimes quite wrong. Remember that Tyrtaeus was not a Spartan.

I took an interest in astronomy almost as early as I can remember; the cause, I think, was a little book we had in the house.

I was brought up in the Church of England and in the High Church party, which is much the best religion I have ever come across. But Lemprière's Classical Dictionary, which fell into my hands when I was eight, attached my affections to paganism. I became a deist at thirteen and an atheist at twenty-one.

I never had any scientific education.

I wrote verse at eight or earlier, but very little until I was thirty-five.

Oxford had not much effect on me, except that I there met my greatest friend.

While I was at the Patent Office I read a great deal of Greek and Latin at the British Museum of an evening.

While at University College, which is not residential, I lived alone in lodgings in the environs of London. *A Shropshire Lad* was written at Byron Cottage, 17 North Road, Highgate, where I lived from 1886 to 1905.

A Shropshire Lad was offered to Macmillan, and declined by them on the advice, I have been told, of John Morley, who was their reader. Then a friend introduced me to Kegan Paul; but the book was published at my own expense.

The Shropshire Lad is an imaginary figure, with something of my temper and view of life. Very little in the book is biographical.

'Reader of the Greek Anthology' is not a good name for me. Of course I have read it, or as much of it as is worth reading, but with no special heed; and my favourite Greek poet is Aeschylus. No doubt I have been unconsciously influenced by the Greeks and Latins, but I was surprised when critics spoke of my poetry as 'classical.' Its chief sources of which I am conscious are Shakespeare's songs, the Scottish Border ballads and Heine.

'Oh stay at home' was written years before the Great War, and expresses no change of opinion, only a different mood. The Great War cannot have made much change in the opinions of any man of imagination.

I have never had any such thing as a 'crisis of pessimism.' In the first place, I am not a pessimist but a pejorist (as George Eliot said she was not an optimist but a meliorist); and that is owing to my observation of the world, not to personal circumstances. Secondly, I did not begin to write poetry in earnest until the really emotional part of my life was over; and my poetry, so far as I could make out, sprang chiefly from physical conditions, such as a relaxed sore throat during my most prolific period, the first five months of 1895.

I respect the Epicureans more than the Stoics, but I am myself a

Cyrenaic. Pascal and Leopardi I have studied with great admiration; Villon and Verlaine very little, Calderon and German philosophers not at all. For Hardy I felt affection, and high admiration for some of his novels and a few of his poems.

I am yours very truly

A. E. HOUSMAN

To Laurence Housman, 24 May 1933

The painful episode is closed; but I may take this sentence from a paragraph which I cut out. 'Not only is it difficult to know the truth about anything, but to tell the truth when one knows it, to find words which will not obscure it or pervert it, is in my experience an exhausting effort.'

I did not say that poetry was the better for having no meaning, only that it can best be detected so.

I hear that Kipling says I am 'dead right' about the pit of the stomach.

I had better tell you before I forget it that the solicitor E.S.P. Haynes, who writes letters to the papers about the liberties of the subject, says in *A Lawyer's Notebook* that Belloc is the best living poet with the possible exception of you and me.

Your still affectionate brother

A. E. HOUSMAN

To Percy Withers, 20 December 1933

It is one of my grievances against the Creator that I always look better than I am (as Emerson said of the Scotch 'Many of them look drunk when they are sober') and consequently receive fewer tears of sympathy than I deserve; but I am really so much better than I have been that I ought not to grumble much at not being really myself again.

To his sister-in-law Jeannie Housman, 3 December 1934

Here is December, bringing round the sad time when we lost Basil, but bringing also this year to me in a letter from Kate the good news that you are wonderfully better in health and have kicked your nurse out of doors. I do beg you to keep it up and not to be weary in well doing. The winter, thus far, is being quite nice to invalids, of whom, however, we have rather a large number here among my friends and acquaintances. One of my best boon-companions died a few months ago, and apparently spoke so much and so well of me in his last illness that his nurse has written to me to engage herself for my death-bed. People, however, are always telling me that I look exceedingly well; so that, I fear, must be a pleasure deferred.

To his sister Katharine Symons, 3 December 1934

I am just about the same, with frequent feelings of fatigue, occasional sinkings at the heart and continual uneasiness at beginning to get up in the morning. I can bear my life but I do not at all want it to go on, and it is a great mistake that it did not come to an end a year and a half ago. This period has been a serious subtraction from the total pleasure (such as it was) of my existence. I am not doing anything important, but putting together notes from my margins to print from time to time. I am much annoyed by being told by everyone how well I look, and being admired for my comparative youthfulness and my upright carriage.

To Percy Withers, 30 December 1934

On your expert advice I left off alcohol for a week, with no effect except the production of gouty symptoms, or symptoms which I am accustomed to regard as such. Your other recipe, a cold douche after my warm bath, is impracticable, because my bath is cold.

To Percy Withers, 20 May 1935

One advantage of living in this charming world is that however bad one may think one's own lot it is always easy to find someone whose lot is worse; but I am sorry that the person to provide me with this poor sort of consolation should be you. I hope that there is no cause beyond your unsettled life in these last months, and that as this experience recedes you will grow better.

To the book-collector Houston Martin, 27 September 1935

Certainly I have never regretted the publication of my poems. The reputation which they brought me, though it gives me no lively pleasure, is something like a mattress interposed between me and the hard ground. The lectures I care very little about.

To the poet Neilson Abeel, 4 October 1935

Dear Mr Abeel,
My heart always warms to people who do not come to see me, especially Americans, to whom it seems to be more of an effort; and your preference of the Cam to the Hudson, which I have always understood to be one of the finest rivers, is also an ingratiating trait.
If you think this note a reward, I shall be pleased.
Yours sincerely   A. E. HOUSMAN

To Katharine Symons, 10 November 1935

I abandoned Christianity at thirteen but went on believing in God till I was twenty-one, and towards the end of that time I did a good deal of praying for certain persons and for myself. I cannot help being touched that you do it for me, and feeling rather remorseful, because it must be an expenditure of energy, and I cannot believe in its efficacy.

To Houston Martin, 22 March 1936

Dear Mr Martin,
I was very ill at the beginning of the year, and I am now again in a nursing home. I hope that if you can restrain your indecent ardour for a little I shall be properly dead and your proposed work will not be by its nature unbecoming. But the hope is not more than a hope, for my family are tough and long-lived, unless they take to drink.
Do not send me your manuscript. Worse than the practice of writing books about living men is the conduct of living men in

supervising such books. I do not forbid you to quote extracts from my letters.

I think you should ask yourself whether you are literary enough for your job. You say that I may think it 'indignant and presumptious' for an American to write such a book before an English one has appeared. By *presumptious* you mean *presumptuous* and what you mean by *indignant* I have no idea.

The best review I ever saw of my poems was by Hubert Bland the Socialist in a weekly paper *The New Age* (1896). The American who called them (I do not know where) the best poetry since Keats is endeared to me by his amiable error.

When an athletic performance, previously the best, is excelled, the *record* is said to be *broken* or *cut*. I am not sure if the latter is really good English, but it was common in sporting circles in my youth.

In philosophy I am a Cyrenaic or egoistic hedonist, and regard the pleasure of the moment as the only possible motive of action. As for pessimism, I think it almost as silly, though not as wicked, as optimism. George Eliot said she was a meliorist: I am a pejorist, and also yours sincerely

A. E. HOUSMAN

NOTES

===

THE TEXT OF THE POEMS

The two volumes published during Housman's lifetime ought to present no textual problems, only the textual difficulty of seeing that there are no misprints. (It was one of life's little ironies, and death's, that the order of the funeral service for this fiercely vigilant critic of misprints should have included an error, possibly a misprint.) Housman made only two changes to the wording of *A Shropshire Lad* ('All other changes, very few, are trifles of spelling or printing,' he wrote); and the text of the first edition of *Last Poems* stands except for the authorised supplying of the missing punctuation in the first two lines of XXVI. The present edition restores Housman's prefatory note to *Last Poems*, silently dropped from all the collected editions; in the first edition of *LP* (1922) it had no heading, but was subsequently 'Preface to First Edition'.

For *More Poems* and *Additional Poems*, things are more vexed. First, there is the question of the true manuscript reading; so, for instance, Laurence Housman's initial 'Above the courts of Kings' (*MP* XXXII) has long since been corrected to 'About . . .' Foremost among the scholars was John Carter, to whose researches the present edition is greatly indebted. Second, there is the matter of alternative readings left standing by the poet. Here the choice is found to be honourably open to question. Again Carter is the scholar trusted here. The edition of the complete poems, by Archie Burnett (to be published by Oxford University Press), is sure to constitute a new stage in substantiated Housman scholarship.

For the story of the posthumous selections, *More Poems* and *Additional Poems*, see the notes on the composition of the poems.

More Poems: Housman published two of the poems, V and XLVIII, both in 1897; his published text is given here. The following are given in the text of *MP*, as revised subsequently by Laurence Housman, not contested by John Carter in these cases: the prefatory poem, I, III, IV, VI–VIII, X, XII, XIV, XVII–XIX, XXII, XXIII, XXVI–XXVIII, XXX, XXXI, XXXVI–XXXIX, XLII, XLIV and XLV. Of these, Tom Burns Haber has variants of wording in his Centennial Edition (1959), in II, VIII,

XVII, XXIII, XXXI, XXXII, XXXIV and XLV. Sometimes Carter and Haber concurred in a change from *MP*; since they were at daggers drawn, this carries weight, and is operative in changes from *MP* within XI, XXV, XL, XLIII and XLVI. In XLIII, 'steadfast' has been changed to 'stedfast', Housman's preferred spelling in *ASL* XXXIII, XLIII and LI. There remain textual choices by Carter such as are necessarily open to differences of judgment, but not here. The present edition treats the prefatory poem to *MP*, 'They say my verse is sad', differently from *MP* and from all previous collected editions, in changing the text from italics to roman; since Housman did not contemplate a further volume of poems, it is misleading to treat the poem as if it were chosen by Housman as a counterpart to his (italicised) prefatory poem to *LP*.

Additional Poems: Housman published three of the poems: XXI (1881) is given as published except for the alteration of 'immortal / Then' to 'immortal / Once' (see the note in those on the composition of the poems); XXII (1894) is given as published; but XXIII (1902) is given not in the published text but from a MS judged by Carter to have greater authority. Of the poems published in Laurence Housman's *A.E.H.* (1937; I–XVIII), the text was not contested by Carter in these cases: I–III, IV (except for supplying a hyphen in 'to-morrow'), VII–IX, XII, XIII and XVI. Carter and Haber concur in some changes from *A.E.H.*, operative within V, VI, XIV, XV, XVII and XVIII. XIX and XX were first published in *Collected Poems* (1939).

Translations: These three translations from the Greek are given as published by Housman in 1890.

Light Verse and Parodies: For the texts of these, see the notes on the composition of the poems.

Single quotation marks are used throughout; *A Shropshire Lad* was printed so, but *Last Poems* had double quotation marks. At half a dozen places, the punctuation and the closing inverted comma have been transposed, it having become Housman's practice to place such punctuation before the closing inverted comma.

THE COMPOSITION OF THE POEMS

These notes are basic and unaspiring; they simply draw upon Housman's letters and upon Laurence Housman; and they are indebted for dates of publication to *A.E. Housman: A Bibliography* (edited by John Carter and John Sparrow; second edition revised by William White, 1982). Dates of composition that are more exact and authoritative will be established by Archie Burnett in his Oxford edition of the poems. Burnett will provide too a full demonstration of Housman's sources and influences. (Burnett's work on Tennyson shows that he has an excellent eye and ear for these things.) There is no point here in providing merely a few such notes; any poem of Housman's (like those of his much-admired Thomas Gray) draws upon, and sometimes alludes to, a multitude of previous poems, and such annotation is beyond the scope of this edition. But until Burnett's edition is completed, those who are interested in sources, analogues and influences should look particularly at the work of John Sparrow (*Nineteenth Century*, February 1934); of G.B.A. Fletcher (an Appendix to Grant Richards, *Housman: 1897–1936*, 1941); of Norman Marlow (*A.E. Housman, Scholar and Poet*, 1958); and of Tom Burns Haber (*A.E. Housman*, 1967).

A SHROPSHIRE LAD

Published 1896

A.W. Pollard records:

A Shropshire Lad, under the name of *Terence*, was ready for publication. Housman knew that books of mine had been published by Messrs Kegan Paul, Trench, Trübner and Co., who had gained rather a special reputation for bringing out prettily printed volumes of verse, and asked me to arrange with them for its publication at his expense. Of course there was no difficulty as to this (I think Housman put down £30 and got it back with a small profit), but my being entrusted with the manuscript led me to suggest that *Terence* was not an attractive title, and that in the phrase 'A Shropshire Lad,' which he had used in the poem, he had a much better one. He agreed at once, and I think the change helped. (*Alfred Edward Housman: Recollections*, a supplement to the *Bromsgrovian*, 1936, p. 43)

Pollard has a note: 'This is all I remember of the title, but I am told that in its fullest form it was *The Poems of Terence Hearsay*.' (Simply, *Poems by Terence Hearsay*, in Laurence Housman, *A.E.H.*, p. 71.) 'Terence' figures in *ASL* VIII and LXII. The phrase 'A Shropshire Lad' occurs neither in the poem as published nor (according to Haber) in the manuscript notebooks; the place where it is most likely once to have been is L: 'When I was a Knighton lad.'

On Shropshire, Housman wrote to Houston Martin, 14 April 1934:

I am Worcestershire by birth: Shropshire was our western horizon, which made me feel romantic about it. I do not know the county well, except in parts, and some of my topographical details are wrong and imaginary. The Wrekin is wooded, and Wenlock Edge along the western side, but the Clees and most of the other hills are grass or heather. In the southern half of the county, to which I have confined myself, the hills are generally long ridges running from north to south, with valleys, broad or narrow, between. The northern half is part of the great Cheshire plain. The Wrekin is isolated. (*Letters*, edited by Henry Maas, 1971, p. 352)

Sir Sydney Cockerell records:

On November 10, 1911, I had a talk with Housman about *A Shropshire Lad*, and next day made the following note in my copy of the book: 'He told me last night that he wrote some of these poems in 1894, but the majority of them in the first five months of 1895 at a time of ill-health, and partly perhaps as a reaction from a learned controversy in which he was then engaged. They came to him willy-nilly, and since then he has written a small number of poems under similar emotional conditions, but not enough to make another volume.' On another occasion I asked him whether he at once realized their merit. His answer was that he had, because they were so unlike anything else that had come to him. (Cockerell's letter to *The Times Literary Supplement*, 7 November 1936, reprinted in Grant Richards, *Housman: 1897–1936*, 1941, pp. 436–7.)

The dates of the poems are from the notebooks, recorded first by Laurence Housman at the end of *More Poems* and then revised by him in *A.E.H.* (pp. 273–5); more authoritative and exact dating will be established by Archie Burnett in his Oxford edition of Housman.

ASL I 1887. Queen Victoria's Golden Jubilee. Housman was to write a vivid description of the celebratory beacons in June 1897, the Diamond Jubilee (*Letters*, pp. 42–3).

ASL III January 1895.

ASL IV January 1895, first draft.

ASL VIII August 1894.

ASL IX February 1895, first draft.

ASL XIII January 1895, first draft.

ASL XVIII May 1895.

ASL XX Housman later wrote that he 'only put it in for variety' (to J.W. Mackail, 25 July 1922; *Letters*, p. 200).

ASL XXI July 1891, first draft. To Houston Martin, 17 October 1934: 'Bredon Hill is Worcestershire on the edge of Gloucestershire. That poem was written early, before I knew the book would be a Shropshire book' (*Letters*, p. 362).

ASL XXVI June (1895?).

ASL XXVII To Houston Martin, 28 March 1933: 'I could not say that I have a favourite among my poems. Thomas Hardy's was no. XXVII in *A Shropshire Lad*, and I think it may be the best, though it is not the most perfect' (*Letters*, p. 331); 'Hardy and I never talked about my poems. I think it was Mrs Hardy who told me his opinion' (27 September 1935; *Letters*, p. 377).

ASL XXVIII January 1895. To Houston Martin, 14 April 1934: 'At Buildwas there is the ruin of an abbey church, not large but fairly complete, of Norman date' (*Letters*, p. 352).

ASL XXIX April 1895.

ASL XXX For Housman's comment on the poem, dismissing a ludicrous illustration, see the notes to the letter of 20 December 1920 (p. 518).

ASL XXXI November 1895, first draft.

ASL XXXIV	To the Librarian of Trinity College, 3 March 1926: 'While the book was printing I took out five pieces and put in the three now numbered XXXIV, XXXVII, and XLI, which are together at the end' [of the manuscript] (*Letters*, p. 235).
ASL XXXXVI	To Richards, 22 April 1922: 'The Oxford dictionary defines *reach* as "to stretch out continuously, to extend," and quotes "how high reacheth the house" (1526) and "the portico reaches along the whole front" (1687). Perhaps your friends are baffled by the subjunctive mood, and think it ought to be *reaches*; but see Psalm 138 6, "*Though* the Lord *be* high, yet hath he respect unto the lowly"' (*Letters*, p. 193).
ASL XXXVII	See the note to XXXIV.
ASL XXXVIII	To Richards, 22 April 1922: 'When you next print *A Shropshire Lad* I want to make two alterations' (*Letters*, p. 193). 'Thick on the wind . . .' became 'Loose . . .' in 1923. To John Sparrow, 19 June 1934: 'I have made only two real alterations, in XXXVIII 10 and LII 9, which were meant to appear in 1922 simultaneously with *Last Poems* but were belated by the publisher's fault. All other changes, very few, are trifles of spelling or printing' (*Letters*, p. 356). (A letter to Richards about this, 6 July 1932, is not in *Letters*; Richards, p. 264.)
ASL XXXIX	February 1893.
ASL XLI	November 1895, first draft. See the note to XXXIV.
ASL XLII	September 1890.
ASL XLIV	Laurence Housman records (*A.E.H.*, pp. 103–4):

On August 6th, 1895, a young Woolwich Cadet, aged eighteen, took his own life, leaving a long letter addressed to the Coroner to say why he had done so. The gist of that letter was quoted in a newspaper-cutting of the day, which I found lying in my brother's copy of *A Shropshire Lad* alongside the poem which begins:

Shot? so quick, so clean an ending?

It is quite evident that certain passages in that letter prompted the writing of the poem; one sentence indeed is almost quoted. I give here only that part of the letter which bears most closely on the poem:

> I wish it to be clearly understood that I am not what is commonly called 'temporarily insane', and that I am putting an end to my life after several weeks of careful deliberation. I do not think that I need justify my actions to anyone but my Maker, but . . . I will state the main reasons which have determined me. The first is utter cowardice and despair. There is only one thing in this world which would make me thoroughly happy; that one thing I have no earthly hope of obtaining. The second – which I wish was the only one – is that I have absolutely ruined my own life; but I thank God that as yet, so far as I know, I have not morally injured, or 'offended', as it is called in the Bible, anyone else. Now I am quite certain that I could not live another five years without doing so, and for that reason alone, even if the first did not exist, I should do what I am doing . . . At all events it is final, and consequently better than a long series of sorrows and disgraces.

How close to that come the lines:

> Oh soon, and better so than later
> After long disgrace and scorn,
> You shot dead the household traitor,
> The soul that should not have been born.

ASL XLVII   August 1895.

ASL L   To Houston Martin, 14 April 1934: 'The stanza prefixed to no. L of *A Shropshire Lad* is traditional. One version is "drunkenest"' (*Letters*, p. 352).

ASL LII   1891–2. In 1923, 'long since forgotten' was changed to 'no more remembered'. (See the note to XXXVIII.)

ASL LIII   December 1894, first draft.

ASL LIV   August 1893.

ASL LVI   March 1895.

ASL LVIII	July 1895.
ASL LXIII	For Housman's account of the composition of this poem, see the closing page of *The Name and Nature of Poetry* and the Notes (pp. 371, 515–6).

LAST POEMS

Published 1922

The progress towards *Last Poems* is recorded in the *Letters*:

28 February 1910: 'The other day I had the curiosity to reckon up the complete pieces, printed and unprinted, which I have written since 1896, and they only come to 300 lines, so the next volume appears to be some way off. In barrenness, at any rate, I hold a high place among English poets, excelling even Gray' (p. 108).

17 May 1911: 'Of course it is nonsense when they talk about my "steadily refusing to write any more poetry": poetry does not even *steadily* refuse to be written by me; but there is not yet enough to make even a small book' (p. 117).

1 October 1912: 'None even of my few unpublished poems have been written within the last two years' (p. 125).

18 November 1917: 'I am obliged by your letter, but I neither have any poem which I wish to publish nor am likely to write one at any early date' (p. 153).

23 May 1919: 'I cannot help being touched and flattered by your anxiety to make me publish . . . But my unwillingness remains, because it is not due to any doubt of the possibility of deluding the public, by printing and binding and so on, into the belief that it is getting its money's worth, but to my own notions of what is proper. However, I shall be contributing a new piece shortly to a MS anthology which is being got up, and in due season I will send you this drop of water to moisten your parched tongue' (p. 162).

18 January 1920: 'Last year I think I wrote two poems, which is more than the average, but not much towards a new volume' (p. 171).

5 September 1920: 'Suppose I produced a new volume of poetry, in what part of the year ought it to be published, and how long would it take after the MS left my hands?' (p. 179)

5 January 1921: '"my new book" does not exist, and possibly never may. Neither your traveller nor anybody else must be told that it is even contemplated. What I asked you was a question inspired by an unusually bright and sanguine mood, which has not at present been justified' (p. 183).

3 November 1921: 'I am flattered by your request, but I have no poems by me which I wish to see in print' (p. 189).

9 April 1922: 'It is now practically certain that I shall have a volume of poems ready for the autumn; so I wish you would take what steps are necessary as soon as they are necessary. But do not mention it to anyone until you are obliged to mention it' (p. 192).

26 June 1922: 'I am bringing out a volume of poems this autumn: will you do me the kindness to look through them first? They are neither long nor many' (p. 198).

18 July 1922: 'I want you to note anything which strikes you as falling below my average, or as open to exception for any other reason . . . You need not be afraid of stifling a masterpiece through a temporary aberration of judgment, as I am consulting one or two other people, and shall not give effect to a single opinion unless it coincides with my own private suspicions' (p. 199).

The dating of the poems derives from Cockerell's letter to *The Times Literary Supplement*, 7 November 1936, except where corrected by J.M. Nosworthy, *TLS*, 11 January 1968 (though again there will be more exact and authoritative dating in Archie Burnett's Oxford edition):

On October 28, 1922, very soon after its publication, I discussed *Last Poems* with him, and he dictated to me the following dates of its contents. Though many of these dates are only approximate, they form a useful supplement to the five dates for this volume given in *More Poems*, and modify those there given for 'In midnights of November', 'The chestnut casts its flambeaux', and 'Onward led the road again'.

LP   *Prefatory note.* Alongside the sentence on printing, Housman wrote in his own copy, 'Vain hope!', with a direction to XXVI (*A.E. Housman: A Bibliography*).

LP   *We'll to the woods no more.* April 1922. Housman had added the four concluding lines; he thought of

485

dropping them, but was dissuaded at the proof-stage by Laurence Housman (Richard Perceval Graves, *A.E. Housman: The Scholar-Poet*, 1979, p. 228).

LP I   Pre-1899 (Nosworthy, correcting Cockerell, *c.* 1905). To J.W. Mackail, 25 July 1922: '"home" and "native land" signify "the sea where they fished for you and me"' (*Letters*, p. 200).

LP II   April 1895 (Nosworthy, correcting Cockerell, *c.* 1900). Published in the *Blunderbuss*, March 1917, with variants (this was a magazine for military cadets then at Trinity College). Reprinted in the *Trinity Magazine*, November 1920.

LP III   1895. Published, as 'The Conflict', with variants, in a leaflet within the *Edwardian*, the magazine of King Edward's School, Bath, December 1915. This was in memory of Housman's nephew Clement Symons; he had been at the school, and was killed in action in 1915. The poem 'had been copied into an autograph book by C.A.S. just before he left England, and entitled by him "The Conflict", as it seemed to him to be the portrayal of conflict in which cowardly fear was vanquished.' (The words are those of Clement Symons's mother, Katharine Symons, in *Memories of A.E. Housman*, from the *Edwardian*, September 1936.) Graves says: 'When he enlisted, Clement, who was in love with a girl whom he hoped to marry, and who had every reason for wanting to live, found that he was "in deadly fear of getting killed". Alfred, hearing of this, sent him these verses, which, according to Laurence Housman, describe "a man in fear of death who conquers his fear" . . . Clement told Kate [his mother] that this poem had helped him overcome his own fears, and he copied it out, and left it with his mother, saying that it would console her if he *was* killed' (*A.E. Housman: The Scholar-Poet*, pp. 139–40). The poem had been set up as XLIII in *ASL*, but was deleted by Housman in page-proof, dated 23 December 1895 (*A.E. Housman: A Bibliography*). Housman wrote to Geoffrey Wethered, 13 September 1933 (G.V.M. Heap, *Housman Society Journal* iv, 1978, 5–6): 'The queen of air and darkness comes from a line of Coventry Patmore's "the powers of darkness and the air," which in its turn is a reference to "the prince of the power of the air" in Ephesians 11 2; and the meaning is Evil'.

LP IV   Published in the *Academy*, 24 February 1900, with variants. Housman wrote to his sister Katharine Symons, 5 October 1915, on the news that her son Clement had been killed in action (see the note to the previous poem): 'I do not know that I can do better than send you some verses that I wrote many years ago; because the essential business of poetry, as it has been said, is to harmonise the sadness of the universe, and it is somehow more sustaining and healing than prose' (*Letters*, p. 141). Reprinted in the *Edwardian*, December 1915, unsigned, with variants, headed 'Illic Jacet./In Memoriam./C.A.S.' (*A.E. Housman: A Bibliography*).

LP V   Time of Boer War.

LP VI   Time of Boer War.

LP VII   April 1922, except last stanza, which was written long ago.

LP VIII   Chiefly 1905.

LP IX   Begun November–December 1895 (Nosworthy). Begun *c.* 1900 (really February 1896); last stanza April 1922 (Cockerell).

LP X   *c.* 1900–1905.

LP XI   1895, intended for *ASL*, but not used. (December 1895, according to *MP*.)

LP XII   *c.* 1900.

LP XIII   Begun *c.* 1901 (Nosworthy). Begun 1905, finished April 1922; based on the tune of a chanty heard at Hereford. (This is the only note from Cockerell that goes beyond dating.)

LP XIV   Drafted pre-1899 (Nosworthy). Before 1910 (Cockerell).

LP XV	1921. At the proof-stage of *LP*, Housman took advice and dropped some poems; Laurence Housman in 1922 persuaded him to keep this (Graves, p. 228).
LP XVI	Composed at intervals, 1900–22.
LP XVII	1902 (Nosworthy). Published in *Wayfarer's Love*, 1904, edited by the Duchess of Sutherland.
LP XVIII	Begun pre-1899 (Nosworthy). First and last stanzas *c.* 1902; finished April 1922 (Cockerell).
LP XIX	Begun before December 1894 (Nosworthy). Begun 1895 (October, according to *MP*); finished *c.* 1905 (Cockerell).
LP XX	April 1922.
LP XXI	Begun 1890–91 and completed *c.* 1899 (Nosworthy). *c.* 1900–1905 (Cockerell).
LP XXII	Finished April 1922; the last two lines are earlier (letter of 3 November 1922; *Housman Society Journal* ii, 1975, 35).
LP XXIII	1895.
LP XXIV	Begun January 1895 (Nosworthy). Begun 1900, finished April 1922 (Cockerell). Moses Jackson, whom Housman loved, returned from India in 1889 (he had taken up a post there in 1887); this, to be married. Housman noted in his diary for 1890: 'Jan: 7. I heard he was married.' (The wedding had been on 9 December, and Jackson had now gone back to India with his wife.) The story is told in Laurence Housman, 'A.E. Housman's "De Amicitia"', *Encounter*, October 1967. (Corrected and supplemented by P.D. Eaton, *Housman Society Journal* viii, 1982, 8–12.) In 1903 Housman prefaced the first volume of his Manilius with a dedicatory poem in Latin to Jackson. (See Appendix, p. 253.) Jackson, gravely ill in 1922 in British Columbia, was sent a copy of *LP* by Housman; it is said (the letter is in very private hands) that Housman's letter with the book spoke of being from 'a fellow who thinks more of you than anything in the world': 'you are largely responsible for my writing poetry and you

ought to take the consequences' (George L. Watson, *A.E. Housman: A Divided Life*, 1957, p. 211). Jackson died in 1923, less than three months after the publication of *LP*; it has been plausibly argued by Norman Page that the knowledge of Jackson's mortal illness incited Housman to consummate *Last Poems*.

LP XXV   *c.* 1900 (Nosworthy). Published in *The Venture*, 1903 (edited by Laurence Housman and W. Somerset Maugham), with variants. (Housman gave Cockerell the date *c.* 1904; this has been thought to cast doubt on some of these datings.) To Laurence Housman, 9 August 1903: 'To write a paper on Patmore would be an awful job, especially in the holidays, so I send you two poems, of which you can print whichever you think the least imperfect' (*Letters*, p. 67). To Houston Martin, 27 September 1935: 'I do not admire the oracle poem quite so much as some people do. The italics, as elsewhere, are equivalent to inverted commas, and give the supposed words of the oracle' (*Letters*, p. 376).

LP XXVI   April 1922. To Richards, 12 October 1922: 'I knew the printers would do something, and I only wondered what it would be. On p. 52 they have removed a comma from the end of the first line and a semi-colon from the end of the second.' Two days later: 'No, don't put in an errata slip. The blunder will probably enhance the value of the first edition in the eyes of bibliophiles, an idiotic class' (*Letters*, p. 204). To J.W. Mackail, 25 July 1922: '"you do lie" is not really for metre's sake, but an imitation, false I dare say, of the ballads which I do imitate' (*Letters*, p. 200).

LP XXVII   Soon after 1900. Housman wrote it out for Percy Withers: 'the shortest of my unpublished poems: unpublished, though I also wrote it for Meynell' (4 May 1920; *Letters*, p. 174).

LP XXIX   30 March 1922.

LP XXX	Begun pre-1900 (Nosworthy). Begun 1910, finished 1922 (Cockerell).
LP XXXI	Begun 1905, finished April 1922. To J. W. Mackail, 18 July 1922: 'The piece I myself am most in doubt about is the longest; and I fear that is not its worst fault' (*Letters*, p. 199). To Mackail, 25 July 1922 (*Letters*, pp. 200–201):

> About 'Hell gate' my troubles were, first, that the whole thing is on the edge of the absurd: if it does not topple over, that is well so far. Secondly, as you perceive, the texture of the diction, especially in the parts which I had to compose, is not what it should be, and I rather despair of mending it. It would not do simply to omit the passages you mention: I should have to put something in their place, and it probably would be nothing better. As to three consecutive initial *and*'s, that occurs in the 'L'Allegro' of my great exemplar; and Shelley in 'The Invitation' and again in 'Ariel to Miranda' has five. On p. 43 I think the repetition has a certain value; on p. 42 it is mitigated by the intervention of a full stop, and offends the eye more than the ear . . . Exception is taken, as I foresaw it would be, to 'spruce' on p. 44. I think it is the right word, and helps, like 'finery of fire,' to keep the piece from being too solemn; and moreover Milton talks about 'the spruce and jocund Spring.' The alternative is 'brave,' which I like less, partly because it has the same vowel-sound as 'failed' in the next line. What do you think?

LP XXXII	After 1910.
LP XXXIII	August 1900. To Mackail, 25 July 1922: 'I must confess I do not know what lines 3 and 4 mean. I find that I originally wrote "forest hut", which may be better' (*Letters*, p. 200). MS, 'the hunter's hut.'
LP XXXIV	Pre-1900 (Nosworthy). *c.* 1905 (Cockerell). Published in the *Cambridge Review*, 29 April 1914, with variants.
LP XXXV	Pre-1900 (Nosworthy). Before 1910 (Cockerell).
LP XXXVI	First stanza 1922, others earlier. To Richards, 28 January 1926, about an anthology: 'The Headmaster of Winchester can have XXXVI from *Last*

Poems, and if he wants a title he can call it "Revolution," which may be of use, as most readers do not seem to see that it is a parable' (*Letters*, p. 234). The title was incorporated in subsequent editions of *LP*; Housman sent word of it to The Richards Press, 17 May 1928 (*Letters*, p. 266). On 16 February 1931, to an American bookseller: 'I find it a trouble to invent titles for poems, and do not think it worth while. I am not alone in this: for instance many of Bridges' *Shorter Poems* have no titles' (*Letters*, p. 308).

LP
  XXXVII

Published in *The Times*, 31 October 1917, under a leading article on 'The Anniversary of Ypres'.

LP
  XXXVIII

Pre-1900 (Nosworthy). After Boer War (Cockerell). Included in a MS presentation volume, *A Tribute to Thomas Hardy O.M.*, 2 June 1919. To Richards, 7 November 1919: 'I enclose the poem. The poems were not supposed to be *addressed* to Hardy, only specimens of our stuff, published or unpublished' (*Letters*, p. 166).

LP XXXIX

1920–22.

LP XL

April 1922. (Confirmed by letter of 3 November 1922; Maas, *Housman Society Journal* ii, 1975, 35.)

LP XLI

To Houston Martin, 17 October 1934: 'Abdon Burf is the highest part of the Brown Clee, which is the highest hill in Shropshire' (*Letters*, p. 362). Housman said in 1922 that the poem was 'quite old' (3 November 1922; *Housman Society Journal* ii, 1975, 35).

MORE POEMS AND
ADDITIONAL POEMS

Though in his letters Housman repeatedly slipped into writing of *Last Poems* as *New Poems*, he meant the obdurate title. The year after *LP* was published, he wrote to Robert Bridges: 'The title of the next volume will be *Posthumous Poems* or *Chansons d'Outre-tombe*' (2 July 1923; *Letters*, p. 213). In reply to a query, he sent a postcard, 15 October 1932: 'Not necessarily the last, but the last volume which will appear in my lifetime' (*Letters*, p. 324). To Houston Martin, 26 September 1934: '*A Shropshire Lad* and *New Poems* will never be joined together while I am here to prevent it, and I think it a silly notion' (*Letters*, p. 361).

More Poems was published in 1936. (The US edition of the same year had many textual differences from the British.)

In the preface to *More Poems*, Laurence Housman reported Housman's testamentary instructions:

I direct my brother, Laurence Housman, to destroy all my prose manuscripts in whatever language, and I permit him but do not enjoin him to select from my verse manuscript writing, and to publish, any poems which appear to him to be completed and to be not inferior to the average of my published poems; and I direct him to destroy all other poems and fragments of verse.

Of the forty-nine poems in *More Poems*, three had been published by Housman but not collected: IV, V and XLVIII. To these, Laurence Housman added eighteen additional unpublished poems in *A.E.H.*, known since as comprising the first of the *Additional Poems*; Laurence Housman's note in *A.E.H.* explains his second thoughts.

The subsequent story is a complicatedly sorry one, even though many of us are glad that the total destruction of the manuscripts did not ensue. John Sparrow tells the story with lucid logic (*The Times Literary Supplement*, 29 April 1955):

Mr Laurence Housman made, and published, his selection from the four poetical notebooks left by A.E.H., and then, as the will directed, destroyed all leaves that contained nothing but unpublished matter. There remained a number of leaves carrying on one side drafts (in varying stages of finish) of published poems, and on the other side jottings and fragmentary drafts of poems which A.E.H. did not publish and which his brother decided were not worthy of publication. He was anxious to preserve the first, but felt himself in duty bound to destroy the second.

In this situation, Mr Laurence Housman should surely have made up his mind one way or the other. If he held his brother's wishes paramount, he should have destroyed all unpublished fragments, even if that involved sacrificing in the process drafts of published poems. If, on the other hand, he thought that the interests of literature required that those wishes should be disregarded, he should have preserved everything. Had he taken the second course he would have had his critics; but, right or wrong, he could have looked them squarely in the face.

Instead, Mr Housman pursued a middle course. From the ambiguous leaves he cut away such portions as bore on both sides unpublished matter: and then, erasing or overscoring in ink or pencil everything, or almost everything, that had not already seen print, he pasted the remaining leaves and parts of leaves on to folio sheets so as to expose to view only the texts of poems which A.E.H., or he himself, had published.

In this unsatisfactory condition the manuscripts were sold to an American purchaser, the right to publish any still unpublished material being reserved to the author's estate. Nothing had been done to remove this restriction when the manuscripts passed by gift to the Library of Congress in 1940. In 1945 the Library authorities removed the leaves from the sheets on which they were pasted, and remounted them with hinges, so that the erased and cancelled texts on the versos were again exposed to view. This was done not with a view to publication but solely in order the better to preserve the manuscripts, on which the adhesive material was said to be having a deleterious effect. It was in 1947 that Mr Tom Burns Haber, of Ohio State University, began to interest himself in the material thus made accessible, and during the summers of 1950, 1951, and 1952 he set to work deciphering what Mr Laurence Housman had taken such pains to hide, and announced his intention of publishing his results.

In 1955, Tom Burns Haber published *The Manuscript Poems of A.E. Housman* ('Eight Hundred Lines of Hitherto Uncollected Verse from the Author's Notebooks'). At once, anger at the violation of Housman's will was compounded by dismay at Haber's mistranscriptions. The dust, as is its way, has since settled. And here too *Nescit vox missa reverti*, the voice sent forth can never be recalled. Just as the only wise alternative to unauthorised approximate biographies of T.S. Eliot will one day be a biography authorised in despite of the poet's wishes, so the only wise alternative to the present messy morass of MSS in Housman's case will be a full and exact edition of all the poems; fortunately, this is in progress, edited by Archie Burnett and to be published by Oxford University Press.

This present Penguin edition does not seek to go beyond the canon established by John Carter and others for the *Collected Poems*; that is, nothing further to *More Poems* and *Additional Poems* is included, nothing from the uncollected juvenilia or from the 'Eight Hundred Lines of Hitherto Uncollected Verse'. The only exception is that for the first time a selection of Housman's *Light Verse and Parodies* is included; see the next part of these notes.

More Poems

MP II ·   John Carter discovered that a final stanza printed in *MP* ('When mixed with me . . .') does not belong to this poem.

MP IV   1890 (*A.E.H.*, p. 254). Published in the *Edwardian*, April 1916, unsigned, 'From an Unpublished MS', with variants of doubtful standing. It had been intended for *A SL* (as XLII), but Housman deleted it in page-proof (*A.E. Housman: A Bibliography*).

MP V   Published in the *Quarto*, vol. 3, 1897. Reprinted in *Trinity Magazine*, March 1922. It is Housman's only published translation from the Latin. There is a memory by Mrs T.W. Pym (*The Times*, 5 May 1936): lecturing in May 1914, 'He read the ode aloud with deep emotion, first in Latin and then in an English translation of his own. "That," he said hurriedly, almost like a man betraying a secret, "I regard as the most beautiful poem in ancient literature," and walked quickly out of the room.'

MP X   February 1893.

MP XIII   Carter noted that this was incomplete, the MS showing that there were two projected stanzas of the conversation, between the second and third stanzas.

MP XV   To Edmund Gosse, 25 October 1922: 'I have copied out a poem for you as you wish. It is one of those which I did not put into the book; for I know you bibliophiles and your passion for *l'inédit* irrespective of merit' (*Letters*, pp. 205–6).

MP XVIII   Dropped from *LP* at the proof-stage, when Housman took advice (Graves, p. 229).

MP XXVI   Dropped from *LP* at the proof-stage, when Housman took advice (Graves, p. 229).

MP XXXIII Dropped from *LP* at the proof-stage, when Housman took advice (Graves, p. 229).

MP XLI	Gerald Jackson (son of Moses Jackson and godson of Housman) suggested to Laurence Housman that XLI, like XLII, refers to his (Gerald's) uncle, Adalbert J. Jackson; dying young, he was buried at Ramsgate (Sotheby's *Catalogue*, 8–9 July 1968).
MP XLII	Laurence Housman records: 'For the first few years of his life in London on taking up his appointment at the Patent Office, he shared rooms in Bayswater with his friend Moses Jackson, and a younger brother named Adalbert, whose death some years later is commemorated in *MP* XLII' (*A.E.H.*, p. 61). A.J. Jackson died in hospital of typhoid fever, on 12 November 1892; Housman's introductory lecture as a professor in London (prompting 'the news' within the poem) had been given the month before. On A.J. Jackson, see Laurence Housman, 'A.E. Housman's "De Amicitia"', *Encounter*, October 1967.
MP XLV	Printed for *LP* but then dropped (*MP*, p. 8).
MP XLVI	Dropped from *LP* at the proof-stage, when Housman was taking advice (Graves, p. 229).
MP XLVII	January 1925. The Dean of Trinity College acknowledged the poem, 9 January 1934 (Sotheby's *Catalogue*, 8–9 July 1968). Printed within the Order of Service, 4 May 1936. Housman noted: 'to the tune of "Brief life is here our portion."' 'The tune to which it was sung was not that suggested by Housman himself when he handed the manuscript over for use "when the time came". The tune he suggested was "rather a commonplace one".' He used to say, "My taste in music is rather vulgar." One cast about and found a better, which was submitted to him and which he approved' (Richards, p. 284). The poem was printed within the order of service without a title, though given on the front as the Hymn; following Housman's name, below it, was 'Melody by Melchior Vulpius, Harmonized by Bach' (note from the MS, *A.E. Housman: A Bibliography*). Published in the *Evening*

Standard, 4 May, as 'For My Funeral'. Gow wrote: 'The title was Housman's, but I suppose he meant it rather as a direction than as a title' (*A.E. Housman: A Bibliography*). Laurence Housman (*A.E.H.*, p. 117) records:

> Though Alfred's health caused him both discomfort and depression during his last years, he was sometimes able to joke about it; and even on the fair copy which I possess of the poem written for his own funeral one finds appended two jocular comments. In the second line of the first verse he had originally written 'Through time and space to roam'; in the rough draft he altered 'space' into 'place', and then, on the fair copy, entered a gibing note about the printers' probable insistence on 'space' as the right word. Finally, below the last verse, he wrote: 'And then, unless forcibly restrained, the choir will sing –' then followed the conventional 'Gloria' – an ascription of praise unsuitable for the very impersonal Power to whom the poem was addressed.

MP XLVIII   Published in *Waifs and Strays*, March 1881, signed 'A.E.H.' Reprinted with variants in *MP* as 'Alta Quies'. *Collected Poems*, 1939, returned to the published text and title.

Additional Poems

AP I to XVIII were published in *A.E.H.*

AP I   Sent to Laurence Housman when he was editing *The Venture* in 1903:

> he kept no fair copy of it; and when I asked him why he had not included it in *LP* he said because it was written in a metre he was so fond of, that he always doubted the merit of any poem in which he had succumbed to its attraction. The fact that he only left a very rough draft, difficult to reconstruct, and nearly impossible had I not remembered the poem fairly well, showed that he had definitely abandoned it (*A.E.H.*, p. 212)

On the metre, see pp. 288, 512 (the note includes the

letter to Mackail, 25 July 1922, on being 'too fond of the Laura Matilda stanza').

AP IV June 1895 (*A.E.H.*).

AP V Published in *The Times Literary Supplement*, 31 October 1936. Written by A.E.H. on the flyleaf of a copy of Manilius, *Astronomicon*, book I, which he gave to Walter Headlam.

AP VI This 'was, I feel sure, put aside by A.E.H. because he had used a refrain made familiar in one of Tennyson's lyrics in *The Princess*' (*A.E.H.*, p. 212); Tennyson's song comes between sections VI and VII of *The Princess*.

AP IX Unauthorised printing, by John Carter and John Sparrow, sent as a Christmas card in 1930: 'A Fragment preserved by oral tradition and said to have been composed by A.E. Housman in a dream.' To Houston Martin, 17 October 1934: '"Fragment composed in a dream" I do not know, or have forgotten' (*Letters*, p. 361). Housman (*A.E.H.*, p. 103) used to 'dream verses of a sort, which he was able to remember and write down on waking. One of these – a poem (the author of which, in his dream, was not himself, but G.K. Chesterton) ran as follows:

> When I was born in a world of sin,
> Praise be God it was raining gin;
> Gin on the house, gin on the walls,
> Gin on the bun-shops and copy-book stalls.'

A notebook entry has: 'I dreamt I was reading a passage of George Eliot, in which was quoted, printed in italics as prose, the verse

> The bogle of the [hairy weid*]
> That beast nor man hath trod
> Must not be seen of you nor me
> Nor aught but hell and God.

*'understood as a heath or moor' (Haber, *The Manuscript Poems of A.E. Housman*, p. 93). There is also a couplet which he dreamed:

Above the soldier's grave there twine
The Woodbine and the Concubine.

(Norman Page, *A.E. Housman: A Critical Biography*, 1983, p. 113.)

AP XI, XIA   A.E.H. published these as one consecutive poem; John Carter corrected this. September 1895 (*A.E.H.*).

AP XVIII   Published in *John O'London's Weekly*, 23 October 1936.

AP XIX   Published in the *Virginia Quarterly Review*, Autumn 1939. *Collected Poems*, 1939.

AP XX   Published in *Collected Poems*, 1939.

AP XXI   Published in *Waifs and Strays*, November 1881, signed 'A.E.H.'. *Collected Poems*, 1939. 'Two years before his death,' Laurence Housman records, 'we talked a good deal about his poems, as I was anxious to make sure of what I might or might not do over any future publication. "New Year's Eve", the poem which he published in a magazine while at Oxford, he ruled out; it smacked too much of the Swinburnian style which he had abandoned. He wrote it, he said, in his twentieth year. "I was then a deist"' (*A.E.H.*, p. 114). To Houston Martin, 26 September 1934: 'One thing I am prepared to do, which might gratify your depraved mind: if you like to send me "New Year's Eve" I can make and initial a correction which I was too late to make before it was printed' (*Letters*, p. 361). Maas notes: 'Housman's correction was "Once" in place of "Then,"' in the twelfth stanza. To Martin, 17 October 1934: 'I have had to make more than one correction in the copy of "New Year's Eve" which I return' (*Letters*, p. 361).

AP XXII   Published in the *Academy*, 22 December 1894; Robert Louis Stevenson, whose 'Requiem' Housman echoes, had died on 3 December. *Collected Poems*, 1939. 'The Fitzwilliam Museum used to exhibit the manuscript of a poem by him, published in a periodical but not reprinted in either volume of verse; and when he gave the museum the manuscript of *LP* he retrieved and burnt the poem he wished forgotten' (A.S.F. Gow, *A.E. Housman: A Sketch*, 1936, p. 22).

AP XXIII Published in the *Outlook*, 7 June 1902. *Collected Poems*, 1939. Carter corrected the 1902 punctuation from a MS. To Witter Bynner, 14 December 1903: 'I have no copy of the piece called "The Olive," which is not particularly good: it was published on the conclusion of the peace in June 1902, in the *Outlook*' (*Letters*, p. 70). The peace ending the Boer War, 31 May 1902.

TRANSLATIONS

Published in *Odes from the Greek Dramatists. Translated into Lyric Metres by English Poets and Scholars*, edited by Alfred W. Pollard (1890). Housman's translations were specially written for the book. He later corrected ('in my Swinburnian translation from Euripides') 'a misprint, *Far-seeking*, which should be *Far seeking*, as *seeking* is noun substantive' (22 March 1933; *Letters*, p. 330). *Collected Poems*, 1939. For his translation of Horace, *Odes* IV 7, see *MP* V.

LIGHT VERSE AND PARODIES: A SELECTION

These are here given lower-case Roman numerals, to avoid confusion with the numbering in *A.E.H.*, where Laurence Housman printed thirteen instances. Housman wrote light verse, parodies and nonsense verse for most of his life; this edition gives a selection from those that have been published.

(i) Published in the *Bromsgrovian*, 15 February and 29 March 1882, within 'A Morning with the Royal Family'. Reprinted in *A.E.H.*

(ii) Published in the *Bromsgrovian*, 8 June 1883. Reprinted in the *University College Gazette*, 1897; *Cornhill Magazine*, April 1901; the *Trinity Magazine*, February 1921; *Yale Review*, 1928; and elsewhere.

Housman sent a copy to Gilbert Murray, 23 April 1900: 'I enclose my own essay at an Andromache, only it is an Alcmaeon' (*Letters*, p. 52). He wrote to Wilbur Cross, 25 May 1927: 'My "Fragment of a Greek Tragedy" was written in 1883 and printed in a school magazine. It has since appeared in two college magazines and also, with more publicity, in the *Cornhill* of 1901. If you think it worth while to print it a fifth time, I can make no objection. I have no copy, but the *Cornhill* is probably accessible to you at Yale. In the circumstances I cannot accept the honorarium you are kind enough to offer, but I should like to see and correct the proofs, as on the last occasion when it was printed I made a few changes which I think are improvements' (*Letters*, p. 252). Gow notes: 'The text of this parody was considerably altered before its second, and again before its third appearance . . . The *Trinity Magazine* makes acknowledgements to the *Cornhill* but contains improvements in ll. 8 and 59 and differs in punctuation. The *Yale Review* speaks of recent changes by the author, but its text, apart from misprints in ll. 10 and 58, differs from that of the *Trinity Magazine* only in reverting to the punctuation of the *Cornhill*' (*A.E. Housman*, p. 77). The text here is therefore that of the *Trinity Magazine*.

(iii) The first stanza was published in 'Memories of A.E. Housman' by Katharine Symons (Mrs E.W. Symons), from the *Edwardian*, September 1936; both stanzas were published in *A.E.H.* From a letter to his stepmother, *c.* 1897, beginning with a reference to what became *Spikenard* (1898), by his brother Laurence (*Letters*, p. 45).

(iv) Published in 'Memories of A.E. Housman' by Katharine Symons, from the *Edwardian*, September 1936: 'About the beginning of this century, he sent a set of verses more elaborately illustrated to his nephew A.D.S.'

(v) Published in the *University College London Union Magazine*, Christmas Term, 1904, unsigned. Reprinted privately, by Housman's permission, at University College in 1935, with 'The Amphisbæna' and 'The Crocodile'.

(vi) Published in the *University College London Union Magazine*, June 1906, unsigned. Reprinted 1935; see the note to 'The Parallelogram'.

(vii) Published in *A.E.H.*, where Laurence Housman says it was 'sent to assist me when I was writing a libretto in 1907'.

(viii) Published in the *University College London Union Magazine*, March 1911, unsigned. Reprinted 1935; see the note to 'The Parallelogram'.

(ix) Published, undated, in Percy Withers, *A Buried Life* (1940), introduced thus: 'The letter containing it was written during the election of a Pope, and after telling me: "No, no more poetry, or at least nothing to speak of," he concludes: [and the poem follows]'. The election must be that of 1922.

(x) Published, undated, in John Pugh, *Bromsgrove and the Housmans* (1974).

(xi) Published, undated, in John Pugh, *Bromsgrove and the Housmans* (1974).

THE SELECTION OF THE PROSE

Most of Housman's appropriate prose is here, with three exceptions. First, there is only a selection from his classical editions, as from his classical papers (which fill three volumes). Second, there is only a selection from his letters. Third, there is nothing of his ceremonial prose. John Carter thought well of this last and included in his *Selected Prose* (1961; with corrections, 1962) five of Housman's formal addresses (to the Master and the Vice-Master of Trinity College; to Sir James Frazer; to the King); but, lacking wit and mischief, they seem to me to have not only less of penetration but less of real dignity than Housman's other prose.

Carter's *Selected Prose* is admirable and it is a pity that it was allowed to go out of print. A later editor is lucky in being able to include two substantial pieces not available in 1961: the Cambridge Inaugural of 1911 (which Carter himself was to edit as a slim volume in 1969), and the essay on Swinburne (likewise published only in 1969). Carter chose to include nothing from the letters.

The selecting which, as a matter of principle, is most contentious is that from the classical editions and papers. Fortunately the precedent was set by Carter, than whom no one, with the possible exception of his friend and collaborator John Sparrow, could have been more respectful of Housman. The excerpts here have been chosen for the life of their insights, arguments and style, for their wit and comedy and passion. They may look as if they demand that a reader know a great deal, but it is no insult to Housman's classical writings to say that they also have a world of instruction and delight to offer to someone who reads them, with modest candour, not as a student of the classics but as someone alive simply to the life of the mind and of a pen. The excerpts have been chosen so as to offer much even to those of us who know little or nothing; but no less important, in excerpting, than a degree of autonomous or self-explanatory power has been the criterion of rhythm, the rhythm of a sentence or a paragraph, of a thought or of a train of thought. Housman's greatness in prose is by no means only a matter of his witty asperity and sense of the absurd, but the right starting-place may still be the isolated remarks in which his brother Laurence Housman delighted (*A.E.H.*, pp. 89–90):

But his treatment of these [targets], though it erred on the side of severity, was mild by comparison with what he meted out to those objects of his special aversion, the pretentious fools who with misled minds strayed mischievously into his own special department of textual criticism. Of the jolly ferocity with which he was prepared to put these into their places, I give here a few samples which had no names attached to them, in order that any who are not readers of the edited classics or the learned reviews, may get an idea of that gift for invective which made him the most feared, and perhaps also the most hated, among the pedants (his own pet phrase) of his day.

'When — has acquired a scrap of misinformation he cannot rest till he has imparted it.'

'Nature, not content with denying to Mr — the faculty of thought, has endowed him with the faculty of writing.'

'I do not know upon what subject — will next employ his versatile incapacity. He is very well – dangerously well.'

'If we all know as little as — does, we should doubtless find the classics as easy as he does.'

'Conjectural emendation as practised by — is not a game, an exercise requiring skill and heed, like marbles or skittles or cat's-cradle, but a pastime, like leaning against a wall and spitting.'

'— usually has the last word in controversy because he incurs exposures which editors do not like to print.'

'I can easily understand why Mr — should not tell the truth about other people. He fears reprisals: he apprehends that they may tell the truth about *him*.'

'If Mr — were a postage-stamp he would be a very good postage-stamp; but adhesiveness is not the virtue of a critic. A critic is free and detached.'

The sources for the text of the prose are listed below (p. 505), and there are notes to the prose (p. 511). No attempt has been made to annotate the classical excerpts, and not solely because the editor is not competent to do so but because of the *kind* of interest that such writings are here believed to have for the readers envisaged; the other prose has been furnished with notes mostly of the sort that simply identifies or locates what Housman is referring to. In the body of the book, titles of works are given in italics as is now standard; in much of what he published in prose, Housman preferred to give titles in roman and without inverted commas, but this was not how, for instance, the classical journals printed him. To put, not *Henry VIII*, but Henry VIII, may leave it uncertain whether the King or the play is being spoken of; and 'the punctual praises of the *Scotsman*' is a different thing from those of the Scotsman.

THE TEXT OF THE PROSE

━━━

Introductory Lecture (1892). Delivered before the Faculties of Arts and Laws and of Science at University College London on 3 October 1892, Housman being about to take up his duties as Professor of Latin. Privately printed in 1892, and in 1933 when Housman corrected his quotation from King George III and wrote in a letter of 5 December: 'I should like to have it stated that the Council of University College, not I, had the lecture printed. I consented, because it seemed churlish to refuse. This is the purport of *Nescit vox missa reverti*' (printed on the title-page; 'the voice sent forth can never be recalled'). Housman spoke of it as 'rhetorical and not wholly sincere' (quoted in the Note by Gow in 1937). 'I don't autograph it, as it is not good enough' (20 December 1933; *Letters*, p. 349). Published posthumously in 1937. The words 'in diffusion' and 'it' have been restored from 1892, in the absence of evidence that Housman intended their removal.

Matthew Arnold. Delivered at University College London, to the College's Literary Society, in the 1890s; these pages are all that survive. Published in *Selected Prose* (Appendix), edited by John Carter (1961; with corrections, 1962), from a typescript among the papers of Housman's sister Katharine Symons (Mrs E.W. Symons). Gow records: 'For the University College Literary Society he produced at one time or another essays on Matthew Arnold, Burns, Campbell, Swinburne, Tennyson, the Spasmodic School, and, in a lighter vein, Erasmus Darwin . . . It is to be regretted that he refused an invitation from the Cambridge University Press to publish them, and gave his executors instructions that they were to be destroyed' (*A.E. Housman; A Sketch*, p. 21). For Housman's account of the Literary Society, see p. 344, his Preface to *Nine Essays* by Arthur Platt.

Swinburne. Delivered at University College London, to the College's Literary Society, in 1910, the year after Swinburne's death. Published, with an introductory note by John Sparrow, in the *Cornhill Magazine*, no. 1061, autumn 1969, from a typescript among Geoffrey Madan's papers. The quotation from Cowper's

'Verses Supposed to be Written by Alexander Selkirk' is corrected here, and 'the death of themes' emended to 'the dearth of themes'. 'A friend once expressed to Housman the hope that the paper on Swinburne might be published, and, on hearing that it was to be destroyed after his death, ventured to suggest that if Housman thought it bad he would already have destroyed it himself. "I do not think it bad," said Housman; "I think it not good enough for me"' (Gow, p. 22).

Cambridge Inaugural Lecture (1911). Delivered at the University of Cambridge, 9 May 1911. 'This lecture,' Gow recorded in 1936, 'was never printed, not because Housman wished to suppress it, but because he was unable to verify a statement which it contained as to the text of Shelley's *Lament* of 1821' (*A.E. Housman: A Sketch*, p. 33). Housman quoted from the lecture in his 1931 Preface to his edition of Juvenal, and again in *The Name and Nature of Poetry* (1933). The Cambridge Inaugural was published, from a typescript, in *The Times Literary Supplement*, 9 May 1968, respectfully omitting the Shelley crux. Further research by John Carter and John Sparrow vindicated Housman's argument (*The Times Literary Supplement*, 21 November 1968), and the complete text, with Preface and Appendix, was published in 1969, under a title supplied by John Carter, 'The Confines of Criticism'. Five 1969 misprints have been corrected here, and at one further place the punctuation has been corrected from Housman's excerpted text of 1931.

The Period of the French Revolution: A Review of The Cambridge History of English Literature. *Vol. XI.* Published in the *Cambridge Review*, 27 January 1915.

A Georgian History of Victorian Literature: A Review of The Cambridge History of English Literature. *Vols. XIII and XIV.* Published in the *Cambridge Review*, 23 May 1917. Two corrections by John Carter of minor misquotations are incorporated (*Selected Prose*, p. 201).

The Application of Thought to Textual Criticism. Delivered at the Classical Association in Cambridge, 4 August 1921. Published in the *Proceedings of the Classical Association* xviii (1922). *The Classical Papers of A.E. Housman*, edited by J. Diggle and F.R.D. Goodyear (1972), iii, 1058–69. Housman wrote to Grant Richards, 21 July 1921: 'I have been away from Cambridge a great deal since the beginning of June, and I now am settling down to work. I am obliged to be here at the beginning of August for a meeting of the Classical Association, damn it: I am not a member, but they have chosen to meet here, and Americans are coming, and I am the only classical professor of Cambridge who is able to deliver an address' (*Letters*, p. 186).

Napoleon III: A Review of Louis Napoleon and the Recovery of France. F.A. Simpson, *Louis Napoleon and the Recovery of France.* Published in the *Cambridge Review*, 25 May 1923.

Preface to Nine Essays *by Arthur Platt*. Published 1927. A subsequent correction by Housman has been incorporated (*Selected Prose*, p. 201). Housman wrote to R. St J. Parry, 17 January 1926: 'I should not enjoy writing an introduction, but I would do it for his sake, and in the interests of scholarship and literature' (*Letters*, p. 233).

The Name and Nature of Poetry. Delivered at the University of Cambridge, as the Leslie Stephen Lecture, 9 May 1933. Published 1933. Housman subsequently corrected 'O mistress mine, where art thou roaming' to '. . . are you . . .' (*Selected Prose*, p. 201). The epigraph from Coleridge, silently dropped by Carter in *Selected Prose*, is here restored. Housman said to Percy Withers: 'Well, you didn't get one because I haven't given a copy to anyone. I take no pride in it. I would rather forget it, and have my friends forget. I don't wish it to be associated with me' (*A Buried Life*, p. 102).

From the *Classical Editions*

The Editing of Manilius: the five books of Manilius, *M. Manilii Astronomica*, were published in 1903, 1912, 1916, 1920 and 1930 respectively; and then in a second edition, with addenda, in 1937. The excerpts here are from book I, and (beginning on p. 387) from book V.

The Editing of Juvenal: the satires of Juvenal, *D. Iunii Iuuenalis Saturae: editorum in usum edidit*, were published in 1905; and then in a second edition, with a further Preface and with corrections, in 1931.

The Editing of Lucan: *M. Annaei Lucani, Belli Ciuilis, Libri Decem: editorum in usum edidit* was published in 1926; and then in a second impression, with corrections, in 1927.

From the *Classical Papers*

The Classical Papers of A.E. Housman, edited by J. Diggle and F.R.D. Goodyear (1972), in three volumes; *CP* below. These volumes do not include the prefaces or notes to Housman's classical editions.

1.   Euripides, *Iphigenia in Tauris* 35. *Classical Review* i (1887); *CP* i 12.

2.   Aeschylus, *Persae* 815–17. *American Journal of Philology* x (1888); *CP* i 19–20.

3.   Aeschylus, *Agamemnon*. *Journal of Philology* xvi (1888); *CP* i 55.

4–6.   T.G. Tucker, *The Supplices of Aeschylus*. *Classical Review* iv (1890); *CP* i 120, 123, 124–5.

7.   I. Flagg, *Euripides' Iphigenia among the Taurians*. *Classical Review* iv (1890); *CP* i 129–30.

8.   Horace, *Serm.* I 3 117–24. *Journal of Philology* xviii (1890); *CP* i 141–2.

9.   The *Oedipus Coloneus* of Sophocles. *American Journal of Philology* xiii (1892); *CP* i 187.

10.   The Manuscripts of Propertius. *Journal of Philology* xxi (1893); *CP* i 242.

11–12.   K.P. Schulze, *Catulli Veronensis liber*. *Classical Review* viii (1894). *CP* i 307, 311–12.

13.   The Manuscripts of Propertius. *Journal of Philology* xxii (1894); *CP* i 347.

14–17.   The Manuscripts of Propertius. *Classical Review* ix (1895); *CP* i 351, 357–8, 361, 366.

18–19.   Ovid's *Heroides*. *Classical Review* xi (1897); *CP* i 380–81, 386.

20.   Lucretiana. *Journal of Philology* xxv (1897); *CP* ii 430–31.

21–5.   A. Palmer, *P. Ouidi Nasonis Heroides*. *Classical Review* xiii (1899); *CP* ii 472, 477, 478.

26–7.   W.J. Stone, *On the Use of Classical Metres in English*. *Classical Review* xiii (1899); *CP* ii 486–7, 487–8.

28.   The *Aratea* of Germanicus. *Classical Review* xiv (1900); *CP* ii 500.

29.   S.G. Tremenheere, *The Cynthia of Propertius. Classical Review* xiv (1900); *CP* ii 517–18.

30.   C. Bailey, *Lucreti de rerum natura libri sex. Classical Review* xiv (1900); *CP* ii 524.

31.   J.P. Postgate, *Corpus poetarum Latinorum, Fasc. III. Classical Review* xiv (1900); *CP* ii 531.

32–4.   *Pharsalia Nostra. Classical Review* xv (1901); *CP* ii 532–4.

35.   Elucidations of Latin Poets. *Classical Review* xv (1901); *CP* ii 547.

36.   Virgil, *Georgics* III 400–403. *Classical Review* xvi (1902); *CP* ii 560–61.

37–8.   Remarks on the *Culex. Classical Review* xvi (1902); *CP* ii 563.

39–40. Ovid, *Ars. Am.* I 337. *Classical Review* xvi (1902); *CP* ii 578, 582.

41–5.   S.G. Owen, *A. Persi Flacci et D. Iuni Iuuenalis saturae. Classical Review* xvii (1903); *CP* ii 602, 605, 607, 610.

46.   H.L. Wilson, *D. Iuni Iuuenalis saturarum libri V. Classical Review* xvii (1903); *CP* ii 614.

47.   Owen's *Persius and Juvenal* – A Caveat. *Classical Review* xviii (1904); *CP* ii 617.

48.   R. Ellis, *Catulli carmina. Classical Review* xix (1905); *CP* ii 625.

49.   Virgil, *Aen.* IV 225. *Classical Review* xix (1905); *CP* ii 628.

50–53. H.E. Butler, *Sexti Properti opera omnia. Classical Review* xix (1905); *CP* ii 632–3, 633, 635, 636.

54–61. Luciliana. *Classical Quarterly* i (1907); *CP* ii 662, 663, 669, 670, 672, 678–9, 683, 684.

62.   Dorotheus of Sidon. *Classical Quarterly* ii (1908); *CP* ii 742.

63.   The Apparatus Criticus of the *Culex. Transactions of the Cambridge Philological Society* vi (1908); *CP* ii 777.

64–5.   G. Némethy, *Ciris epyllion pseudouergilianum. Classical Review* xxiii (1909); *CP* ii 795, 797.

66.   A. Ratti, *Reliquie di un antico codice delle satire di Giovenale. Classical Review* xxiv (1910); *CP* ii 815.

67.   A Transposition in Propertius. *Classical Quarterly* viii (1914); *CP* ii 884.

68.   AIOC and EIOC in Latin Poetry. *Journal of Philology* xxxiii (1914); *CP* ii 895.

69–70. S.G. Owen, *P. Ouidi Nasonis Tristium libri quinque.*
       Cambridge Review xxxvii (1915); *CP* iii 903, 904.

71.   Ovid, *Ibis* 512. *Classical Quarterly* ix (1915); *CP* iii 905.

72–4. The *Thyestes* of Varius. *Classical Quarterly* xi (1917); *CP* iii
       941, 944, 948–9.

75–7. Juvenal and Two of His Editors. *Journal of Philology* xxxiv
       (1918); *CP* iii 964, 966, 967–8.

78–80. Transpositions in the *Ibis* of Ovid. *Journal of Philology* xxxiv
       (1918); *CP* iii 969, 976, 977.

81–2. J.P. Postgate, *Phaedri Fabulae Aesopiae.* *Classical Review*
       xxxiv (1920); *CP* iii 1007, 1010.

83–4. De Nihilo. *Classical Review* xxxiv (1920); *CP* iii 1012, 1014.

85.   The *Ibis* of Ovid. *Journal of Philology* xxxv (1920); *CP* iii
       1040.

86–7. The Codex Lipsiensis of Manilius. *Classical Quarterly* xv
       (1921); *CP* iii 1046, 1048.

88.   E.T. Merrill, *Catulli Veronensis liber.* *Classical Review*
       xxxviii (1924); *CP* iii 1090.

89.   W. Morel, *Fragmenta poetarum Latinorum.* *Classical Review*
       xlii (1928); *CP* iii 1152.

90.   H. Bornecque and M. Prévost, *Ovide, Héroïdes.* *Classical
       Review* xliii (1929); *CP* iii 1158.

91.   H.J. Izaac, *Martial I–VII.* *Classical Review* xlv (1931); *CP* iii
       1174.

92–3. Notes on the *Thebais* of Statius. *Classical Quarterly* xxvii
       (1933); *CP* iii 1217, 1219.

94.   N. Vianello, *D. Iunii Iuuenalis satirae.* *Classical Review* l
       (1936); *CP* iii 1249.

From the *Letters*

From *The Letters of A.E. Housman*, edited by Henry Maas (1971), except for the excerpt of 19 August 1929 which is from Grant Richards, *Housman: 1897–1936* (1941). Maas says he prints about half of the 1,500 letters that he traced; but P. Naiditch says that 2,114 letters survive, of which 'some 1,492' have been published. Naiditch's exact and important article on the letters (*Housman Society Journal* ix, 1983, 53–69) makes one wish that he would re-edit them more comprehensively.

Notes to the Prose

p. 265   *Johnson*. To Boswell, 19 October 1769, with a comic concession: 'Shakspeare never has six lines together without a fault. Perhaps you may find seven: but this does not refute my general assertion.'

p. 266   *King George III*. To Fanny Burney, 19 December 1785, continuing: 'Only one must not say so.'

p. 266   *The Winter's Tale*. III iii 25–6.

p. 267   *Four speedy Cherubim. Paradise Lost* II 516; the two subsequent quotations are IV 555 and IV 810–11.

p. 269   *to carry to my lips . . . Iliad* XXIV 505; considered by Arnold one of 'the most essentially grand and characteristic things of Homer'; *On Translating Homer: Last Words* (delivered 1861, published 1862).

p. 269   *out of print*. The original three lectures *On Translating Homer* were published in 1861; Housman spoke in 1892; there was to be a 'Popular Edition' in 1896.

p. 271   *Hamlet*. IV iv 36–9.

p. 271   *Dante. Inferno* XXVI 90–124.

p. 276   *Gerard Hamilton*. Quoted by Boswell in the closing pages of the *Life of Johnson*.

p. 280   *Thy face . . .* 'Mater Triumphalis'.

p. 283   *The blackbird . . .* William Cowper, 'The Poplar-Field'.

p. 283   *There is mercy . . .* Cowper, 'Verses Supposed to be Written by Alexander Selkirk'.

p. 283   *Out of Dindymus . . .* 'Dolores'.

p. 284   *In the darkening . . .* 'Hertha'.

p. 284   *There lived a singer . . .* 'The Triumph of Time'.

p. 285   *Night wanes . . .* Byron, *Lara*, opening of Canto II.

p. 285   *Thee too the years . . .* 'Anactoria'.

p. 286   *Wordsworth*. 'It is not to be thought of that the Flood', *Poems Dedicated to National Independence and Liberty*.

p. 286   *How delicious . . .* Thomas Campbell, 'Song'. I owe this attribution to Elsie Duncan-Jones.

p. 287   *Fairer than feigned . . . Paradise Regained* II 358–61.

p. 288 *Many a long blithe wave* . . . *Tristram of Lyonesse*: 'Joyous Gard'.

p. 288 *The celebrated stanza*. 'Dolores'.

p. 288 *Rejected Addresses.* By James and Horace Smith (1812); the parody of the Della Cruscans, 'Drury's Dirge' by 'Laura Matilda'. Dropping what became *A P* I from *L P*, Housman wrote to J. W. Mackail, 25 July 1922: 'I believe I am too fond of the Laura Matilda stanza, which I think the most beautiful and the most difficult in English' (*Letters*, p. 200; *A.E.H.*, p. 212). Maas notes that this is the stanza of *A S L* IV and XXXV, and of *L P* VIII. Housman wrote to Robert Bridges, 18 December 1925: 'Along with your novelties I am glad to see you using the old and beautiful stanza, now unjustly despised because so often ill managed . . . which ought not to be left to Laura Matilda' (*Letters*, p. 231).

p. 288 *Grace Darling*. 'Grace Darling', *Astrophel* (1894).

p. 291 *And the night* . . . 'A Channel Passage'.

p. 291 *Hurry me, Nymphs* . . . George Darley (1795–1846), from Canto I of *Nepenthe* (privately printed 1835, published 1897). Housman wrote to Laurence Housman, 12 May 1897: 'George Darley was the writer of the excellent sham 17th century song "It is not beauty I demand" which Palgrave printed as genuine in the second part of the *Golden Treasury*. Because it was so good I read another thing of his, a sort of fairy drama whose name I forget, and was disappointed with it and read no more. But the piece you quote about the sea is capital' (*Letters*, p. 41).

p. 292 *Ere frost-flower* . . . 'March: An Ode'.

p. 293 *Tale of Balen*. Part VI; indenting of the last line corrected here.

p. 295 *The elegy*. 'Ave atque Vale', *Poems and Ballads: Second Series* (1878).

p. 301 *Johnson*. To Boswell, 6 April 1772: 'Why, Sir, if you were to read Richardson for the story, your impatience would be so much fretted that you would hang yourself.'

p. 301 *Uncontrolled truth*. Undisputed (*OED*, which quotes Swift).

p. 305 *William Rossetti*. Carter and Sparrow note that 'Housman left out *and* when citing Rossetti's reading.'

p. 311 *ergastulum*. 'A kind of prison on a large estate to which refractory or unreliable slaves were sent for work in chain-gangs' (*Oxford Latin Dictionary*).

p. 315 *A bird* . . . 'A Character':

> Thus, his own whim his only bribe,
> Our Bard pursued his old A. B. C.
> Contented if he could subscribe
> In fullest sense his name Ἔστησε;
> ('Tis Punic Greek for 'he hath stood!')

p. 315 *Written in the worst prose.* By Herbert J.C. Grierson.

p. 316 *A chapter on Wordsworth.* By Émile Legouis.

p. 317 *Will no one tell me* . . . 'The Solitary Reaper'.

p. 317 *No motion has she now* . . . 'A slumber did my spirit seal'.

p. 317 *My eyes are dim* . . . 'The Fountain'.

p. 317 *And I can listen* . . . 'To the Cuckoo'.

p. 319 *Ces enfants* . . . La Bruyère.

p. 319 *The tuneful quartos* . . . Francis Jeffrey, reviewing Felicia Hemans, *Edinburgh Review*, October 1829.

p. 321 *A writer.* A. Hamilton Thompson.

p. 321 *On Tennyson.* By Herbert J.C. Grierson.

p. 321 *The worst chapter.* By Alfred Perceval Graves.

p. 321 *An interesting chapter.* By W. Murison.

p. 322 *Coleridge. Biographia Literaria*, chapter 22.

p. 328 *Mare's-nests.* 'In conversation his more usual attitude towards such offenders was a tolerant contempt which on one occasion at least framed itself in verse. A scholar, whose imagination often outran the evidence, evoked the couplet

> When — 's roaming footsteps fieldward fare,
> Quakes for her callow young the brooding mare'.

(Gow, p. 31).

p. 340 *aftermath.* The previous year, Housman had used 'after-math' with exact felicity: 'In aftermaths of soft September' (*LP* XL).

p. 349 *Anima Poetae* has 'as far as he goes'.

p. 349 *I used these words.* His words differ, in small but interesting ways, from those of the typescript of the Inaugural; see p. 302.

p. 350 *Patmore*. Housman directed a correspondent to Patmore's 'Essay on English Metrical Laws' (*Letters*, p. 345; Maas notes, 'First published as "English Metrical Critics" in the *North British Review*, 1857; reprinted in Patmore's *Poems*, 1879').

p. 350 *Myers*. In his essay on Victor Hugo (*Essays Modern*).

p. 351 *Now Gilpin* . . . William Cowper, 'The Diverting History of John Gilpin'.

p. 351 *Come, worthy Greek* . . . Samuel Daniel, 'Ulysses and the Siren'.

p. 352 *Cuckoo*. 'Ode to the Cuckoo', by John Logan or Michael Bruce.

p. 352 *Johnson's lines*. 'On the Death of Dr Robert Levet'.

p. 353 *Duncan is in his grave* . . . *Macbeth* III ii 22–3.

p. 353 *defined by Johnson*. Not so in his *Dictionary*, but in his *Life of Cowley*.

p. 353 *Two walking baths* . . . Richard Crashaw, 'Saint Mary Magdalene, or The Weeper'.

p. 354 *salt*. To H.F. Newall, 7 February 1918: '*Circle* is one of those English words (like *salt*) on which you men of science have laid hands and wrested them out of their original meanings' (*Letters*, p. 413).

p. 355 *Arnold*. 'The Study of Poetry' (1880).

p. 355 *Nonne's Priest's Tale*. To Katharine Symons, of Bridges, 3 January 1924: 'He has a large number of correct opinions, and is delighted when he finds that I have them too, and shakes hands with me when I say that *The Nun's Priest's Tale* is Chaucer's best poem' (*Letters*, p. 217).

p. 356 *Riches, like insects* . . . Pope, 'Epistle to Bathurst: Of the Use of Riches'.

p. 357 *As one* . . . Andrew Lang, 'The Odyssey'.

p. 357 *Lo! where* . . . Gray, 'Ode on the Spring'.

p. 359 *Till frowning skies* . . . *The Hind and the Panther* III 437–8, 1283–4, 175–6.

p. 360 *hymns . . . burdens every bough*. The 'comparison' then is not only that within the metaphor but a comparison with a poetry greater than the Augustans': Shakespeare's Sonnet 102:

Not that the summer is less pleasant now
Than when her mournful hymns did hush the night,
But that wild music burdens every bough.

p. 361   *Watts.* 'A Cradle Hymn'.

p. 361   *What gentle ghost* . . . Ben Jonson, 'An Elegy on the Lady
Jane Pawlet'.

p. 362   *What beck'ning ghost* . . . 'Elegy to the Memory of an
Unfortunate Lady'. Pope wrote 'step'.

p. 364   *Coleridge. Anima Poetae*, p. 5.

p. 365   *The only poem.* 'A Song to David'.

p. 365   *One of the best poems.* 'He spoke in warm praise of Ralph
Hodgson's "Song of Honour", adding "Yes, but what a
debt it owes to Smart's 'Song to David!'"' (Percy Withers,
A Buried Life, p. 59).

p. 366   *Take O take* . . . *Measure for Measure* IV i 1–6.

p. 368   *Tho' thou art* . . . Epilogue to 'For the Sexes: The Gates of
Paradise'.

p. 369   *Sorrow, that is not sorrow* . . . Wordsworth, *The Prelude* XIII
246–9.

p. 369   *Though love repine* . . . Emerson, 'Sacrifice'.

p. 369   *Milton.* 'Song', *Arcades*.

p. 369   *I replied.* To Seymour Adelman, 6 May 1928 (*Letters*, pp.
264–5).

p. 369   *A spirit* . . . Job IV 5.

p. 370   *one of Keats's last letters.* To Charles Brown, 1 November
1820: 'Every thing that I have in my trunk that reminds me
of her goes through me like a spear.'

p. 370   *Wordsworth.* Preface to *Lyrical Ballads* (1800).

p. 370   *Burns.* To Alexander Cunningham, 11 March 1791. (Burns
wrote 'rather than from the impulse'.)

p. 370   *a secretion.* Housman will have remembered (even if for
private pleasure) *Of the Art of Sinking in Poetry*, chapter III,
'an undoubted Physical Maxim, that Poetry is a *natural* or
morbid Secretion from the Brain'.

p. 371   *the piece which stands last. A S L L X III*, 'I hoed and trenched
and weeded'. Housman wrote, 12 April 1935: 'I have
received several guesses at the order of some or all of the
stanzas, but I do not let the truth be known, because then

everyone would begin to pretend that it was obvious to them. If I had to guess myself, I am sure I could not tell which was last and which last but one; though I think I could guess which two came first' (*Letters*, p. 369). Laurence Housman noted a page torn from the notebooks: 'I surmise that on that page was written the last poem in *ASL* . . . He refused more than once to tell anyone the answer; I suspect that the answer was on the missing page, and that he purposely cancelled it, in order that his riddle might remain unsolved' (*A.E.H.*, p. 255). F. W. Bateson speculated on the order, *Housman Society Journal* i (1974) 3–6. For the principle, there is Housman's letter to J. W. Mackail, that a particular poem 'dissatisfies me too, but not quite in the same way. The first and last stanzas came into my head; the middle ones are composed' (25 July 1922; *Letters*, p. 200).

p. 373   *thou ailest here* . . . Matthew Arnold, 'Memorial Verses':

> When Goethe's death was told, we said:
> Sunk, then, is Europe's sagest head.
> Physician of the iron age,
> Goethe has done his pilgrimage.
> He took the suffering human race,
> He read each wound, each weakness clear;
> And struck his finger on the place,
> And said: *Thou ailest here, and here!*

p. 374   *plies his desperate hook.* Pope, *Imitations of Horace*, Epistle II i: 'Not that I'd lop the beauties from his book, / Like slashing Bentley with his desperate hook.' Hook, both an implement for lopping and a bracket; Bentley lopped *Paradise Lost* by putting 'between two hooks' (as he said) lines which he imagined had been foisted into the text. Housman discusses Bentley's Milton in the Introductory Lecture (p. 267).

p. 380   *Byron. Childe Harold's Pilgrimage* I 860.

p. 397   *Pascal. Pensées* II 80.

p. 412   *hippomanes.* An aphrodisiac.

p. 432   *Direness* . . . Following 'horror', this adapts (from 'My . . . me') *Macbeth* V v 13–15.

p. 438   *The thes. ling. Lat.* See p. 311 for Housman on this, 'the latest and most elaborate' of Latin dictionaries.

p. 439 *What I tell you* . . . Lewis Carroll, *The Hunting of the Snark*.

p. 443 *Milton. Paradise Lost* II 392.

p. 451 *The verse*. Of *A S L*, published the previous month. Kate is their sister Katharine.

p. 452 *the poem. A S L* LXI.

p. 452 *Arnold*. 'The Church of Brou'; on Arnold's 'factual inaccuracies' and his source, see the headnote in *The Poems of Matthew Arnold*, edited by Kenneth Allott, revised Miriam Allott (1979).

p. 452 *publishers*. Grant Richards.

p. 452 *Green Arras*. Laurence Housman: 'I had designed for the cover of my own book, *Green Arras*, a very elaborate, and, as I thought, beautiful cover of gold scroll-work' (*A.E.H.*, p. 76).

p. 453 *the finances of the first edition*. Sold at 2s. 6d.

p. 453 *Kegan Paul*. Housman had arranged that they publish *A S L* at his expense; Macmillan and Company had turned the book down.

p. 454 *Sic notus Ulixes?* Maas notes *Aeneid* II 44 ('Is this the Ulysses we know?').

p. 455 *this college*. University College London.

p. 455 *a novel*. Maas notes an anthology, rather: *Wayfarer's Love* (1904), which contained what became *L P* XVII.

p. 456 *our joint work*. The latest edition of *A S L*.

p. 457 *E. Thomas*. The poet Edward Thomas.

p. 457 *Quiller-Couch*. Editor of *The Oxford Book of English Verse* (1900).

p. 458 *Gurney*. The poet and composer Ivor Gurney.

p. 458 *Mrs Taylor's poems*. Maas notes *Rose and Vine*, by Rachel Annand Taylor.

p. 458 *the second Lord Lytton*. The poet 'Owen Meredith'.

p. 459 *here*. Cambridge.

p. 459 *The type-written text*. Of the second book of Manilius; Housman sends Richards five instructions.

p. 460 *only the Bible that has performed*. Richards (Maas's source) prints 'that' and not, as Maas does, 'which'.

p. 460 *Hopkins*. His poems, then first published (1918), edited by Bridges.

p. 461 *The letter to Jackson*. The ceremonial letter to Henry

Jackson, drafted by Housman (14 July 1919; *Letters*, pp. 162–3).

p. 462   *Constable*. Maas notes that Messrs Constable and Company had in 1917 published *L. of C.* (*Lines of Communication*) by James Agate, in which *ASL* XXV was printed without permission; a recent Grant Richards advertisement (*The Times Literary Supplement*) had now given prominence to Agate.

p. 462   *Rothenstein*. Gow (pp. 23, 58–9) lists five drawings of Housman by William Rothenstein, three of 1906 and two of 1915. Of the second 1906 one, Gow notes: 'The Library of Trinity College, Cambridge, possessed a drawing of him by Sir William Rothenstein which Housman disliked. In 1933 he obtained leave to substitute for it another drawing by the same artist and burnt the one he thought inferior.' This is the 'full face' one in the letter, the others of 1906 being profile.

p. 462   *Lovat Fraser's designs*. Illustrations to *ASL*. Among Housman's detailed asperities are those on: *ASL* X, 'Poem on March illustrated by tree in full leaf'; XXX, 'Poem contrasting the passions of youth and the unwholesome excitement of adultery with the quiet and indifference of death, illustrated by figure of obese old man: possibly the injured husband'; and LII, 'The poem is about black poplars growing by pools and whispering at night when there is no wind. The illustration displays Lombardy poplars in broad day and a furious gale: no water anywhere about, except suspended as vapour in a cloud' (Richards, pp. 181–3).

p. 463   *the Queen's doll's-house*. Maas notes: 'An ambitious scheme designed to show posterity an English Queen's way of life in the twentieth century and to incorporate the work of leading artists and craftsmen. The house itself was designed by Sir Edwin Lutyens . . . Apart from Housman's, each book contained an original story written for the occasion. The only author who refused was Bernard Shaw' (*Letters*, p. 212).

p. 465   *less haughty*. Macmillan then turned the offer down (the book was published by Blackwell); see also p. 466, Housman to Sir Frederick Macmillan and the note.

p. 465 *literary criticism, referring opinions to principles*. Johnson: 'It is, however, the task of criticism to establish principles; to improve opinion into knowledge' (*Rambler*, no. 92, 2 February 1751).

p. 466 *Macmillan*. See Housman's offer, p. 464. Maas notes: 'On 22 December 1926 he wrote to Housman asking if the firm might publish his edition of Lucan after all. "I remember thinking at the time that this was possibly a case in which it would be wise to relax our rule but I expect that what decided us not to do so was a phrase in your letter describing us as 'haughty'. . . . It may be that it is too late, but this letter will at all events convince you that the quality of humility has not been omitted from our composition"' (*Letters*, p. 245).

p. 466 *Symons*. A.J.A. Symons, seeking to include Housman in *A Book of Nineties Verse* (1928).

p. 466 *hanging*. By Charles Duff (1928).

p. 467 *Shelley's Skylark*. Housman's letter was published in *The Times Literary Supplement*, 20 December 1928. Maas notes: 'In *For Lancelot Andrewes*, 1928, T.S. Eliot wrote à propos Shelley's "Ode to a Skylark": "I am still ignorant to what Sphere Shelley refers, or why it should have silver arrows, or what the devil he means by an intense lamp narrowing in the white dawn." The book was reviewed in *The Times Literary Supplement* on 6 December 1928. The following week T. Sturge Moore contributed a letter to say that "a schoolgirl would know that the 'silver sphere' is the moon."'
'*Egeria*': the nymph who instructed Numa Pompilius, the second King of Rome.

p. 467 *Huxley's*. Aldous Huxley (Maas notes), to whom Wilson must have addressed a query.

p. 468 *Patmore*. Maas notes: 'The essay to be included in *The Great Victorians* edited by H.J. Massingham, 1932. It was eventually written by Herbert Read.'

p. 468 *Pollet*. Maas notes: 'Teacher of English literature at the Lycée d'Oran, Algeria. In the course of preparing a monograph on Housman he drew up a questionnaire (printed in Richards) [pp. 267–9] which was submitted to Housman.'

Housman ignored some of the questions, notably this one: 'Have you ever disclosed the names of some of those friends of yours who are made the subject of some of your poems; and if not, do you think that you would, as it were, give them away, in handing their names to the public?' Sometimes Housman diverted the question drily. His final paragraph answers Pollet's specific listing of these names; that is, Housman here volunteers no names.

p. 468   *Tyrtaeus*. Maas notes: 'National poet of Sparta (seventh century B.C.); according to tradition, an Athenian.'

p. 469   *pejorist*. The Supplement to the *OED* now has: 'One who believes that the world is becoming worse'; from 1919 and including this from Housman. George Eliot's sense of meliorism is as much that first given in the *OED* ('The doctrine . . . which affirms that the world may be made better by rightly-directed human effort') as that given second ('The belief that society has on the whole a prevailing tendency towards improvement'); Housman's pejorism probably opposes both of those.

p. 470   *Cyrenaic*. 'Belonging to the school of the Socratic philosopher Aristippus of Cyrene, whose doctrine was one of practical hedonism' (*OED*).

p. 470   *The painful episode*. Giving his lecture *The Name and Nature of Poetry* on 9 May.

p. 470   *Basil*. Housman's brother, Jeannie Housman's husband; he had died 1 December 1932.

p. 471   *One of my best boon-companions*. R.V. Laurence, of Trinity College (*Letters*, p. 363).

p. 473   *The New Age*. 16 April 1896.

p. 473   *the* record. A gloss on *A S L* XIX.

BOOKS ON A.E. HOUSMAN

Biographical

A.S.F. Gow, *A.E. Housman: A Sketch* (1936).

Laurence Housman, *A.E.H.* (1937). Published in the USA as *My Brother, A.E. Housman* (1938). See also his essay, 'A.E. Housman's "De Amicitia"', *Encounter*, October 1967.

John Pugh, *Bromsgrove and the Housmans* (1974).

Richard Perceval Graves, *A.E. Housman: The Scholar-Poet* (1979).

Norman Page, *A.E. Housman: A Critical Biography* (1983).

Bibliographical

A.E. Housman: A Bibliography, edited by John Carter and John Sparrow; second edition revised by William White (1982).

Critical

John Sparrow, Introduction to *Collected Poems* (1956).

Norman Marlow, *A.E. Housman, Scholar and Poet* (1958).

Tom Burns Haber, *A.E. Housman* (1967). See also his *The Manuscript Poems of A.E. Housman* (1955); and *The Making of A Shropshire Lad* (1966).

A.E. Housman: A Collection of Critical Essays, edited by Christopher Ricks (1968). Includes poems by W.H. Auden, Ezra Pound and Kingsley Amis; and essays by Edmund Wilson, John Wain, W.H. Auden, Cyril Connolly, Randall Jarrell, Cleanth Brooks, Richard Wilbur, Christopher Ricks, Morton Dauwen Zabel, F.W. Bateson, J.P. Sullivan and John Sparrow.

B.J. Leggett, *Housman's Land of Lost Content* (1970). See also his *The Poetic Art of A.E. Housman* (1978).

C.O. Brink, *English Classical Scholarship: Historical Reflections on Bentley, Porson and Housman* (1986).

A.E. HOUSMAN:
A CHRONOLOGY

=====

1859   Born on 26 March at the Valley House, Fockbury, Worcestershire.

1870–77   Attended Bromsgrove School.

1877–81   At St John's College, Oxford.

1879   Gained First Class Honours in Classical Moderations, his first Public Examination at Oxford.

1881   Failed in Greats (Final School of Literae Humaniores), his final Public Examination, and so left Oxford without a degree. (He later qualified for a pass degree.)

1882–92   After taking the Civil Service Examination, accepted a Higher Division Clerkship in Her Majesty's Patent Office and lived in London. During the latter years of this decade, wrote and published many papers on Greek and Latin authors.

1892–1911   Professor of Latin at University College London.

1896   Published *A Shropshire Lad*.

1903   Published his edition of Book I of Manilius, *Astronomicon*. (Book II, 1912; Book III, 1916; Book IV, 1920; Book V, 1930.)

1905   Published his edition of Juvenal's satires.

1911–36   Professor of Latin at Cambridge University, and Fellow of Trinity College.

1921   Lecture to the Classical Association: 'The Application of Thought to Textual Criticism'.

1922   Published *Last Poems*.

1926   Published his edition of Lucan.

1933   Leslie Stephen Lecture at Cambridge: *The Name and Nature of Poetry*.

1936   Died on 30 April.
     More Poems, edited by Laurence Housman.

1937   *A.E.H.*, by Laurence Housman, which included *Additional Poems* I–XVIII.

INDEX OF TITLES AND FIRST LINES
OF POEMS